C0-BKV-993

The Best of Smithsonian

The Best of
Smithsonian

An anthology of
the first decade of Smithsonian magazine

Smithsonian Exposition Books, Washington, D.C.

Harmony Books, New York, N.Y.

First Edition

Copyright © 1981 Smithsonian Institution
All rights reserved. No part of this book may be
reproduced or utilized in any form or by any
means, electronic or mechanical, including pho-
tocopying, recording, or by any information
storage and retrieval system, without permission
in writing from the publisher.

Harmony Books is a registered trademark of
Crown Publishers, Inc., One Park Avenue, New
York, N.Y. 10016

**Library of Congress Cataloging in
Publication Data**

Main entry under title:

The Best of Smithsonian.

  "Most of these articles have appeared in issues
of Smithsonian magazine"—T.p. verso.
  I. Smithsonian
AC5.B4225 1981   081   81-6534
ISBN 0-89599-007-5   AACR2
ISBN 0-517-54526-8 (Harmony Books)

Manufactured in the United States of America
Printed and bound by Holladay Tyler Printing
Corp.

Table of Contents

ENERGY AND TECHNOLOGY

PEOPLE AND HISTORY

JANUARY 1975,
PP. 28-29

Look—and then look more closely

To reproduce the line above from American poet Theodore Roethke's *"The Far Field"* required innumerable experiments over eons of time. For each letter has been etched into the wing of a moth or a butterfly

through a never-ending series of trials and errors known as natural selection. No one knew the letters could be found there in the wings until Kjell Sandved, staff photographer for the Smithsonian's National Museum of Natural History, perceived them. Imagine, then, what else there is to be seen in the wing of a moth, or the water above a sunken tree, or in the memory of a single person.

The view from the castle

The mission of Smithsonian *magazine, as of the Institution itself, is to persuade its readers that knowledge is indivisible*

In April 1970 the first, rather slim, issue of *Smithsonian* magazine appeared. It was to serve as a medium of expression for the Institution and a link with our National Associate members scattered far and near. The purpose of the Associates has been to promote a sense of extended interest in what the Smithsonian itself is doing and thinking, both now and for the future. In this communication of ideas we have sought to remind our members and readers that the Institution belongs to all Americans, and that it is their right to expect us to pursue the "increase & diffusion of Knowledge among men," as James Smithson's will put it, in continuing process. We view the results of this diffusion as extended education and the refreshment of interest.

Joseph Henry, the celebrated Princeton scientist, became the first head, or Secretary, of the Smithsonian in 1846, and for more than 30 years led the American scholarly community in attempting to increase research in this country and develop a network of communication with kindred workers abroad. He often quoted a far-sighted and practical thought of our enigmatic English benefactor: ' Knowledge should not be viewed as existing in isolated parts, but as a whole. Every portion throws light on all the others."

Now in 1981, as in past years, mankind is in danger of losing sight of this valuable maxim through the emphasis on specialization, or the tedium of self-concern and introspection. And so, in the first issue of our magazine, our bias was in favor of art and beauty, the understanding of the meaning of history, and the interpretation (as best it can be transmitted) of the observation made in science. We believed then as now that the Institution must reflect the whole of material culture, of humanism and of curiosity. To do so would lead to a consciousness of the unity of thought, and the moral and intellectual concern that we all must possess if the creations of Man are to be preserved, let alone our own home range on this fortunate planet.

Our task in the Smithsonian should be to cultivate the spirit of conservation, of the saving of objects, so that men may benefit in the future. Thus, perhaps, our spirits may be so enriched in the process as to remove, at the least, some small part of that cruelty and rage which cause the destruction of our history and deny our claims as human beings.

With the endless quest for self-knowledge is tied a restless seeking for other selves, other worlds and other planets to know. And this is all very well, but a discipline must be assumed if the whole is to be comprehended. I firmly believe that the future is mirrored in the past, especially now that we have the awesome capability of creating our own future—perhaps blindly or willfully—with the fruits of our technology. More than ever now it is worth remembering that we should interest ourselves in every scrap of evidence of the uniqueness of our own creation and the environment in which we live.

If our reaching out through this magazine to our Associates and their friends can accomplish a tithe of this, then all the history of the Institution will have been worthwhile.

S. Dillon Ripley

...and from the operations desk

*This anthology provides a provocative
and rewarding tour of the expanding*
Museum Without Walls

The late 1960s, when *Smithsonian* magazine was contemplated, did not provide an obviously favorable climate for new magazines. Furthermore, comparable publications, starting at about the same time, had around $5 million each in start-up funds, while the Smithsonian Institution had nothing to spare. It seemed, however, that there could be a niche for a group of readers distinguished mostly by college educations and a wide variety of cultural interests.

When I discussed with Smithsonian Secretary S. Dillon Ripley the prospect of becoming editor and publisher, I volunteered the opinion that there wasn't enough subject matter to sustain a periodical devoted to the Institution as it was at any given time. It turned out that he didn't want a pure house organ either. He suggested we include anything that interests the Institution—and what might interest it. This provided a broad mandate indeed.

With unlimited time and money—neither was available—perhaps a staff could have been trained from scratch. The alternative was to recruit professionals who were in sympathy with the Institution's goals and had the journalistic know-how to render the arcane knowledge of specialists into accurate words, photographs, and drawings.

An announcement was inserted in other periodicals. It promised that "fresh, carefully selected articles will probe Man's disasters . . . and ever join the battle for his improvement. We will decry the *blind* growth of technology but never lose sight of the Bad Old Days

that technology bettered. Always we will give the reader a sense of participation as well as information . . . We are basically pragmatic yea-sayers."

In guiding the magazine to its present successful state, the staff adhered to a concept articulated by the late André Malraux, the great French abiter of taste—which he called the "Museum Without Walls." In *The Voices of Silence* he observed that even a privileged 19th century traveler on the Grand Tour was able to sample relatively few formal museums.

The Museum Without Walls, he wrote, shows that "one and the same impulse gives rise to works as diverse as those of Renoir, Roualt, Matisse, Braque and Picasso. . . . From Polynesian art to the great periods of China and India . . . a large share of our art heritage is now derived from peoples whose ideas . . . were quite different from our own."

Malraux noted in the early 1950s that "color reproduction is coming into its own." Thus, in creating the Museum Without Walls, *Smithsonian* magazine relies heavily on photography. It isn't only for representing painting and sculpture: photography extends the confines of institutions such as natural history museums into living nature itself and it helps explain the complexities of technology.

In this anthology, then, you will be listening in vicariously on the possible noises of Creation with the Very Large Array of radio telescopes or participating in Man's technological march to the future with Sir Peter Medawar. As in the unfolding issues of *Smithsonian* magazine, you are touring an ever-growing portion of the Museum Without Walls.

Edward K. Thompson

Phenomena, comment and notes

Before long almost everyone connected—however tangentially—with scientific matters feels the urge to pontificate about science. As this column swerves out of anonymity this month, the temptation will be indulged here just this once—and never again.

A recent poll has reassured the National Science Foundation by telling it that 70 percent of all Americans feel that science has been generally beneficial. There are of course extreme views not shown in this poll: A few people (most of them scientists) see science as the crown of civilization; others believe it to be the seat of evil. Both sides may be right, but one thing *can* be said of science: Unlike other exalted human endeavors, such as the arts and the law which also seek the truth, science is quintessentially progressive and fair.

In the tradition of Western scientific inquiry, at least, a theory works or it doesn't (technology is quite another matter). Scientists have to publish their results in as precise a manner as they can (often requiring language that seems to us laymen like deliberate obfuscation). The results stand or fall on their own merits. Bad science always fails sooner or later; good science holds out until replaced by even better science. Salesmanship simply doesn't work in the long run and no other profession can make that statement.

Sometimes, of course, jargon overcomes thought; a prior investment in a concept can delay the acceptance of a more appropriate one. Scientific knowledge can be—and is often—misused. And sometimes the little parcel of truth a scientist seeks to illuminate seems downright silly. Never-

theless, whether you like it or not, the self-corrective system of accumulating scientific knowledge is by far the closest we have yet come to a foolproof and just means of inching towards the truth.

That is something worth keeping in mind whenever one enters the expanding storehouse of scientific insights and oddities and rummages around with wonder, delight and, now and then (it must be confessed), befuddlement.

November 1973
p. 16

Black holes cropped up as the subject of what a *New Scientist* reporter found to be the shortest question-and-answer period during a week of scientific meetings of the British Association in Canterbury:

Participant: "Did the big bang start with a black hole?"

Speaker: "I don't know."

Chairman: "Next question, please."

November 1973
p. 14

For a while there it seemed that Neanderthal man had been rehabilitated and was slipping closer to the mainstream of human evolution, but the situation remains fluid. As has been reported in these pages, Neanderthals are known to have buried their dead with flowers, a clear sign of humanlike sentiment. But then a British scholar found that Neanderthals' thumbs were barely opposable and, without our opposable thumbs, anthropologists imply, we humans would be oafs. Yet even oafs

talk, and now two scientists have looked into the Neanderthal vocal tract and found what could be bad news for Neanderthal sympathizers.

Philip Lieberman, a linguist from the University of Connecticut, and Edmund Crelin, an anatomist from Yale University, modeled the talking apparatus of contemporary human adults and newborns, chimpanzees and fossil hominids, including the classic Neanderthal from La Chapelle-aux-Saints in France. Reconstruction from the fossil skulls was based on anatomical clues such as the marks muscles leave on bones, and a computer helped determine the possible range of sounds that could have been made by each type of vocal tract. They concluded that classic Neanderthal man just didn't have the equipment to produce the full

A totally reconstructed Neanderthal.

range of sounds (particularly certain vowels) necessary for human speech, although other fossil hominids may have.

Many anthropologists object to these findings about Neanderthals and, while that debate continues, Lieberman may have started another among zoologists: He believes, from the modeling, that chimps have the ability to produce enough sounds and manual gestures to establish a useful language of their own. "Perhaps we're just too dumb to understand what they're saying," says Lieberman. Or perhaps the chimps just don't want to interrupt.

November 1973
p. 10

Pictured below is an ultimate achievement of the human imagination—a perfect tool. However humble it may seem, there is really no *better* way to open a can than to use this tool. All changes in design since wrought thereupon have been a waste of time.

An ultimate human achievement.

Consider: A manual can opener screwed to a wall adds virtually nothing to the speed or ease of the process, uses more materials to make, and is more difficult to keep clean. An electric can opener is not much quicker (who needs to measure their lives in seconds anyway?) and any convenience gained by not using the wrists to open a can is surely exercise ill lost. It also uses more materials to make, and electricity to boot.

The basic type of can opener pictured here has none of these disadvantages; it has fewer moving parts, it is plenty fast enough and, importantly, its is portable. It is an instance where technological

progress could have ceased to no one's real disadvantage—an instance where "improvements" have simply not improved the tool. (There could be one variant: a left-handed edition.)

Since it is becoming quite clear that our society cannot go on in the rampant manner we are used to, since there is a vast and real need for technological improvements in other arenas, it may well be that inventiveness among us should be more precisely focused, that a moratorium should be declared on all unnecessary technological alterations.

There must be many other cases where technology has already basically fulfilled a function adequately, instances where no further "improvements" were necessary. This column would be delighted to publish short, well-described, well-argued examples.

May 1975
pp. 24-26

To an outsider observing the field, there are two kinds of science—hard and soft. Hard science is the kind that is experimentally verifiable so that even a layman can understand its powerful truth. Soft science is the kind where nothing much is certain even after long exercises in reasoning and data processing.

The physicist and the chemist seem examples of hard scientists, while psychologists and sociologists best represent the soft side of science. Biology fits somewhere in between. Biologists can be pretty certain that x will happen to an organism if they do y to it, but at the same time their technological brethren, the people of the medical profession, seem pretty soft on an awful lot of subjects like swine flu vaccine.

There is another distinction to be made between hard and soft sciences: hard sciences are generally optimistic ("We have just isolated the enzyme bionucleoacetatophile cardboardius, which, we have reason to believe, is the cause of mental disintegration") whereas the soft sciences are generally pessimistic ("The conclusions we have reached from our stochastic analysis of senior class members graduating from Midwestern junior colleges and whose names begin with the letter R is that we may face a generation of nontaxpaying heterosexuals with no savings accounts and no interest in dus-

trial design.") Those social scientists, by the way, who are optimistic get into high government positions and, as a result, lose their tenure at the university, and then wind up running for the U.S. Senate.

In any event, quite aside from science, it is now February in the nation's capital, the worst possible time of year, so one is inclined to believe the soft scientists that nothing really works and nothing really improves. The sense of pessimism slops over even to the natural (semihard) science of paleontology at this time of year.

February 1977
pp. 10-12

The rolling of stones has always provided Man with food for mythology, from the ancient hopelessness of Sisyphus to the present aimlessness of what with some merit could be called our Deafened Generation. One wonders then, why so little mythology has arisen from a phenomenon that has long been known to occur in Nevada and California (the latter being the champion region of the world in the spontaneous generation of myths). There, in dry lake beds, stones weighing from around six pounds to a third of a ton have been discovered to have moved *by themselves*, sometimes several hundred feet, leaving readily distinguishable tracks across the ground.

Pet rocks in search of masters? Von Danniken-like dabblings in the orderly processes of nature? One explanation which was suggested was that moving sheets of winter ice transported the stones, but this left two California scientists unsatisfied. So, nine years ago, Robert P. Sharp and Dwight L. Carey set out to do a little rock-watching.

They labeled and named a bunch of rocks at Racetrack Playa in Death Valley National Monument, marked their positions with metal stakes and, in some cases, surrounded the stones with a corral of seven stakes wide enough apart for the stones to escape but close enough to effectively eliminate the action of a moving sheet of ice. (One imagines the stones sitting quiet but alert and watchful during these arrangements, cleverly sensing distance and angle.)

In seven years, 28 or 30 stones stole away from their markers, generally in a north-northeasterly direction. A stone named Nancy, an attractive 250-gram

Across the valley floor, rocks make tracks.

the entire social fabric—all of which depend for existence on people looking the other way while someone else tells a fib (*i.e.*, diplomacy)—will come to a screeching, ear-shattering, heart-breaking halt. Truth will reign and the world will be at an end.

Let the floods come.

April 1978
p. 24

cobble of syenite, moved 201 meters—possibly, Sharp and Carey estimate, at a breezy clip of as much as one meter per second.

And breezes—or to be more specific, winds—seem to be the motive force in the movement of the rocks.

It seems that at least 24 hours after the playa surface is wetted by rain, a thin film of slippery water-saturated fine clay forms over the firm base of the playa. A strong blast of wind, it is averred, then can dislodge the stones, and a continuing high wind thereafter keeps them sailing across the well-lubricated surface.

No one, of course, has ever seen this happen and romantics can cling to whatever explanations they wish. The two scientists, as if caught up in the spirit of the phenomenon, are quoted in *Scientific American* (Vol. 236, No. 2) as saying: "Some immutable law of nature probably prescribes that movements occur in the darkness of stormy moonless nights, so that even a resident observer would see newly made tracks only in the dawn of a new day."

April 1977
pp. 10-11

It probably doesn't make much difference one way or the other if we lose all that real estate to the vanishing Antarctic glacier, but the end of civilization as we know it is now clearly in sight. This sad event is presaged by an electronic device a bit larger than a pocket calculator that has red and green lights that blink under certain circumstances. It is called a Hagoth and advertisements for it have been appearing in recent months. It is a voice-stress analyzer and its maker says that, plugged in to your phone, it will enable you to tell if the salesman at the other end if lying and, if so, whether the lie is of the white variety or more severe. Green lights indicate truth; red ones untruth. The more red ones that blink, the deeper the deception.

This doomsday machine is available for $1,500—it's being pitched at businessmen now and, like the polygraph, does not yet produce evidence admissible in court—but probably its price will plummet before too many more months go by, putting it (like calculators) in the hands of anybody—everybody. Then, the party will be over. Marriages, parent-child relations, communities, economics, politics,

The perceptions of the women's movement have begun to influence our understanding of species other than ourselves, and so it should come as no surprise that women zoologists are in the forefront of zooliberation.

Since Darwin's time biologists have been interested in sexual dimorphism, which means that, among many species, one sex is larger or more colorful than the other, or has antlers or some other bodily difference. An extreme example is the northern fur-seal bull, which weighs four-and-a-half times as much as the cow. Another is the male bird of paradise, whose flamboyant nattiness seems all the more flamboyant because of the total dreariness of the female. It has generally been accepted that sexual dimorphism has evolved in cases where one sex has to compete vigorously for a mate and it has been rather smugly assumed that this is generally a male "initiative."

Hold on just a moment, cautions Dr. Katherine Ralls of the Smithsonian's own National Zoological Park. She found some species of mammals where the females were larger than the males, especialy among bats and rabbits, and some baleen whales (as at right), seals and antelopes. Why should this be?

One theory is that whichever sex makes the smaller parental investment will compete for mates and will be inclined to be larger. But in most mammal species where females exceed males in size, the males make little contribution to the care of the young, and the males are also the aggressive ones, competing for available females.

The answer may lie in the fact that a bigger mother tends to be a better mother—having larger (or more) young and being better able to feed and defend them. It seems, then, that in some cases the forces of natural selection affecting the females are stronger than those affect-

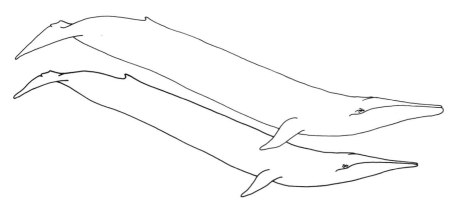

In this pair of typical blue whales, the female (top) is 88 feet long, or seven percent longer than male counterpart. The weight difference is even greater.

ing the males. With an insight women readers will no doubt understand, Dr. Ralls suggests that zoological theorists classically focused too much on the males, thus producing a "one-sex" model. This will now have to be replaced with a "two-sex" model.

And to get in a bit of female macho by way of redressing the sins of her brethren, Dr. Ralls points out that the largest animal that has ever lived on the Earth is the blue whale, or more accurately, the *female* blue whale.

Humans, of course, exhibit sexual dimorphism (for which one can be nothing but grateful), but in its subtler forms it can be quite unfair. A recent study showed that common old everyday aspirin had a significantly beneficial effect on men who are stroke prone. This confirmed lab studies showing that aspirin retards blood clotting.

According to *Medical World News* (Vol. 19, No. 7), 12 Canadian medical schools, in a 6½-year study of nearly 600 patients, found a 48-percent reduction of stroke and death for aspirin-taking male patients. Unfortunately, for women the aspirin made no difference at all.

July 1978
p. 20

There has been, in recent months, some discussion in the public press about heroes or, to be more precise, how our spotlighted, fast-changing and faddish times do not permit heroes to exist. This is a highly debatable point and one which is, like football games, more exactly considered after the fact.

On November 15, 1978, one of my heroes left the family of mankind which, indeed, had been the subject this hero of mine had spent the better part of 76 years thinking about. I've encountered few heroes in any life—they are after all, special . . . and personal. One was a curmudgeonly naturalist with a heart of mush named Marston Bates. Another was Hamilton Gibson, the headmaster of a school in New England long before I met him and a wonderful storyteller in retirement. He was also something of a naturalist and tried to teach me to sit still in the presence of chipmunks. Another was Margaret Mead.

Like millions of others, I read her stuff. Like thousands, I knew her a little bit—for a few fleeting wondrous moments while hanging around the American Museum of Natural History where *she* hung out when home. She broke all the rules of

Photograph © 1978 by Jill Krementz

Margaret Mead, teaching at Columbia.

her academic discipline by going public, in order to prepare anyone who would listen to think about the nature of mankind and what we do, usually blindly, to and for each other.

She had, quite simply, the most humane and tough mind around.

I haven't the faintest idea how the discipline of anthropology plans to produce another such benison for us all, but I wish it would hurry up because I feel lonely.

January 1979
pp. 22-24

Predicting what's going to happen in a marriage is something even the most foolhardy marriage counselor avoids, but biologists step into this arena with confidence. At least Wanda K. Pleszczynska, of the University of Ottawa, did.

Each spring, in the short-grass prairie lands of the Dakotas, some very striking birds called lark buntings arrive. The males come first, establish territories and mate with females who blow in over a nine-day period starting a week after the males. Some of the females arriving, on the average, on days five and six became secondary females to already mated males. What, wondered Dr. Pleszczynska, could be the cause of this?—especially since about 20 percent of the males remain bachelors and since she could find no difference among any of the males.

It must, she thought, have to do with what we would call the quality of the environment. Some males must choose superior territories. It's as though the earliest-arriving females picked up with males with good territories, some mid-arriving females chose to play second fiddle to another to live in a nice place, and late-arrivers simply had to settle for poorer neighborhoods.

And what makes a nice neighborhood? Dr. Pleszczynska studied everything from the abundance of food and the nearness of predators to the incidence of solar radiation (temperature) on the nest site. She found, surprisingly, that the temperature on the nest correlated most closely to the incidence of mate sharing—the cooler the better. (Naturally females know what they're doing: studies also showed greater fledgling success from the nests with less light.) Thus armed, she headed off to Colorado and measured light-incidence in lark bunting nesting sites. Her predictions about plural unions there were correct 28 out of 31 times.

This ability to predict the mating habits of lark buntings is probably fairly low on the scale of Earth-shattering scientific breakthroughs, but it is gentle science, reminding us that we all do relate to the sun in subtle ways.

December 1978
pp. 26-28

On the subject of monsters, it is rare enough to find a new species of anything even the size of a lizard (Italian scientists did find a new lizard a few months ago). How rare, then, to find a new species of an animal 14½ feet long weighing nearly a ton. Nevertheless, it happened.

Called Megamouth, this is just what we need: a brand-new species of shark.

Not long ago a Navy torpedo recovery vessel dropped a sea anchor into 500 feet of water off Hawaii. Instead of a torpedo they later hauled in a suffocated shark of the dimensions given above. It was characterized, according to *Science News* (Vol. 110, No. 25-26 by a bathtub-shaped lower jaw, an enormous, short-snouted head and 484 vestigial teeth. The teeth apparently got fouled in the vessel's parachutelike sea anchor.

The shark, unquestionably a new species, apparently ate shrimp and is, for the nonce, known to science as Megamouth, until ichthyologists find an appropriately classical taxonomic binomial. Megamouth, awaiting further analysis, resides in the California Academy of Siences in San Francisco because, *Science News* says, the usual destination for such oddities, the Smithsonian, is too far away and doesn't have a crane big enough to reel Megamouth into its halls. This last is, of course, nonsense: the Smithsonian has reeled such creatures as DC 3s into its halls.

March 1977
pp. 30-34

If one new shark species, added to the presently known 350, makes the zoological heart palpitate, imagine the addition of 64 shark species all found in one place. That is precisely what has occurred, the specimens having been found in Montana in an uneponymously named placed called Bear Gulch. The sharks, of course, are fossils from Carboniferous times 300 million years ago when a shallow sea covered western North America.

One four-foot shark had a dorsal fin that was hinged like a rudder, making it the probable all-time champion in maneuverability. Another had a hornlike protuberance, somewhat like a unicorn's; yet another had crablike pincers protruding from its snout. So well preserved are these many specimens that their discoverer, Dr. Richard Lund of Adelphi University, even found fossil shrimp in a few fossil shark stomachs.

To discover this mostly unknown shark fauna is something akin to finding a few million years' worth of previously unknown dinosaurs all at once: it will take years to sort it all out.

What is fairly clear is that long ago the versatile sharks evolved into such diverse forms that they filled all the available ecological niches that bony fish now inhabit. A question arises, asked by *New Scientist* (Vol. 73, No. 1033): Why, if they were so well adapted, did so many of these shark species die out, to be replaced by bony fish? Not, says Dr. Lund, because the bony fish were better adapted, but probably because of some major climatic change that wiped out many species of sea and land animals all at once, leaving behind just a few selected shark and bony fish species to repopulate the seas.

Moral: even paleontology textbooks should be loose-leaf affairs. Also, we should consider raising the budget for climatological research.

The first Western naturalist to see a giant panda thought it was a kind of bear; the next one placed it among the raccoon family. And for the last century the giant panda has been bounced from one family to the other, a black-and-white Ping-Pong ball of taxonomy.

The latest volley—as decisively delivered as a forehand smash—is from Vincent M. Sarich, of the University of California at Berkeley, who uncompromisingly asserts that giant pandas are bears. His opinion, in *Nature*, is based on analysis of certain characteristics of serum proteins from the blood of the late Chi-Chi of London. These blood proteins mutate at a known rate, it is believed, therefore providing a kind of clock to help trace the evolutionary paths of various species. As measured in Berkeley, panda blood is no farther from bears' than dog blood is from foxes'. Also, it's quite far from the blood of raccoons.

Prior to the appearance of Sarich's findings, Chinese zoologists (and those at the Smithsonian's National Zoological Park) had taken the position that pandas —the giant kind and the lesser-known lesser pandas—form a taxonomic family of their own. What of the new findings? "If you take all this blood serum business too seriously," says a recently interviewed National Zoo researcher, "then you've also got orangutans in the same family as Man.

"Taxonomists don't really have a good definition of family; it's just a category to put a whole lot of genera in. And furthermore, what's a bear?"

Pong. The game goes on.

December 1973
pp. 12-14

This spring Arthur C. Clarke, the science-fiction writer, addressed a Frank Nelson Doubleday lecture audience at the Smithsonian National Museum of History and Technology and described the research by paleontologists as a kind of "time machine" permitting us to "see" the world millions of years ago. So precise are the techniques, said Clarke, that one can chronicle the changes of day to night by examining growth lines of certain fossils.

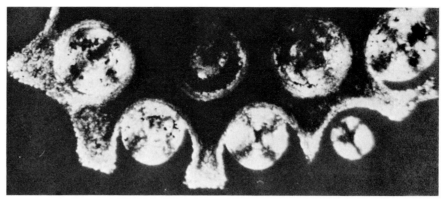

Lenses in sliver of trilobite's compound eye, seen through microscope.

A trilobite, 500 million years old.

Next door, in the National Museum of Natural History, a scientist has taken a different approach. He has given us a glimpse of how a trilobite might have seen its world. Trilobites are those small oval-shaped fossil arthropods that evolved some 500 million years ago and, until they died out, they were one of the Earth's dominant creatures, plying the Cambrian ocean bottoms and swimming near the surface by means of feathery branches on their legs.

Kenneth Towe of the Smithsonian's paleobiology department has been looking into the trilobites' eyes—more specifically into their lenses which, he found, were impregnated with calcite while the animal was alive. What is almost unbelievable, says Towe, is that the crystal structure of the calcite is such that the lenses have the optical properties of glass. Some living arthropods have calcified lenses, too, but those of the trilobites were

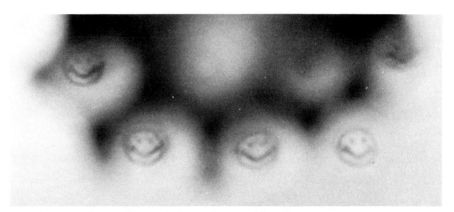

Same lenses as above still permit sharp, if not prehistoric, image.

better, says Dr. Towe, who has looked through them.

He mounted some in clear epoxy, face down on glass slides, and peered at objects through them with a microscope. It is not known, he says, if the trilobites had the equipment to convert the images that passed through their lenses into actual perceptions of form, but it is clear that at least some trilobites had the optical equipment to form relatively sharp images over a depth ranging from a few millimeters to infinity (see photographs, previous page).

May 1973
pp. 6-8

Blue jays, rude and slovenly but at least well-dressed, also are clever. Just how clever has been shown by two psychologists at the University of Massachusetts, Thony B. Jones and Alan C. Kamil.

A northern blue jay in their laboratory was seen on several occasions to rip a piece of newspaper from the pages kept beneath its cage, crumple it up and then thrust it between the wires of the cage,

raking in food pellets that were too far away to be reached by beak alone. Given other objects—a piece of straw or plastic bag tie—the jay did the same.

When there were no pellets to be garnered, the jay would occasionally drop a piece of paper into the water dish, sweep it around the food can, picking up food dust in the process, and then pick off the food dust or simply eat the piece of paper.

When subsequently tested, only one of eight other jays in the psychologists' hand-reared colony showed no sign of such tool-using behavior. They suggest, in *Science* magazine, that one jay chanced "serendipitously" upon the utility of this behavior and the others learned it from observing the lucky pioneer. In any event, although jays are not known to behave this way in the wild, they can now be placed alongside the few other animals—chimpanzees, baboons, Galápagos woodpeckers and humans—which use tools.

—James K. Page Jr.

Around the Mall and beyond

Ever determined to take up cudgels for wildlife, I whizzed over to the Smithsonian's National Zoological Park recently to see about the vultures. I'm referring to native American vultures, as "wild" as any bird can expect to be which spends much of its time soaring over the nation's capital. For decades they have dropped in at the zoo to feed and roost and sometimes breed. They have become an old, though hardly cherished, tradition. But this year they have gone.

Guy Greenwell, Curator of Birds, says that though the vultures often flake off in the heat of summer, this year they never attained their normal spring buildup. He blames all that new construction that is going on, renovating our old zoo. Some trees have to go, and the snarl of power saws from dawn until dark, day after day, proved just as discouraging to the vultures as to you and me.

I tried to talk to Greenwell in his office in the basement of the bird house. "Tried" because there was raucous competition from an assortment of macaws, cockatoos and other noisy exotics having their own conversation in some special cages outside Greenwell's door. The barks, howls, squeals, honks and whistles sounded like a dog fight in the midst of a Paris traffic jam.

I gleaned that the zoo hosted the two eastern American species of vulture, the black (*Coragyps atratus*), common enough in nearby Maryland and Virginia, and the turkey (*Cathartes aura*), a much shyer bird that looks somewhat like a sunburned businessman: black suit, bald red head and bags under the eyes.

Greenwell shouted—against the vehemently stated opinions of a macaw—that the black vultures sometimes nested, but that the turkey vultures came just to roost, not to breed. The birds would often line up on the railing above the bear den hissing and shouldering until they were evenly spaced, about six inches apart, like guardsmen on parade. Then they would take turns flapping down to swipe a dead fish from the bears.

After feeding, the vultures would take off and get in a little soaring on the thermals rising from Washington's hot streets and rooftops. Finally they would sail off to the high banks of the Potomac and ride the hill currents there.

"Did they ever lay any eggs?" I yelled.

"We incubated one," Greenwell bellowed back.

It turns out that Mike Johnson, biological technician for the bird unit, raised a small black vulture named Vernon who now lives in a cage with a hooded vulture from Africa. Vernon is confined right now because one evening, when Greenwell had been working late and was the only one of Vernon's friends around, Vernon followed him home. Greenwell walks to and from work and on this particular evening stroll, there was Vernon waddling and flapping along beside him, hissing at passersby. And when Greenwell noticed, and picked him up to carry him back to the zoo, Vernon bit him.

Vernon's fellow vultures may come back when the reconstruction project is finished—first the bold blacks, then, cautiously, the turkeys. But some of the zoo's neighboring Washingtonians would hard-

ly shed a tear if they never saw another vulture. Residents at the nearby Kennedy-Warren apartments used to find the sight of 180 or so wheeling vultures, silent and ever watchful, right over their roof, uncomfortably portentous, especially to someone with a nasty hangover. But the birds had their share of fame in Washington. Foreign zoos sometimes requested a shipment of them. Mrs. Sybil Hamlet, Public Information Officer at the zoo, told me (in a normal voice, after I had bade farewell to Guy Greenwell and his high-decibel companions) that in the 1950s zoo people would box-trap a few vultures and send them off.

"Then the wire netting got all rusty, and we painted it with lovely black enamel," she said, "and from then on, not one bird would go inside. That was the end of our trapping."

Which proves that what seems lovely to a human does not necessarily seem lovely to a vulture. And, come to think of it, vice versa.

On one rather famous occasion, a zoo vulture—a griffon vulture from western Asia, Africa and southern Europe—escaped and took a roost at the Alban Towers Apartments on Massachusetts Avenue (Embassy Row, no less). The residents there rather liked their new neighbor and sent food up to it. "It was some kind of big," recalls one young man who was living there. "When it flew by my window the whole sky darkened."

The zoo people tried every which way to recapture the griffon, but it took off. Probably out there in Des Moines by now, making better friends than he would back in western Asia, Africa and southern Europe. Another prophet without honor. . . .

One of the first places in the zoo to get renovated was the monkey house. Already visitors are getting used to it, but I wonder how my friend *Lagothrix lagothrica* is making out. I first met him when his splendid new quarters were opened at a ceremony in May. It was a hot afternoon, and guests lined up at the two tables which had been set up in the air-conditioned expanse between the display rooms. These latter are sealed off with glass to keep out the air conditioning, which would give tropical animals chills, muffle the noise of sightseers and, as Zoo Director Theodore Reed said in his dedicatory remarks, "keep the monkeys from having to smell the people."

Now, Lagothrix is a woolly monkey from the Amazon Basin. He eats leaves, fruit and insects. Take it from me, he also can use a vodka and tonic if you offer him one.

The trouble was that, at the opening ceremony, no one did. So he sat at his window—cut low so children can look in —resting his hairy forearm on the sill and glowering. Just waiting.

I suppose that not everyone has been in a quiet local bar on a Tuesday night when the whole gang has cleared off except for one miserable old toper, hunched at one end of the mahogany, silently hoping that the bartender will relent and slide a pony of Old Apple up to him. After all, he really can't help it if he's a mean drunk. He really didn't intend causing all that trouble earlier in the eve-

ning. All he needs is just one more glop and he'll be good. Honest.

Well, that was my friend Lagothrix. The same patient waiting, the same disgusted glower at the waiter.

"Very little is known about behavior in the wild," says the legend on his window.

I know something. He's obviously got the reputation of being a mean drunk.

August 1975
pp. 22-25

For some years now, I have been going to and from my daily job by passing directly beneath two of the world's most famous aircraft—the Wright "Flyer"—the first plane to get off the ground successfully—and Charles A. Lindbergh's *Spirit of St. Louis*—the first plane to make it from New York to Paris. Both have been hanging from the ceiling of the Smithsonian's old Arts and Industries Building for decades.

The Wright brothers' plane seemed to be soaring low toward the front entrance, and the fabricated figure of Orville Wright, prone under the lower wing, stared ahead with a glazed look as though he were just realizing he could never get through the door. Behind him, and higher, the silver *Spirit* gleamed, her wings slightly tilted as though she were straightening out for that historic landing at Le Bourget in May 1927.

When our Air and Space Museum began the move to its enormous new quarters just down Independence Avenue (scheduled to open July 4, 1976), I noted with some excitement that we ordinary people, with a little luck, would have a chance to see these great old planes on the ground, at close quarters. The time came, last August, and my luck ran out. I was in California.

Fortunately, however, one of my colleagues on this magazine is a pilot and she made a personal point of approaching the *Spirit of St. Louis* on the ground, wings removed, and making its acquaintance. She reports that, aside from nearly 30 years of previously unreachable dust, the cockpit where Lindbergh sat for 33 hours looks pretty comfortable. The seat is padded, the instruments and gadgets reasonably familiar to a pilot today.

My friend and I had forgotten that the late General Lindbergh toured many countries, mostly in Latin America, in the *Spirit* after his Paris flight. Each nation he visited is noted by a small flag, neatly painted on the metal cowling of the engine. These are not decals, mind you. They seem to be hand-painted flags, carefully rendered and then varnished.

Who did this meticulous job, we wonder. Surely not the great man himself? And yet there is something about the task that is like him—the total accuracy, the endless attention to detail.

Our pilot admits that before saying farewell (for now) to the *Spirit of St. Louis*, she perpetrated what is traditionally considered the most heinous of all museum crimes, on a par with talking in a public library. She touched the plane. She says she thought about the story of the French crowd that swept onto Le Bourget field to greet Lindbergh, and how the souvenir hunters swarmed about his plane, swamping it with humanity, tearing pieces of fabric from its ribs while he strove to save it.

Just to see if the scars had healed all right, my friend gently ran her fingers across the silver fabric. She says it was as tight as a drumhead, slick and smooth. It felt almost like new.

The *Spirit* is now at the preservation and restoration division of the Air and Space Museum. This is a sprawling complex out at Silver Hill, Maryland, on the outskirts of Greater Washington. It deserves—and I hope will get—a column to itself one day, but, as a tantalizer, you should realize that just about every plane that ever made a historic flight is out there getting fixed and shined up for the new museum.

I returned to Washington in time to get a look at the Wright plane before it, too, was bustled off for the tender loving care due such a fragile old-timer. The wooden wing spars looked sound, though darkened by 72 years. One wing strut was slightly bent. The muslin of the wing surfaces is also brown with age—it was originally unbleached white—but it looked taut and sound. If you think I had the nerve to touch it, you are wrong. Had I done so, a lightning bolt would have sizzled all the way from Dayton, Ohio, and reduced me to a pot of tallow.

Dayton was the Wrights' hometown, where much of the work on the wings was done. Myriad stitches that attach the fabric to the wing spars were done by hand. I'm told that an old lady of Dayton recently recalled answering an advertisement seeking someone to do "plane sewing." She thought it meant "plain," got the job and found herself working on a wing for one of the Wright planes.

The Wright "Flyer" used to hang in a London museum until 1948, when it came to the United States largely through the efforts of Paul E. Garber, Historian Emeritus of the Air and Space Museum. Garber says it made the voyage in the old Cunarder *Mauretania,* but landed at Halifax instead of New York because of a strike. He got the U.S. Navy to ship it on down to Washington.

Garber felt the plane needed a man's figure in it to show how it was controlled, and also to indicate front from back, for the shape of those early birds is a lot different from that of a jumbo jet. What better figure to copy than that of Orville Wright, who actually made the first flight?

A sculptor friend of Garber's did Orville's head, based on a likeness (he had died early the same year), and Garber himself banged together a sort of body frame to lie on the wing the way Orville had—prone, with hips fitting into a yoke that controlled the warping of the wing, right elbow supporting himself and left hand in charge of the plane's elevator, making it rise or descend. Garber used himself as a model, adding a few inches since Orville was taller.

When it came to dressing the mannequin, Garber found he could get one of his old suits—soberly dark blue, which Orville would have liked—onto the frame without too much wrist and ankle showing. He also sacrificed a white shirt, but he drew the line at giving up a pair of his own shoes to a dummy. Garber bought some, he thinks at a cut-rate shoe store.

One item of clothing gave Garber a lot of trouble. Men's fashions of 1903 dictated a stiff high collar, even for unpretentious bicycle-shop owners who just happened to go around inventing planes. And the Washington, D.C., shops of 1948 had left that style far behind. Garber tried everywhere with no luck, then asked the elderly proprietor of a haberdashery in the old Willard Hotel.

"What size?" responded the haberdasher, as if he listened to that particular request every day of the year and was a bit bored by it all.

Garber choked down his surprise and automatically gave his own size, 15½.

"How many?" asked the man.

Swallowing again, Garber decided on two for openers.

And after a little rummaging in the back, there they were—two high-standing collars right out of the Edwardian age. Delighted, Garber asked how in the world the haberdasher happened to stock them. "I was a great admirer of Herbert Hoover," replied the haberdasher. "He wore these when he was President, and if he should someday return to office I want to be prepared for him."

When the new Air and Space Museum opens, new mannequins will probably adorn the planes and space capsules that require them, although no one seems to know for sure whether there will be a new, shiny, plastic Orville lying on the lower wing of the "Flyer." If so, Paul Garber will presumably get his white shirt and blue suit and cut-rate shoes back again. As for the high-standing collar, the chances are fair that it's the only one left in the whole United States. And now that President Hoover has left us, Orville may well wear it again.

October 1975
pp. 20-26

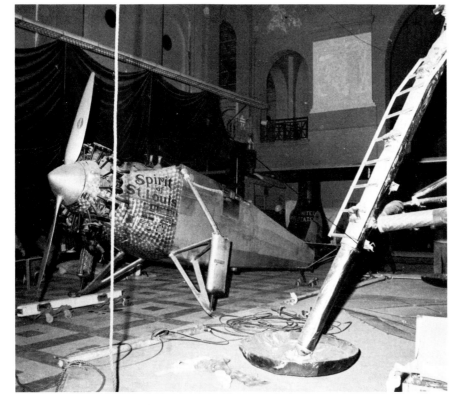

They got the big steam engine running the other day. It's one of those delightful old machines that awed the spectators at the Philadelphia Centennial Exhibition in 1876, and will do so again when the Smithsonian recaptures that marvelous display this year—beginning in May. These engines, with their polished steel drive shafts and great barrel-like cylinders and massive flywheels, fascinate us today because they are so much the product of human craft and devotion instead of the automated processes we are accustomed to. They even have decorative stripes and flowers painted on their cylinders and along their spokes. They undoubtedly had names, too.

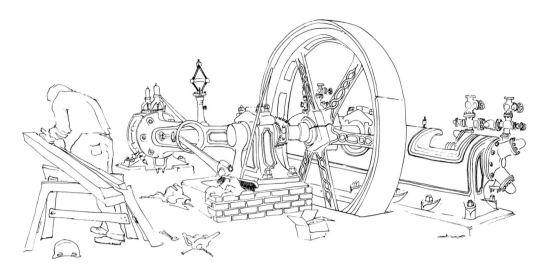

Anyway, the people who have been putting the engines together in the Arts and Industries Building hooked up a compressed air hose to the steam inlet and after several urgings, adjustments and imprecations, away she went, the piston rod flashing in and out, the crankshaft winking back reflected lights as it muscled the flywheel around, the spokes blurring, the governor whirling and the whole hall filled with the sound of motion. It was a deep stage whisper with muffled ticks and knocks as consonants.

The young men who got the big engine going looked at each other with silent pleasure, then walked lovingly around the thing, touching a bearing here, laying hands on a connecting rod there, feeling for too much heat, listening critically to the ancient voice. This particular engine was used by the Wiessner (later American) Brewery of Baltimore to compress ammonia used in the refrigeration system. It had not been operated for 25 years.

The longer it ran and the more often it was started, the better it sounded. It was quite demonstrably running in— "finding itself" as the old expression went. And as it did so, the stage whisper dropped to a lover's words, breathed in the night.

Not without some help. One of the young men, on his meticulous inspection, paused beside the crankshaft and listened. Then, in the half-second while the crank was at the upper arc of its rotation, he smacked the steel bed under it with a hammer. Instantly, the sound he had heard, whatever it was, vanished, for he moved on.

I recognize these steam mechanics as belonging to a type that gathers at the Smithsonian as naturally as eels in the Sargasso Sea. Some people are so attuned to the past that their forced involvement with 1976 seems almost a cruel hoax. Many keep struggling to preserve the motives and rewards of the past, no matter what nasty shots the present takes at them. This bunch often ends up in politics, as we all know. But others are materialists, preoccupied with old engines, old ships, old apothecary jars and gilded eagles and pipes and kites and bicycles. These *thing* lovers all eventually seem to wind up somewhere in the Institution— and that's good.

A great many of these unnamed, unsung aficionados are presently engrossed with "1876: A Centennial Exhibition," the repository of these engines—and some 29,000 other old *things* as well. Visitors will see the treasures for themselves, three months from now, but they may not appreciate all the human effort and skill and special devotion that have been going into the exhibit.

February 1976
pp. 32-34

Our Bicentennial has lured a spate of foreign dignitaries to the United States, and the Smithsonian Institution has given a hearty welcome to most of them. Like the millions of everyday sightseers who visit our museums every year, these crowned heads and prime ministers are drawn to our displays. But the difference between a VIP and a tourist is clear.

The potentate's tour is of brief, prescribed duration. He or she is led by the proper greeters to a few specific displays— things that are interesting to the ruler and which also fall within the demands of security.

The tourist, in contrast, wanders happily at will, gazing at everything, lingering in front of something that intrigues him, spurning something else that bores him. He stays all morning if he feels like it, then steps out on the Mall to chomp down some popcorn and gooey ice cream before hitting another museum later in the day. He may come back tomorrow if he doesn't have to head home to Albuquerque or Cleveland or Des Moines.

The tourist has that advantage over Queen Elizabeth. She—our most recent royal guest—arrived at the Smithsonian castle exactly as she was supposed to (*Around the Mall,* July 1976) and was duly greeted by our own institutional dignitaries: Secretary Ripley, Chief Justice Burger, Chancellor of the Board of Regents, and Vice President Nelson Rockefeller, all suitably begowned in their academic regalia.

The Queen was then shown three specific areas: the crypt which holds the remains of our founder, James Smithson, an exhibit in the Great Hall called "The Federal City: Plans and Realities" which shows how Washington has changed over the years, and a few other items on display in the Associates' Lounge.

Queen Elizabeth handled her assignment with smooth expertise, standing properly silent before Smithson's tomb, for, after all, he *was* an Englishman, even though illegitimate. With her was James Smithson's half-brother's great-great-great-great-grandson, the Duke of Northumberland, come to visit his friend,

Secretary Ripley, and point up the family interest in the Institution.

Queen Elizabeth's appearances are traditionally the best engineered in the world. They click off like clockwork. Sometimes it is hard to realize that the pretty little lady in the big royal hat who walks sensibly into a room, surrounded by tall and respectful men, and looks at various things with a sort of determined interest, is really a warm-blooded human being. I was near her in the castle when Secretary Ripley (who towered decorously above her) made some lighthearted remark. And she turned and looked up at him with a warm and nicely naughty smile. She has kind of a generous mouth and when she smiles she lights up and turns into someone you feel you'd like to know better. I had trouble restraining myself from suggesting to her that I knew a nice quiet place around the corner and would she like to bust away from all this and come and have a quick one?

After this appearance at the castle, Queen Elizabeth went to look at "The Eye of Jefferson," the exhibition at the National Gallery, (see June SMITHSONIAN). This was obviously *her* choice of what she could see and yet remain safeguarded. I can't imagine that Elizabeth was most fascinated with "The Federal City" and its models of how Washington looked in 1900 and other years. Her empire never even bothered to take over the city back in 1814 after capturing it and burning the White House. But Jefferson's taste—that may be of special interest to the same Royal Family from which Jefferson led his countrymen in the Declaration of Independence. "The Eye of Jefferson," however, is a huge exhibit—far too extensive for the Queen to absorb in her allotted time. She would have seen more as an ordinary tourist.

The Queen did her bit with all the savoir-faire we have come to expect of her—the incredible coolness, the ability to hurry from one place to another without, er, perspiring, the gracious little speeches delivered in those precise accents that sound so disturbingly like Carol Burnett imitating Queen Elizabeth. She left me, for one, an unregenerate Anglophile and an unrepentant royalist.

The Duke of Northumberland, aside from paying his respects to his more-or-less relative, James Smithson, gave us, on extended loan, a famous Gilbert Stuart portrait of the Indian chief Joseph Brant, an educated warrior who fought for the Crown during the Revolution and proved himself a formidable foe. The painting now hangs at the National Portrait Gallery.

Earlier this summer, I had done some rubbernecking at Juan Carlos, King of Spain. He and Queen Sophia pulled up at the Museum of History and Technology, were met by Mr. Ripley and Museum Director Brooke Hindle and were led inside to look at the new exhibit of Colum-

Queen Elizabeth, with Secretary Ripley as her guide, views a model of "The Federal City."

Chief Justice Burger is to the left of the Queen, and beside him Vice President Rockefeller.

bus memorabilia—some fascinating maps, gold from the New World, armor, chests and other items, also on loan to the Smithsonian. They were then shown the "We the People" exhibit and had a look at the First Ladies' gowns.

Carlos is youthful, handsome, upright, charming—very much your average, everyday king. His wife is a youthful, pretty, charming blonde, originally the Princess Sophia of Greece. But what struck me most about Juan Carlos was the ring of his title. As I was standing outside the museum, rubbernecking, a cute stenographer from the Department of Commerce hurried to join the crowd.

"What's going on?" she asked excitely. "Who is it?"

I turned around to tell her it was the King of Spain, but the words came out as though I were standing beside a medieval trumpeter, making an announcement to the court: "The King of Spain!" I proclaimed, letting the words roll forth like thunder.

She looked at me round-eyed with awe. *The King of Spain,* she repeated eagerly. "Wow!"

I wonder why those four words are impossible to utter without an effect like the crash of cymbals. Elizabeth II is really closer and more important to us royalty-happy Americans, yet her title is unwieldly, even relatively unknown. You can't call her the "Queen of England" because she's more than that, and you can no longer get in that nice bit about her being "Empress of India (pronounced 'Injah')," so you're left with the awkward combination of Great Britain and Northern Ireland.

No, none of our present monarchs can touch Juan Carlos for the resonance of his title. The King of Spain. Whoo, boy!

September 1976
pp. 30-32

Dr. Theodore H. Reed, director of our National Zoo, who talks about pandas on p. 44, sometimes drives around his domain in a sort of golf cart which can negotiate the footpaths and slip around the road barriers without going fast enough to pose a threat to man or beast. It's a privilege of rank. If you're famous or have done something extraordinary like donate a live yeti to the zoo, or if

The late Mohini Rewa, "Enchantress" of the National Zoo.

you're just plain lucky, you might get a ride in the cart with Ted Reed.

I got one, either for the last reason or because he got me confused with someone else. We drove past the birds that had been so amorous during the burgeoning of spring and found them merely languid in the heat of summer. We ventured down the new Beaver Valley, which opened in May, and found that the timber wolves were no longer restlessly digging, but were simply panting in the heat, accepting their new home; that the otters were not endlessly rolling and wrestling in play, but were lying side by side in a shady spot; that the beavers were not catatonic, stunned by their new surroundings, but had settled in nicely. They had obviously met the neighbors and knew which ones to borrow a quarter-pound of butter from; they approved of the school and they knew which days the trash collectors came. The sea lions, lively and unabashed when they first arrived in Beaver Valley, were quite irrepressible now. They dashed around their pool, shoving each other off favorite rocks and crowding clamorously around their keepers at mealtime. It was a wonderfully entertaining sight.

My host, however, seemed absent-minded, almost morose. This was especially true as we drove around the old Lion House hill, and I ascertained that Ted Reed was still quietly mourning his old queen, the regal Mohini Rewa, the white Bengal tigress that died last April.

Everyone knows about the white tigers (SMITHSONIAN, April 1971). Mohini's arrival in 1960 was well publicized and the birth of her cubs got breathless attention in the press. "It's difficult to say how much the zoo owes that cat and her cubs," says Reed. "They drew attention to the facility and made all our recent improvements so much easier."

Reed recalled that Mohini lost a piece of ear to her first mate and sire of her first litter. This tiger, with white genes, was Samson, Mohini's uncle. On one of his early meetings with Mohini he nipped her ear as she leaned against the door of his cage. An Irish engineer at the zoo saw the episode and remarked admiringly, "Shure, 'tis the perfect lover!"

At the towering age of 20, Mohini began to suffer from kidney troubles and her legs started giving out. She was put to sleep. Ted Reed left town on the day it was done.

September 1979
pp. 26-28

—EDWARDS PARK

Wildlife and Environment

On any given day, Smithsonian scientists may be studying sea urchins on the reefs of Belize, elephants in Sri Lanka, monkeys in Panama, birds in Antarctica. The Institution's concern with the biota of the biosphere goes back at least as far as its interest in the energy input: the solar radiation that drives all life. Thus it is no accident that the first article in the first issue of *Smithsonian*—and the first article in this section—is an appreciation of the interconnectedness of all life on Earth by the biologist/philosopher, René Dubos. The magazine began in April 1970 with an Earth Day all its own.

The Institution studies life and the magazine celebrates it. Birds are accessible to almost all of us and many of our readers are birders, so Charlton Ogburn's distillation of the joys of birding is an invitation to a celebration in every backyard and park, field and thicket, swamp and shore in America.

There is bad news as well as good. A professional ornithologist who happens to run the whole Smithsonian complex (and who decided to start the magazine), S. Dillon Ripley, reminds us of some of the magnificent creatures lost in recent times, although he offers the hope of others saved and restored to the wild. (He is pleased to report that the tiger, although threatened, now is known to number considerably more than the 1,000 mentioned on page 49.) Botanist Edward S. Ayensu, who directs Smithsonian conservation efforts, alerts us to some of the 20,000 plant species now considered endangered.

These days habitat destruction is the most common culprit, and John Hay details the throbbing life, the drag line attacks, and efforts (all too frequently unsuccessful) to save one of the most valuable and vulnerable of all habitats, the coastal salt marsh.

To know what's really in a marsh, or any ecosystem,

we must have the baseline biology known as taxonomy, the scientific description and differentiation of species. Howard E. Evans and artist Fred Gwynne show how a vocation that sounds so tedious is in reality a calling for the liveliest, most curious minds of all.

No matter how deep our understanding of ecosystem and biosphere, our appreciation of how scientists study life and sometimes save it, it is after all the living organisms themselves that we really want to know. Wildlife is the category in which we editors find it most difficult to limit ourselves (to keep a balance of subject in the magazine) and the area with the most qualified writers. In this anthology we also limit ourselves, in this case to three wildlife stories, or really two and a half. The "half" is the picture story of a baby rhinocerous born at the National Zoo, an arm of the Smithsonian. The text gives the facts, but the photographs tell all. More typical of the magazine's love affair with wildlife is Alison Jolly's account of lemurs in Madagascar. And in a marvelously understated blend of scientific observation and emotional attachment, Durward L. Allen tells of the community of foxes that joined a community of scientists studying the wolves and moose of Isle Royale.

Finally, dessert: Gerald Carson and illustrator Brenda Tilley round up some of the most improbable critters dreamed up by spinners of tall tales all over America. Consider just the cross between mosquito and bumblebee: a stinger at both ends.

All about us dwell other nations, the living things that were here before us: clams and condors, lichens and redwoods. The cliché of the Seventies, that we are all part of one whole, is true. A better understanding of the wildlife with which we share the planet is in our own best interests, and these articles supply some of the most interesting reading that we offer.

—John P. Wiley jr.
Board of Editors

A polar bear and her cub plod across a frozen section of Hudson Bay at sunset near the small town of Churchill, Manitoba. Residents seek to coexist with these magnificent animals. From "Polar bears aren't pets, but this town is learning to live with them" February 1978 pp. 70-79.

Drawings by Robert Osborn

"All the elements of nature have evolved
and continue to evolve together"

26

by René Dubos

Life is an endless give-and-take with Earth and all her creatures

*If these processes continue, all is well
—but certain aspects of the present
situation have no precedent in history*

Our blue planet. Our green planet. It was worth the 21 billion dollars spent on the Apollo missions to make us perceive, through the eyes of the astronauts and with our own eyes, the color and inviting richness of the earth in contrast to the bleakness of space. Now that we have experienced the grayness and drabness of the moon and that the photographs taken by the Mariner spacecrafts have dispelled our illusions about the existence of canals and of life on Mars, we appreciate even more, because we know it to be so unique in the solar system, the sensuous appeal of Earth with her blue atmosphere and her green mantle.

But there is much more to the quality of the earth than the pleasure it gives our senses. Our blue planet is responsible for our very nature because human beings are shaped, biologically and mentally, by the environment in which they develop.

One need not be a learned biologist to understand the large implications of James Baldwin's words: "It means something...to live where one sees space and sky or to live where one sees nothing but rubble...." And: "We take our shape...within and against that cage of reality bequeathed us at our birth...." Just try to imagine a child developing on the desolate surface of

René Dubos is a microbiologist and experimental pathologist, and a professor at Rockefeller University in New York. He is the author of many books, among them So Human an Animal, *which shared the Pulitzer Prize for nonfiction in 1969.*

the moon or on Mars. However favorable his heredity, nutritious his food, comfortable his dwellings, he could never acquire the mental and emotional attributes that we identify with humanness. The earth is our mother not only because she nurtures us now, but even more because our biological and mental being emerged from her during evolutionary times and is constantly maintained and shaped by the stimuli we receive from her during our present existence. We could not long remain true human beings if we were to settle on the moon or on Mars, and we shall progressively lose our humanness if we continue to destroy the unique qualities of the earth by pouring filth into her atmosphere, befouling her soil, lakes and rivers, and disfiguring her landscapes with junkpiles. Man is of the earth, earthy. The quality of his life is inextricably interwoven with the quality of the earth and of the life she harbors.

How Earth transcended her material

Astronomers describe the earth as just another planet, and a minor one at that, with no special distinction among all the countless celestial bodies that gravitate mechanically and perhaps aimlessly through the limitless universe. But this is a view of reality distorted by scientific professionalism. The more interesting and more important truth is that the earth transcended her material and mechanistic nature when she began to harbor life more than two billion years ago. Without life, the earth would indeed be just another drab fragment of the solar system. Fortunately, however, living things have converted the inanimate matter of her crust into a living substance. The sensuous quality of her blue atmosphere and of her green surface derives from the activities of the countless microbes, plants and animals that she has

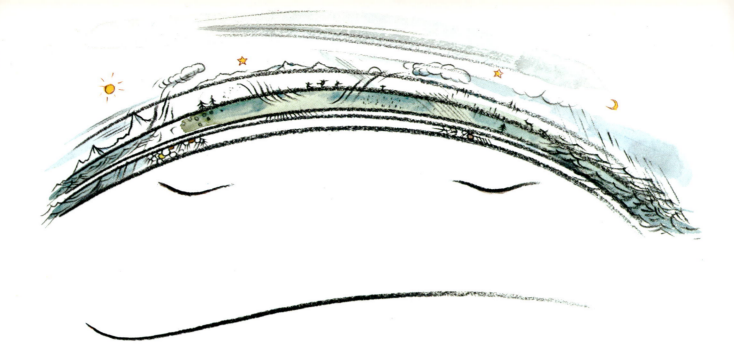

nurtured and that have transformed her substance. We human beings exist and enjoy the world only by virtue of the environmental conditions created and maintained by all the other forms of life. The earth is a home suitable for man because her crust is literally a living organism.

All the elements of nature have evolved and continue to evolve together. Living things are transformed by the responses they make to environmental stimuli, and these responses in turn transform the environment which stimulated them. For example, the chemical composition and the physical texture of the soil are determined not only by its mineral basis and by the effects on it of atmospheric conditions, but also by the activities of the microbial, plant, and animal life it harbors. Even more impressive is the fact that the concentrations of oxygen and carbon dioxide that exist today in the earth's atmosphere differ profoundly from those that prevailed before the emergence of life. The present atmosphere owes most of its oxygen and carbon dioxide to biological phenomena that have been going on uninterruptedly since the emergence of life and on which our own life depends today. It is this fact which accounts for the gravity of the persistence and accumulation of the new synthetic pesticides throughout nature, and particularly in the ocean plankton where they interfere with the production of oxygen by microscopic plants.

The benefits of reciprocity

The complex and endless give-and-take between living organisms and the environments in which they function has been described as "cybernetic relationships" or "feedback processes." These phrases apply not only to nature as a whole but also to local situa-

Without her living crust, Earth would be . . .

tions. Each type of organism selects a special kind of environment in which it creates its own niche and thereby transforms this environment to make it even more suitable to its needs. For example, social bees have an environment that differs from that of solitary insects living in the very same field, in part because they do not use the same kind of local resources, but also because they create their own microclimate inside the beehive (illustration, p. 12). The land under an oak forest differs from that under a pine forest because pine needles do not produce the same kind of humus as do oak leaves.

Under normal conditions most changes that occur as a result of the interplay between a particular organism and its total environment are beneficial to both in the long run. These reciprocal changes account for the exquisite fitness that is often encountered in undisturbed nature and now and then in the works of man, especially when he creates them in close association with nature.

Ancient civilizations all over the world derive much of their appeal from the fitness of their ways of life and of their cultural forms to natural surroundings. One of the charms of travel in old countries is that their buildings, and especially their roofs, vividly reflect the constraints imposed by the climate and by the topographical characteristics of each region. This is true especially for primitive people in economically poor areas. The adobe houses of the Pueblo Indians and the snow houses of Eskimos exhibit ecological fitness just as do the very different types of dwellings evolved centuries ago by the civilizations of the Mediterranean or

... another drab fragment of the solar system

Scandinavia, where prevalence of sun or snow determined biological needs and architectural forms.

In the past, farming communities created, probably in an unconscious manner, environments that were often aesthetically and operationally successful because they were so closely related to the ways of life and therefore to natural conditions. All over the world, some aspects of the landscapes left by ancient societies constitute now their most enduring memorials—as for example the medieval farmlands of Western Europe, the dry stone walls of New England or the terraced mountainsides of Bali.

The diversity and fitness resulting from a continuous series of feedbacks between natural forces, man-made artifacts and human activities generally persisted until the Industrial Revolution. According to the English archaeologist Jacquetta Hawkes, the interplay between the people and the landscape of Britain came close to achieving a desirable equilibrium during the 18th century. In her words, "... Men had triumphed, the land was theirs, but had not yet been subjected and outraged. ... Communications were good enough to bind the country ... but were not yet so easy as to have destroyed locality and the natural freedom of the individual that remoteness freely gives. Rich men and poor men knew how to use the stuff of their countryside to raise comely buildings and to group them with instinctive grace."

The environmental crisis we are experiencing now is the expression of the fact that fitness can no longer be achieved by the spontaneous processes that were effective in the past. Ecological adjustments cannot keep pace with the disturbances caused in nature by population growth and by the impact of technology. Man cannot adapt rapidly enough, and in many situations cannot adapt at all, to the new surroundings and ways of life he is creating.

The optimist has good historical reasons to justify his confidence that the present environmental crisis will eventually be overcome. Mankind has experienced many similar types of crisis in the past and has taken them in stride. A century ago, the great cities of Europe and America were far more polluted, unsanitary and crowded than they are today. Their inhabitants were plagued with nutritional and infectious diseases such as rickets, tuberculosis or typhoid fever of which the seeds rooted in the dank surroundings and flowered in the polluted air of squalid cities. Human life was made miserable by socially inflicted neuroses of the kind which provided Sigmund Freud with abundant clinical material. Fortunately, many of these organic diseases and neuroses which were so common during the late 19th century have all but disappeared in the Western world, even if they have been replaced by others which constitute the so-called diseases of modern civilization.

Modern life's all-too-solid wastes

Since the resilience of nature and of the human constitution is as great as ever, one can hope that the defects of modern life will be corrected as have been those of the past. Certain aspects of the present situation, however, have no precedent in the history of the earth or of man. As a consequence, it cannot be taken for granted that the self-corrective processes which used to operate in nature and in human life will prove effective in the present crisis.

Two life-styles in the same field

economic cycle. The viper of industry must learn to swallow its tail.

In the concentrations used, DDT and related chlorohydrocarbon insecticides possess little toxicity for man and for most animals. However, many of these new synthetic substances not only resist microbial decomposition but are chemically stable. As a result, they accumulate in nature and increase in concentration as they pass from one organism to the other along the food chains. According to recent reports, shrimp from Utah's Great Salt Lake contain DDT in concentrations of seven parts per million; laboratory crabs fed on these shrimp die in an early phase of development. Most shocking of all, the concentration of DDT in the milk of American women now greatly exceeds the maximum level allowed in food products by the U.S. Food and Drug Administration.

The environmental pollution problem has thus taken a very new aspect in consequence of the fact that neither man nor other living forms have had any experience in the course of their evolution with the host of synthetic substances produced by industrial civilization. The microbes present in soil or water cannot develop enzymatic mechanisms to decompose automobile tires, plastic containers, DDT and other synthetics, let alone the bathtubs, washing machines, refrigerators, television sets and other gadgets that are discarded everywhere and disgrace the American landscape. Similarly, there is little if any chance that man will ever develop truly effective biological mechanisms of resistance to automobile exhausts, industrial pollutants and the countless new synthetic products which are now part and parcel of this daily life—yet are so different from the substances he experienced during his evolutionary past.

Consider for example the problems posed by the disposal of solid wastes. In the past, solid wastes consisted chiefly of wood, paper, cotton, linen, wool, leather and other organic substances derived from natural sources. When deposited on the earth or thrown into the water, such organic residues were rapidly attacked by microbes and thus eliminated through decomposition. This happened naturally because there exist in water and in the soil a great many different species of microbes that have evolved since the beginning of life in contact with the various types of natural products. All over the world, it has long been the practice to use organic residues as fertilizers, either by spreading them directly on farmlands in the form of so-called night soil or by processing them first in the farmer's manure pile or in the gardener's compost heap, where they undergo microbial decomposition. Microbes, however, have had no prior experience with the new products of industry.

The need to recycle junk

The junk and dirt of primitive societies was and is objectionable, but fortunately it did not accumulate because it was reintegrated into nature through the action of the microbes. In contrast, there is no natural mechanism to decompose and reintegrate into nature —to recycle, as the expression goes—the junk of industrial civilizations. The solid wastes of modern life will continue to accumulate, and soon bury us, unless scientific technology develops ways to destroy the artificial products it creates in such nauseating profusion, or—more usefully—ways to reintroduce them into the

Microbe vs. new product of industry

Like the problem of environmental pollution, the population problem is now presenting itself under aspects for which there is little precedent in prehistory or history. Despite what is usually believed, however, crowding *per se* is not the new factor. Surprising as it may seem, most cities of the Western world are less densely populated today than they were in the Middle Ages and during the Renaissance, or even a generation ago. The population density in American cities—even in New York—is lower than it is in the cities of continental Europe and Asia. And yet American cities give the impression of being more and more crowded.

Why the crowd seems to be closing in

The painful experience of crowding so common in the prosperous industrial countries comes not from greater population density than in the past, but from the greater impact made on the environment by the modern city dweller. He owns automobiles that emit irritating fumes, create confusion, make unbiological noises, and require ever increasing space in the form of concrete highways and garage facilities. He uses air conditioners which cool his individual dwellings but generate heat for the city as a whole and thereby increase the demand for more air conditioning and for more electric power. And so it goes. Each gadget that saves physical effort, each piece of equipment that adds to the gross comfort of modern life, inevitably increases the impact of the city dweller on his environment and thereby makes crowding more stressful, even though population density is actually decreasing in many urban settlements.

The most publicized effects of the environmental crisis are those influencing the supply of natural resources, and those threatening human health. I shall not consider these effects, not because I doubt or minimize their importance but because they are obvious and have been extensively discussed by scholars in economics, sociology and medicine. I shall instead deal with the more elusive problem posed by the effect of the environmental crisis on the quality of human life.

Before proceeding, however, I must reaffirm my conviction that the human species cannot develop effective biological mechanisms of adaptation to stimuli with which it has had no experience in its evolutionary past—for example, to the pollution of air, water and food with new synthetic chemicals, to the shrill noises of certain technologies, to the sudden changes in human relations resulting from excessively rapid social and geographic mobility. One can expect therefore an increase in the prevalence of the so-called diseases of civilization—those man-made maladies which are caused by our failures to respond successfully to the new environmental stresses of man's own making. Granted these failures, I doubt nevertheless that the threatening ecological crisis will lead to irreversible disasters and to the extinction of mankind. Its more certain effect will be to cause a progressive degradation of the quality of human life.

A legacy of soot and dirt

I shall introduce the subject with a personal experience which certainly has its counterpart in the life of most persons living in the technological world.

I spent my school years in Paris, until the age of 24. At that time, the historic buildings of Paris were dark, covered with black soot. We used to believe that this somber tonality—caused by dirt!—gave antique refine-

"Progressive degradation of the quality of human life"

ment to the Parisian atmosphere. Indeed, there was an outcry of anger when André Malraux proposed that the Paris buildings should be washed. Then a miracle happened. When the soot was removed from 18th-century monuments, their surfaces revealed the golden hue of the building stone, as subtle and warm as young human flesh. For more than a century Parisians, and the rest of the world, had become accustomed to the gloomy mood created by the soot and dirt of the Industrial Revolution. Sensitive life had been impoverished by this conditioning. How I wish now that, as a young boy, I had seen the Gothic cathedrals when they were still white, and the 18th-century buildings when they proudly displayed colorful stones and marbles.

Memories of the dark sooty buildings in the Paris of my youth always come alive when I hear from some of my young friends that they have never seen the Milky Way. They are sensitive and perceptive persons, but have had the misfortune of being born and raised in New York City. Living in an environment which is always polluted, they hardly ever have the opportunity to experience a luminous, vibrant night, a truly blue sky, the intoxicating fragrance of an early spring day, or the poetical melancholy of autumn. Industrial civilization has robbed them of the immensely enjoyable sensations which have heretofore nurtured the desirable attributes of human nature, and which are still as essential as ever for biological and mental health. Biologically, mentally and emotionally, man is still

"Noise, ugliness and garbage in the street"

shaped by his environment and depends on it for the satisfaction of his acquired needs.

Experiments with laboratory animals and studies of human populations have demonstrated that biological and mental individuality reflects the influences exerted by environmental stimuli on the developing organism. In scientific jargon, this means that, contrary to what is often believed, genes do not determine all the traits by which we know a person; what they do, rather, is to govern his biological and mental responses to the stimuli that impinge on him. These responses become indelibly inscribed on the body and mind, thus providing patterns which impose a direction on further development. As a result, each one of us is constantly being shaped by his total environment as much as by his genetic endowment.

The environmental influences experienced during the very early phases of development—prenatal as well as early postnatal—have the most profound and lasting effects on the characteristics of the adult. Hence the critical importance of the environment to which the child is exposed, since this determines to a very large extent which parts of his inherited potentialities become activated and the manner in which they develop to shape his adult individuality. The greatest crime committed in American cities may not be murder, rape or robbery, but rather the wholesale and constant exposure of children to noise, ugliness and garbage in the street, thereby conditioning them to accept public squalor as the normal state of affairs and diminishing their future enjoyment of life.

In the preceding paragraph, I have used modern biological jargon to express the common awareness that most human characteristics are the expression of environmental forces. But this truth had been recognized long before the advent of modern science, for example by Greek philosophers and physicians almost three thousand years ago. In a striking passage of his famous treatise on *Airs, Waters and Places,* Hippocrates boldly asserted that the topography and climate of a region are as important as the quality of food and water in determining the physical stature of the inhabitants, as well as their political institutions, military prowess and general behavior. This was written in the 4th century B.C. So ancient is the wisdom which modern scientists now try to restate in formulas and equations.

Ralph Waldo Emerson expressed the same view in other words when he wrote in his essay "Uses of Great Men," published in 1850, "Men resemble their contemporaries even more than their progenitors." We resemble our progenitors because we inherit from them our genetic endowment. But we resemble our contemporaries even more because, within a given country and social group, most members of a given

"America is redolent of loose fits everywhere"

generation are simultaneously exposed during the formative stages of their early life to similar environmental conditions and stimuli. For example, a very general effect of the environment created by the modern world during the past decades had been the acceleration of growth and the earlier sexual maturation among children of the countries that have adopted the ways of Western civilization. Examples of this phenomenon can be observed today in Israel where teenagers and young adults born and raised under the conditions prevailing in the collective homes of the kibbutzim are bigger than their parents who emigrated from the ghettos of Eastern and Central Europe. Likewise, Japanese teen-agers are much taller than their prewar counterparts, not because they are different genetically but because the conditions of life in postwar Japan differ profoundly from what they used to be. It can be taken for granted that larger size and accelerated sexual development have behavioral consequences that will affect the course of civilization. One may wonder how a population of tall and husky Japanese can function happily and effectively within the exquisite daintiness of the kind of architecture and landscaping that characterized traditional Japan.

Japan provides one of the many illustrations in the preindustrial but civilized world of the development of fitness between man and his total environment. The very word *Nippon* evokes a wonderfully integrated composition of natural scenery and climate, humanized landscape and architecture, formal ways of life and functionally elegant furniture. Such fitness could hardly be achieved through conscious design. It must have developed more or less spontaneously in the course of the slow interplay between man and his total environment.

All over the world in the preindustrial era, tools, architectural forms and social structures exhibited a high degree of fitness not so much as a result of conscious design as because the very process of inventing and building involved a slow, continuous and highly personal contact between man and his creations. Since the problems that had to be dealt with were usually rather simple, only limited knowledge was needed to create artifacts or institutions well suited to the needs. Then, tradition and the almost unconscious response to new needs maintained the fit as culture evolved and became more complex.

A formula for a contented life

In Southern China, it has long been a custom to select village sites according to the doctrine known as *fêng shui,* wind and water. It teaches that buildings should be located in such a way as to be protected against storms and floods, exposed to warmth and attractive views, and readily accessible to farmlands, streams, and groves of trees. What better formula could there be for a contented life? And why should it surprise us to learn from Bernard Rudofsky in *Architecture without Architects* that the architecture of preindustrial people is often better than our own?

It is easy to imagine how accidental influences determined at the beginning certain choices and courses of action which were largely intuitive and even subconscious, because the purpose to be fulfilled was not clearly defined and the goals to be reached were uncertain. Desire for a certain form of worship, the needs of collective life, or simply the search for comfort and safety, evoked responses that were organic rather than cerebral in nature. The body made the decision, as it were, and the mind followed. Local opportunities determined the slight bias in techniques, forms and attitudes which was at the origin of the process. And as time went on, this bias progressively became more con-

"The belief that man has conquered nature"

scious and more strongly expressed, evolving into better-defined standards of beliefs, behavior and tastes.

In modern societies, however, technological and social innovations are so numerous, extensive and rapid that they do not provide the conditions or the time for the spontaneous adaptive processes that used to be so effective in the past. This has been especially striking in the United States since the 19th century, for the simple reason that growth and change then became dominant criteria in the American way of life.

Sixty years ago William James wrote to C. A. Strong: "*Tight fit* is what shapes things definitely; with a loose fit you get no results, and America is redolent of loose fits everywhere." At least two different kinds of reason may account for this lack of fitness in America life. One is that the massive and virtually uninterrupted waves of immigration during the past century made it extremely difficult for most of these people to become rapidly and completely identified with the environments, often entirely new to them, that they found in their country of adoption. Around the turn of the century, a large percentage of Americans had no deep roots in the American soil. Another reason is that technology developed faster and to a greater extent in the United States than in other countries, thus making it more difficult than elsewhere for the adaptive processes which generate fitness to keep pace with the rate of change.

Now that social and technological changes are too rapid for the spontaneous development of successful adaptive responses, modern societies will have to depend on conscious design for the achievement of fitness. I prefer to speak of "design" rather than "planning" because I want to emphasize the need to create social and ecological patterns in which the potentialities of persons and places can achieve expressions that are humanly desirable.

We belong to a generation which has been brainwashed into the belief that man has conquered nature and can transform it for his own purposes in any way he pleases. But this formula inevitably leads to degradation of the environment and to the destruction of human values. In reality, each place has its own peculiarities, which limit the range of what can be safely done with it and which indeed determine the kinds of successful expressions it can achieve. One could almost say that places, like persons, are well suited to only a very few tasks.

The belief that places have a calling—a vocation as it were—is probably as ancient as mankind. At least from the beginning of recorded time, people of all races in all parts of the world have imagined that each particular place or region is endowed with a "genius" or "spirit" which they commonly personified by a god or goddess. We have not outgrown this belief. Agnostic as we may be, and scornful of any thought that there is a ghost in the machine, we still know deep in our hearts that there is pragmatic truth in expressions such as "the genius of New England" or the "spirit of the Far West." Who can doubt that Naples and New York each have their own *genius loci,* which will make them and their inhabitants evolve differently irrespective of technological standardization?

As used in the classical phrase *"genius loci,"* the word genius does not denote gifts or achievements of a superior quality, but rather a special array of attri-

butes—including limitations as well as potentialities—that accounts for the uniqueness of each particular place or region. Design can be lastingly successful only if it takes these attributes into consideration. As Horace Walpole wrote after returning from a trip to France, ". . . They can never have as beautiful landscapes as ours, till they have as bad a climate."

Progress in a civilized world

Human beings are so adaptable that they can survive, function and multiply despite malnutrition, environmental pollution, excessive sensory stimuli, ugliness and boredom, or high population density and its attendant regimentation. But while biological adaptability is an asset for the survival of *Homo sapiens* considered as a biological species, it can undermine the attributes that make human life different from animal life. From the human point of view, the success of adaptation must be judged in terms of values peculiar to man. The cultivation of these values does not imply a retreat from civilized life, but it will require a change of emphasis in economic and technological enterprise, which is quite within our present capacities. Progress should not mean, as it does now, doing faster and faster on an ever increasing scale what we are already doing. In a truly civilized world, progress will mean a social design in which the economic and technological effort will be focused on the creation of the environmental values best suited to the development of human potentialities. These values cannot be dissociated from the qualities of the earth.

The enchanting diversity of Earth comes from the multiplicity of the living forms she harbors, each fitted to a particular place and contributing to its genius. Although modern man has placed himself somewhat outside natural systems, he can and should play a creative role in the achievement of fitness by substituting for the contemporary doctrines of conquest and exploitation, a philosophy of conscious design based on ecological knowledge which will eventually lead to a theology of the earth.

Landscapes and civilizations emerge from the interplay between external nature and man's nature. And so do human individualities. We shall be successful in shaping the world around us, and in advancing the human condition, only if we learn to integrate our unchangeable biological nature with the natural forces and living forms which together constitute the *genius loci*. Man's daily life and his aspirations cannot be thought of apart from natural events because they are the ultimate expressions of our living Earth.

This is the first in a series of articles on Man's relationship to his environment. In the next issue Senator Henry M. Jackson, author of the National Environmental Policy Act of 1969, will write about legislative priorities.

Man and nature reconciled

If it weren't real and entirely natural, this picture of a loon, arrowing its way across the blazing face of the sun, might be a feverish theatrical backdrop.

By Charlton Ogburn

In fall's clear skies birds part the air and raise the spirit

To spend the whole of a day lying on one's back in the soft, green grass, looking up at birds in the air, is to be close to heaven

I fell in love with birds at the age of 11 and have never fallen out of it. I am an *ornithophile* rather than an ornithologist, though during most of my adolescence I hoped to become the latter. Had I done so I should probably not be setting forth as I am to try to account for a lifelong ardor. I should have known too much about birds and have stood overwhelmed by all that could be said about them, and doubtless I should have regarded the human response to birds as irrelevant and distorting. A title such as *The Adventure of Birds* would hardly have occurred to me and would have put me off if it had been suggested. What would it have meant? That birds are an adventure for life on Earth to have undertaken? That the pursuit of birds is an adventure for us? (It means both, really.)

Although in my youth I was often without other company than my own and that of birds, and felt consoled and elevated by the latter, I was at the same time coming to share in the general fascination and concern of my species with itself. Even the most devoted disciple of nature must attach a high importance to humankind if for no other reason than without it the object of his fealty would be denied understanding and remain uncelebrated.

However, if my love of birds has not been preemptive and I have had other preoccupations, it has been constant. It preceded and has not been displaced by the others. In half a century there has been scarcely a day when the sound of an unusual bird's voice would not have brought me up short; when the form of any bird, however barely glimpsed, would not have registered on my consciousness, demanding recognition of what it was and what doing. And in all those years I have had to be sorely pressed indeed not to be susceptible of delight and excitement from a fresh revelation of the charm of birds or of the drama of which they are so expressive. . . .

In the central Atlantic states, autumn, to choose a season at hand, begins in the middle of April. That is when dandelions and little early white mustards will have made their first seed—their versions of the ripe pumpkins and red apples of October. After another month almost all the other first spring flowers will have done likewise. As the days and weeks roll on, more and more plants will have passed through the springtime of flowering and matured their crop.

If there is autumn in spring, there is equally spring in autumn. Wild sunflowers and goldenrod light up whole fields early in September. Blue spires of pickerelweed blossoms rise from the tidal flats of our estuary, on which jewelweed blooms abundantly, the little pouting, orange trumpets evenly distributed on the shrub-sized but delicate plants of bluey foliage, looking misted.

If summer spans the three warmest months of the year and winter the three coldest, then autumn, intervening between the two, begins about September 5th. But here in northern Virginia the woods then are almost as green as ever. Only in the high mountains to the west, as a rule, has there been a frost.

Autumn began for us last year on August 18th when the dogwood berries were getting red: a young Blackburnian warbler appeared at the birdbath. Three days later it was back, or another like it, with a female Blackburnian, a female Canada and a Tennessee. (The little visitors are comical in their ablutionary impulses. They flit nervously to the water and bounce off as if scalded.) The 24th brought an extraordinary flurry. At one time a Blackburnian, a Canada, a hooded and a blue-winged warbler were all bathing in a row.

The Canada lingered longest, a beautiful male, suede gray above with necklace of black slash marks against a glowing yellow breast. Like the others, he could have no idea of what he was flying all the way to Peru or Ecuador to escape, may never have known a cold day. Or am I being parochial? Perhaps by his lights he was going back to where he belonged, in a South American rain forest, after a long and perilous excursion to raise his young in the comparative security (no threatening monkeys or lizards and few

The Adventure of Birds *by Charlton Ogburn, ornithophile, will be published this month by William Morrow & Co. © 1975 Charlton Ogburn.*

Migratory grackles sit like black bobbins on a snow-framed loom. Streaming in floods

snakes) he would find in the Canadian-zone woods.

There is, indeed, probably validity in the view that our wood warblers (orioles and tanagers), as is certainly the case with hummingbirds, are tropical species that come north to breed, taking advantage of the annual springtime opening up of the vast, underpopulated (or under-avianated) lands vacated by the snows—in human terms as if the settlement of the New World from Europe were a yearly occurrence. By contrast, our thrushes, sparrows, crows and jays, pipits and larks might be considered northerners that retreat southward before the rigors of winter.

However it may be, that this sunbeam mite of birdity, this Canada warbler, should twice yearly journey from one to another of two such mutually exotic homes 4,000 miles apart—*four thousand miles, please*—is to me utterly fantastic.

September 21st:

Remarkable descent of warblers upon concrete birdbath in early afternoon of mild temperatures and brisk, southerly breeze. Two brightly colored parulas bathing at same time. Followed by a redstart in dull female plumage, then another. Also an immature blackpoll and a red-eyed vireo. Then three Tennessee warblers in fall plumage, quite greenish yellow. Two shortly afterward in earthenware bath on other side of house. Bathed vigorously, up to their mid-parts in water, for a good five minutes—quite extraordinary. One alone would surely never have remained so long. Charming to think of this companionship, conceivably throughout migration.

The next morning I stood in the driveway finding it hard to go indoors. Blue jays were deep in vocal exchanges in the trees. Like crows, jays become very garrulous on resuming their social life in the autumn after the constraints of the breeding season. These were carrying on in a conversational undertone of quacking or "queeking" with now and again voices raised in a harsher, louder discourse. Surely this was truly talk! "Purty, purty, purty," one would say. What could it mean? Suddenly an outcry from them heralded trouble: jays are great ones for rousing the woods to danger, not, presumably, because they are sharper-eyed than other birds, but because where others freeze in silence they yell to high heaven.

Trouble fluttered in fast through the trees in the form of a sharp-shinned hawk, which put down on a branch above the driveway. Patterned in brown and larger than the jays, it was a young female. But the hunting had been spoiled and without wasting time she crouched, was off and had sped away. A bay-breasted warbler I had been watching, with some of the bay remaining on its flanks, had simply evaporated, not to be seen again.

Most small birds do their main migrating at night. From radar observation, it would appear that they fly usually at between 1,500 and 3,000 feet, though migrants traced by an aircraft carrier crossing the Mediterranean sent back echoes from between 4,000 and 6,000 feet. In darkness the migrants are safe from hawks, at whose mercy they would be by day. (In Europe, Eleonora's falcon, smaller than a peregrine

across the sky, they fill the woods with a
discordant symphony of cluckings and shrillings.

With wings spread like an Indian chief's bonnet,
a junco is stopped by a shutter in midair.

and proportionately longer of wing and tail, which is skilled at capturing and consuming prey on the wing, nests semicolonially on rocky Mediterranean isles, beginning in midsummer, to insure its young a supply of autumn migrants attempting to cross the sea and having no means of escape.)

But what is probably of equal importance to safety is that by migrating at night, normally diurnal birds leave the day free for feeding, which darkness would preclude. Swallows, swifts and nighthawks, which capture their fare on the wing and can feed as they go, and are strong flyers besides, migrate by day. So, too, does the kingbird, "always active and exuberant," as Jean Dorst, of the Muséum National d'Histoire Naturelle in Paris, says; its migrating flocks of up to several hundred are conspicuous in Central America.

Bands of blue jays winging by at 100 or 200 feet in businesslike silence against a sky matching their azure are as much a part of autumn's rites in the East as the incarnadining of the multitudinous woods beneath them. But of all migrants the most difficult to overlook are the grackles. Beginning as a rule in late afternoon, they come by in rivers overhead, also usually at between 100 and 200 feet, from horizon to horizon. Last year there was one of these processions as early as July 19th. "Grackles have been everywhere in the

past four or five days," I wrote on September 22nd, "pouring over the fields and through the trees to settle briefly on the branches, adding black foliage to green, or to forage over the ground, filling the woods with soft cluckings, gratings and shrillings."

To spend the whole day lying on one's back on the grass, I thought, would be the thing. There would be the luminous blue of the sky to watch for nighthawks that come by on wings that seem to work on springs; swallows of our six species; hawks passing swiftly in power flight at treetop level or, with sails set, circling serenely in a buoyant, southward-drifting cushion of rising warm air; perhaps a loon streaking by like a flying bow and arrow.

Oh, to a watcher of the sky anything is possible: a white ibis, a raven like a black cross, an eagle in lordly disdain of the earth. And looking up into the trees at the wood's edge for warblers to materialize, three or four together, may be as good a way to catch them as to go seeking them out. One who knows how difficult it can be to spot a butterfly-colored male in spring, singing its head off in the crown of a tree only half leafed out, can appreciate what the odds are against noticing one of the little sprites as it moves in silence, rummaging restlessly through the heavy foliage of September. When you do detect one, you still have to

But after the breeding season most male warblers lose their brilliance of color, which the juveniles, who outnumber them, have yet to acquire. On the southward trek, moreover, instead of coming through hard upon one another's heels in about a month, often in a wave when favored localities will be alive with them, the warblers drift through undramatically and nearly voiceless during a period almost twice as long. So when you say "fall warblers" you explain why for every five or ten birders in the Arnold Arboretum, or in Central Park, or on the Chesapeake and Ohio Canal on a May morning, there is only one on a morning in September.

Yet many birders, if they had to settle for one season or the other, might well choose autumn. There are more birds then, and the erratics are likeliest. Some displacement of migrants to east or west is apt to occur both spring and fall, but the postbreeding season is, above any, a time of wandering. Now, too, for those of us in the East, is the best time for strays from the West —though the excitement of recording one must be offset by knowledge of the fate that probably awaits it.

Recalling how, one August, he had seen three western kingbirds perched on electric wires along a road on Monhegan Island, some 16 miles off the coast of Maine, while friends of his had seen two others elsewhere on the island, the able nature columnist Irston Barnes comments that "instead of flying south, these birds had flown northeast," and judges that "for all practical purposes such birds are permanently lost. They probably do not have any means to correct and set a new course." What is most extraordinary about his report is that there were five of the aberrants. Since it is hardly conceivable that the internal compasses of all five would have been off just so much as to bring them to the same place 1,000 miles away, it must have been that four of them followed a misguided fifth.

pray that it will hold still in the open for the two seconds you need to get your glasses on it and its image on your retina, and that it will not prove to be one of those greenish or tannish indeterminates that do not quite correspond to any picture in the field guide.

All these uncertainties are comprised, for the birder, in the term "fall warblers." And when we speak of going out for the migration, it is above all (among the small land birds) the warblers we have in mind. In their number of species as of individuals, in the floral variety and brightness of their colors as in their delicacy and animation, they are a birder's delight; in the mid-Atlantic states there are some 35 species he has a good chance of seeing in May or September. They have his gratitude, too, in that their songs give him the means of identifying them even when they cannot be seen. (Said an uncle of mine to stimulate my interest in Wagner when I was 14, "Think of the motifs as warbler songs.")

Perched across the bottom of these two pages, resplendent in their

bejeweled coloration, quiescent and yet vibrant with life's

heartbeat, is a panoply of birddom. From far left, and in order, are:

The East Coast may for another reason be favored in late summer and early autumn by visitors many hundreds of miles out of orbit. That is the season of hurricanes. Caribbean seabirds caught in the eye of one of these circular storms will, rather than fight the 75-plus-miles-per-hour winds raging around it, accompany the relative calm of the eye as the storm pursues its course until its winds eventually diminish or it moves inland, and end up as notable vagrants on some fortunate birder's checklist.

But autumn has more with which to move us than the spectaculars it may bring. Stand out-of-doors at night in September and hear the call notes faintly raining down from the dark sky, some recognizable, like those of thrushes and the "peents" of bobolinks. Let yourself visualize the little forms peppering the obscurity, winging all in one direction, high above black forests and fiery-glowing towns, above rivers, bays and seas shimmering like dragon skin in the moonlight. There is poignancy in the matching of insignificance against overpowering distances of as much as thousands of miles for some of the migrants; and this is especially so in autumn when as many as half or more of the hastening specks, cheeping in exchange of assurances, are only weeks old and on their way, as Barnes puts it, "to an unknown destination by an unknown route . . . impelled by forces which they do not understand."

Then if you back away far enough to see in the mind's eye all North America and the vast breadth of Eurasia, there is as much drama as you can encompass in the draining southward of dustings of birds rising from, passing over, settling upon every shore, waterway, fen, marsh, spinney, meadow, heath and acre of forest the hemisphere around, clamorous or silent, by ones and twos and by thousands—hummingbirds, larks, cranes, waterfowl—in a living tide not otherwise exampled even in great hidden realms of the deep.

The Southern Hemisphere, we may note, witnesses no such phenomena—though that domain of the oceans has its own version in the seasonal movements of its myriad myriads of seabirds. Below the equator, few considerable landmasses obtrude into the middle latitudes, and of those that do, only the narrowing South American peninsula has winters slightly comparable to those assailing the immense territories of the upper northern latitudes. Some species desert Tasmania and southern Australia, a few reaching Indonesia. Many South African birds migrate the relatively short distance to the Congo and Tanzania and many from lower South America to the broad beam of the continent; two Patagonian swallows make it to Central America and even Mexico. But not a single land bird of the Southern Hemisphere—or any other but a few petrels—has the migratory impetus to carry it through the tropics to the summer temperate zone, as so many birds of the Northern Hemisphere have.

By the last week of October, autumn's final chapter is under way. On the 19th, at the epitome of its glory, the first white-throated sparrows appear while the two kinglets are still much in evidence—tiny creatures so compact as to be neckless—and the last olive-backed thrush is at the birdbath. From the bank of the stream a winter wren skedaddles—a dark little peg-tailed gimmick; you would think it would be lonely. The next morning the fields are rimed in four degrees of frost. A heavy fall of leaves follows. Hard freezes on the 21st and 22nd bring the first juncos and a brief stopover by two hermit thrushes in the dogwood near my window. Silent in movement as two small brown shadows, motionless in repose after the characteristic lifting and subsidence of the tail on alighting, the thrushes seem mere thoughts of birds, as yet uncorporealized. The hardy myrtle warblers have acquired the appear-

a Canada warbler, a northern oriole; a tufted titmouse; a summer tanager; a female belted kingfisher; a predatory sharp-shinned hawk, true to form, with a hapless evening grosbeak.

ance of winter birds in brown, furry-looking plumage.

There are reprieves. On October 28th a horned grebe, bird of the rough winter seas, is to be seen on the river and, nearby, the first group of the raft of ruddy ducks that winters here—so many floating tea-pots with tails for spouts. The day is mild and sunny, an extension of spring's lease.

But for all its color and excitement and regretful looks backward to times of song and flowering, autumn is a losing season.

Yet all is not over. It is for this stage that nature reserves a crowning demonstration, heralded by one of its great voices. The sound is one you are seldom immediately sure of, when the first audible presentiment comes downwind of a clamor in the northern sky. The geese! It is out-of-doors then in a rush. What a summons it is, that high, broken, incessant baying out of the wild and solitary spaces of the north, like the sounds of an army returning with battle honors from a frontier beyond the imagination of stay-at-homes. And there they come, the dark, strongly beating forms, forward-striving in the outstretched necks, all in one rank, wing tip to wing tip in that extraordinary, broad V-formation—an incredible sight in the humdrum sky above the suburbs. Cry havoc! No, it is not havoc they cry but the untamed and untamable, the unquench-able springs of our common vitality, clarioned in the heavens by the passing phalanx that all may hear.

Only the setting-in of the hard freeze in the north could send those stalwarts southward down the sky roads. When the Canada geese come through, winter cannot be far off.

Heralded by one of nature's great combined voices, a skyful of geese begins its annual migration.

By S. Dillon Ripley

Extinction's tide and the ripples and eddies of hope

There are species gone and species going.
A few we still can save and, occasionally,
a mourned species turns up alive and well

"Whatever happened to the white-winged guan?" an ornithological friend of mine asked me the other day. This pheasantlike bird is known to science only by three mounted specimens, one of which is in a museum in Lima, Peru, and it was the specimens about which my friend was worried. "I can't find out what happened to the other two," he said.

The other specimens are said to be in Warsaw and London, but I'm not sure. Moreover, no one knows where the white-winged guan itself is, beyond the fact that it was found in 1876 near Tumbez on the northwestern slopes of the Peruvian Andes and described by Count Taczanowski in 1877. Having thus been described and registered for science as part of the inventory of living things that the great 18th-century encyclopedists felt was the way to record the six days of Creation, the white-winged guan disappeared from human sight. It hangs there like a dangling participle.

Is it worse really not to know?

We *do* know a good deal about the dodo. It lived, though we don't of course know how long, on the tiny Indian Ocean island of Mauritius. Before 1628 the Dutch landed pigs on the island, in Robinson Crusoe fashion, to maintain God-fearing shipwrecked sailors. Pig reproduction and appetites being what they are, the dodos lasted barely 50 years after this mistaken

In addition to his duties as the Smithsonian Institution's secretary, biologist S. Dillon Ripley is writing a book on the marsh birds of the world.

Illustrations by Daniel Owen Stolpe

Among the annals of the forever lost are
the solitaire of Réunion (lower left corner),
the dodo and (upper right) the red rail.

Huddled in the lower right and also extinct are
the blue rail, the Mauritian pink pigeon
and, again from Mauritius, the pigeon hollandais.

piece of Dutch philanthropy, having disappeared by 1681. Now we know about the dodo from fewer than a dozen sketches and paintings, a collection of bones from a Mauritian swamp where the birds were evidently trapped by their own weight and clumsiness, and by some skin and head fragments at Oxford—pieces from what was the only preserved specimen.

In 1755 the curator of the museum in Oxford saw a moth fly out of the stuffed dodo as he passed by.

"Take that dodo out and burn it. It has a moth," he said. The skin and head fragments were salvaged—by someone unknown—from the little conflagration in the courtyard, so we are at least tantalized by fragments. Are we better off knowing even that much about the dodo?

During many years in India I had always dreamed of seeing a pink-headed duck, an angular bird, its body clothed in sober brown plumage with a little creamy gray on the wings. Its real glory was the head and neck which, in the male, were a brilliant shade of pink, Schiaparelli "shocking pink"—a most implausible creature.

None has been seen since before World War II. The last place where they seemed to occur in the wild was Darbangha, the state of a rich maharaja in the Himalayan foothills in Bihar.

In 1948 I heard from a Mr. Danby, a retired agent for the maharaja, and my saddest thoughts were confirmed. "Each winter," Mr. Danby wrote, "the maharaja's hunters trapped a good number of migratory duck on the local *jheels* (ponds), and brought them to a large aviary which the ruler had constructed. I remember occasional pink-headed ducks, which were of course rare, and local, caught in pairs.

"During the winter, the maharaja ate all the duck, the aviary serving as larder." How sensible of him, but how sad to think that as he ate the last cooked pink-

headed duck, probably boiled for a curry, the maharaja didn't even realize what a special gustatory triumph he was enjoying. How many people in the world have ever eaten a pink-headed duck?

So we know the fate of the pink-headed duck and the dodo, if not the white-winged guan, but what good does it do to know? Perhaps it is only morbid to eulogize these minor disappearances. Perhaps they only tell us something about ourselves that we would rather not be told again.

Of course evolution is far older than we are. To be sure, long before Man's appearance, many life forms had become extinct as the result of vast climatic changes, mountain-building and continental movements. But from my own subjective point of view, what fascinates me is what has happened in the last two million years since Man arrived. That is merely 1/1,250th of the time during which life has existed on Earth, but it is a big enough fraction of time for me, and what is intensely interesting is the effect Man has had on his surroundings in that period.

For example, it seems likely that the present problems of the Middle East, which are economic problems as much as anything else, had their origin long before written history in the discovery of how to domesticate animals—sheep, then goats and then migrations of flocks from settlement to settlement. From North Africa to India, a limited rainfall supported acacia forests, a dry savanna land of limited species of grasses and shrubs and large populations of a few animal species ranging from lions and ostriches down through antelope and game birds and a variety of smaller orga-

Bustards once ranged widely over the world.
Now endangered, they are protected in many areas.

nisms. It was a fragile environment, and grazing by domestic animals, once begun, was irreversible. Destruction of savanna forests is a one-way street. Perhaps the nomads never should have left the Middle Eastern hillsides where more ample rainfall guaranteed a higher yield.

All over the world we can see the result of overgrazing: the creation of deserts in former savanna land. From experiments recently performed in western India, it seems highly probable that once the desiccating process begins, rainfall is itself affected. It seems to rain less in areas of man-made desert, and a "dustbowl" phenomenon results, made worse as political stability replaces nomad life and as populations concentrate and breed mightily in cities, making even heavier demands on the surrounding countryside.

It is too bad that historians or political scientists don't make more of this sort of thing. Politicians normally have no knowledge of their nation's biological past. In the Middle East, President Bourguiba of Tunisia knows the menace of goats. Through his tree-planting schemes he has begun to try to change the face of Tunisia. The cedar is the national emblem of Lebanon; a huge welcome sign to Beirut has a cedar tree appropriately cupped by hands in prayer.

The depredations of early Man

The drastic effects of human activity on the environment are not new, and today we reap the harvest of actions taken long, long ago, even those taken well before written history.

Large and dangerous wild animals such as the cave bear, cave hyena and cave lion of northern Europe and Asia seem to have been exterminated by early Man. These fierce creatures would have been difficult to kill; the simplest way would have been to kill off the young. Remains of young cave bears have been found in circumstances that indicate death at human hands. The gradual removal of the younger, more easily hunted animals would lead to the extermination of the species. So it must have been over much of the emerging world of the hunter.

Traps, deadfalls, overhanging cliffs, culs-de-sac into which stones and spears could be hurled—all contributed to the charnel heaps of old bones we now find. In the United States there are the remains of stone walls placed on hillsides into which herds of bison could be guided, only to stampede over a low cliff and die in large numbers—probably in larger numbers than were necessary. It is possible, though, that the Indians husbanded their wild supply of food and tried to kill only a few animals at a time.

In any event, the bison probably got a temporary reprieve when the Spanish introduced the modern

The fearless moa of New Zealand towered 12 feet high but it fell to early Polynesian settlers.

horse into North America in the 16th century. With increased hunting skill, the Indians would have been able to take more mature animals rather than young ones, and vigorous, young breeding stock would have grown rapidly. Then, of course, white buffalo hunters with skills even more efficient than those of the Indians finally attacked all age classes of the animals and nearly extirpated the species altogether, until Dr. William Temple Hornaday of the New York Zoological Society painstakingly reared some bison and in the early 1900s began shipping them west to recreate the herds now found.

Of course, it is difficult for us today to be sure how many animal species have vanished since Man developed fire and weapons. Added to the unfolding tale of the prehistoric hunter and of agricultural Man, the changer of whole environments, is the subsequent exploration of the world and its remote territories and islands. Vulnerable, isolated, flightless and fearless species fell like ninepins to skillful human explorers.

Not just Western Man: New Zealand had a whole family of flightless birds called moas, ranging from turkey-size to 12-foot giants. In the tenth century Polynesians came and within eight centuries, as Captain Cook arrived, the moas—all of them—were gone.

Lee M. Talbot, Smithsonian ecologist and senior scientist on the President's Council on Environmental Quality, has pointed out: "Since the time of Christ, Man has exterminated about two percent of the known species of the world's mammals. . . . However, more than half of these losses have occurred since 1900. During the past 150 years the rate of extermination of mammals has increased 55-fold." If the same rate were projected into the future—hopefully a most unlikely possibility—"In about 30 years all of the remaining 4,000 species of mammals could be gone," except presumably domestic species, including humans.

Scientists question such projections. Projections are not, after all, facts. When Rachel Carson published *Silent Spring,* plenty of scientists rallied to the pesticide industry and said that so long as all her suppositions were not proved, her statements about the dangers of insecticides were not only exaggerated but therefore possibly erroneous. At least they were nothing to worry about until they were proved. Scientists often forget that the French physiologist, Claude Bernard, said it is *not* against the rules for a scientist to make a supposition and believe it until he can prove it.

Orthodoxy in science comes from following the rules and subscribing only to proven facts, but if that is the only path to follow, science would have perished years ago.

In my own case I have been interested in the tiger since I first came across it in the wild as a boy of 13. In the 1920s there were maharajas in India who had records of 500 or more tigers killed by themselves. It was the "hairy-chest syndrome"—a grand piece of one-

upmanship. Colonial officials in Asian countries where the tiger occurred were given their quotas. Retiring governors in India always had the chance of one last ceremonial "durbar" at some maharaja's court and a "camp" somewhere with a tiger beaten up to the butts by scores of villagers, to be picked off by the governor's rifle. The governor might have a palsied hand or fading sight, but the maharaja's son or another keen young sportsman would be sitting beside the nabob in his tree platform, ready to press the trigger of his no. 2 gun so that there would be no failure, and the trophy would go safely home to be mounted, snarling out into dusty space.

War came to Asia and with it guns fell into everybody's hands. Forest and game departments of former colonial regimes withered under the new republics, and a tide of destruction was unleashed as economic development speeded up with new technologies.

In the last 50 years the tiger in India and Pakistan has shrunk in numbers from being "abundant," whatever that means (let us say more than 40,000 animals at least), to what I would guess is fewer than 2,500, perhaps only 1,000, and exists only in limited areas at that. Poaching, $7,000 women's coats (most unsuitable —tiger fur wears out and rubs badly) and occasional tourist hunts with a chance for the sportsman to bag one of the trophies (the same old hairy-chest stuff for the new rich), have accounted for the big decrease. So has grazing by cattle in former forest preserves, thus

The Arabian oryx once patrolled most of the Middle East. Its chances now rest with zoo keepers.

One could guess that the tiger will be extinct
in 25 years. Perhaps only 1,000 now live in the wild.

eliminating the tiger's natural food of deer and pig.

Three years ago I made a dangerous statement in a speech before a naturalists' society in Bombay, to the effect that the tiger would be extinct in 25 years. It made the newspapers and people were incredulous. I jeopardized my reputation as a biologist by speaking out without provable statistics—merely hazarding a guess, based on 40 years of visits to India.

But surely a scientist can have a hunch. I feel in my bones that the tiger can disappear in a twinkling, leaving hardly a trace. It is a supposition and one I would like to see *not* proved. But the odds are not good these days for wild creatures, and it seems unwise to wait for all the facts to be proved before acting.

Take birds: Some 95 species and almost as many subspecies and local populations have been recorded as having disappeared since 1600. Presumably there are others we don't know about. Presently almost 200 species and perhaps an additional 150 subspecies of birds are listed as endangered. Project *that* rate. How long before the rest of the 8,600 known bird species follow the mammals? Another unprovable supposition, perhaps, but it is well to consider the odds against the birds. Consider the widespread development of the Earth's more remote places since World War II, the vast increases in human populations, the eradication of human diseases by new chemicals and the general dissemination of arms.

The old codes of hunting still persist. The sport is no more sport, the food is not a vital necessity, but the old customs die hard. In the deserts, new rich men hunt game by age-old prerogative. Thus, for example, the houbara bustard, royal game of old, has disappeared from Arabia and is making its last stand in Pakistan. What to do? We could let them all vanish without a trace. But if that is our course, as Alfred Russell Wallace wrote in 1863, "future ages will cer-

tainly look back upon us as a people so immersed in the pursuit of wealth as to be blind to higher considerations. They will charge us with having culpably allowed the destruction of some of those records of Creation which we had it in our power to preserve; and while professing to regard every living thing as the direct handiwork and the best evidence of a creator, yet, with a strange inconsistency, seeing many of them perish irrecoverably from the face of the earth, uncared for and unknown."

Wallace was in favor of museum specimens and the value of this scientific record. Better, to Wallace, to know that there was a mounted white-winged guan or a pink-headed duck and to look at them once in a

Blackbuck antelope, mostly gone from the plains of India, gained a reprieve on Texas ranches.

while like visiting old gravestones. And of course, there's always the chance that we might have been fooled all along, and the creature might just be hiding, not extinct. We live on hope.

One course of action, and perhaps the only one at this time, is to keep breeding stocks in captivity, waiting until education has replaced outworn rituals.

A wild animal in captivity is not an ideal arrangement. Speeding over the desert sand dunes, the Arabian oryx is an ethereal-looking animal; in a California or Arizona zoo, it seems a rather squat, dumpy creature with odd needle-shaped horns (O horns of symbolism—of the unicorn and the virgin, of prowess and virility—those symbols will kill you in the end if you don't watch out). But in zoos, in captivity, these animals can be bred successfully. The same goes for the blackbuck antelope, now virtually gone from the plains of India but being bred in plenty on Texas ranches. Already a first shipment of live blackbuck has been flown to a new preserve in Pakistan.

We all hear of disasters. As the president of the International Council for Bird Preservation, I am likely to hear early of certain kinds of successes. Last July, for example, the first nesting of the lovely little Hawaiian goose since perhaps the turn of the century was observed on the island of Maui. It was feared on the verge of extinction, the victim of poaching and the destruction of its nests by wild dogs and cats. But it reappeared, was saved by a few dedicated men, reared in captivity and flown back to be released on its old and now protected range, first on the main island of Hawaii, now on Maui.

The Aleutian Canada goose, a geographically isolated miniature of the Canada goose, was thought extinct until sighted on Buldir Island in 1962. Now, at this writing, the U.S. Fish and Wildlife Service and a group of cooperators including my wife and me are rearing young Aleutian geese for eventual release on those islands of the chain that are fox-free. There are more Aleutian geese in captivity right now (nearly 100) than there were left on Buldir Island in 1962.

There are ups and downs in this business. Bermuda petrels, also called cahows, are good to eat, especially young fat ones. The 17th-century colonists on Bermuda ate most of them. A few survived on rocky islets until the 1940s, when the bird apparently vanished. Suddenly, in the 1950s, a few were found on an offshore islet, causing such an ornithological sensation that it was kept quiet at first for fear of over-eager birdwatchers. There were some left, we whispered among ourselves, perhaps a dozen. We took measures to protect the young petrels against the attacks of white-tailed tropic birds which also nested there, and all was serene for a while. The colony built up to 24 nesting pairs this year, with 50 percent reproductive success. But the birds are full of DDT, ingested at sea, presumably from the bodies of tiny Atlantic shrimp and other planktonic food. The cahow seems doomed all over again.

Another success is the takahe, a huge gallinule—flightless, with purplish blue irridescent feathers and a powerful-looking reddish bill. It was described by A. B. Meyer in 1883 from a single specimen that reached the Dresden Museum. It had come from a lake on South Island, New Zealand, and the species was not seen again after a dog caught one in 1898. Not, that is, until 1948, when climbers found a colony of fewer than 100 birds in a tiny steep-sided valley high in the Murchison Mountains. Protection may yet save it, just as vigilance may save other vanishing species like the whooping crane and the California condor.

Just after World War II, but before the takahe had been rediscovered, an ornithologist asked me, "What ever happened to the takahe, the specimen I mean?"

"You mean the one in Dresden?" I replied. "Don't know, just vanished." It is nice to be able to report now that the live takahe still exists, whatever the fate of the specimen. I suppose we must be content with small triumphs, but they are rarer every year. All over the world today species are dropping off, in a twinkling, like the lights of fireflies, into limbo.

Whatever happened, whatever happened? Often now we don't have the answers.

Whatever happened . . .? Sometimes I feel the voices are trailing off like those of very old men talking about former, and now lost, acquaintances.

Long thought extinct, the gaudy takahe (left) was found again on New Zealand; the Hawaiian nene has been brought back by dedicated men.

By Howard Ensign Evans

Taxonomists' curiosity may help save the world

Many say there's neither time nor need to try cataloguing all the world's creatures. A scientist says it is necessary that we try

It was in the autumn of 1728 that a young medical student with a passion for botany and a young divinity student with a passion for fishes met at the University of Uppsala—and the spark that leapt between them was to ignite a flame that is still burning. This was the age of enlightenment, the era of exploration—a time when the study of natural history had become respectable, and when expeditions to distant parts of the globe were reporting plants and animals previously undreamed of. What could be more important than to inventory all of the things of nature? But seven years later Peter Artedi, the divinity student, stumbled into a canal and was drowned, and it remained for Carl Linnaeus to bring their plans to fruition.

This he did with great success. His *Systema Naturae* went through 13 editions, each one something of a scientific best seller for its day. Furthermore, he set in motion what is often called "the Linnaean age," a long period when nothing seemed more worthwhile than to describe and classify species. Taxonomy—the science of classification—was a calling of the highest repute.

In retrospect, Linnaeus' system of naming organisms hardly seems revolutionary. Giving things double names—one a group (generic) name and the other specific—is as natural as speech itself. For example: red maple, grizzly bear, honeybee. Linnaeus used Latin, the scholarly language of his day, and very logically put the group names first: hence *Acer rubrum, Ursus*

Illustrations by Fred Gwynne

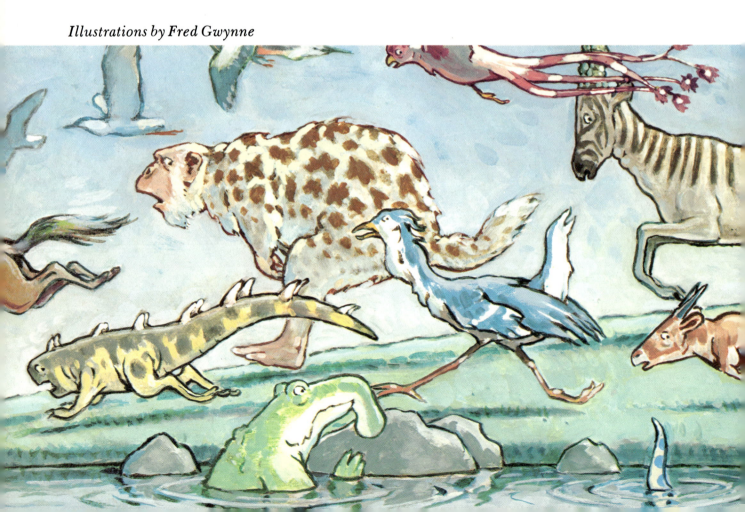

horribilis and *Apis mellifera*. It is true that Latin is no longer part of the education of most of us, but if Linnaeus had used his native Swedish, his system of names would hardly have become universal. And, as a dead language, Latin has no political connotations; to a Russian or a Japanese or anyone else, *Acer rubrum* is still *Acer rubrum*.

Such names can roll off the tongue like a song. I well remember how, as a college freshman, I delighted in surprising my friends with the name of the green sea urchin, *Strongylocentrotus dröbachiensis*. What a wonderful name, enough to give a computer indigestion! But let's not let automation squeeze *all* the poetry out of life. And the cold fact is that those who find Linnaean nomenclature cumbersome have yet to propose a successful alternative. To a considerable extent, we are still in the Linnaean age, for we still use his system of binomial nomenclature; and taxonomists, by and large, are still committed to the belief that a complete systematic inventory of living things is not only possible but a matter of high priority. Nevertheless, both Linnaean nomenclature and the hope and need for a total inventory of nature are now being seriously questioned.

Linnaeus in his *Species Plantarum* (1753) recorded about 7,300 species of plants, and in the tenth edition of *Systema Naturae* (1758) some 4,200 species of animals. But today the number of described species of flowering plants exceeds 300,000, and slightly more than a million kinds of animals are known. Many Linnaean genera are now regarded as families, and a host of new categories have been devised to accommodate all of these names. Classification has become so complex that textbooks can present only the barest outline (and hardly any two agree). The detailed classification of specific groups is often known to but a handful of people scattered widely about the globe—and they are unlikely to agree on all particulars.

In a recent article in *Science,* Peter H. Raven, Brent Berlin and Dennis E. Breedlove stated that there are approximately ten million kinds of organisms, and despite more than two centuries of effort we have still described only some 15 percent of them. Furthermore, "the rapid growth of the human population will cause most of the remainder to disappear from the earth before they are seen by a taxonomist." So much for the dreams of Linnaeus and Artedi.

"The complete description of life on earth . . . is impossible," wrote Paul Ehrlich of Stanford University almost ten years ago. And, more recently, Ernst Mayr of Harvard, one of the most widely respected figures in the field of systematics, expressed his opinion that "we need work in alpha taxonomy [that is, species] only in the areas where such knowledge is essential." Unfortunately, he provides no rigid standards for deciding what is essential, and I suspect that the average

In this visual fable, which was inspired by (and starts sequentially below) Dr. Evans' reasoned plea for more taxonomic research, a multitude of fantastic animals stream across the scene, yet . . .

businessman, congressman or (for that matter) college administrator would, on this basis, sweep all of taxonomy into the wastebasket.

I doubt that scientific progress has ever resulted from pursuit of the "essential." Rather, it has emanated from persons who were, above all, *curious.* And to accept any of the dicta quoted above is to say that to be curious about the diversity of nature is to be misguided. As R. J. Herrnstein of Harvard University has pointed out, "what looks 'important' at any time reflects a consensus based upon what is already known." If this is true (as it surely is), one could make a strong case for the deliberate pursuit of what seems unimportant and nonessential (as I would).

A year or two ago I became interested in an obscure group of South American spider wasps of unknown relationships. I was puzzled because no females had ever been discovered, although males of several species were not uncommon in the collections of several museums. All of these males were banded with yellow and brown like many of the social wasps of the tropics, which are abundant and armed with powerful stings. After careful study of museum material and discussions with persons who had collected these wasps in the field, I concluded that the females must have been placed in a different genus because, in overall form and in coloration, they were utterly unlike the males. All had, in fact, blue-black bodies and orange wings, and were evidently mimics of tarantula hawks and other widespread wasps of similar color.

This proved to be the first known case of what I called dual mimicry; that is, a case in which the females and males of the same species belonged to very different mimicry complexes. It happens that in these wasps the two sexes spend most of their time in different habitats. Under these conditions it evidently had survival value (vis-à-vis vertebrate predators) for each sex to adopt a color pattern like the most pernicious stinger in its habitat. Having drawn these conclusions, I re-examined several other puzzling groups and found several additional examples.

Now I would be the last to claim that this research was essential, but it was gratifying; it fitted a few "loose pieces" into place and it resulted in a hypothesis of at least limited application. By some standards, no doubt I should have junked my manuscript. Recycled, the paper might have provided the wrapper for a package of spaghetti or some other essential commodity. As it is, I have added to the glutting of our libraries simply to satisfy idle curiosity. But I wonder whether most of what we do now know about our en-

Dr. Evans, author of Life on a Little-Known Planet *and* Wasp Farm, *recently moved from Harvard's Museum of Comparative Zoology to Colorado State University. Mr. Gwynne is a stage and TV actor.*

. . . how less fantastic is the true range of diversity among creatures that really inherit the Earth.

vironment didn't come about in much the same way.

Fortunately, there are many people who still find living things so terribly exciting that they cannot leave them alone. We live on a planet where, through several billion years, vast numbers of distinctively different kinds of organisms have evolved from simple primordial molecules. The processes we can now deduce, though with some uncertainties, and the products we can study in nature and in the holdings of our museums. To thinking persons they provide a drama without parallel. We have spent billions of dollars to collect a few sterile rocks on the moon—and are still devoting endless pages in our journals to their analysis. Has the dead moon become more essential to us than the living Earth?

I agree that as human populations continue to expand, the delicately balanced environments of more and more living things will be destroyed; we see this happening every day. That is all the more reason to make an all-out effort to describe the diversity of life, for without such an effort we shall simply never know. And a case can be made for our greater dependence on the things of nature as the human population approaches saturation. The sperm whale is nearing extinction, but we read in SMITHSONIAN (April 1972) that an obscure desert plant called jojoba produces a liquid wax very similar in chemical properties to sperm oil. We hear that a little-known beetle produces cortexone,

a medically important drug, in amounts equivalent to the adrenal glands of 1,300 cattle. How can we know what organisms may enrich our lives—or permit us to survive a bit longer—if we cease to inquire? How can we be sure that we are not, this year, bringing about the extinction of a species that we may desperately need 50 years hence?

At the moment much research is being conducted on prostaglandins, very potent hormones that occur in minute quantities in most animal tissues and exhibit a startling array of pharmacological properties. Among other things, they appear to mediate inflammation, and a better understanding of their precise role may some day lead to more effective treatment of such persistent maladies as asthma and arthritis. A few years ago it was found that compounds closely related to prostaglandins occur in quantity in a gorgonian (soft coral) inhabiting West Indian reefs. The very limited supply of mammalian prostaglandin is expected to be supplemented soon by large quantities obtained by synthesis from precursor compounds in the gorgonian. This is exciting news for researchers and for pharmaceutical companies, one of which is already planning to harvest the reefs—one hopes with appropriate caution and good sense.

Paul D. Hurd jr., chairman of the Entomology Department of the Smithsonian Institution, has been studying, along with several coworkers, the systematics

and host relationships of bees of the genus *Peponapis*. These bees collect pollen only from the blossoms of *Cucurbita,* a genus that includes our cultivated squashes and pumpkins, and there is evidence that the bees and their host plants evolved together in warmer parts of the Western hemisphere.

Not only has the systematics of the bees provided clues as to how cultivated squashes may have evolved from wild ancestors, but it appears that it may be possible to increase the yield of these crops in the Old World (where they were brought from America long ago, without the bees) by establishing species of *Peponapis* in suitable habitats. Hurd and a coworker have described about a third of the species of *Peponapis,* and it is quite possible that the groundwork they have laid may prove far more relevant in retrospect than it ever did at the time.

Examples such as this could be supplied ad infinitum. In 1885 Carlos Berg, in the course of his studies of the Argentinian insect fauna, described a small moth as *Cactoblastis cactorum*. Did he foresee that 40 years later 60 million acres of Australian countryside would be overrun by alien cacti and that of 150 cactus-feeding insects surveyed, *Cactoblastis* would prove the key to the problem—nearly wiping out the cactus in a few years? Of course he didn't.

Could anyone have predicted the current search for "wonder drugs" in diverse and often poorly studied parts of the plant world? The discovery in recent years of antibiotics, muscle relaxants, hypo- and hypertensive agents, cortisone precursors and a startling array of hallucinogens has led Richard E. Schultes of Harvard to remark that "the Plant Kingdom represents a virtually untapped reservoir of new chemical compounds, many extraordinarily biodynamic, some providing novel bases on which the synthetic chemist may build even more interesting structures." Professor Schultes cites an estimate that perhaps a fourth of the vascular plants of the New World tropics—a proven source of new drugs—have yet to be described, and many of the described species remain poorly known. Is it appropriate to throw up our hands in despair, when we can be quite sure that discoveries of many kinds await those who work toward them?

Every blueprint for survival on Earth includes the substitution of biological control methods for chemical pesticides. Why is this proving so difficult? Because the parasitic wasps and flies that we wish to rely upon are so poorly understood. These are very tiny insects, requiring detailed study of their structure, life histories and host relationships. A good friend of mine who has devoted many years to the study of ichneumon wasps, perhaps the largest of all groups of parasites of pest species, had his research funds cut off, doubtless by persons convinced that we can "no longer afford" to be curious.

The opinion that taxonomists should discriminate species only "where such knowledge is essential" is hardly novel. One of my favorite quotes to taxonomy classes is the following: "It seems to me sufficient to consider those kinds [of organisms] which prove to us that they deserve to be distinguished. . . . It seems to me that the many hundreds and hundreds of species of gnats and very small moths . . . may be left confounded with one another."

This is from the Introduction of Réaumur's *Mémoires pour servir à l'Histoire des Insectes,* published in 1734, one year before the appearance of the first edition of Linnaeus' *Systema Naturae.* Are we to return to pre-Linnaean times simply because the task proved far more difficult than supposed?

I would like to reconsider, too, the statement mentioned earlier that we have only described some 15 percent of the ten million kinds of organisms. It is commonly agreed that most species of birds have been described, and a high percentage of the species of mammals, butterflies and several other "popular" groups. In the group I know best, the Aculeata wasps, I would estimate that more than 90 percent of the species north of Mexico have been described (though admittedly the tropics do not fare so well).

Speaking of the insect fauna of Australia—one of the most inadequately studied groups from one of the less well known continents—K. H. L. Key estimates that the description and naming of species may be 70 percent completed (although I think this percentage is a bit too high). Flowering plants continue to be described at the rate of about 3,700 species a year, but here (as in many groups) there is a certain amount of "overdescribing"—that is, the creation of unnecessary names in regional studies when more comprehensive monographs would demonstrate that several supposed species are one and the same. Of course, it is as much the function of good taxonomy to point out such synonymies as it is to discover novelties.

It is true that there are vast groups in which many thousands of species remain unrecognized, groups such as the nematodes, mites and parasitic wasps—ironically, groups showing much host-specificity and of potentially great importance to agriculture. Nevertheless, I cannot go along with the estimate that only 15 percent of all organisms have been described; surely 50 percent is much closer to the truth.

And if this is the case, and about 1.5 million have so far been described, then the total may not exceed three million. This is depressing enough, or challenging enough, depending on one's mood. But it is not a cause for alarm. The task can and should be accomplished. Given the cost of only one moon shot, a great deal could be done in a few years, at least in a preliminary way.

Of course, no one pretends that to describe and

Time, unfortunately, appears to be running out for many species whose names we might never know.

Are they, in the words of an old nonsensical song, about to be "kicked in the head by a butterfly"?

name a species is to "know" it. This is only the first step to knowledge, but it is an essential step, not only because one needs to have a name for it, but because by placing it in a family and genus of organisms, one has the basis for predicting many things about it. This in itself serves as a guide to acquiring further knowledge. For example, I am currently describing a new wasp from Peru, placing it in the family Pompilidae (all members of which prey upon spiders and use one spider per nest-cell, so far as is known) and in the genus *Aporus* (known species of which prey on trapdoor spiders and have structural modifications associated with this behavior). Thus something has been grasped in the realm of the unknown and placed in a position where more can readily be learned about it— one knows where to look and, in gross terms, what to look for. Such a matter might be critically important in medicine or agriculture; and no one can predict to what use such knowledge might be put in elucidating the structure of an ecosystem or in demonstrating some principle of evolution or animal behavior.

Members of a genus share certain common features of structure and biology just as the genera comprising a family have fundamental similarities. A sound classification has enormous information content. Although the many categories recognized by the modern systematist may seem ponderous to the layman, in fact they reflect in remarkably concise fashion a vast body of sophisticated data. For Linnaeus, five categories sufficed. Such is our knowledge of living and fossil members of some groups that we now use more than 20 categories, from kingdom down to subspecies. The non-specialist may use as much or as little of this as suits his purpose. He may feel confident that if the classification is sound, it will lead him to almost any information he might require.

In the words of George G. Simpson, systematics "gathers together, utilizes, summarizes, and implements everything that is known about animals [and plants], whether morphological, physiological, or ecological." Our system of organizing this knowledge may not be perfect—but what is?

The time, also, is long past when taxonomists contented themselves with the gross features of dead museum specimens. They are studying organisms in all stages of their life cycle; they are revealing minute, wholly unexpected structural details by the use of scanning electron microscopy; they are analyzing behavior patterns, chromosome configurations, and even the sequence of amino acids in protein and nucleic acid molecules.

Modern classifications, of course, reflect these sophisticated approaches. This is a cause for alarm in some taxonomic quarters, as what seemed to be one species has sometimes proved to be several. By analyzing song patterns, B. B. Fulton and R. D. Alexander

have demonstrated that "the" field cricket of eastern North America is in reality seven species; although they could not be differentiated on the basis of dead specimens, they fail to interbreed in nature. Studies of egg color and structure, along with other biological features, revealed that "the" malaria mosquito of Europe was actually six species, only two of which actually transmit malaria effectively. Use of a minute parasitic wasp to control the California red-scale insect, a serious pest of citrus, led to inconsistent results until Paul DeBach and his colleagues discovered that what was thought to be one was actually seven different species, each having its own biological characteristics. This discovery provided a vastly improved basis for control and permitted the introduction of several new species of scale-insect parasites.

Such discoveries are exciting and of fundamental importance. We still pay homage to Linnaeus, but we have gone very far beyond the brief Latin descriptions of superficial features that sufficed for his day.

It is ironic that in our time, when ecology has truly become a household word, young systematists are having even more difficulty than usual in finding positions. In the words of Edward O. Wilson, writing in the journal *Ecology:* "Most of the central problems of ecology can be solved only by reference to details of organic diversity. Even the most cursory ecosystem analyses have to be based on sound taxonomy. . . . The food nets, the fluctuation of population numbers . . . the colonization of empty habitats . . . and most other basic topics of ecology, require a deep understanding of the biology of individual taxa." Yet there are large groups of organisms having only one or two specialists in the entire world, and sometimes none at all.

"It is the exclusive property of man to contemplate and to reason on the great book of nature. She gradually unfolds herself to him who, with patience and perseverance, will search into her mysteries." As a person caught in the turmoil and surfeit of our times, I have become blasé about a great many things and a doubter of many human enterprises and supposed values. But I have never questioned the sentiments expressed by Linnaeus in the above sentences from the introduction to his *Systema Naturae.*

I am not sure whether, at this stage, a more profound knowledge of the biosphere—including, as a first step, an inventory of living things—would save us from destroying the Earth as a viable habitat for Man. Perhaps not. But it would be nice to think that we tried at last to acquaint ourselves with the cast of that greatest of all dramas that began with a primordial soup and one day yielded a superb green world filled with remarkable creatures, including, at least for a few ticks of the cosmic clock, a being that imagined himself master of the Earth.

The curious naturalist may chase only the butterfly, but he'll find a lot more after he catches up.

Edward S. Ayensu

Calling the roll of the world's vanishing plants

New international Red Data Book *reveals how grazing, logging, development, pollution and other pressures could doom many species*

Now-famous Furbish's lousewort is threatened by proposed dam on St. John River (background), but careful conservation measures may yet save it.

While the plight of endangered creatures such as blue whales and whooping cranes is widely appreciated, it is less well known that from 20,000 to 25,000 of the world's *plant* species face extinction. Today botanists are trying to locate, identify and protect these species; it is an enormous task, complicated by considerations involving law, land use, economics and large doses of human emotion. In many parts of the world the flora is so little known that the exact status of a given plant is difficult to determine. In 1973, at an international conference on endangered species, some countries, out of national pride, proposed for endangered status native plants that proved to be common, even weeds; rectifying this situation at later meetings involved delicate diplomatic maneuvering.

More recently, the International Union for the Conservation of Nature and Natural Resources (IUCN) appealed to botanists around the world to supply accurate information about endangered species in their countries. The IUCN's Threatened Plants Committee, of which I am the chairman for North America, has assembled these data for a new publication to "highlight the growing and continuing threats to the world's natural ecosystems and the diversity of species they contain." This *Plant Red Data Book* is being prepared in London by the secretary of the Threatened Plants Committee, Grenville Lucas, and should be available by the end of the year. Although it will cover only 250 of the thousands of species the IUCN feels need protection, these species include some of the plants that are in the gravest danger, or are particularly spectacular, useful or interesting.

The plants listed in the book have become endangered for a wide variety of reasons—overgrazing by domestic or feral animals, herbicide spraying, fires, cutting for timber or firewood, damage by off-road vehicles (SMITHSONIAN, September 1978), forest clearing and collecting by plant fanciers. (Ironically, no plant has become threatened because we eat it—societies maintain their important food plants through careful stewardship.)

The case of Furbish's lousewort

Today the most celebrated of all endangered plants is an unprepossessing member of the snapdragon family (left), Furbish's lousewort (*Pedicularis furbishiae*), which was named for Kate Furbish, an American turn-of-the-century botanical artist of considerable repute. After a careful search, the U.S. Army Corps of Engineers has located only about 1,000 individual plants—all of them along a 120-mile stretch of the St. John River in northern Maine and a much shorter stretch of the river in New Brunswick. The surviving louseworts occur in the area of the proposed

Dickey-Lincoln hydroelectric project, which, if constructed, would inundate them. Because of the special protection endangered plants and animals have been given in the United States, the future of the Dickey-Lincoln project has been called into question.

The case has aroused intense emotion, both on the part of the environmental groups who want to see the dam halted—the free-flowing St. John not only provides a riverbank habitat for the lousewort but runs through a beautiful 140-square-mile wilderness area—and of proponents of the dam. The feelings of the latter were articulated in a letter to the editor of *Time:* "For heaven's sake, the species was thought extinct anyway—let's make it official and drown it under a few billion gallons of water." It appears now that the dam will be built—but with special conservation measures to save the plant.

Invasion by subdivisions and rooikrans

Other American plants are endangered by much smaller development projects. One such is the Dehesa beargrass or San Diego nolina *(Nolina interrata)*, a lovely relative of the lily that bears a flower stalk about five feet high (right). Only about 150 individual plants are known to exist, and they are all distributed along the margins of two or three small gullies in San Diego. Since the locality has recently been designated as a residential area, the chances are that this elegant plant will be lost forever.

It is not only in the United States that plants are under pressure. The temperate Cape flora of South Africa, dominated by heaths and proteas—flowers that look like roses made of porcelain—is one of the most varied and spectacular in the world. Yet it has been estimated that approximately 1,500 species in the Cape flora are threatened. One of the rarest proteas, *Mimetes hottentotica*, is being invaded and ousted by weedy Australian trees such as hakeas and rooikrans.

Even more disquieting is the illegal trade in South African cycads. These plants are so coveted by collectors that recently a specimen of *Encephalartos woodii* was stolen from the Durban Botanic Gardens and is said to have sold for $65,000. Another endangered cycad, *Encephalartos barteri* (p. 64), is being destroyed because it has a seed from which a hallucinogenic drug can be extracted—thieves even stole seeds from a specimen in Great Britain's Royal Botanic Gardens at Kew.

The African violet *(Saintpaulia ionantha)*, widely known as a house plant, is exceedingly rare in its native habitat, the damp cliffsides of eastern Tanzania. There its precarious existence is threatened by the removal of forest trees that normally provide the shade in which it grows best.

Indeed, throughout the tropical regions of the

Dehesa beargrass thrusts up its stalk in a ravine in San Diego. This lilylike plant is under even greater pressure than the more celebrated lousewort.

Bare of leaves in the dry season, massive baobabs dominate the Senegal landscape. Traditionally

world the forests are being cut down at an alarming rate. Exploitation on this scale could, in the opinion of many ecologists, ultimately affect global climate. The disappearance of these lush but fragile ecosystems could alter the amount of carbon dioxide in the air, the rates of vaporization of moisture, and the albedo—the amount of solar radiation reflected by the atmosphere—and thus could trigger major changes in the entire biosphere.

Rain forests contain many particularly vulnerable, rare and famous species that are disappearing before the ax. A number of the striking displays of rhododendrons that used to grace the Himalayan foothills have been so depleted that there are now much grander displays in the Royal Botanic Garden at Edinburgh, Scotland. In the Himalayan orchid jungles, many endemic, epiphytic orchids used to be safely supported by specialized microclimatic conditions. The effects of primary forests being clear-cut for timber, along with pressures of urban and agricultural expansion, as well as collecting by commercial plant hunters, are dooming extensive, beautiful populations.

The rain forests of eastern Australia, along the coast of Queensland and New South Wales, are threatened by a number of activities, including replacement of native forests by monocultures of the hoop pine *(Araucaria cunninghamii),* itself an Australian species. A relative of the Australian araucaria that is native to Chile and Argentina, the monkey puzzle tree *(A. araucana),* is being rapidly reduced by the demand for it in the manufacture of plywood. The gigantic Chilean larch *(Fitzroya cupressoides)* may become extinct in ten years, as stands of this tree are being cut

Dr. Ayensu is Secretary General of the International Union of Biological Sciences and the Director of the Smithsonian's Office of Biological Conservation.

at a fantastic rate; all the remaining forests of southern Chile are potential wood pulp for foreign—generally Japanese—paper companies.

Japan, the world's largest importer of wood products and pulp, is expanding its industrial timber operations into the forests of Brazil, Borneo, Malaysia, Sarawak, Indonesia and New Guinea. The chronic and desperate desire for wood and wood by-products is now threatening the Sumatran home of the world's largest flower, *Rafflesia arnoldi* (pp. 66-67). This rare parasitic plant, which grows on the forest floor attached to roots of tropical grapevines, has a flower that can be three feet wide. Its habitats are dangerously near the Japanese timber concessions, and it suffers another threat from the trampling feet of curiosity seekers.

The islands of Malaysia and Indonesia are the home of many species closely related to tropical fruit trees such as the durian, breadfruit, citrus, mango and banana. It is important to save these plants in order

regarded as symbols of fertility and protected by taboo, these trees are now being stripped for firewood.

At a restaurant in China's capital, Peking ducks cook above fire made from wood of *Zizyphus jujuba.*

to investigate them for the characteristics of fruit quality and disease resistance that their genes may carry.

More research into the biology of declining plants is urgently needed. A case in point is the endangered *Lodoicea maldivica*—the coco-de-mer or double coconut—which grows in only three reserves on Praslin Island in the Seychelles (p. 65). Its reproductive habits and life history must be studied in the field in order to find methods of cultivating it (I am inclined to doubt that it can be successfully bred in botanical gardens without further research). The double coconut has an excessively low rate of fruit production, and though some researchers have predicted that it will die out even if left undisturbed, I am confident that scientific knowledge, combined with determination, can save this curious plant.

It is impossible to calculate the potential value of the genetic material carried by such plants. Let us consider the origin of wheat, the world's most widely

and intensively cultivated crop (an estimated 381 million metric tons this year). The genetics of one of the common wheats known as Wild Emmer indicates that it comes from a cross between a wheat called Wild Einkorn and a wild grass, possibly *Aegilops speltoides.* This hybrid is cultivated in such places as Ethiopia, Yugoslavia and southern India. Had *Aegilops,* the wild grass, been wiped out, the loss to mankind would have been incalculable.

It is obvious that for agriculturalists to breed stronger, disease-resistant varieties, obscure species that could be useful as parental stock must be rescued from possible extinction. To this end a National Seed Storage Laboratory was established in 1958 at Fort Collins, Colorado. It houses more than 100,000 samples of all sorts of seeds, and has a capacity for more than 500,000. There are seed banks in Mexico that store wheat and corn, a bean bank in Colombia, a bank for pearl millet and pigeon pea seeds in India, and a rice bank in the Philippines.

As populations grow in developing countries, pressures increase on forest and savanna lands. Overgrazing by domestic animals, in particular, is causing deserts to encroach upon grasslands. In North Africa, overgrazing results in the creation each year of 247 *thousand* acres of new desert.

Some 1.5 billion people, more than a third of the world's population, depend on wood for cooking and heating. Eighty-six percent of all the wood consumed annually in the developing countries is used for fuel. At least half of this is for cooking.

Pressure on the forests because of demands for fire-

Pineapple-size fruit of this rare cycad is the source of pharmaceuticals—and a hallucinogen.

Lady's slipper orchid is disappearing throughout Europe, in England survives in only a single locality.

wood is a serious factor in India, central Africa south of the Sahara, Central America, the Andes and the West Indies. Trees are renewable resources and certain fast-growing species can be ready for firewood harvesting in five or six years. But most developing countries do not have adequate reforestation programs. In the mountains of Nepal it takes a whole day to gather a supply of firewood, and in some areas of West Africa a villager has to walk 15 miles to find wood.

The need is so great that wood is poached from officially protected forest preserves. In West Africa people cut each other's hedges at night, and remove scaffolding from building sites. Where wood does not exist at all, as is now the case in parts of India, the Near East and Africa, people burn dung as an alternative—some 400 million tons of it annually. Formerly, much of it was used as fertilizer to enrich the soil.

Drought and famine are again this year gripping the Sahel belt of West Africa. With so little vegetation left, even the majestic baobab tree (*Adansonia digitata*) has become vulnerable (pp. 62 - 63).

The baobab is virtually the botanical symbol of the hot African countries, and traditionally has been protected by taboo because of its prominence in African religious beliefs. At the mouth of the Senegal River the French botanist Michel Adanson, for whom the genus is named, found trees with European names carved in the bark from the 14th and 15th centuries, and some specimens are reputed to have lived for 5,000 years. The baobab's spongy, swollen trunk can

be as much as 100 feet in diameter and serves to store water; its imposing stature and shape make it recognizable even on a distant horizon. Unfortunately, these great trees are now being stripped and mutilated by people desperate for fuel.

Last year, I encountered an unusual case of preservation of a firewood species during a visit to China—a country that now takes the conservation of flora very seriously. At the Peking Duck Restaurant in the Chinese capital, the wood of *Zizyphus jujuba* is used in the cooking and smoking of the delicious meat in order to bring the duck's bouquet to perfection. Because of its value in preparing this feast, the source of the wood is kept a closely guarded secret, known only to the elite restaurateurs, so that the trees will not be cut down indiscriminately (p. 63).

China recently has established several floral reserve areas and Japan, too, is now taking stringent measures to preserve her few remaining natural habitats of native plants.

The flora of the heavily populated Japanese islands has suffered great damage in the past. Indeed, island ecosystems in general are particularly vulnerable to destruction. The Hawaiian Islands are a good example. The progenitors of the present-day Hawaiian flora arrived at infrequent intervals over thousands of years, and in the isolation of the islands speciated into new plant forms, of which 97 percent exist nowhere else in the world. In these islands plants assumed special characteristics. Some developed shallow roots to

Paphiopedilum venustum, an orchid of the Himalayan foothills, is vanishing as its habitat is destroyed.

The coco-de-mer, noted for its big double coconuts, is nearing extinction in the Seychelle Islands.

spread horizontally throughout the thin soil. Others developed without defensive thorns or spines—so common among plants in similar mainland habitats—since mammalian foragers and tramplers were absent. Weird-looking plants emerged with leaves confined to dense rosettes at the tips of spindly branches; some families, such as the violet, which are small herbaceous plants elsewhere, evolved into tree-sized giants.

Then the native Polynesian Hawaiians and the European colonists arrived. Human occupation has resulted in logging, massive erosion, introduction of troublesome exotic weeds and fast-growing exotic trees such as the *Eucalyptus,* overgrazing by feral goats and swine, and massive land clearing. Overall, more than 50 percent of the native Hawaiian flora is endangered, threatened or already extinct.

Throughout the world there has always been a demand for stimulating brews that will restore flagging spirits, cure diseases and increase sexual appetites. The ginseng root (SMITHSONIAN, February 1976) has long been believed to be a source of such powers, and recently there has been an upsurge in its use—and price. The ginseng of world commerce comes from two plants, one Asiatic, the other North American. The Chinese are great users of ginseng tea, and on my first trip to China in 1975 I noticed a comfortable supply of ginseng products in local shops. But on my return visit last year, the shops were bare owing to the insatiable demands of Japanese tourists who had been purchasing all the ginseng in sight.

In 1977 the United States exported 380,000 pounds of ginseng valued at $26.5 million. Of this, about half came from farms in Wisconsin and about half from the wilds, where the plant has been depleted.

Many other plants, of course, are used for their therapeutic values and this has a twofold effect on the world's flora. On the one hand, the demand for herbs, particularly in parts of Africa and Asia, has brought some plants near extinction. On the other hand, the growing evidence that herbal medicine is not without scientific foundation has made it imperative that no plant species should be wantonly destroyed without analysis of its chemical constituents.

Recent studies of Latin American orchids, for example, may offer new insights into the aging process. Bees that visit the orchids collect chemicals from them, which they store and possibly metabolize. It is now known that the male bees that collect these fragrant compounds live longer than males that do not. Do the compounds, then, control aging in some way? If the orchids disappear, we may never know the answer.

Even the simplest plant may have a future importance that we cannot predict. Recently, we have learned that certain species of lichens, which are healthiest in pure, uncontaminated air, often shrivel up and die from pollution. Thus they have become useful indicators of atmospheric problems.

Pollution is detrimental to many plants. Some of it originating in the United States is now blowing across the Atlantic Ocean to the extremities of Western Europe. Similarly, England's locally manufactured pollution is wafted eastward; Scandinavians believe it may affect their vegetation. This eastward chain reaction, if heavy metals and chemical particles fall onto orchards and croplands, could reduce European food production.

Conservation of the world's flora requires a commitment to preservation of natural landscapes and perpetuation of natural vegetation. This commitment is being made by a number of governments, and also by ordinary people who are simply trying to combat the degradation of their homelands. Last year in India, in order to resist the felling of a forest, the people of the Alaknanda River Basin in Uttar Pradesh peacefully demonstrated against the cutting by joining hands around the trees to ward off the loggers. The forest was subsequently saved.

The celebrated British tropical botanist, E. J. H. Corner, related a comparable incident in Australia: "A few years ago, not a national park but a car park was planned in Sydney. It would have necessitated the felling of some stately trees of the Moreton Bay fig [*Ficus macrophylla*]. It was not the officials, however, that saved them, or an august body of scientific representation, but the labourers of the Builders' Federation who threatened to strike if the trees were cut."

Saving the world's plant resources calls for more protection and management, more research, and an increasing level of public awareness about our vanishing heritage. The *Plant Red Data Book*, it is hoped, will help to generate that awareness.

In Sumatra the world's largest flower, *Rafflesia arnoldi*, produces a blossom three feet across. This photograph is by Smithsonian's Kjell Sandved.

Pinkish vetch adds a flash of color to marsh
reeds at the edge of the wetlands' grassy plain.

Photographs by Farrell Grehan

By John Hay

Making peace with the marshes of New Jersey

*A new law grants a reprieve to what's left
of the quiet, rhythmic tidal lands of
the nation's most densely populated state*

New Jersey has had a bad press from people like myself who drive out of New York City into regions that seem incapable of sustaining any life other than human beings whose capacity to stand sterile surroundings and to breathe poisoned air seems fantastic. In reality, of course, nature saves us all, up to a point. The water can be relatively purified, the oxygen gets to our lungs along with the particulate waste matter, and we survive. And seemingly ruined areas like the marshes and water courses near the big cities still contain a surprising amount of life.

In the marshlands along Newark Bay the tall phragmites grass plumes in the wind, black ducks fly up, muskrats tunnel into grimy shores, and killifish, tolerant of low oxygen and polluted waters, manage to make a reasonably good living, as do eels and crabs. But saltwater fish rarely reach these inland wetlands since they have to swim through heavily polluted Newark Bay to get there, and it lacks enough oxygen to sustain them.

Marshes have had another kind of bad press from people who think they are smelly, useless for anything but mosquitoes and should be filled in. We are only beginning to be aware of how great a role their diversity plays in the great productive interaction between land and sea, but in many parts of urbanized New

*A longtime celebrant of the Atlantic coast, John
Hay is president of the Cape Cod Museum of
Natural History and author of* In Defense of Nature.

Jersey diversity has been forgotten. The Hackensack Meadows, for example, have been filled in at the rate of 30,000 tons a week in recent years. As if to show on which side the scales are weighted, New Jersey's marsh areas have been valued at the exorbitant sum of $70,000 an acre, not as life systems for themselves alone, but as landfill. In other words, organic material from salt marshes is being used to destroy them.

If you look at a road map, you can see first of all that New Jersey's coastal plains occupy more than half of it. A large part of the state, aside from its hills and lakes to the north, is invested by the sea. Wide marshes border its low shores; streams, tidal rivers, inlets and estuaries lace it like the veins in your hand, and it is the kind of region where you can find a wide variety of natural food for Man. Such wetlands are one of the most productive environments on Earth.

As you continue to look at your road map or out of the window of your car as you speed down another giant turnpike, you can also see the evidence that New Jersey is the most densely populated state in the Union, with 953 people per square mile. Fair Haven, an average town, has a population of 4,000 people per square mile. It is evident that a city like New York, one of the most heavily concentrated knots of human power and effort ever known to civilization, exerts enormous pressure on the lands beyond it, and the

One of the world's most productive habitats:
a shallow salt pond set in the spike-grass.

Autumn

same is true to a lesser extent of the Philadelphia, Camden and Chester regions. The wetlands are being subjected to a squeeze.

The cities press and push, and money sometimes talks louder than the landscape. The real estate business claims to speak for people and progress, an argument against which undeveloped wetlands have not had enough defenders. There may be up to 400,000 or 500,000 acres of marshland in the state, and though only ten percent may have been destroyed so far, the pressure against the remainder continues to build. New Jersey is a dredge and fill state, where the developers have been able to use methods fairly economical to them in order to destroy salt marshes and make a clear profit. Fortunately, now the state has a new Wetlands Act, being seriously and conscientiously implemented, and perhaps times are changing.

I drove down to New Jersey last spring, past some of the nearly petrified pleasure domes and palaces of Asbury Park and other beach cities, with plaster deer standing on their lawns beside the sea. It was on the shores of Great Bay, south of Tuckerton, that I saw what a salt marsh could really be, in natural ease stretching away for miles between the shore and the sea horizon.

These marshes are for the most part without beaches, except those which are man-made. Out on their far edges the sea laps and pushes against low shelves and lips of peat held by spartina grass and periodically floods the meadows behind them, back

Autumn sun and coastal goldenrod form
a temporary court for migrating monarchs.

70

toward the lift of the shore. The marine plants that make up the marsh and its great bodies of peat are salt tolerant and are variously adapted to being flooded by the tides. Cordgrass, *Spartina alterniflora,* can stand being half or totally submerged for many hours; it is the pioneer plant in the building of marshes, growing the farthest out toward the sea. Salt hay grass, *Spartina patens,* and spike-grass, *Distichlis spicata,* grow on slightly higher, drier, less saline levels. Mixed in with these grasses and others, are flowering plants, and fleshy glassworts grow there with a nice salt taste to their jointed stems. Just listing a few plants gives no idea of the dynamic way they create shelter and stability in an essentially hostile zone open to the sun, the tides, the sea winds.

A marsh is a region of great subtle strength and elasticity; it reaches out, it reaches in, and you only have to meet a few of the life forms there to realize just how much it accommodates. Grass shrimp dart between the stems of reeds or grasses along a muddy bank. You catch sight of a blue crab slicing edgewise through the water, or a terrapin swimming hurriedly away. There are piles of empty oyster and clam shells along one bank of a tidal creek where it passes a small fishing settlement. You may hear a low "wuhk wuhk" from a surprised bittern that flies up out of its hiding place in the reeds.

The salt marshes are a vast nursery for the young of such fish as weakfish and the bluefish so much prized by the sportsmen. It is estimated that young bluefish grow as much as an inch a week on the food of the estuaries, protected there from predators. Americans who depend more on hamburgers than fish may not be expected fully to appreciate it, but some 70 percent of the species of our Atlantic fish depend on the estuarine zones for some part of their existence.

I think of these great marshes not only in terms of their productivity (although that may be a useful term in trying to coax a produce-minded culture into valuing them) but of their timing. They, and their brown creeks with waters running blue-hued from the sky, take the year to themselves. Even in winter they serve as a refuge for some species of fish and for thousands of waterfowl. Life is never entirely absent in these wetlands that serve as meeting places between the land and the more temperate sea. From spring until fall there is a gradual change in growth and color in their plants and grasses, from one week to another.

New Jersey's great width of salt meadows, with their waving, coarse-bladed grasses, seem more blended with the land behind them than with many similar regions to the north. They seem quiet, almost domestic. Their waterways move easily into low shores. Though there are definite transition zones between one type of vegetation and another, so that you can define the area of a marsh fairly readily, even the areas miles inland from it seem like comfortable partners.

From a highway a marsh may look flat and featureless, but when you are down in its inner meanderings it seems endless and full of unexpected turns. In some areas, you can see new sections of marsh building up where the fine tips and stems of the tough cordgrasses wave above the water offshore. And then you can follow coiling and curving inlets back toward the land, past banks where fishermen, for generations, have driven in their posts for mooring boats or for use as small landing stages.

Rhythm and reclamation

Now and then you see a boat lying along a creek bank like a tired horse. Islands up an estuary may have a house or two on them. The older fishing settlements along the shore have the kind of gray shacks built on stilts that accommodate rather than impose. Land and sea have a companionship here and the results, when allowed, show in an easy, rhythmic diversity. You could eat well and live well here and find yourself a part of both intimate locality and ample space. No wonder the Lenni-Lenape Indians who lived in these coastal regions of New Jersey were reputed to be a peaceable and well-settled people.

The Indians lived with these complex life communities without taking away anything essential to them, but we wielders of the bulldozer, the dredge and the crane not only add destructive materials that pollute the environment, but we are also able to change it so drastically as to destroy its capacity to regenerate.

Off on the horizon, beyond the waving marine grasses, there is another great section of marsh replaced by promontories of glaring sand, divided by channels and covered with small one-story houses.

Marsh grass stretches for miles in natural
ease, a quiet shelter for wetlands' life.

Omnipresent laughing gulls congregate
at the grassy edge of a tidal pool.

A grapevine wends its way through the bright
green spring growth of the marsh's grasses.

They are called lagoon developments and are particularly thick from Barnegat south to Tuckerton. Each row of houses has its ditch or channel, made by dividing the claimed marshland into a grid. None of the original plant life is left on the former marsh level where the houses are built; there is not even very much grass.

Inland, behind the developments, patches of unaltered woodland stand out dark with cedar, oak and pitch pine. The higher trees have an undergrowth of holly and blueberry, laurel and shadblow, or serviceberry, with blossoms starting out white and lacy in airy spring days. The natural woodland and marsh is dark and glossy, a repository of light and shadow. The man-made land stands out bright, gray and dry under the sun.

Don't these people, getting away from the city's pressures and troubles for a while, deserve their houses for rest and company? The answer is that of course they do, but perhaps they also deserve a far less sterile relationship to the land they live in. Reclaiming the organic environment is a dead-end street; there is a point at which it will sustain no more people.

Dery Bennett, director of the American Littoral Society of Sandy Hook, who has been testifying about the ecological value of marshlands in court cases involving them, says: "Those who are trying to restrain the developers are not so much against them as against their methods."

The method of destroying a marshland is to build bulkheads and sod dikes and then dredge out peat and estuarial mud to fill in behind and, when this material dries out, of course, its organic capacity is dead. The gridlike pattern of lagoons, especially where it comes closer to inland banks and higher land, is beyond reach of the continual flushing action of the tides, which means that these artificial channels become too high in nutrients, their waters become loaded with algae and deficient in oxygen.

Putting a system out of business

The developers' methods result in putting a life-giving, nourishing, circulatory system out of business, and since it has been profitable for them, they move on to new areas wherever these can be bought up. Until recent years at least, they have been able to do so almost without restraint. They were obligated to get permits from the New Jersey Department of Conservation and Economic Development, but the department's general policy seems to have been to keep leases, grants and permits from piling up on its desks.

Nevertheless, it has become evident in New Jersey, as in several other eastern states before it, that unless some positive restrictions and definitions were established with respect to laws and regulations governing the use of coastal wetlands, they would eventually be destroyed. Under a new governor, William T. Cahill, the Department of Conservation and Economic Development was broken up so that the responsibilities of economic development were given to the Labor Department, and a new Department of Environmental Protection was formed, with Richard J. Sullivan as its commissioner.

A new law for the wetlands

In November 1970, the legislature passed a Wetlands Act which declared the vital importance of the estuarine zones of the state in protecting the land from the force of the sea, in moderating the weather, in providing a home for waterfowl, fish and shellfish. The act ordered the Commissioner of Environmental Protection to make an inventory and maps of the wetlands by the end of 1972. In addition, it authorized him to make regulations restricting or prohibiting dredging, filling, removing or polluting the wetlands. The act provided fines for violators and makes them liable for the cost of restoring wetlands in so far as possible to their previous condition.

The new law defines coastal wetlands in general as lowlands subject to tidal action along outer shores and inland waterways, streams and estuaries that are subject to tidal reach. Specifically this refers to land flooded to an elevation of one foot above the line of extreme local high water, and this is to be defined as exactly as possible in terms of the vegetation growing there. All the tidal lands below that as far as mean high water are now subject to regulation by the state. Previous to that they had only been subject to home rule or local restrictions.

To establish these tidal lines by means of their vegetation clearly means very careful mapping. The state would not be able to enforce regulations based on cloudy, incomplete or poorly designed inventories and boundaries. Nor do officials of the commission, based on past information, know where all the wetlands are. Therefore aerial mapping is now being undertaken with color and infrared photography with the help of a satellite. Base maps are at an image scale of one to 12,000 (one inch = 1,000 feet) and are of the dimensions to fit overlays of tax-plan maps.

In September 1971, the state issued its first maps and regulations in two test areas, to be followed by a public hearing as required by law. One of these was in Tuckerton, with about 30 square miles of coastal marsh. This is an area where development has dredged thousands of acres and where thousands more are threatened. The Mystic Development Corporation had already been enjoined by the state to stop its dredging

Male flowers of a black oak start a new cycle in the dew of wetland spring.

Low-growing honeysuckle blossoms begin to emerge beneath reeds and viburnum.

and restore the land to its prior condition, as far as possible. (It might be said, in editorial fashion, that a marsh can be wrecked in a day, but for all the legal, perhaps necessary, emphasis on restoring it, that is in reality an almost impossible thing to do.)

In any event, a notable beginning has been made, one that follows the precedent of other states like Massachusetts, which initiated wetlands legislation about ten years ago, as well as Connecticut, Maine and Maryland later on. New Jersey has a unique approach to the problem, and all other regions faced with diminishing coastal resources can only hope for its success.

I drove down to New Jersey again last summer and headed for the inlets and the salt marshes, to the slow easy rushing of salt water against peat banks on the outer shores to the quiet creeks, and the grasses where innumerable seaside and sharp-tailed sparrows are always making short flights ahead of you and dropping out of sight. The full summer wind poured across wide bands and patches of yellow and yellow-green on the salt meadows that also wore darker, running shadows under the clouds.

Clam shells were piled along the bank and roadway where I talked with a local clammer and fisherman who knew the wetlands intimately, even patriotically. He showed me a rig called a "shinnecock," a scoop with rakelike teeth, having a handle that could be ex-

tended to 30 feet to drag the bottom for clams. He could feel it when the rig was on the right kind of ground for a clam, or the wrong one: "It's like feeling a bit of seaweed between your teeth."

The fisherman's feeling about wetlands was in effect very much like that of some state officials, the conservationists, other fishermen and local inhabitants who respected their environment for its own sake.

He felt that the developers were taking almost everything. He also felt that if enough local people who really valued the coast and the living it provided them could always be on the alert for violations, things might be better.

"They can't be expected to see everything from Trenton."

Land and intimate human use should not be divided. Seen through local eyes, respectful through long acquaintance with all the details in the landscape, the marshes, the estuaries, the creeks and inlets, the grasses, birds and salt pools are a tremendous resource worth far more than billions of dollars. Compared to such a resource, the value of speculative "growth," ruining what it feeds upon, amounts to no more than a gutted clam shell tossed into the sea.

The warm wind poured in hard, roughing up the shore waters, swimming through seas of grass. I was reminded of the great plains of the west. "There's nothing more pretty in the world," said this fisherman as I left him for a bypass, an expressway to the north.

A frieze of egrets, four snowy and one common, patiently stalks the marsh's riches.

Like a dramatically lit sculpture, cordgrass
gleams in the late afternoon sun.

On parade, a troop of ring-tailed lemurs strolls about at the Berenty Reserve. Although primarily

By Alison Jolly

Some tall tails: remarkable lemurs of Madagascar

Primate cousins of apes and men fight duels with scent, control their populations and live in close harmony with their environment

Text begins on following pages

arboreal, the troops come down several times a
day to feed. These two pictures are by Russ Kinne.

To begin the day, ringtails warm their sparsely
furred bellies and thighs in the morning sunshine.

Madagascar's remarkable lemurs

Like most lemurs which are protected in preserves, battle-scarred One Eye showed little fear of humans.

One Eye (right) limped after his troop's parade. The ringed tails rose in a series of pert question marks that swayed with the movement of the haunches, but One Eye's tail dragged in the sand behind him. His right foot gave way at each step. When the troop (preceding pages) stopped to stretch out arms and bellies towards the warmth of the morning sun, One Eye dropped heavily to the ground. Another male turned back from the rest, to touch muzzles with him, in the ancient mammalian gesture of greeting and reassurance.

One Eye was dying. He was not dying from disease or the scars of any particular battle. He had lost his eye years before, but still leaped from branch to branch 50 feet above ground. One Eye was dying of old age, a rare privilege for a wild animal. His death, in turn, would make room for another lemur to live in his isolated forest patch in the southeast corner of the Malagasy Democratic Republic (Madagascar).

He lived at Berenty on a 240-acre reserve of gallery forest by the Mandrary River. The Berenty Reserve has been guarded for more than 30 years by the de Heaulme family. The animals there are trusting, so that over and over scientists have "discovered" Berenty as a study site. I went there first in 1962, and am only one of many who have conducted research there.

One startling fact has emerged from the studies and censuses. The populations of ring-tailed lemurs and white sifaka lemurs in that tiny forest seem to be stable, and their habitat undamaged. Those few lemurs, unlike their distant human cousins, apparently live in equilibrium with their environment.

What are lemurs, and what is their environment? They are primates. They are of the same mammalian order as monkeys, apes and men. They are prosimians; however, their long muzzles and narrow skulls make them more distantly related to true monkeys than

Primatologist Alison Jolly has written extensively about lemur behavior. She is now working on a book about Madagascar for the World Wildlife Fund.

monkeys are to people. Present-day lemurs resemble our earliest primate ancestors.

Lemurlike animals of 70 million years ago left their fossils in North America. A few of their prosimian descendants survive still in Africa, Asia and Madagascar. When the monkeys evolved on the larger continents, bounding through the trees in chattering bands, the less domineering prosimians were forced to remain or to become nocturnal, small, solitary and largely insectivorous creatures, such as the bush babies and pottos, tarsiers and lorises. But as lemurs developed in isolation on Madagascar, some of them evolved as diurnal, social creatures.

Lemurs are a parallel line of evolution, a natural experiment in primate behavior, because they inhabit the living museum of Madagascar. Continental drift wrenched Madagascar loose from Africa perhaps a hundred million years ago. Mammals had probably scarcely begun to evolve, but as the Mozambique Channel slowly widened, a few mammals rafted across to the new land. One, or several, were popeyed ancestral lemurs, clinging with all four hands to the wave-washed twigs.

When they arrived, they found not an island but a small continent, largely or wholly covered by trees. Madagascar is a thousand miles long. Its climate varies from semiarid to superhumid—20 to 450 centimeters of rain per year—and its landscape ranges from rain forest to desert. Small wonder that the plants and animals that did reach here have speciated explosively. In a natural Madagascar forest, some 90 percent of all species are unique to the island continent. Like Australia, this is a laboratory of evolution.

But Madagascar is under enormous pressure from Man. If you fly to the Malagasy Republic, you know that the jet is near the coast when the Indian Ocean turns red. The center of Madagascar is bare of trees, the result of centuries of slash-and-burn agriculture. Three-quarters of the land is now cleared. The water is red because the eroding hills bleed red clay down to the sea.

To see the Malagasy forests, then, you must travel to the ring of surviving woodlands around the coast. There you will find mouse lemurs (p. 84), dwarf lemurs, and hapalemurs crunching bamboo like miniature pandas. You may hear the variegated lemurs roar or the indris sing.

Elsewhere, in different habitats, are brown lemurs, nocturnal mongoose lemurs, white sifakas (p. 86), aye-ayes (p. 85), forked lemurs and, in the far south, the jaunty ringtails that swagger through the scrub.

The adventures of Domino

For the ringtails of the Berenty Reserve, spring comes in September. Early one morning when I was there, from the shadowed foliage of a great old tamarind tree there hung 20 black-and-white ringed tails, like huge fuzzy caterpillars. The tails twitched, attached to arched gray backs. Out of the shadow appeared raccoonlike face masks. Then a female sat back on her haunches. The first lemur infant of the season clung to her belly fur.

It was very new, still damp, about three inches long. Its head was almost spherical, like a Ping-Pong ball with black eye-and-muzzle spots painted on. The tail dangled in a minute corkscrew, its stripes like a dashed line drawn in soft pencil. What to call him? Domino! A little masked domino with three round spots for eye, eye, muzzle.

Domino clung with hands alone, his feet almost

While feeding, this lemur lets its tail hang free. Tail is used for balance, but is not prehensile.

Baby ringtail clutches mother's belly fur. Infants have reflexes similar to those of human babies.

helpless in his mother's belly fur. Development proceeds from front to back. Domino could suckle, could lift his head, although he did so rarely, and could pull himself with his hands toward the nipple. In a few days the nerves would function better down the length of his spine. He would cling and push more strongly with his hind legs, and his tail would curl into a prehensile belt round his mother's waist.

Domino did not look like a human infant, yet many of his reflexes were the same. Newborn babies, like newborn lemurs, can clutch with their hands and push with their arms and often lift their heads, as long as they are placed with tummy against something —our ancestors' position of ventral contact with the mother. If you let a human newborn's head drop sharply, or slap its bed, its arms and legs flap wildly toward the midline and its hands clutch in midair. This is Moro's reflex, used for many years by doctors to test babies' coordination. Not until the 1960s did we realize that the Moro is the ancient clutching of a primate infant for its mother's belly fur when she jerks into movement.

And the mother's response to all these fixed gestures of groping, holding, nursing? The human beams at her child; the mother ringtail drops her chin on Domino's head and licks his tufted ears. So begins the process of learning and teaching. With every action and reaction, mother and child create a new and personal bond. Biologist Helen Blauvelt has filmed the newborn's reflex contact behavior being stimulated by expressions of affection from the mother.

On this morning the troop of lemurs stretched, defecated, began to click and grunt—the sign for the day's first promenade. One, then another, leaped downward from branch to branch. They thumped onto the path. Soon all 20 of the animals paraded toward the forest edge, tails in S-curves over their backs.

A group of females and more dominant males kept roughly together at the front of the troop, but two more males lagged behind. As they passed a sapling, one sniffed it, seized it with palms and wrists, then jerked his shoulders from side to side. The perfumed spurs on his forearms gouged horizontal scars on the bark. Favorite marking trees grow permanently scarred, and the incisions last for life, like African tribal cicatrices.

The male sniffed the bark again for good measure. Ringtail males know each other's marks and those of males from neighboring troops. If you plant a total stranger's mark in their path, they go berserk, sniffing and overpainting their scents violently. The tree scarring occurs at sites along all the troop's paths, and communicates individual, not just group, information.

The troop reached the goal of the parade, trees in fruit. The lemurs bounced upward, crawled out to branch ends, reached out and hooked the fine twigs toward their muzzles. They gobbled ripe fruit, stripped the new leaves, sometimes licked the flowers.

A female I called Jessica, her stomach taut with her unborn babe, saw that the troop's lead male was

In the open, three ringtails keep 180-degree watch.
Unlike some lemurs, they find safety in numbers.

ensconced among a clump of golden berries. She
bounced to his branch. He did not wait to be clouted
over the ear, but sprang away hastily, in the direction
of male number two. The second male had been
watching his superior, for male ringtails keep a rank
order throughout the year, reinforced by chases,
threats and fights. Insouciant females, on the contrary,
have priority over males for space and food. Jessica
settled to eat with never a backward glance at the
quarreling males.

Male two leaped off his branch with a high-pitched
call, the corners of his mouth drawn back. Male one
swaggered toward him, stopped to glare, then, order
restored, settled back and spread his arms out wide,
with white belly fur toward the sun. Malagasy legend
says that lemurs worship the sun, holding their arms
out in prayer. Scientists say their temperature fluc-
tuates more than other mammals', so that after the
night's chill they use the sun to raise their body heat
to proper functioning.

After an hour of feeding, the troop was interrupted
by the arrival of a neighboring troop—15 animals
promenading toward the same clump of trees. With

ringtails, there is absolutely no predicting the reaction. The troops may mingle, apparently amicably.
One or the other may move off, fast or slow, with no
obvious signals given. Or, they may fight. If they fight,
it seems that females do most of the challenging,
scratching, wrestling and knocking each other off
branches. The core of a ringtail troop seems to be the
band of females; males operate under different rules.

In this case, the troop moved off without fighting,
Domino's mother and Jessica well to the fore. Two
males lagged behind, as before. Then one of the other
troop came forward to stink-fight.

The new male rocked back on his haunches, and
drew his tail between the spurs on his forearms. His
muzzle flared, his eyes narrowed, his ears lay back
along his scalp. Then he stood and held his tail above
his back, pointing at his adversaries. He shook it, quiv-
ering it like an outraged feather duster.

Then he simply sat down and waited, while one of
Jessica's males marked a twig, in the same gestures he
had used alone by the trail. Jessica's male bounded
forward—all of half a meter, though he could have
easily closed the five-meter distance in one leap. He

Nocturnal mouse lemur, the size of a field mouse, is the smallest primate. It nests in holes in trees.

then paused, while the new male took his turn to mark.

The tournament involved a good 20 minutes of tail waving, branch marking and rushing in place. Neither animal gained ground. Only once did they make a mistake in timing, and both tail-waved simultaneously, the two backs and tails arching toward each other in answering pattern like two halves of a heraldic design. The whole procedure was as ludicrous as a medieval joust, and ended with each male turning back to its troop.

It was apparently pointless, yet such stink-fights in the long run determine the males' chance of ever siring offspring. The individual scent marks, the individual challenges, are not defense of troop, but a jockeying for position, an attempt to find the most suitable troop before the next breeding season. In November as many as one-quarter of the males change troops. Then they are in position for their final challenges in April.

November and December bring the rains. January and February bring cyclones that rage inland from the Indian Ocean. At last, in March, the summer storms are over and the lemurs work up to their own private storm of the mating season.

For six weeks before mating the tension rises. Males stink-fight more and more frequently. Females cuff males, and one another. The infants, weaned, have grown into playful juveniles, although when not in bouncing play groups of their peers, they still follow their mothers closely. The juveniles have matured to subadults. Their genitalia are too small for breeding, but they strut around, sniffing and posturing as adults do. The woods are filled with lemur calls—the click, rattle and meow of the restlessly moving troops, coyote howls and answers from neighboring males.

At last the first female comes into estrus. She is receptive for a day at most, probably for only two to four hours. The males leap at her and at each other. They start to jump-fight, prancing and springing upward on hind legs. This is no mock battle, but an attempt to grapple with an opponent and slash him with a downward stroke of the upper canines. The males wound each other in ears and limbs and flanks with three- or four-inch gashes. When one male appears victorious, he goes to join the female, but others pursue him. He mounts, but then tears off the female to resume the fight. At last the rivals lose heart and let victor and female go off alone, as a consort pair.

Strangely, the winner may be a subordinate. The jealously preserved male hierarchy falls to pieces in the violent jump-fighting, and a third- or fourth-rank male may be the troop's Don Juan. Then, after the brief two-week orgy of the mating season, the Don Juan resumes his old status, and he and the others sprawl exhausted on the branches.

Repeatedly, lemur watchers confirm that subordinates may do the mating, but that only males within a troop seem to mate with the females of that troop. Males from neighboring troops try, but appear to be driven off by in-troop males. Somehow, then, a ringtail male must use all the information he has, from scent marks and howling and chasing, to place himself among all the males of the neighborhood. Clearly, "dominance" among lemurs is more complex than a simple pecking order.

We also suspect that it is the core of females that probably gives the troop its continuity. Indeed, lemur females have priority on food and space, while, among our nearer relatives, the monkeys and apes, males

Cat-sized black lemur is diurnal, roams forest in small groups.

The aye-aye, one of world's rarest mammals, uses big ears to listen for wood-boring insects, which it then captures with long fingers.

The squirrel-like lepilemur is a nocturnal, solitary creature.

have priority. This female dominance is a trait shared by ringtails, brown lemurs, sifakas and indris—that is, all the social lemur genera whose behavior has been closely studied in the field—and it appears to be an inherited characteristic.

Among most of the apes—orangutans, chimpanzees, gibbons and siamangs—the females forage alone, but female lemurs travel together, feed together, groom each other, and wrestle and cuff the females of neighboring groups when there is a troop confrontation. Why is it in their interest to stick together?

There are two reasons, both relative to size. Lemurs are small, and the trees are not. A fruit tree that could satisfy one female chimpanzee can hold a whole troop of ringtails. The distance from tree to tree varies with the forest's richness, but is not necessarily different for lemur or chimp. Even though a large animal can maintain its body temperature more efficiently than a small animal, it is less economical for a large animal to move, so a lemur spends less energy moving from tree to tree than would a similar weight of chimp. Therefore, similar forests can support more small fruit eaters than large ones.

The second reason for sticking together is predator pressure. The apes are large and powerful creatures. Lemurs are not. The social group has more eyes and ears to warn against attack. Malagasy eagles and harrier hawks frighten lemurs into screaming pandemonium, and sifakas into a bellowing roar. When the screaming starts in a troop, all the lemurs stream downwards under cover of leaves. Also, the short mating season in April and two-week birth season in December may serve to "swamp" predators. The large number of young in a single troop may present the predator with more opportunity than it can handle.

Lemurs are also preyed upon by the fossa, a lynx-sized animal that resembles a cat but in fact is a member of the aberrant Madagascar viverrid carnivores, a group unique in the world. When the fossa wanders into the woods, lemurs mob it as birds mob an owl. There is safety, or at least better safety, in numbers.

It seems, from repeated counts, that the populations of ringtails and white sifakas in the Berenty forest have remained stable for at least 12 years. This is extraordinary in two ways: first, the few other primate populations for which we have long-term data have fluctuated wildly—from climate change, epidemics, or no obvious reason. And the lemurs are probably a closed population in an island reserve. If they remain at about 150 ringtails and 100 sifakas in a 240-acre reserve, with little chance for in- or out-migration, they have surprising delicacy of balance with their environment.

Zoologist Vero Wynne-Edwards proposed that social animals may keep themselves at optimum population density, guarding food and other resources against bad times. It is clear that individuals guard space in their own interests beyond their immediate physiological needs. This is crude biological foresight, like getting hungry and eating somewhat before the body tissues are in dire need. Animals can also guard extra space in the interests of close kin, even at some detriment to their own interest.

Ring-tailed lemurs and sifakas seem to do just this. The surprising thing is the accuracy of their calculations. In wet years of plenty and dry years of famine there are always about the same numbers of lemurs.

Again, there is a question of scale. Ringtails can live in captivity for more than 20 years. Sifakas, being larger, would probably live longer if we could keep them in captivity at all. This is enough for even one animal to see several cycles of good and bad years. It is in an individual's interest to keep enough space for its own lifetime, and also in the overlapping interests of close kin.

But why don't a troop's own offspring expand to overcrowd their own space? There are only two possibilities: birth control and death control.

Birth control is not as silly as it sounds. Many animals have evolved to have fewer offspring, and to put more care into each one. Where a species' environment is fairly stable, predictable and full, individuals will have to compete for the available space. The best-

Acrobatic sifaka lemur leaps from branch to branch.
It will rotate in air and land with hind legs first.

endowed offspring, then, are the winners. If the environment is fluctuating, unpredictable and at least sometimes empty, the parents who have many offspring are the winners. We see just these choices among people—if your children face famine, rioting and infant epidemics, better for your genes to have eight offspring and hope some make it through the likely shipwreck of the family. If your children will probably survive, better have two, then lavish on them the kind of exceptional support that will incline them to produce your grandchildren and finance them through, say, medical school.

Primates as a group are "K-selected"—that is, they maintain rather stable populations—as opposed to "r-selected" animals, whose populations are apt to boom and crash, and may become plagues. We are back to Domino, with his four-and-a-half-month gestation, his six-month dependence on his mother and his two-and-one-half years till first mating. A cat of the same size can breed at less than a year of age and bear her litter after two months' pregnancy.

Even so, about 50 ringtails and 20 sifakas are born in the reserve each year. They would be enough, if all lived, to swamp the precarious balance of nature. They die—from falls, predation, perhaps from other causes. Half survive to a year of age, and half of those to adulthood. Apparently that is enough to replace the One Eyes, laboring farther and farther behind as the troop forages, growing thinner and more ragged of fur in the harsh September days.

This is the season of birth. It is also the season of death. The One Eyes who will not survive to eat the new tamarind leaves make way for a few of the newborn Dominos.

The final question: if they can do it, why can't we? In 1962, when I first saw that Madagascar woodland, there were five million Malagasy people. Today there are nine million. There were three billion of the human race. Today we are more than four billion.

The Malagasy cut and burn their forest, and watch their cleared land erode into the sea, and no one family behaves as though it lives on an island. A person in the rich countries consumes many times as much as an average Malagasy, and very few of us behave as though we have just one planet to share.

We can trace our personal beginnings to a baby like Domino, just starting the fusion of learning and instinct which will give him his role in life. We can trace our evolution from the prosimians that first began to specialize in learning, long life, social dependence and care for their young, and eventually became more complex in mind than any other animals. We can see that the lemurs, relative to other mammals, have few young, buffered over a long life against their varying environment.

Why have we, who are the outcome of the primate line, failed to learn this lesson?

Photographer Kinne finds a pensive sifaka.
Defenseless, trusting, it cries "chi-fac" at intruder.

Photographs by Yoichi Okamoto

Nose to nose with baby rhino

It took only 16 months of pregnancy, but this hemisphere's first newborn Indian rhinoceros now cavorts in the National Zoo

Patrick is the first Indian rhinoceros born live in the Western Hemisphere and almost certainly the first one anywhere to be named for an Irishman (technically an Irish-American, Daniel Patrick Moynihan, the U.S. ambassador to India).

The mother is more traditionally named—Rajikumari, which means little princess; she weighs only about two-and-a-half tons. Raji had her firstborn a little later than some rhino mothers—she was 11 in April—and her courtship with Tarun, five years her senior, was nothing if not dramatic. It began back in the spring of 1972—daily visits filled with whistling, scenting and other rhino rituals, including a light-footed dance by Tarun and a great deal of initial confusion. Eventually, under the direction of the Na-

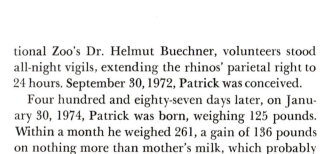

tional Zoo's Dr. Helmut Buechner, volunteers stood all-night vigils, extending the rhinos' parietal right to 24 hours. September 30, 1972, Patrick was conceived.

Four hundred and eighty-seven days later, on January 30, 1974, Patrick was born, weighing 125 pounds. Within a month he weighed 261, a gain of 136 pounds on nothing more than mother's milk, which probably will be his sole sustenance until mid-1975, when he will weigh nearly a ton.

For now, amid the chirpings of the squirrel monkeys that run free in the National Zoo's Elephant House, Patrick plays vigorously with his mother and sleeps a lot. And since he is one of only 700-odd Indian rhinos in the world, he and his parents are a significant reason to hope that an endangered species will survive.

Bitch Kitty, here ten months old, was a favorite of wolf researchers on Isle Royale. The foxes that lived around the cabin became relatively tame from being fed at the camp and the lodge in summer.

Two males roll on ground in a real fight to settle a dominance question. Most such problems are resolved by stereotyped behavior, but occasionally challenge is serious enough to result in open combat, as here.

Article and photographs by Durward L. Allen

Lives and loves of some sly foxes on Isle Royale

Winter after winter, scientists charted evolving relationships in these lake-locked animals—and became attached to them

A professor of wildlife ecology at Purdue University, Durward L. Allen spent 18 winters at Isle Royale National Park on Lake Superior studying the wolf and moose populations and all the other wildlife. Animals came from the mainland during rare periods when the ice was solid. The fox community provided a unique opportunity to study behavior over the years. This article is excerpted from Allen's book, Wolves of Minong, *to be published this month by Houghton Mifflin Company.*

In the early 1960s, when we first began to see "tame" foxes around the Windigo camp, we did not recognize the beginning of an era that would afford unparalleled opportunities to observe their behavior. Foxes were breeding in the area, and young animals were fed by help at the lodge kitchen (until its closing in 1973) and by the families of other summer workers.

In 1962 we saw "the fox" around occasionally, and in the next two years Sleepy became a part of the establishment. He was succeeded from 1966 to 1969 by Fido, alias "Heikki" (Henry), as he was known by residents of Finnish extraction. Other vulpine visitors were around, which we did not try to identify, except that one was a distinctive grayish female. From physi-

© 1979 by Durward L. Allen

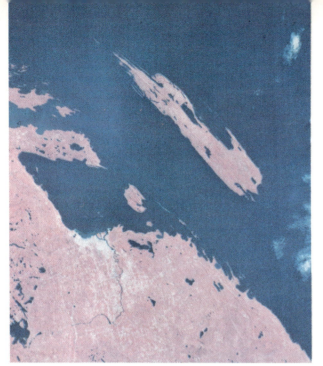

A satellite view of Isle Royale. East is at the top; Thunder Bay, Ontario, at left; Minnesota, lower right.

cal characteristics, we thought this female and Fido founded the fox dynasty that began in 1970 and was so much a part of our winter scene for six years. These included a new Heikki, whom we gradually came to call by his real title, Dominant Male or just DM; Vixen, a young female; and Blackie (p. 97), a subordinate male—a young silver fox—who spent a lot of time on the outskirts or hiding under a building.

We learned early that foxes would have to be taken into account in our daily operations. When snowshoes were left stuck in the snow by the back door, their bindings were chewed off. One February day in 1966 I made a large kettle of chili—up to the top of a three-gallon pot. I set it out in the snow to cool and then forgot it for a couple of hours. On going out the back door I found the cover 20 feet away and about an inch of chili gone. Chili was splashed on the snow in a ring around the pot, which had melted down even with the snow's surface. Fox tracks left no doubt about the culprit. I brought the kettle in to freeze in the back room. It was the way we kept our soup fresh.

Unlike wolves, foxes do not socialize well with people. Our familiar animals could not be touched, and their chief interest in us was as a source of food, which meant practically anything of organic origin except uncooked vegetables.

No chivalry was involved in food competition. When something was thrown onto the snow, the dominant males usually got it. The strategy was always the same; the successful fox grabbed the morsel and presented its back to the others, body-checking sidewise any animal that tried to get at the prize. Obviously, in

these routines there are rules at work; a fox does not attack a superior individual from behind. In a real fight no animal turns its back. Actual fights (p. 91) are rare, but when they occur the blood flows, with each animal grabbing the other by the snout or jaw.

The system of food monopoly that went along with dominance, regardless of sex or condition, irritated Donald E. Murray, our pilot, wolf observer and willing helper. Don would fare forth with a pan of moose-autopsy leavings (which he always brought back for his friends) in one hand and often a stick in the other, and would attempt to bring some justice and morality into the system (pp. 94-95). Actually he seemed at times to make his point, to the extent of a faint indication that the foxes were taking turns. From one day to the next, however, Don always had to start all over again with basic principles.

It is the nature of foxes to curl up on the highest perch available where the view around is advantageous. The turned-up roots of a windthrow, a fallen log, or any high mound of snow would be used as a resting place by our local animals. After snow was dug off the roof, it piled up in the southeast angle of our building nearly to the eaves, giving the foxes ready access to the roof (p. 94). Frequently one or more of them could be seen looking down through our kitchen window as they sought their rooftop napping places. Sometimes these habits resulted in the marking of chimneys or the anemometer, degrading the quality of icicles we used for coffee water.

The arrival of Whiney

In 1971 two young animals joined our winter group, obviously tame as a result of summer conditioning. The female was with us only one season. The male was light in color, like our dominant male, and his character was unmistakable. He was totally subordinate to DM, whose sufferance he cultivated by a perpetual caterwauling from a crouching posture of submission (p. 93). We were to see much more of this fox, who soon earned the name of Whiney.

Vixen produced a litter of six in 1971, according to Windigo ranger Frank Deckert. One of them was still around the following winter. Our new female, yclept Bitch Kitty (p. 90), was a gracile and winsome adolescent with the dark throat and general appearance of Vixen. Ingenuous and trusting, she became a favorite with all. She would be a member of the fox community through 1975.

By the second year it was evident that Vixen was the grande dame of local society and, in an undemonstrative way, the chosen one of DM. Modest and withdrawn, she did not participate in the mad scrambles for food. As someone said, Vixen was the kind of fox you would like to take home to Mother. When we arrived each winter, she was in noticeably better condition than the others, and her droppings attested to honest endeavor. They contained the fur of hares caught in fair chase. In a winter when cage traps were set for hares in the campground, someone got to running them and pulling the animals out through the wire. But that could not have been Vixen.

There were many more fox characters, but only one is essential to our story. In 1973, probably from a litter produced by Bitch Kitty, we acquired a glossy light-red, piquant and impish female whom we called, simply, the little female or Little One.

After 1971, when a male named Scarnose disappeared, we never had two truly competing males. We got a distinct impression that in any aggregation of foxes a single male is the quota. DM efficiently repelled all nonfemale joiners except Whiney, who got along passably through his self-debasing tactics. He was an annoyance, but no threat to the system.

When foxes convene at a food source there is aggressive testing, and the same applies to disputes over land tenure. Evidently the males are territorial and the females more inclined toward sharing. However, our females sometimes ran off aliens of the same sex—judged by DM's lack of interest in the matter.

In the typical interaction, two foxes would stand on their hind feet, pawing at one another with their forefeet. Ears would be flattened, tails kinked in an S-curve, and jaws gaping widely. Both uttered a staccato snarling "kuc-kuc-kuc-kuc-kuc-kuc-kuc-kuc," obviously threatening bodily harm. Usually the **known** subordinate quickly backed down, which meant he crouched and sometimes cried in a high-pitched wavering yowl. This was the fate of any strange males that moved in to challenge DM.

After an encounter, the beaten fox would be further humiliated as our head animal deliberately turned his back and went into a full-dress dominance display. This consisted of a magnificent piloerection—head, shoulders, back and tail—that increased his size impressively. He dropped his tail straight down and humped his back like a Halloween cat. Then DM would stalk away stiff-legged to freshen up his nearest scent post. The interloper would be devastated.

Challenges and dominance testing were frequent and elaborate between males, but often they were male-female and female-female. Young animals sometimes were left crouching in the snow, noses a few inches apart, both crying in a seeming uncertainty of threat and submission.

Through February social tensions mounted, and more foxes would drop in at times to complicate things. By the end of the month there was increasing absenteeism, and it was suggestive when DM and Vixen were gone at the same time.

At home DM displayed a grave interest in the scent marks of all females, and any of the latter might be involved in coquettish tail switchings and slitherings about in the snow. Sometimes DM slithered, too. From 1971 to 1974 Whiney was not much involved. With rare exceptions, he kept shop at the shack while others were off on more interesting missions.

Whiney, second male in the group, survived only by frequent caterwauling, adopting submissive postures.

Whiney later acceded to supremacy when dominant male disappeared; humans found him unconvincing.

Pilot Donald Murray tries to break food monopoly enjoyed by the dominant foxes in the group. It

The foxes make frequent use of elevated perches, here the roof of the researchers' cabin, for a better view.

When Whiney was the only male around, we heard little caterwauling, and there was less emphasis on status. Things were much different when DM got back from "a business trip," and it took a few days to reduce Whiney to his usual size. This was especially so on an afternoon in 1973 when DM returned, an ominous kink in his tail. Like Odysseus of old, he found things in what he considered a state, and we were exposed to a degrading spectacle.

Whiney crouched in the snow and cried for quarter, then took refuge behind a screen of small birches. DM was not to be appeased. Swelled out in awesome display, he approached, humped and glowering, hissing and snarling. Repeatedly he struck the bushes with a sidewise slam of the hips. The stricken Whiney was reduced to a psychological shambles, as the Great One turned his back, then eventually moved away to lift a leg at appropriate places. It was the most vulgar exhibition of temper we ever saw, and DM seemed to realize he had achieved something extra. For the rest of the day he sat aside, squint-eyed and flat-eared,

sometimes seemed to work, but he always had to start over each day. Later all fox feeding was stopped.

aloof and grand, gazing imperiously off into the woods, exuding charisma.

I never was able to define the criteria for many changes in status and attitude that took place almost on a day-to-day basis in the second half of February and early March—the mating season. In February of 1974 DM and Vixen disappeared for nearly a week. On February 26 they were back again, and Whiney got the treatment; he raised a continuing racket. I fed DM some bones, which he crunched up and swallowed. Little One was crouching about 20 feet away, and as I stopped at the door, something happened. Suddenly she blasted off like vengeance incarnate, straight at the big male.

DM knew instantly that his fate hinged on a quick getaway. In total abandonment of alpha dignity, he fled over the snow yammering like the most abject subordinate. A red streak of terror, he circled the premises, Little One hot on his tail in deadly resolve to eat him alive. Three times the male sped around the lot, up the ramp and over the roof. On the west

Kitty had no trouble climbing a ladder to get food left for the jays. She then came down head first.

A fox moves in on the remains of a moose killed by wolves. Sometimes foxes wait days for their turn.

side he launched himself into the blue to land in a snowdrift with all four feet spinning. As he emerged in a flurry of white, the young female plumped into the snow behind him.

This was Little One's finest hour. It was no stylized attack, but honest murder in the making, and the boss fox had no doubts. In a wild burst of energy, they skirted the edge of our compound, passed behind the trail-crew cabin, and disappeared in the woods.

Half an hour later they were behind the shack as though nothing had happened. Experimentally, I gave DM a worn-out soup bone. He walked away and buried it. Vixen dug it up, and he appeared not to notice—nor did Little One, although I had a feeling she had come up in the world.

On a February night two years earlier, four of us were in the kitchen eating supper. There were five of our neighborhood foxes in the back lot, all well-fed from the proceeds of a field trip to a moose carcass: about 60 pounds of head, organs and bones. The foxes had been burying food against harder times.

There was a thump and a slight commotion at our door. Don went to the window and looked out. "Would you believe that there's a fox dying on our back step?"

We found a strange fox breathing its last in the shoveled-out entranceway. Whiney had been perched on the snowbank at one side, and the others were scattered about taking it easy. None appeared to have attacked the dying fox. We injected the body cavity with formalin and froze the carcass, later taking it back for autopsy in the veterinary lab. The fox was an old eight-pound male that had lost part of its teeth. But there was no wound and no evident cause of death.

My personal diagnosis was "shock," obviously a noncommital term. I suspected that this fox, driven by hunger, had invaded a strange territory occupied in force by the rightful proprietors. The adventure could have produced a social strain of colossal proportions. By the time he had pursued the enticing aromas to our door, was the buildup of stress just too much for an individual well past his prime? Exactly what occurred we will never know.

A couple of years later I felt a bit better about my guessing while reading S. A. Barnett's *Instinct and Intelligence.* He was discussing crowding and social stress: "An extreme example, which I have studied in laboratory groups of wild rats, *Rattus norvegicus,* is sudden, unexplained death. An adult male, intruding in the territory of others, is attacked by a resident: the attack consists of a threat posture, leaping and brief biting. The biting is usually harmless. The intruder may nevertheless die—indeed, often does so; there are then no postmortem changes to account for the collapse."

I am led to believe that social sufferings are among the worst that befall an animal, including the most sentient of them all, the human. Especially tragic and punishing are frustrations long continued. They lead to desperation and physical breakdown.

The terrors of misfitism and insecurity were evident in the plight of Blackie, although some of this is part of the usual trials endured by young animals. In particular, the potentially territorial males must travel during their first fall and winter. They wander through unfamiliar fox-inhabited country in an attempt to settle down somewhere. Unless there is a high death rate in the population, some will never make it, but will remain unestablished, opportunistic vagrants. Or they can accept the status exemplified by Whiney, which would not always work.

Blackie needed food, but we had difficulty getting any to him when other foxes, including females, were present. When threatened by another of our boarders —which was nearly always—he would flatten his ears, half crouch, tremble, urinate, defecate and appear to be on the brink of a nervous breakdown. Then he would dash under the building next door. Blackie was inferiority personified.

In the wild the fox is exquisitely adapted for its role as a minor predator in the food chain. Its senses are keen and it is incredibly quick and agile.

The environmental awareness of a fox must be constantly whetted by odors brought on every breeze. The animal readily locates cached food anywhere, and twice I have seen them detect an approaching fox that was out of sight in the woods between 200 and 300 yards away. After one of our moose autopsies in the early 1960s, I bunched up some visceral fat in a wire holder and hung it about six feet up on a tree trunk for the birds. Our familiar Sleepy was trotting

Beaver-gnawed tree, like anything unusual along trail, becomes part of the territorial scent-marking system.

Another time we saw her climb six feet up the trunk of a ten-inch yellow birch in an attempt to get suspended food. She clasped the trunk with her forelegs and pushed with her back feet, using them alternately. Red foxes like Bitch Kitty, in contrast to grays, are not supposed to be able to climb trees.

On the latter occasion the food in question was a hard loaf of bread I forgot to take out of the oven. I tied it with a cord and hung it up for the squirrels. The first squirrel nearly made a mistake. It clung to the loaf, then severed the string with one bite. Bread and squirrel dropped within three feet of a fox. Both of the animals moved instantly, but the squirrel got up the tree.

In February 1966 we had three feet of snow, and our war-surplus vehicle, a Weasel, had made deep tracks behind the cabin. Don saw one of the squirrels running on the packed snow in the Weasel trail. The animal was too low to see Fido standing nearby, but the fox was aware of the squirrel. As it passed, Fido leaped into the trail and snapped it up. Don said the bones crunched as Fido began eating the squirrel at the head end, and the last thing to disappear was the tail's tip.

I watched both Fido and a wilder fox hunt squirrels that winter. The snow was sufficiently firm so that squirrels were active. One day the wild fox came in for a handout, and later I saw it curled up on a log about 60 yards behind the cabin. It was watching squirrels and whisky jacks intently. It lowered its head flat to the log as our tame (and very fat) squirrel worked closer in traveling over the snow. Finally the squirrel ran between trees only 20 feet away, and the fox made its move. With several bounds it nearly caught the squirrel, which kept about two feet ahead as it made two circles, each time bouncing off trees to keep from getting caught. Finally the squirrel hit the side (rather than the middle) of a tree and circled behind and up. The fox simply walked away.

through the woods about 30 yards away when he got downwind of the suet. He instantly whirled, nose in the air, came directly to the tree, leaped up to jerk off the feeder, and sped away with it.

On an afternoon in 1972, researcher Rolf Peterson hung part of a moose head in a tree for the benefit of the whisky jacks, the Canada jays. It soon became evident that Bitch Kitty was interested. She pointed her nose up and circled the tree. Rolf had left the ladder leaning against the trunk, and soon we saw the fox at the top of it (p. 95) chewing on the meat. When we went out of the door she came down *head first,* the pads of her small feet hitting the rungs of the ladder with dainty precision!

Blackie shows the rare silver-color phase. For every silver fox there may be many hundreds of red animals.

His star was risen and his underprivileged past forgotten. By default he had become a dominant male. Now he was first at the food, first on the mound and first in the hearts of his ladies.

The change in social status had obvious physiological effects on this fox. He openly courted Bitch Kitty, his testes enlarged, he began to scent-mark, and he was in breeding condition for the first time in his life. It was another example of those stopgap adaptabilities that so often appear among wild creatures.

We had difficulty adjusting to all this. Perhaps Whiney showed to disadvantage against the high standard of leadership we had known in previous years, but for me his alpha-ism never quite came off. He had been a career subordinate, and his exaltation in one easy leap was a bit much. But inadequacies could have been in the eye of the beholder—his supporting cast did not seem to know the difference.

In particular, he and Bitch Kitty seemed to have much in common. However, she was gone for a time, and on her return it appeared she had been in the wrong company. I heard something in the backyard and went to the window. Ten feet from the door, Bitch Kitty and Whiney were touching noses, something rarely seen. Kitty was in a deplorable state.

Her coat was rough, she looked thin, her left front leg was swollen and useless. I thought it was broken. There was a two-inch gash at the elbow, and when she put her paw on the ground she closed her eyes in a grimace of pain. Pieces of lip were missing and there were cuts on her nose. Blood marked her tracks. She seemed so weak she could hardly get around.

With visible misgivings on the part of Little One and Whiney, we got some food to Kitty, but we had scant hope she could come out of it. In the next few days she spent much time off in the brush, where she was haunted by Little One, who seemed to be taking dominance liberties. Rolf tracked them and kept up on the situation. By that time I had left the island; it was the last of my winter work. Surprisingly, Rolf reported that in another week Bitch Kitty had nearly recovered, and she seemed her old self when they closed the camp.

In one starkly realistic way Whiney was a success: he lived to be at least five years old. Rolf saw him last at Windigo in May 1975. By 1976 the no-feeding policy had dispersed the fox community and returned the winter camp to the squirrels, pine siskins and whisky jacks. An era was at an end, and I was glad to have been a part of it.

Fido used the same technique, crouching on the snow at a vantage point with head up and ears cocked. As a maneuvering squirrel got nearer, the head of the fox hugged the snow between its forepaws. I spoiled the hunt by taking pictures, and Fido walked off in disgust. A few days later I found tracks where a squirrel and a fox had rounded a high mound of snow from opposite directions. A patch of blood told the story. There was more blood among the fox tracks on top of the mound.

In 1976 William Kohtala, Windigo maintenance mechanic, told me he saw a fox catch a squirrel by lying quietly near the base of a tree until the squirrel worked its way down the trunk. Then the fox leaped up, knocked it off with a paw, and deftly caught it on the ground.

After we had been in camp for a few days in 1975, it became evident that something was missing; we had not seen Vixen, and DM obviously was not there. The back lot was quiet, and it appeared that the days of Don's "reform school" were over. We were now under the burden of a Park Service mandate not to feed foxes. Each summer the prospering litters had been a nuisance around the campground at Windigo, and our top pair could have been the victims of a deportation program of some sort. We understood the food embargo and did our best to cooperate, although there were occasional emergencies.

I never tried to find out what happened to DM. The truth was, of course, that his churlish cant was not just personal cussedness, but a part of the system. If you overlook the occasional tantrums, he was a forceful personality, one not likely to be replaced.

We did have a dominant fox in 1975—Whiney, no less—and he presided over the remaining females (Bitch Kitty and Little One) according to the rules.

As winter ended, researchers left, knowing that they would be missed. They were watched by a lone fox.

By Gerald Carson

Fantastic animals prowl tall timber of our mythology

From the long-clawed, green-scaled gowrow to the weeping squonk that melts in its tears, here's America's wild and woolly taxonomy

The extent of the animal kingdom is almost beyond imagining. The total fauna amounts to some thousands of creatures which Man has loved, hated, feared, worshiped, eaten, exploited and often exterminated. All the while, in addition, fable and legend have given us an apocryphal biology based on hearsay or faulty observation. We have the unicorn, the basilisk, the winged bulls of Assyria, the frightening griffin of the Hittites, the chimera, the phoenix, sphinx, sirens and sea horses. This amounts to a vast archive of European and Oriental mythical animals.

What is less widely known is the distinctly American contribution to this menagerie that never was. Historically, Americans have always had a taste for droll stories and odd bits of misinformation, imparted with artistry and a straight face. So exuberant wonder tales have grown around queer critters that crawled, leaped, marched, prowled, bounded, swam, flew or burrowed.

The information presented here has been gathered with diligence and loving care, and it is believed to be either reliable or unreliable or somewhat doubtful. Following this caveat, I quote from sources, named and nameless, who have enriched North American animal mythology.

Early hunters, explorers, land agents and settlers told entrancing tales of the snake that takes its tail in

Author of many books, Gerald Carson will have his most recent, Men, Beasts and Gods, *published by Scribner's this fall.*

Our mythical menagerie was born of the tall stories of hunters, farmers, loggers, salesmen and housewives.

Strange beasts were inspired by our vast and varied landscape which this composite creature stalks.

Illustrations by Brenda M. Tilley

its mouth and rolls toward its victim (to outrun it, climb over a fence—it has to unhoop to get through). New Englanders wrote letters to their rats, telling them to depart, where to go and how to get there. Greased, rolled up and tossed into ratholes, the letters were "duly read, marked and inwardly digested."

From backwoods settlements have come descriptions of the sidehill gouger, the squonk, the hodag, the cactus cat, the gumberoo, the wampus cat and the augerino. This last is an enormous corkscrew-shaped worm that drills underground. It exists for the sole purpose of letting water out of irrigation ditches.

Some stories deal with the surprising things familiar animals do (squirrels that migrate across rivers by launching shingles and hoisting tails for sails) or strange powers they possess (unproductive men in North Carolina who ate the teeth of the alligator's right jaw to restore potency). The beaver's tail, the hare's eggs, the cod's head were devoured for the same purpose. Other yarns come straight from the lips of venerated Americans. Benjamin Franklin described, for English consumption, American sheep with tails "so laden with wool, that each has a little car or wagon on four little wheels, to support and keep it from trailing on the ground." He also insisted that whales were so fond of codfish that they pursued them *up* Niagara Falls, making a grand leap "esteemed by all who have seen it, as one of the finest spectacles in nature."

A more surprising bit of nature-faking comes from the pen of Cotton Mather. A bulwark of Boston Puritanism, Mather was no gay deceiver. But he had a taste for marvels, especially if they bordered on the maca-

Sheep with tails so laden with wool that each has a little wagon to keep it from trailing on the ground.

bre. So we find the divine, who was enormously proud of being a member of the Royal Society of London, passing on the news in the Society's *Philosophical Transactions* that if a rattlesnake bites the edge of an ax, the poison discolors the metal, and the affected section will chip away when used.

Another clergyman, Samuel Peters, wrote spitefully about his town of Windham, Connecticut, after he was roughly handled by Liberty Boys for his Tory sympathies during the Revolution. He claimed that a frog army, led by bullfrogs and followed by peepers, hopped through Windham one night looking for the Winnomantic River, and the townsfolk thought the French and Indians were attacking. They ran for their lives, then sneaked back to find someone they could surrender to.

Even John James Audubon played games with fanciful species. He was visited in 1818 by Constantine Samuel Rafinesque, an eccentric French naturalist, who was delighted by the plants and animals of the American Middle West and developed a passion for announcing new species. Rafinesque was also gullible. Audubon may have wearied of those announcements of new varieties of fish. In any case he could not resist supplying Rafinesque with sketches of ten nonexistent species of fish. Rafinesque rushed into print with descriptions—and so disrupted for years the science of ichthyology. In his *Ichthyologia Ohiensis or Natural History of the Fishes Inhabiting the River Ohio*, Rafinesque hailed one of Audubon's creations, the Devil-Jack Diamond-Fish (*Litholepis adamantinus*), as the "wonder of the Ohio." Naturally. It supposedly grew to a length of from four to ten feet, was known to weigh as much as 400 pounds and was cov-

New Englanders wrote letters to their rats, telling them to depart, where to go and how to get there.

ered with diamond-shaped scales so hard that a bullet could not penetrate them. Rafinesque, poor fellow, said that he had been shown some of its "singular scales" and had personally seen a Devil-Jack Diamond-Fish, "but only at a distance."

In the journal of his first voyage, Columbus recorded a Haitian Indian tale that the New World contained men born with one eye in the middle of their foreheads. A later explorer, Père Marquette, saw two hideous dragons or birds, carved and painted, high on a Mississippi River bluff between the mouth of the Illinois River and the site of present-day Alton. I grew up nearby and understood the enchantment and sense of menace in the stories of these petroglyphs and pictographs. "They are as large as a calf," wrote Marquette, "with head and horns like a goat; their eyes red; beard like a tiger's; a face like a man's. Their tails are so long that they pass over their heads and between their forelegs, under their belly, and ending like a fish's tail. They are painted red, green, and black. They are so well drawn that I cannot believe they were drawn by the Indians."

Later, Father Louis Hennepin, another friar-explorer, also described the pictures. They were known, together, as the "Piasa bird" ("man-devouring"). Passing Indians offered tobacco to appease the Evil Spirit, for they said the monsters once lived in this bluff country and carried away humans to be torn apart and eaten. One wonders whether the Piasa bird could represent a dim racial memory of the earliest form of bird.

Toward the middle of the last century, the Piasa bird was painted over with patent-medicine advertisements. Some of the rock face was blasted away to provide building stone for a state prison.

Modern breeding techniques have contributed some useful animals. The U.S. Signal Corps has been saluted for crossing a homing pigeon with a woodpecker. The result is a bird that not only delivers the message but knocks on the door. A species of Arkansas bees produces twice as much honey as the ordinary bee. Having been successfully crossed with a lightning bug, they can still gather honey into the night.

Paul Bunyan, legendary hero of the logging camps, imported some bumblebees to combat the giant mosquitoes of the Chippewa River region. The two species fought for a while. Then the woods became almost unbearable because the hymenopterous and dipterous insects interbred and produced progeny with stingers at *both* ends.

A traveling salesman, William Miller, is credited with bagging a huge reptile near Marshall, Arkansas, in 1897. He gave it the name gowrow. No one saw the beast locally because Miller said he shipped the skin and skeleton to the Smithsonian. But museum officials have disclaimed any knowledge of the gowrow. It was

reportedly thick-skinned, 20 feet long and enormously tusked, with short legs, webbed feet, a vicious claw on each toe, a body covered by green scales and a back bristling with stubby horns. Pete Woolsey, who used to run a restaurant in Bentonville, Arkansas, was offended when a visitor was skeptical about the gowrow.

"I don't see nothin' so unreasonable about it," he said. "Them scientists over at the State University are tellin' people that there used to be elephants right here in Arkansas. *Elephants,* mind you, with red wool on 'em two-foot long! Would you rather believe them professors, talkin' about red elephants in Arkansas before America was *discovered* even, than my Grand-paw's story of what happened in his own lifetime?"

The sidehill gouger (*Membriinequales declivitatis*) flourishes in hilly country. Through evolution it has developed two long legs on the downhill side and two short ones (by a good 4 inches) on the uphill. Thus equipped, the animals always run around their hills in one direction—some going clockwise, some counterclockwise. Not being able to dodge each other, a terrible fight ensues when the two varieties meet. The gouger or hoofer, as it is also called, has been likened to a cross between a buffalo and a mountain goat.

The gouger is dangerous, but easy to avoid. If you are chased by one, take a couple of steps up- or downhill. The gouger cannot turn without falling and breaking its neck. There is a certain hollow in Marion

Crossing a bee with a lightning bug produces offspring that can gather honey after dark.

The goofus bird builds its nest upside down
and flies backward in order to see where it has been.

cat has thorny hair, the thorns being especially long
and rigid on its ears. Its tail is branched, and upon its
forearms above its front feet are sharp, knifelike blades
of bone. With these blades it slashes the base of giant
cactus trees, causing the sap to exude. This is done
systematically, many trees being slashed in the course
of several nights as the cat makes a big circuit. By the
time it is back to the place of beginning the sap of the
first cactus has fermented into a kind of mescal, sweet
and very intoxicating. This is greedily lapped up by
the thirsty beast, which soon becomes fiddling drunk,
and goes waltzing off in the moonlight, rasping its
bony forearms . . . and screaming with delight."

Another denizen of the Rockies is the photophobic
Ratchet Owl. This curious bird always faces away
from the sun—westward at dawn, eastward at sunset.
Its neck is equipped with a ratchet that permits a
clockwise adjustment as the Earth moves around the
sun. At night the bird releases the ratchet so it can
return its head to the west-facing position. The un-
winding ratchet can be heard afar.

Lumberjacks have made many contributions to ornithological lore. They reported the gillygaloo, or hill-
side plover, which lays square eggs that cannot roll
from the nest. Hard-boiled, they serve in the lumber
camps as dice. Another inhabitant of the deep forest
is the goofus bird. It builds its nest upside down as
does the fillyloo crane. The latter's eggs are lighter
than air; if pushed out of the nest, they ascend. The
goofus bird or flu-fly bird also flies backward instead of
forward. Old-timers say it doesn't care where it is going, it only wants to see where it has been. It has a
marine relative, the goofang. This odd fish swims backward to keep the water out of its eyes.

Among the shyest of woodland creatures is the
hodag, like the squonk given to weeping. The reason
is that it is ugly and knows it, being buck-toothed,
short-legged, spiny-backed and spear-tailed. The animal has *some* admirers, at least in Wisconsin, where
the "World's Largest Snowmobile Marathon," held
annually at Rhinelander, is known as the Hodag 50.

I wish I could bring you encouraging news about the
hinge-tailed bingbuffer and the chipmunks which
feasted on prune stones discarded from Bunyan's cook
shanty and grew so large and fierce they could tackle
a bobcat; also the upland trout which nested in trees.
But the bingbuffer has been declared extinct: The last
one was killed in Osage County, Missouri, about 1881
—maybe the spring of 1882. The others are on the endangered species list of mythical animals, victims of
our times. It is the familiar story of shrinking habitats,
real-estate developments, four-lane highways, shopping centers, snowmobiles and outdated thinking in
state and federal conservation departments. No sight-
ings have been reported for years and years.

County, Arkansas, reportedly half full of gouger bones.

Much speculation surrounds the squonk *(Lacrima-
corpus dissolvens).* Jorge Luis Borges, professor of English and American literature, University of Buenos
Aires, and onetime visiting professor at the University
of Texas and Harvard, says that the squonk's range is
limited to the hemlock forests of Pennsylvania. Since
it weeps constantly, hunters follow it by its tear-stained
trail. The tears dissolve it. Another authority notes:
"Mr. J.P. Wentling, formerly of Pennsylvania, but now
at St. Anthony Park, Minnesota, had a disappointing
experience with a squonk near Mont Alto. He made
a clever capture by mimicking the squonk and induc-
ing it to hop into a sack, in which he was carrying it
home, when suddenly the burden lightened and the
weeping ceased." When the hunter investigated, he
found "nothing but tears and bubbles."

From Idaho comes the wampus cat with a right arm
which works on an extension system like a folding
pruning hook. The wampus cat is incredibly fast in
thrusting this arm out to catch its prey. It is especially
fond of eagles—which may explain why conservationists are anxious about Idaho's eagle population.

Another member of the cat family once ranged the
dry Southwest. This cactus cat *(Felis spinobibulosus)*
lived on cactus and was especially plentiful between
Prescott and Tucson, Arizona, but is now practically
extinct. It was well described in 1910 by William T.
Cox, an expert on nonacademic zoology: "The cactus

Buck-toothed, short-legged, spiny-backed hodag
weeps copiously because it is so ugly.

Energy and Technology

Technology is news every day, some of it good news and some not so good. We learn of new things and new ways of doing things. And every day seems to bring new problems, new threats to our health and safety from existing technology. Magazines fill an important niche in that they can take a long, measured look at the news and the alarms, providing the background and perspective to put the issues in context.

Of the seven articles presented here, just one is an unabashed report of a technological advance, the Very Large Array radio telescope. Another explains a natural phenomenon, the killer waves that rise out of a storm at sea to sink ships; technology cannot stop such waves, but it can help captains avoid them. The concept of net energy, even more pertinent now than it was in 1974, is examined by a writer whose articles in the first half of the decade alerted *Smithsonian* readers to alternative sources for energy.

Three of the articles deal with problems caused by technology: disposal of nuclear wastes, the possible destruction of the life-shielding ozone layer by supersonic jets and aerosol spray, and the growing impracticality of the flush toilet. The first article is the only one here by a scientist: a philosophical consideration of humans as technological beings and of technology as the only answer to problems posed by technology.

Just as Sir Peter Medawar uses technology to define human beings, we can use it to define America. What better image than the Yankee tinkerer and the basement inventor, the huge industrial laboratories developing nylon and transistors? It is no accident that one of the Smithsonian's major buildings was called, until recently, the Museum of History and Technology (now the Museum of American History). It continues

to house early farming implements, steam locomotives, and the latest in lasers and nuclear reactors.

The magazine's broad mandate has resulted in articles such as these during its first decade. They are more than a sample, they are a veritable biopsy of the 1970s. They come from free-lance writers, an energy consultant, a *Wall Street Journal* reporter, a *Newsweek* editor, and, of course, an eminent British scientist.

No sample is complete, naturally, and no magazine can cover everything. Relieved of that responsibility, the editors are free to concentrate on subjects in which they feel they can add some light to the heat, or move into areas few people have thought about at all. Just what are the problems with nuclear waste? What's the real dope on these scare stories about ozone? Do you know the real cost of flushing a toilet?

A magazine can be a year late, waiting for more facts before offering an assessment. Sometimes, in giddy foresight, it can be five years early, seeing the import of a technological idea long before it hits the headlines. But for every issue, month in and month out, the editors can pick and choose from a world bubbling with technological fermentation. The only problem there is an embarrassment of riches.

Here, then, is a taste of technology in the 1970s, as it appeared in the pages of *Smithsonian* magazine. When an article worked well, it became a flare over the battlefield, allowing us to orient ourselves in the smoke and confusion. It helped us to appreciate, in the sense we learn to appreciate music, the very technology that is part of our humanity. It made us increasingly literate citizens of an increasingly technological world.

—John P. Wiley jr.
Board of Editors

Whither technology? From a special Bicentennial issue dealing with America's immediate future, artist John Huehnergarth fancifully depicts some of the revolutionary hardware of the communications industry. From "So you think TV is hot stuff? Just you wait" July 1976 pp. 78-84.

By Sir Peter Medawar

What's human about Man is his technology

*A distinguished British scientist argues
that we are inseparable from our tools
and must now choose to evolve a new set*

The use of tools has often been regarded as the defining characteristic of *Homo sapiens*. It has been thought of as the taxonomically distinctive characteristic of the species. But there is evidence that non-human primates and even lower animals can use tools —something Jane van Lawick-Goodall has shown to be true of chimpanzees and baboons and that is true also of the Galápagos woodpecker. In light of this, the view is now gaining ground that what is characteristic of human beings is not so much the devising of tools as the communication from one human being to another of the know-how to make them.

For example, it was not the devising of a wheel that was distinctively human, we may suggest, but the communication to others, particularly in the succeeding generation, of the way to make one. This act of communication, however rudimentary it may have been—even if it only took the form of a rudely explanatory gesture signifying "It's like this, see," accompanied by a rotary motion of the arm—marks the beginning of technology or the science of engineering.

Everyone has observed with more or less wonderment that the tools and instruments devised by human beings undergo an evolution themselves that is strangely analogous to ordinary organic evolution, almost as if these artifacts propagated themselves as animals do. Aircraft began as birdlike objects but evolved into fishlike objects for much the same fluid-dynamic reasons as those which caused fish to evolve into fishlike objects. (Even toothbrushes have evolved, though not very much. I have never seen Thomas Jefferson's toothbrush, but I don't suppose it was very much different from the one we use today; the Duke of Wellington's, which I *have* seen, certainly was not.)

To some Victorian thinkers, such as Herbert Spencer, facts like these served simply to confirm them in the belief that evolution was the fundamental and universal modality of change. The assimilation of technological to ordinary organic evolution had substance, because all instruments are functionally parts of ourselves. Some instruments like spectrophotometers, microscopes and radio telescopes are sensory accessories inasmuch as they enormously increase sensibility and the range and quality of the sensory input. Other instruments like cutlery, hammers, guns and automobiles are accessories to our effector organs; they are not sensory but motor accessories.

A property that all these instruments have in common is that they make no functional sense except as external organs of our own: All sensory instruments report back at some stage or by some route through our ordinary senses. All motor instruments receive their instructions from ourselves.

It was for reasons like this that the great actuary and demographer Alfred J. Lotka of the Metropolitan Life Insurance Company invented the word "exosomatic" to refer to those instruments which, though not

In front of Greenough's *Washington,* Lady Medawar and Sir Peter arrange his notes for his Frank Nelson Doubleday lecture at the Smithsonian's Museum of History and Technology. Sir Peter is a former director of England's National Institute of Medical Research and a Nobel laureate (medicine and physiology). This article has been adapted from his lecture on evolution and technology.

What is distinctively human is not devising, say,
the wheel, so much as passing the idea along.

Illustrated by Robert Osborn

parts of the body, are nevertheless functionally integrated into ourselves. ("Exo" signifies "out of" or "beyond"; "soma" signifies "the body.")

Everybody will have realized from personal experience how closely we are integrated psychologically with the instruments that serve us. When a car bumps into an obstacle, we wince more through an actual referral of pain than through a sudden premonition of the sour and skeptical face of an insurance assessor. When the car is running badly and labors up hills, we ourselves feel rather poorly, but we feel good when the car runs smoothly. Wilfred Trotter, the British surgeon, said that when a surgeon uses an instrument like a probe, he actually refers the sense of touch to its tip. The probe has become an extension of his finger. Jane van Lawick-Goodall defines a "tool" as a functional extension of an organ such as the hand or the mouth.

I do not think I need labor the point that this proxy evolution of human beings through exosomatic instruments has contributed more to our biological success than the conventional evolution of our own (or "endosomatic") organs. But I do think it is worthwhile calling attention to some of the more striking differences between the two.

By far the most important difference is that the instructions for making endosomatic parts of ourselves like kidneys and hearts and lungs are genetically programmed. There is no learning process in ordinary genetic heredity. We can't teach DNA anything. Instructions for making exosomatic organs, on the other hand, are transmitted through nongenetic channels.

There was for a time a theory of biological evolution called Lamarckian after the French biologist, Jean Baptiste Lamarck. This theory held that characteristics acquired by an organism during its lifetime could be passed along to the next generation. That is, in a highly exaggerated example, an Olympic swimmer could transmit to his children the musculature already suitable for championship swimming. Genetics simply does not work that way. In Darwinian evolution, variations are ready-made and those which give their possessors an advantage are selected and become the prevailing type.

Through the direct action of the environment the human body does, in a sense, "learn" to develop a thicker skin on the soles of the feet than elsewhere. But information of this kind cannot be passed on genetically and there is no known mechanism by which it could be. Each set of human feet must "learn" it afresh. It is only in exosomatic heredity that ac-

Technological evolution can parallel biological evolution. Planes began as birdlike objects.

As extensions of our own organs, tools are very definitely part of human evolution.

quired characteristics can be transferred. We can learn to make and wear shoes and pass this knowledge on to the next generation. Indeed, we can even pass on the shoes themselves.

Thus exosomatic heredity is Lamarckian or instructional in style, rather than selective. By no manner of means can the blacksmith transmit his brawny arms to his children, but there is nothing to stop him from teaching his children his trade, so that they grow up to be as strong and skillful as himself. The evolution of this learning process and the system of heredity that goes with it represents a fundamentally new biological strategem—more important than any that preceded it—and totally unlike any other transaction of the organism with its environment.

Another important difference is this: Genetic evolution is conceivably reversible just as it is thermodynamically conceivable that a kettle of water put on a lump of ice will boil. It's very unlikely, that's all. On the other hand exosomatic evolution is quite easily reversible. Everything that has been achieved by it can be lost or not reacquired. This is what specially frightens us when we contemplate the consequences of some particularly infamous tyranny which threatens to interrupt the cultural nexus between one generation and the next. This reversion to a cultural Stone Age is what each political party warns us will be the inevitable consequence of voting for the other. To bring the idea of reversibility to life one should contemplate the plight of the human race if for any reason it did have to start again from scratch on a desert island. As every mother knows, it is not heaven but the old Stone Age that lies about us in our infancy.

I have been looking around in my mind for some

Planes then became fishlike objects for much the same reasons that fish became fishlike.

one word or phrase to epitomize what I understand by our human inheritance through nongenetic channels—through indoctrination, that is, and the conscious transfer of information by word of mouth and through books. A new book by the philosopher Karl Popper, called *Objective Knowledge,* supplied the answer. (Popper is the author also of *The Open Society and its Enemies,* for many the most important work of social philosophy since Karl Marx's *Das Kapital,* of which it is in some senses a refutation.) Let me introduce you to Popper's concept of a "third world."

According to the philosophic views we specially as-

Artifacts of the mind have an existence of their own: We "grasp" ideas and we "handle" numbers.

sociate with the name of George Berkeley, the apparently "real" world about us exists only through and by virtue of our apprehension of it. Thus sensible things and material objects generally exist only as representations or conceptions or as "ideas" in the mind—hence the name "idealism." Berkeley argued persuasively, and James Boswell (always on the lookout for copy for his great biography of Johnson and not too proud to create it) very well knew that Berkeley's argument was of just the kind that would enrage Dr. Johnson. When Boswell teasingly said it was impossible to refute Berkeley's beliefs, Johnson said, "I refute it *thus,*" kicking a large stone so violently that he "rebounded" from it, thus simultaneously refuting Berkeley and confirming the second Newtonian law of motion which declares that every action has an equal and opposite reaction.

Even those, however, who take a sturdily Johnsonian or commonsensical view of Berkeley's philosophy as it relates to the real world of material objects, sometimes hold a Berkeleian or subjectivist view of things of the mind. They tend to believe that thoughts exist by reason of being thought about, conceptions by virtue of being conceived and theorems because they are the product of deductive reasoning.

Man's major inheritance

Popper does away with subjectivism in the world of the mind. Human beings, he says, inhabit or interact with three quite distinct worlds. World 1 is the ordinary physical world or a world of physical states; World 2 he describes as the mental world or world of mental states. The "third world" (you can see why he now prefers to call it World 3) is the world of actual or possible objects of thought, the world of concepts, ideas, theories, theorems, arguments and explanations —the world of all artifacts of the mind. The elements of this world interact with each other much like the ordinary objects of the material world: Two theories interact and lead to the formulation of a third.

Again, I mention for what it is worth that we speak of things of the mind in a revealingly objective way: We "see" an argument, "grasp" an idea and "handle" numbers expertly or inexpertly as the case may be. The existence of World 3, inseparably bound up with human language, is the most distinctively human of all our possessions. This third world is not a fiction, Popper insists, but exists "in reality." It is a product of the human mind but yet is largely autonomous.

This then was the conception I had been looking for. This third world is the greater and more important part of human inheritance. Its transmission from generation to generation is what above all else distinguishes man from beast.

"I refute it *thus!*" roared Samuel Johnson,
painfully disproving Bishop Berkeley's idealism.

Popper has argued strongly that although the third world is a human artifact, it has an independent objective existence of its own—and is indeed quite largely autonomous. I have already pointed out that the third world undergoes the kind of slow, secular change that is described as evolutionary. That is, it is gradual, directional and integrative in the sense that it builds upon whatever level may have been achieved beforehand. The continuity of the third world depends upon a nongenetic means of communication and the evolutionary change is generally Lamarckian in character, but there are certain obvious parallels between exosomatic evolution and ordinary organic evolution in the Darwinian mode. Consider again, for example, the evolution of aircraft and of automobiles. A new design is exposed to pretty heavy selection pressures through consumer preferences, "market forces" and the exigencies of function, by which I mean that the aircraft must stay aloft and the cars must go where they are directed. A successful new design sweeps through the entire population of aircraft and automobiles and becomes a prevailing type much as jet aircraft have replaced aircraft driven by propellers.

I hope it is not necessary to say that the secular changes undergone by the third world do not exemplify and are not the product of the workings of great impersonal historical or sociological forces. Just as the third world, objectively speaking, is a human artifact, so also are all the laws and regulations which govern its transformations. The idea that human beings are powerless in the grip of vast historical forces is, in the very deepest sense of the word, nonsensical. Fatalism is the most abject form of this aberration of thought, which Popper calls "historicism." Its acceptance or rejection has not depended upon cool philosophic thought but rather upon matters of mood and of prevailing literary fashion. There was quite a fashion for fatalism in late Victorian and Edwardian England, admirably exemplified by Fitzgerald's famous stanza in *The Rubáiyát of Omar Khayyám:*

> *'Tis all a Checkerboard of Nights and Days*
> *Where Destiny with Men for Pieces plays:*
> *Hither and thither moves, and mates, and slays,*
> *And one by one back in the Closet lays.*

Some people believe we have injured the ecology of Earth so badly that we should be punished.

Man and technology

This is a comfortable doctrine insofar as it spares us any exertion of thinking, but we may well wonder why it was so prevalent in late Victorian and Edwardian England. The answer surely is that it fits very well with that high Tory and latterly Fascist philosophy according to which, regardless of his upbringing and of any efforts he may have made to improve his condition, a man's breeding and genetic provenance fix absolutely his capabilities, his destiny and his deserts: A man not born a gentleman or, say, a German could only at best merely simulate gentility or Germanity.

This kind of fatalism sounds very dated today but

we should ask ourselves very seriously whether there is not a tendency nowadays to take the almost equally discreditable view that the environment has now deteriorated beyond anything we can do to remedy it—that man has now to be punished for his abandonment of that nature which according to the scenario of a popular Arcadian daydream should provide for all our reasonable requirements and find a remedy for all our misfortunes. It is this daydream that lies at the root of today's rancorous criticism of science and the technologies by people who believe and seem almost to hope our environment is deteriorating to a level below which it cannot readily support human life.

My own view is that these fears are greatly and unreasonably exaggerated. Our present dilemma has something in common with those logical paradoxes that have played such an important part in mathematical logic. Insofar as any weapon can be blamed for any crime, science and technology are responsible for our present predicament but they also offer the only possible means of escaping the misfortunes for which they are responsible.

The coming of technology and the new style of human evolution it made possible was an epoch in biologic history as important as the evolution of man himself. Indeed, the two cannot be considered separately. We are now on the verge of a third episode as important as either of these: that in which the whole human ambience, the human house, is of our own making and becomes as we intend it should be, a product of human thought—of deep and anxious thought, let us hope, and of forethought rather than afterthought. Such a union of the first and third worlds of Popper's scheme is entirely within our capabilities provided it is henceforward made a focal point of creative thought. A blueprint for such an effort is described in the book, *Only One Earth,* by Barbara Ward and René Dubos, written in preparation for the U.N. World Conference on the Human Environment held in Stockholm last year.

The word ecology has its root in the Greek word *oikos* meaning "house" or "home." Our future success depends upon the recognition that household management in this wider sense is the most backward branch of technology and therefore the one most urgently in need of development. An entirely new technology is required, one founded on ecology in much the same way as medicine is founded on physiology. If this new technology is accepted, I shall be completely confident of our ability to put and keep our house in order.

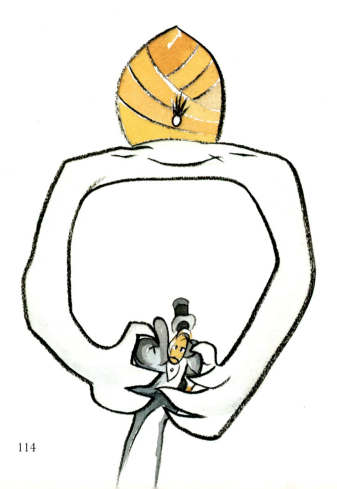

Criers of ecologic doom are as misguided as fatalistic Edwardians who were enthralled by Omar Khayyám.

The word "ecology" derives
from the Greek for "house,"
and household management
is the most backward
branch of our technology.
It is time for us to create
an entirely new technology.

A plane with wing scoops for collecting air samples flies over a steel plant in Fontana, California.

Ozone is one pollutant monitored; it has been found as far as 70 miles downwind from power plants.

By Mariana Gosnell

Ozone—the trick is containing it where we need it

Man may break it down in the stratosphere, where it's essential, and produce too much of it down here, where it is poison

You heard the news. First, that a fleet of 500 supersonic transports, flying at over 50,000 feet seven hours a day for one year, could emit enough nitrogen oxides in their combined exhaust to wipe out a portion of the stratospheric gas layer that guards all life on Earth from ultraviolet rays. Then came the warning that heat from the fireballs of nuclear explosions could tear into the same gas shield, breaking the plant and animal food chain needed on Earth by survivors of a nuclear war. Perhaps most ominous of all was the prediction last fall that the innocuous sprays in some household aerosol cans could be changed by sunlight into free chlorine, which would attack and destroy even more of the gas band, causing thousands of new cases of skin cancer and altering the Earth's climate.

What is in that precious, vulnerable gas band? A substance with bizarre properties and a dual personality: In the stratosphere it acts as a shield to protect us from deadly ultraviolet radiation, but on Earth it is one of the most toxic pollutants known. Ozone—invisible as a gas, deep blue as a liquid, blue-black as a solid—is an allotropic form of oxygen with three atoms instead of two. It is therefore highly unstable, ready at any time to give up its extra atom to other molecules. This is what makes it toxic (more poisonous than cyanide or strychnine or carbon monoxide), given to producing unexpected, violent explosions, and a more powerful oxidant than oxygen itself.

Its name comes from the Greek, meaning "to smell." People have described its odor variously as like new-mown hay, pungent, like freshly ironed sheets, acrid, disagreeable, sweet, like chlorine bleach and as something that "gets you at the back of the nostrils." Created when a spark passes through dry air (splitting oxygen molecules into single oxygen atoms, which then mate up with more O_2 to form O_3), the smell of ozone can be found near toy electric trains, leaking power lines and lightning.

Heralded for years as a disinfectant, bleach, deodorizer, and air sterilizer for asthmatics, ozone had something of a "good guy" image. Then, in the 1940s, Los Angeles tire dealers began noticing deep, wandering cracks in their stored tires, and housewives complained that rubber-lined washtubs, guaranteed for five years, didn't last more than one. Ozone was eventually identified as the culprit, a pernicious though hitherto unsuspected ingredient of smog, created in the Los Angeles bowl by a mixture of hydrocarbons, nitrogen oxides and a lot of southern California sunshine. It was soon found to be affecting far more than rubber tires and tubs: the lettuce and spinach of local truck farms, playground equipment, city trees, petunias and hibiscus, and—in one of the many little ironies of the ozone story—the lungs of asthma victims.

Though all the effects of ozone on the human body are not understood, it is definitely known that it is an irritant to the lungs, causing coughing, tightness, pain and fatigue—especially in the very young, very old, very sick or very active, and there is some indication that it may affect the blood, lower resistance to infection and even, in combination with other chemicals, be a cocarcinogen.

Over the last 20 years, readings of ozone levels have been taken in Los Angeles at least once every single minute (one early method, still used for demonstration purposes, is to hang a one-inch strip of rubber in the

A blanket of smog, including ozone, presses down on San Bernardino-Riverside area of California.

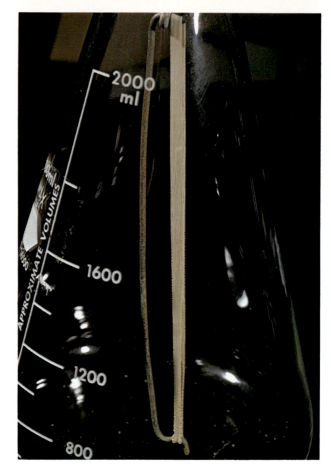

In these pictures taken a few seconds apart, a
rubber band placed in a flask of ozone first begins
to crumble, top, and then to crack, bottom.
Now a demonstration, it was once a test for ozone.

ambient air, pinch it, and see how fast it cracks—sometimes that takes no longer than a minute and a half).
The readings are regularly included in local weather
broadcasts, and are the basis for calling alerts, can-
celing gym classes and keeping poor risks indoors.
Although the number of alerts has dropped off in recent years because of a strict auto-control program
(both hydrocarbons and nitrogen oxides come chiefly
from auto exhaust), last year the city exceeded the federal air quality standard of 80 parts of ozone per billion parts of air on 237 days. Ozone is still the Los
Angeles area's number one air pollution problem.

Recently, ozone levels well above 80 parts per billion (ppb) have also been recorded at rural stations
well away from such photochemical cooking pots as
Los Angeles—on a mountaintop in New York, a farm
in central Ohio, a ship in the Atlantic.

How much, some researchers were asking, does nature contribute to ozone buildup? Although not much
is known about the interchange between the stratosphere and troposphere, it is generally assumed that
there is some slow, downward mixing of stratospheric
ozone, which reaches Earth after a couple of years, and
that tongues of upper-level ozone are sucked suddenly
to the ground during violent storms as well. But the
contribution of such "background" ozone was always
considered minor. Starting last year, two scientists at
the New York State Department of Environmental
Conservation, William N. Stasiuk and Peter E. Coffey,
have bagged samples at mountain and valley sites, as
well as at the top of the World Trade Center in Manhattan. From their readings, and others, they reported
uniformly high levels over large areas—"from here to
Wisconsin and up to Ottawa," says Coffey—"for days at
a time, usually when there was a high-pressure system
with winds from the southwest." This led them to the
controversial conclusion that "there are regional blan-

kets of ozone, and high urban loads are mainly the result of ozone-rich air being carried into the city from the surrounding air mass." "Man's contribution," Coffey speculates, "may be small."

To confuse matters, a second "natural" source of ozone is the greenery of needle-bearing trees and other plants, which gives off hydrocarbons known as terpenes. Though different in structure from the hydrocarbons in auto exhaust, like them terpenes react with sunshine and nitrogen oxides in the air to form ozone. Tons are released every day by plants (perhaps 55,000 tons, more than half as much as autos put out), yet the chemistry of ozone formation is so complex and skittish that nobody can say for sure what the contribution of vegetation to the ozone burden is.

There are guesses, though. The current best ones for the sources of earthly ozone are 20 to 40 ppb from the stratosphere, 20 to 30 ppb from forests, and the rest—"what pushes us over the edge," according to Lyman A. Ripperton at the Research Triangle Institute in North Carolina—is from Man. "Wherever we have found ozone," says Ripperton, who disagrees with Stasiuk and Coffey about the importance of human input, "we've found acetylene, the biggest source of which is gasoline combustion."

As might be expected, depending as it does on sunlight, ozone is especially rich, and especially corrosive, during the spring and summer growing seasons. It causes the greatest damage to plants of any pollutant in the country, attacking sweet corn, red clover, citrus fruits, alfalfa, beans, celery, radishes, tobacco and grapes, among others. To combat ozone burn, and more subtle effects such as retarded growth and reduced yield, scientists are trying to develop resistant strains.

Despite all the evidence of wrongdoing, however, ozone has begun to regain a bit of its old Mr. Clean reputation. It's being considered as an alternative or accompaniment to chlorine for purifying drinking water. Chlorine has come on hard times of its own, as it forms compounds that are harmful to fish and other stream life, and perhaps to man as well. Ozone is known to kill only bacteria and viruses, which it does 100 times faster than chlorine. It breaks down pesticides and detergents and, best of all, leaves no aftertaste or smell. But it is also expensive, requires a lot of electricity to generate, and has no residual germicidal power since it disappears by the time the water hits the tap. There are hundreds of ozone water systems abroad—the first was set up on the French Riviera in 1906, and Paris and Moscow now have large operations—but less than a handful in the United States.

Today ozone is also used to treat industrial wastes

The author is an associate editor at Newsweek, *where she covers science and medicine.*

Some lima bean plants can tolerate ozone better than others. Variety at left shows discoloration and leaf damage. The middle one is turning yellow. The resistant plant at right is almost injury-free.

and municipal sewage, but it seems to be most popular in controlling odors. Despite its name, ozone doesn't mask other smells with its own; it removes the offending molecules by oxidizing or "burning" them.

For all the ozone on Earth, produced by automobiles, lightning and trees, it's a minuscule supply compared to what's in the stratosphere—where we want it. There is perhaps 100 times as much ozone aloft as below—but even that is a tiny amount as far as gases go. If the ozone belt, which extends from 10 to 20 miles above the Earth's surface, were moved to an area of standard temperature and pressure, it would measure only one-tenth of an inch thick. Yet without it, surface life on Earth would probably never have evolved.

Millions of years ago, there were no molecules of oxygen on Earth, but there was lots of water vapor. Sunlight broke up the vapor, releasing hydrogen atoms into space. The remaining oxygen atoms formed molecular oxygen; then, as more accumulated, ozone. One theory goes that ultraviolet energy from the sun, before there was an ozone layer to block it, helped convert some of the simple gases on Earth into simple amino acids, precursors of biotic life. As the ozone shield developed, the amino acids began to form more complicated molecules, such as DNA, the basis for the genetic code in all living organisms, which can be broken down by ultraviolet radiation. Thus the absence of the ozone shield allowed the life process to begin; its appearance assured that the process would continue. Today ozone absorbs 99 percent of the sun's ultraviolet rays at the most lethal wavelengths, 300 nanometers and below.

The ozone band doesn't shield all parts of the Earth

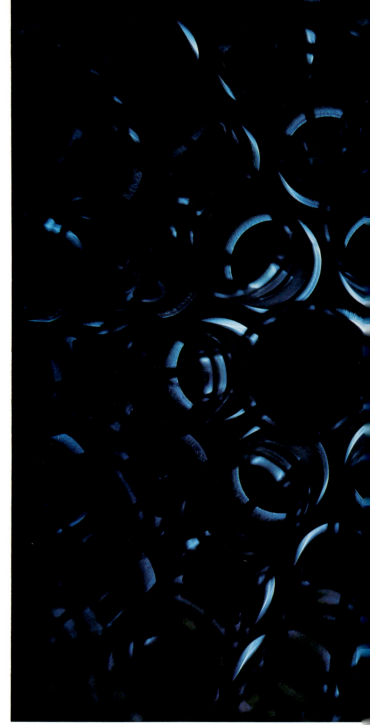

equally, however. Its upper and lower edges lift and fall, and its density changes drastically according to season, weather, latitude, and what the sun is doing. On a typical day, the amount of ozone over Minnesota is 30 percent higher than it is over Texas, 900 miles to the south. But even in Minnesota it may be 25 percent higher on one day than another.

Despite its shifts, bulges and peculiarities, the ozone belt is considered stable. The only natural catastrophe believed possible is a supernova explosion 50 light-years or less away, which could remove 90 percent of the ozone for up to a century. However, such explosions occur only about once every 300 million years.

The first indication that man might be altering the equation came five years ago when scientists who were contemplating the possible effects of SST exhaust on the stratosphere warned that water vapor could diminish the ozone layer by one or two percent. Soon afterward, Harold Johnston, professor of chemistry at the University of California at Berkeley, made the startling suggestion that damage due to water vapor would be nothing compared to what nitrogen oxides would do: speed up the destruction of ozone by a factor of 4,600. In only one year of full-scale operation, he said, 500 SSTs could destroy half of the ozone layer.

Since Johnston first sounded the alarm, at least eight other investigators have made computations on the stratosphere and have come to similar conclusions, although estimates of the degree of loss have been reduced to about 10 to 20 percent as a result of new information about the stratosphere. The latest word was pronounced early this year by the Department of Transportation after a comprehensive three-year study. Its panel of experts concluded that although the planes currently in use present no real hazard, "serious consequences [can be expected] if either supersonic or subsonic [or, one day, hypersonic] fleets are

Inside an ozonator, brilliant electric arcs split oxygen molecules into single atoms; the free

expanded to large numbers without imposing a strict limitation on engine emissions."

Another, graver threat to the ozone layer was discovered "by accident" during the SST inquiry. Intense heat from nuclear bombs, rising more than eight miles into the air, would produce enormous quantities of nitrogen oxides (a single-megaton blast can generate 10,000 tons of nitrogen oxide), which would remove

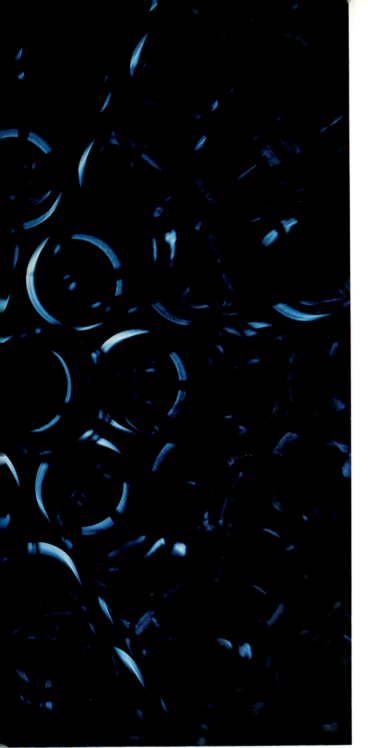

atoms then combine with other oxygen molecules
to form the three-atom molecules making up ozone.

even greater quantities of ozone. But the damage
wouldn't stop there: The nitrogen oxides would recycle, in an extended chain reaction, and ozone would
continue to be depleted for many years after an explosion. During 1961 and 1962, when the United
States and the Soviet Union set off about 300 megatons
of nuclear explosives, the ozone layer is thought to
have shrunk by about 4 percent. A nuclear war, the

Banks of ozonators form ozone from oxygen in
the air at the Cincinnati plant of Emery Industries.

Pentagon admits, could destroy ozone over the temperate regions by 50 to 75 percent.

Yet probably the greatest menace to the ozone supply is an absurdly small, weak item, compared to
supersonic jets and nuclear warheads. As satirist Russell Baker put it, "[I'm] destroying the Earth for whis-
ker removal." The common everyday household aerosol can, which squirts underarm deodorant, bug killer,
air freshener, oven cleaner and hairspray on people's
bodies, furniture and houses at the rate of 600,000 tons
a year, also squirts the can's propellants into the air.
Nearly all sprays used on the human body and as many
as half of the others have as their propellants chloro-
fluoromethanes or fluorocarbons.

These gases are inert, which makes them invaluable
as propellants: They aren't dissolved by water, absorbed by plants or soil, or broken down by other
chemicals or the contents of the cans. They may have
lifetimes of decades in the troposphere, where everyone considers them harmless. Once they enter the
lower stratosphere, it takes many more years for them
to reach higher elevations in the stratosphere where
they were also considered harmless, until recently.
Last year two chemists at the University of California
at Irvine, F. Sherry Rowland and Mario J. Molina,
figured that "hard" ultraviolet light, available only
above the ozone layer, would break fluorocarbons
down and release free chlorine atoms—which are six
times more powerful in annihilating ozone than nitrogen oxides.

Hurriedly, other scientists calculated, too: Michael
B. McElroy and Steven C. Wofsy of Harvard University estimated that if the production of fluorocarbons
were stopped immediately, an unlikely occurrence in
a $3 billion-a-year industry, the ozone layer would

Courtesy Time-Life Nature Science Annual

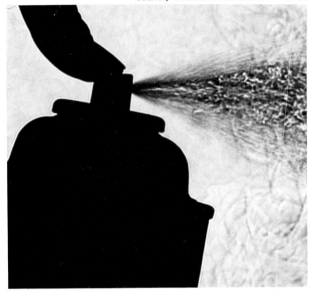

A shadowgraph shows discharge from a spray can; the turbulence above and below is the propellant.

still be depleted 1½ percent by 1985. If production increased at 10 percent a year, the ozone layer would go down 15 percent by the year 2000. Since it takes anywhere from 10 to 200 years for the molecules to reach a level where they can be split by sunlight, the effects of the gases already released might be felt well into the 21st century—or longer.

Why all the fuss? What would happen if the ozone layer were destroyed? The most immediate fear is of widespread skin cancer. Estimates are that a 5 percent decline in ozone would mean 30,000 new cases of skin malignancy (including the dreaded melanoma) added to the present 300,000 cases a year in the United States.

What plants and animals might suffer is more speculative. Ultraviolet radiation appears to slow the growth of some plants, and cause increased mutation rates and decreased photosynthesis in others, but little has been measured so far. Contrary to popular belief, ultraviolet light does penetrate water, to depths of several feet. Plankton, the basis of the ocean's food chain, has proved sensitive to an increase in ultraviolet radiation in the lab, and if it is sensitive in the sea as well, the entire marine ecosystem could be disrupted. As for insects, most see in the ultraviolet range and a change in intensities might disrupt their celestial navigation, recognition of flowers and mating behavior as well as cause genetic damage.

A long-term effect of a weakened ozone belt could create a turnabout in the world's climate. As an absorber of ultraviolet, as well as infrared and visible radiation, ozone is the heat source of the stratosphere. A thinning of the layer could mean temperature and

wind shifts in the stratosphere, which in turn might induce tropospheric variations, leading to changes in growing seasons, the location of deserts and rain belts and the levels of the seas. Stephen Schneider, deputy head of the climate project of the National Center for Atmospheric Research, predicts that a 50 percent reduction in ozone would create a cooling, by almost 1 degree F, which is as large a global change as the Earth has seen in the last two centuries.

Some scientists have called for an immediate ban on aerosols—"the benefits gained," says Rowland, "aren't worth the risks we're taking"—and suggested using roll-ons, pump valves and fingers instead. Meanwhile, investigators are preparing to barrage the sky with balloons, aircraft, rockets and satellites to measure fluorocarbons and other chlorine-bearing compounds (they expect to have evidence whether the fluorocarbon threat is real or not within three years).

James E. Lovelock of Britain's University of Reading estimates that the supply of natural chlorine compounds in the stratosphere (the most abundant being methylchloride from the sea) is much higher than previously assumed. If further research confirms his findings, fluorocarbons may win "a stay of execution," says Lovelock. A Dupont spokesman, Ray McCarthy, makes this point: "The planet has compensated over the last four billion years for some very dramatic changes. . . . I think the biosphere has feed-back mechanisms that maintain the equilibrium so that life on Earth goes on."

Other researchers claim, however, that ozone's capacity for self-healing will be limited in the face of unnatural, man-made attacks, and depletions could be one-way rather than cyclic. Three years ago, Mariner 9 discovered ozone on Mars but it appears mostly in wintertime and only over the polar regions. Presumably, all impurities such as water vapor are frozen out during Martian winters, allowing ozone to form, but in warmer months they either attack the ozone directly or inhibit its formation. On Venus, where nobody has yet seen any ozone, clouds of hydrochloric and sulfuric acid may be interfering with ozone genesis. "That shows what a fortunate situation evolved here," says Charles A. Barth, director of the Laboratory for Atmospheric and Space Physics at the University of Colorado. But we may not remain fortunate: "Almost any impurity will end up destroying ozone," says Barth. "Instead of worrying about each new complicated molecule we put into the atmosphere, we might as well worry about all of them."

Cooled blue ozone is adsorbed onto silica gel granules in a University of Maryland chemistry lab.

The tanker *Siri* plunges her bow into a wall of water off the coast of Japan during Typhoon Judy in 1963.

In the artist's conception at right a tanker encounters a giant wave of the sort that can form during a storm.

By Peter Britton

Nightmare waves are all too real to deepwater sailors

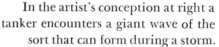

When a storm heaps the sea into a towering horizontal avalanche, the largest ships in the world are in mortal danger of foundering

Although several other ships came through unscathed, the 44,000-ton *Michelangelo* took a terrific interior beating in that fierce April storm 12 years ago. With 775 passengers, she was suddenly struck by an enormous wave some 800 miles from New York City. The pride of the Italian Line came away second best.

The gigantic wave inundated the entire forward half of the ship, breaking heavy glass 80 feet above the waterline. A large hole was gouged in the ship's curved superstructure. The flare of the ship's bow was crumpled. Forty feet of railing and bulwark were torn away. Seventy feet above the sea, tons of water crushed bulkheads and cascaded into the ship.

Two passengers and a crewman died. Many were injured. Passengers spoke unabashedly of terror as the vast length of the liner "seemed to whip back and forth as though she were flexible." The *Michelangelo* limped into port and thousands of New Yorkers gazed in awe at the twisted metal inconceivably high above the waterline. Could this possibly be the work of a single wave?

The answer is yes, and this kind of open-ocean en-

counter is not as rare as it might seem. Thousands of seagoing craft around the world—liners, tankers, trawlers, warships, pleasure craft—as well as assorted offshore structures, have had similar meetings with the scariest and most dangerous of maritime phenomena: the sudden and often overwhelming giant wave that forms unpredictably during a storm at sea.

It was a wave like this that came close to causing what would have been the worst transportation disaster in history, surpassing by tenfold the lives lost in the *Titanic* disaster. Late in the winter of 1942 the English coast was weathering an unusually vicious gale. Seven hundred miles to the west the *Queen Mary* was laboring through extremely heavy seas caused by the same storm. Aboard her were nearly 15,000 American troops bound for war in Europe. A gigantic wave caught the *Mary* broadside. An eyewitness account stated that the thousand-foot, 81,237-ton Cunard liner came within inches of capsizing and "immersion." *The Daily Mail* reported: "She listed until her upper decks were awash and those who had sailed in her since she first took to sea were convinced she never would right herself. Her

safety depended on no more than five degrees. Had she gone those inches farther to port, the *Queen Mary* would have been no more."

It is difficult if not impossible for most people to imagine what these waves are like. "Mountainous seas" and "giant" waves are terms essentially meaningless to the layman until they are assigned dimension and given human perspective. Blair Kinsman, I found, could supply the latter and I met with him at the Marine Sciences Research Center in Stony Brook, Long Island. There, in his incongruously snug office, I asked the oceanographer, yachtsman and author about giant waves.

Kinsman gazed at me for a long moment. "Imagine yourself on the bridge of a tanker in a Force 10 gale. And imagine, if you can," he said, carefully limning his image, "imagine a green-black mass, the height of a seven- or eight-story building, maybe half a mile long, suddenly before you, rushing towards you at 50 miles an hour. You're on a roller coaster plummeting down into its trough; this monster towers above you, alive, shifting, breaking, roaring, hunching. There's

Paintings by Pierre Mion

"Normal" storm waves, such as this one hitting the Wolf Rock Lighthouse off England, can be awesome.

In this reconstruction the *Queen Mary*, with 15,000 U.S. troops aboard, is rolled to port by a giant

no place to hide; then it's on top of you. The top third breaks off. Thousands of tons of deadweight water hurtle down on you."

Giant ocean waves formed by the wind are known by a number of names: freak, rogue, solitary, phenomenal, episodic and pyramidal. The most chilling term of all is the "non-negotiable wave" of the yachtsman. They are neither tidal waves nor tsunamis. The latter (known incorrectly as tidal waves) are caused by undersea earthquakes or volcanic eruptions. In the open ocean tsunamis are practically undetectable, traveling at speeds up to 500 miles an hour and in heights of a few feet. When tsunamis reach shore they slow down and steepen, sometimes into waves that tower 100 feet and cause extensive damage.

Knowledge of waves in general, of course, has been of utmost importance to mariners and shipbuilders for centuries. Yet there was little intensive scientific study on the force of waves, or on how to predict their size. It took World War II to start that. Perilous troop landings on unknown enemy shores made study of

A former newspaperman, Peter Britton is a New York free-lance writer specializing in stories on science, technology and energy.

wave conditions vital. Structure and behavior had to be understood to assess occurrence and impact. These studies led to further work on open-ocean waves.

But giant waves were something else, a breed apart, as elusive as the giant squid and possessed of a mythic aura. Current knowledge comes from actual, though rare and often disputed, observations through the years; from at-sea measurements taken by devices and trained personnel on weather ships and offshore oil rigs; from the results of a wave's onslaught on vessels; and from extrapolating the meteorological records of hurricanes, typhoons and North Atlantic winter gales.

Basically, waves are built by the action of wind on water. They travel in trains of varying frequency and energy and speed. Two wave trains going in the same direction can eventually get "in step" for a moment and produce a wave that is higher than either component. Infrequently, three or more wave trains get in step, concentrating their bulk, energy and motion in one wave that is exceptionally high.

This "combination" or giant wave will live for a minute or two until the components separate. In a stormy sea, where waves are large to start with, the results can be a transient, awesome, turbulent heap of water well over a hundred feet high that bounds

wave. Eventually the top decks were awash and the ship was within five degrees of going under.

The bow lookout runs for his life as a rogue wave threatens his ship; the view is from the bridge.

along, sometimes breaking, in a kind of horizontal avalanche—and then quickly dissipates after several minutes' life, and dies. The laws of probability say that this is certain to occur, but they say nothing about where or when.

Many elements come into play. The intensity of the wind; the length of time it blows; the distance over which it blows (the "fetch"); prevailing weather conditions; sea and air temperature; a series of closely spaced storms; swells arriving from storms in remote regions; sea currents; bottom topography—all these factors can affect sea state and hence giant wave formation. The complexity is such that even present-day computers are unable to handle it and tell ship masters what they would dearly love to know: exactly when and where the giants will strike.

Out of this tangle of possibilities there appear to be three types of conditions under which giant waves form. There are the deep-sea storm waves resulting from coinciding trains. There are waves formed along continental shelves where topography, current and weather factors conspire to heighten and steepen waves and provide a dangerous preceding trough. And there are "pyramidal" waves that form abruptly in relatively shallow areas, as refraction from bottom or shore features causes two wave trains to intersect.

Research on waves is being carried on today by many private and governmental agencies, and indeed has become a billion-dollar business. Most vigorously pursuing the truth about wave heights and forces are those most directly affected: the oil companies and their partners in offshore exploration. The reason is twofold. Offshore platforms and other structures can't sail around storms, as can ships, and must be built to withstand the worst that nature can stir up. And waves from ten feet on up tend to disrupt operations and can cost a company up to $100,000 per day.

When the first offshore platforms were built in the Gulf of Mexico after World War II, the power of the great waves was grossly underestimated. Maximum wave heights for the Gulf of Mexico, for example, were thought to be 40 feet during hurricanes. But a number of offshore catastrophes, including the Texas Tower tragedy (an Air Force radar platform in the ocean off New York City that was washed away with a loss of all hands), soon proved that some waves got far bigger than anyone had thought.

Offshore oil structures are now designed for the maximum wave (the so-called 100-year wave) that could occur within an area in the 30-or-so-year life of

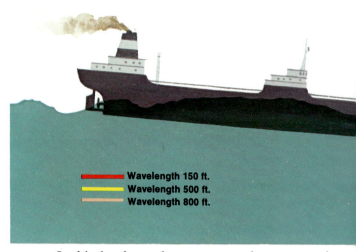

In this sketch a tanker encounters three wave trains, each with a different distance from crest to crest. When the wave trains get "in step," as is happening

the structure. This means that in addition to structural strength there must be enough room for the maximum wave's crest to pass beneath the vulnerable deck. In the North Sea, for example, this wave is now thought to reach about 111 feet (the highest so far actually measured there is said to be 75 feet).

Dr. Willard Pierson of the City University of New York's Institute of Marine and Atmospheric Sciences has a deep interest in waves and their effects. On a recent sabbatical he did some research for the Intergovernmental Maritime Consultative Organization (IMCO) and its ad hoc committee for the study of external forces affecting ships at sea. He was particularly interested in the distress of ships off northern Europe. Two examples caught his eye. In the winter of 1965 the trawler *Blue Crusader* disappeared 25 miles east of the Orkney Islands, and the trawler *Boston Pionair* disappeared midway between England and Denmark off Dogger Bank. Authorities suspected that both vessels were "suddenly overwhelmed by the sea."

Pierson found that in these two cases wave refraction, or bending, was the culprit. Relatively shallow bottom contours affected waves in each area in two ways. They increased waves to a significant height of as much as 36 feet. One wave in a hundred could reach about 55 feet. But, more important, these already high waves, refracted by variations in underwater topography, would advance on a hapless vessel from two directions at once. If the one-two punch of the waves didn't get it, the massive pyramid that was formed as they coincided would.

Refraction of waves is a special case that applies in precisely defined areas. Another set of circumstances surrounds the waters off North Carolina's Cape Hatteras, which have been known for years as "the grave yard of the Atlantic." Quick storms, tumultuous seas,

opposing current, shoals: all combine to destroy vessels sailing along the coast.

Perhaps the most tragic of recent Hatteras tales is that of the *Texaco Oklahoma*. In March 1971, the 632-foot tankship was carrying 222,000 barrels of fuel oil from Port Arthur, Texas, up the coast to Boston with a crew of 44. She had run into bad weather off Florida. The weather deteriorated steadily and by ten o'clock on a Friday night she reported whole gale conditions: winds were blowing from the northeast at 70 miles an hour and waves up to 40 feet were washing over the decks. The ship, according to the National Transportation Safety Board, was "rolling and pitching moderately to heavily," proceeding at the greatly reduced speed prescribed for such conditions.

"During a combined forward pitch and starboard roll at 0330 Saturday," the report said, "some of the crew members on the stern section heard a loud 'crack' followed by a 'bumping' sensation a few seconds later." The *Texaco Oklahoma* had broken in two, just about amidships. None of the 13 crew members on the bow section survived. The stern stayed afloat for 27 hours. Thirty-one crew members died, including all of the officers.

The exact cause of the ship's splitting in half may never be known for sure. But Dr. Richard James of the Naval Oceanographic Office in Washington has an intriguing theory which may explain why the waters off Hatteras are so treacherous. James has found that storms of the same size can vary greatly in intensity. They are most intense, he feels, when there is a pronounced temperature difference between air and water.

Northeast of Cape Hatteras, in precisely the spot

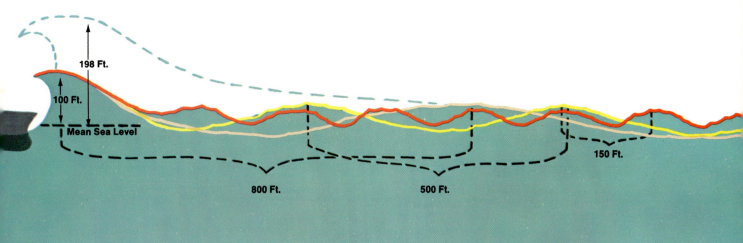

| 198 Ft. |
| 100 Ft. |
| Mean Sea Level |
| 800 Ft. | 500 Ft. | 150 Ft. |

just in front of the ship, a wave much larger than its components forms briefly. In more severe sea conditions, a giant wave could theoretically reach the height of the dotted line at top. In advance a trough would form, into which the ship, like many before it, could vanish.

where the *Texaco Oklahoma* broke apart, a complicated ocean-air temperature exchange takes place in the winter months. The "north wall" of the Gulf Stream is a narrow band of extreme horizontal temperature change. In February and March the temperatures to the north are at their coldest while the Gulf Stream remains warm, a difference of some 30 degrees. As frigid air from the north passes over the Gulf Stream, it is warmed, rises and is replaced by colder air. This colder air brings down strong winds from above, creating still rougher seas.

There is no doubt as to the cause of a long string of accidents and losses off the southeast African coast. There mariners have reported frightful waves and accompanying "holes in the sea" for more than a century. With the closing of the Suez Canal in 1967, tankers and other ships had to go around the Cape of Good Hope, joining the larger tankers that were too big for the canal. They all were sitting ducks for the monster waves—especially so the oil tankers. The ships were lying low in the water, heavy with Middle East crude, riding the swift Agulhas Current in an effort to save time and fuel, semi-ignorant of the potential for disaster that lay ahead. The conditions were right for the inevitable. It was the loss of the 28,000-ton tanker *World Glory* in 1968—broken in two and sunk by a giant wave 65 miles east-northeast of Durban—that should have sounded the final alarm and made the area off limits under certain weather conditions. It did, at least, start J. K. Mallory, professor of oceanography at the University of Cape Town, on his definitive study, "Abnormal Waves on the Southeast Coast of South Africa."

Mallory found that a certain sequence of weather events and ocean activity was needed to create the maximum waves that do the most damage. A falling barometer, a fresh northeasterly wind, a sudden change to strong southwesterly wind—these can combine to create ten-foot local waves. Other waves called Cape Rollers sweep in from storms in the remote Southern Ocean. These superimpose on the local waves, and the large resulting waves now run up against the swift Agulhas Current, moving at up to five knots just outside the 100-fathom line. Waves 60 feet high and more with precipitous faces can result.

The combination, reports Mallory, is extremely dangerous. With a large vessel, he wrote, there is often a tendency to believe she can plough through the normal sea (up to 25 feet) at full speed. "Without any warning the bow falls into a long sloping trough, probably greater than the length of the ship, so that she virtually ends up steaming downhill with increased momentum."

The result is amply illustrated by the case of the Norwegian tanker *Wilstar*. On May 17, 1974, the 132,000-ton vessel, fully loaded with crude oil, was moving in a southwesterly direction at reduced speed in gale conditions off Durban, South Africa. She was in the right spot, ten miles east of the 100-fathom line where subterranean canyons cut into the continental slope. The weather was right; a low had moved across South Africa and caused an abrupt wind change hours earlier. And sure enough, a giant wave was there.

It nearly sank the *Wilstar*. The master reported that the waves were coming in sequences of seven. In one sequence the seventh wave did not hit them; instead, there was "no sea in front of the ship, only a hole." The bow fell into the hole and then the seventh wave, higher than the bow and very steep, crashed onto the ship, submerging the bow and main deck. The *Wilstar* lost her bulbous bow. Steel hull plates almost an inch thick were torn away. Beams thicker than railway tracks were snapped. The damage: $1.2 million.

Halfway around the world scientists and mariners are coming to grips with a different, and perhaps worse, set of giant waves in the increasingly important Gulf of Alaska. There, a group of 13 oil companies is conducting a four-year, $1.8-million wind and wave measurement study. Wilfred McLeod, coordinator of the oil company study, says that extreme waves there are no higher than those in the northern North Sea: around 100 feet. But the investigators have also made an estimate based on the characteristics of the worst storms that have traversed the area in the last 20 years. Their conclusion is that the maximum possible wave could reach an incredible 198 feet.

The giants continue to roam the world's waters. Less than two years ago, some 400 miles southwest of Bombay, India, the Cypriot tanker *Cretan Star* vanished, leaving only an oil slick and a final radio message reporting that she had been hit by a huge wave. In December 1976 the 18,700-ton Panamanian tanker *Grand Zenith* disappeared in a storm 30 miles east of Cape Sable, Nova Scotia. The suspicion: a giant wave snuffed her out.

A giant wave washing over the deck of an offshore drilling platform could be fatal to all on board.

This 132,000-ton tanker lost its bulbous bow in an encounter with a giant wave off South Africa.

It takes energy to get energy; the law of diminishing returns is in effect

In the mid-19th century, a British company launched the *Great Eastern*, a coal-fired steamship designed to show the prowess of Britain's industrial might. The ship, weighing 19,000 tons and equipped with bunkers capable of holding 12,000 tons of coal, was to voyage to Australia and back without refueling. But it was soon discovered that to make the trip the ship would require 75 percent more coal than her coal-storage capacity—more coal, in fact, than the weight of the ship herself.

Today the United States is embarking on an effort to become independent in energy production, and such a program deserves the kind of analysis that the British shipbuilders overlooked. Indeed, our civilization appears to have reached a limit similar to that of the *Great Eastern*: The energy which for so long has driven our economy and altered our way of life is becoming scarce, and a number of respected experts are suggesting that, without significant changes, our society will go the way of the ship that needed more fuel than it could carry.

In recent years, energy growth in the United States has expanded at a rate of nearly four percent per year, resulting in a per capita consumption of all forms of energy higher than that of any other nation. U.S. energy consumption in 1970 was half again as much as all of Western Europe's, even though Europe's population is one-and-a-half times ours.

As energy consumption has increased in this nation, our energy resources have drastically declined. According to M. King Hubbert, a highly respected energy and resource expert, the peak for production of all kinds of liquid fossil fuel resources (oil and natural gas) was

Wilson Clark, a Washington consultant, has written often in Smithsonian *about alternative energy sources. His book,* Energy for Survival, *is just out.*

The elephantine *Great Eastern,* designed for nonstop voyages from England to Australia, required more

reached in this country in 1970 when almost four billion barrels were produced. "The estimated time required to produce the middle 80 percent [of the known reserves of this resource]," Hubbert says, "is the 61-year period from 1939 to the year 2000, well under a human lifespan."

As available domestic oil and gas resources have declined, we have turned more and more to foreign imports—but, since 1973, the price of this essential imported oil has quadrupled. Recoiling from the specter of another embargo, federal officials and industrialists have suggested that the nation develop alternative energy sources such as nuclear power, and fossil fuels such as coal and oil shale, to bridge the energy gap and enable the nation to become self-sufficient.

According to John Sawhill, former chief of the Federal Energy Administration, "the repercussions of Project Independence will be felt throughout our economy. It will have a dramatic impact on the way 211 million Americans work and live." The price tag placed on pursuing the energy goals of Project Independence has been estimated to fall somewhere between $500 billion and $1 trillion. Raising such capital for energy development may prove to be the greatest

*When economics and energy flows are
combined, some analysts see the dollar value
of a tree and an end to industrial growth*

By Wilson Clark

Illustrations by Jan Adkins

coal than the ship could carry. Some experts are
beginning to wonder if we aren't in the same boat.

financial undertaking in the history of the United
States. A growing number of experts, however, say the
goal of Project Independence may be unreachable.

The central problem is simply that *it takes energy to
produce new energy.* In other words, in every process
of energy conversion on Earth, some energy is inevitably wasted. The laws of thermodynamics, formu-
lated in the last century, might be viewed as describing
a sort of "energy gravity" in the universe: energy constantly moves from hot to cold, from a higher to a
lower level. Some energy is free for Man's use—but it
must be of high quality. Once used, it cannot be recycled to produce more power.

Coal, for example, can be burned in a power plant
to produce steam for conversion into electric power.
But the resulting ashes and waste heat cannot be collected and burned to produce yet more electricity. The
quality of the energy in the ashes and heat is not high
enough for further such use.

Numerous studies have indicated that the United
States has enormous reserves of fossil fuels which can
provide centuries of energy for an expanding economy,
yet few take into account the thermodynamic limitations on mining the fuels left. Most cheap and accessible fossil fuel deposits have already been exploited,
and the energy required to fully exploit the rest may
be equal to the energy contained in them. What is
significant, and vital to our future, is the *net* energy of
our fuel resources, not the *gross* energy. Net energy is
what is left after the processing, concentrating and
transporting of energy to consumers is subtracted
from the gross energy of the resources in the ground.

Consider the drilling of oil wells. America's first oil
well was drilled in Pennsylvania in 1859. From 1860
to 1870, the average depth at which oil was found was
300 feet. By 1900, the average find was at 1,000 feet.
By 1927, it was 3,000 feet; today, it is 6,000 feet.
Drilling deeper and deeper into the earth to find
scattered oil deposits requires more and more energy.
Think of the energy costs involved in building the
trans-Alaska pipeline (see SMITHSONIAN, October
1974). For natural gas, the story is similar.

Dr. Earl Cook, dean of the College of Geosciences at
Texas A. & M. University, points out that drilling a
natural gas well doubles in cost each 3,600 feet. Until
1970, he says, all the natural gas found in Texas was
no more than 10,000 feet underground, yet today the
gas reserves are found at depths averaging 20,000 feet

and deeper. Drilling a typical well less than a decade ago cost $100,000 but now the deeper wells each cost more than $1,000,000 to drill. As oilmen move offshore and across the globe in their search for dwindling deposits of fossil fuels, financial costs increase, as do the basic energy costs of seeking the less concentrated fuel sources.

Although there is a good deal of oil and natural gas in the ground, the net energy—our share—is decreasing constantly.

The United States has deposits of coal estimated at 3.2 trillion tons, of which up to 400 billion tons may be recoverable—enough, some say, to supply this nation with coal for more than 1,000 years at present rates of energy consumption. And since we are dependent on energy in liquid and gaseous form (for such work as transportation, home and industrial heating), the energy industries and the Federal Energy Administration have proposed that our vast coal deposits be mined and then converted into gas and liquid fuels.

Yet the conversion of coal into other forms of energy, such as synthetic natural gas, requires not only energy but large quantities of water. In fact, a panel of the National Academy of Sciences recently reported that a critical water shortage exists in the Western states, where extensive coal deposits are located. "Although we conclude that enough water is available for mining and rehabilitation at most sites," said the scientists, "not enough water exists for large-scale conversion of coal to other energy forms (*e.g.*, gasification or steam electric power). The potential environmental and social impacts of the use of this water for large-scale energy conversion projects would exceed by far the anticipated impact of mining alone." In fact, the energy and water limitations in the Western states preclude more than a fraction of the seemingly great U.S.

To maintain the average American at present comfort levels requires 21,600 pounds of nonmetal resources such as sand and gravel and salt, 1,450 pounds of metal substances and 18,600 pounds of fossil fuels, plus coal deposits from ever being put to use for gasification or liquefaction.

The prospects for oil shale development are not as optimistic as some official predictions portend. Unlike oil, which can be pumped from the ground relatively easily and refined into useful products, oil shale is a sedimentary rock which contains kerogen, a solid, tarlike organic material. Shale rock must be mined and heated in order to release oil from kerogen. The process of mining, heating and processing the oil shale requires so much energy that many experts believe that the net energy yield from shale will be negligible. According to *Business Week*, at least one major oil company has decided that the net energy yield from oil shale is so small that they will refuse to bid on federal lands containing deposits. And even if a major oil-shale industry were to develop, water supplies would be as great a problem as for coal conversion, since the deposits are in water-starved Western regions. The twin limiting factors of water and energy will preclude the substantial development of these industries.

Nuclear power is seen as the key to the future, yet an energy assessment of the nuclear fuel cycle indicates that the net energy from nuclear power may be more limited than the theoretically prodigious energy of the atom has promised.

Conventional nuclear fission power plants, which are fueled by uranium, contribute little more than four percent of the U.S. electricity requirements at present, but according to the Atomic Energy Commis-

a little less than one ounce of uranium each year. That amount of energy, nearly twice what the average European uses in a year, is the equivalent of each citizen having 300 slaves working 24 hours per day.

sion, fission will provide more than half of the nation's electricity by the end of the century. Several limitations may prevent this from occurring. One is the availability of uranium ore in this country for conversion to nuclear fuel. According to the U.S. Geological Survey, recoverable uranium resources amount to about 273,000 tons, which will supply the nuclear industry only up to the early 1980s. After that, we may well find ourselves bargaining for foreign uranium, much as we bargain for foreign oil today.

According to energy consultant E.J. Hoffman, however, an even greater problem with nuclear power is that the fuel production process is highly energy-intensive. "When all energy inputs are considered," he says, such as mining uranium ore, enriching nuclear fuel, and fabricating and operating power plants and reprocessing facilities, "the net electrical yield from fission is very low." Optimistic estimates from such sources as the President's Council on Environmental Quality say that nuclear fission yields about 12 percent of the energy value of the fuel as electricity: Hoffman's estimate is that it yields only 3 percent. That advanced reactors might have a higher net yield is one potential, but largely unknown at present, since such reactors have not yet been built and operated commercially. Other nuclear power processes, such as nuclear fusion, have simply not yet been shown to produce electricity, and so they cannot be counted upon. Even the more "natural" alternative energy sources, such as solar power, wind power and geothermal power, have not

been evaluated from the net energy standpoint. They hold out great promise—especially from a localized, small-scale standpoint. Solar energy, for example, is enormous on a global scale but its effect varies from one place to another. However, the net energy yield from solar power overall might be low, requiring much energy to build elaborate concentrators and heat storage devices necessary.

What about hydrogen as a replacement fuel? By itself, hydrogen is not at all abundant in nature, and other energy sources must first be developed to power electrolyzers in order to break down water into hydrogen and oxygen. The energy losses inherent in such processes may result in a negligible overall energy yield by the time hydrogen is captured, stored and then burned as fuel. An indication of the magnitude of this problem has been given by Dr. Derek Gregory of the Institute of Gas Technology in Chicago, who points out that to substitute hydrogen fuel fully for the natural gas currently produced would require the construction of 1,000 enormous one-million-kilowatt capacity electric power plants to power electrolyzers—more than twice the present entire installed electrical plant capacity of the nation.

While much of this kind of analysis is apparently new to most energy planners, it also represents more than an analogy to the cost-accounting that is familiar to businessmen investing dollars to achieve a net profit. The net energy approach might provide a new way of looking at subjects so seemingly disparate as the natural world and the economy.

Dollar values of natural systems

An outspoken proponent of the net energy approach is Dr. Howard T. Odum, a systems ecologist at the University of Florida. In the 1950s, Odum analyzed the work of researchers trying to grow algae as a cheap source of fuel, and found that the energy required to build elaborate facilities and maintain algae cultures was greater than the energy yield of the algae when harvested for dry organic material. The laboratory experiment was subsidized, not by algae feeding on free solar energy—which might have yielded a net energy return—but by "the fossil fuel culture through hundreds of dollars spent annually on laboratory equipment and services to keep a small number of algae in net yields."

With his associates at the University of Florida, Odum began to develop a symbolic energy language, using computer-modeling techniques, which relates energy flows in the natural environment to the energy flows of human technology.

Odum points out that natural sources of energy—solar radiation, the winds, flowing water and energy

Some ecologists believe swamps could recycle urban wastes as well as treatment plants do—with no fuel.

stored in plants and trees—have been treated as free "gifts" rather than physical energy resources which we can incorporate into our economic and environmental thinking. In his energy language, however, a dollar value is placed on all sources of energy—whether from the sun or petroleum. To produce each dollar in the economy requires energy—for example, to power industries. The buying power of the dollar, therefore, can be given an energy value. On the average, Odum calculates, the dollar is worth 25,000 calories (kilocalories, or large calories) of energy—the familiar energy equivalent dieters know well as food values. Of this figure, 17,000 calories is high-quality energy from fossil fuels and 8,000 calories low-quality energy from "natural" sources. In other words, the dollar will buy work equal to some mechanical labor, represented by fossil fuel calories, and work done by natural systems and solar energy.

Odum's concept of energy as the basis of money is not new; a number of 19th-century economists thought of money or wealth as deriving from energy in nature. The philosophy was expounded earlier in this century by Sir Frederick Soddy, the British scientist and Nobel Laureate, who wrote that energy was the basis of wealth. "Men in the economic sense," he said, "exist solely by virtue of being able to draw on the energy of nature. . . . Wealth, in the economic sense of the physical requisites that enable and empower life, is still quite as much as of yore the product of the expenditure of energy or work."

Odum views natural systems as valuable converters and storage devices for the solar energy which triggers the life-creating process of photosynthesis. Even trees can be given a monetary value for the work they perform, such as air purification, prevention of soil erosion, cooling properties, holding ground water, and so on. In certain locations, he says, an acre of trees left in the natural state is worth more than $10,000 per year or more than $1 million over a hundred-year

period, not counting inflation. Last year, he calculated that solar energy, in conjunction with winds, tides and natural ecological systems in the state of Florida, contributed a value of $3 billion to the state, compared to fossil fuel purchases by the state's citizens of $18 billion per year.

The value of the natural systems to the state had never before been calculated. "These parts of the basis of our life," says Odum, "continue year after year, diminished however, when ecological lands that receive sun, winds, waves and rain are diverted to other use." He is now developing a "carrying capacity" plan for the future development of the state which has attracted the interest of the state legislature.

Odum's work may lead to eminently practical applications, by indicating directions in which our society can make the best use of energy sources and environmental planning. One application is to use natural systems for treating wastes, rather than using fossil fuels to run conventional waste-treatment plants. "There are," he says, "ecosystems capable of using and recycling wastes as a partner of the city without drain on the scarce fossil fuels. Soils take up carbon monoxide, forests absorb nutrients, swamps accept and regulate floodwaters." He is currently involved in a three-year program in southern Florida to test the capability of swamps to treat wastes, and demonstrate their value to human civilization as a natural "power plant." The work, supported by the Rockefeller Foundation and the National Science Foundation, has drawn the attention and interest of many community and state governments.

According to Odum's energy concepts, a primary cause of inflation in this country and others is the

If dollars buy work and work takes energy, the value of a dollar can be calculated in terms of energy.

pursuit of high economic growth with ever-more costly fossil fuels and other energy sources. As we dig deeper in our search for less-concentrated energy supplies to fuel our economy, the actual value of our currency is lessening. "Because so much energy has to go immediately into the energy-getting process," he notes, "then the real work to society per unit of money is less."

Economists, who generally resent intruders on their turf, have not embraced this equation of energy and money with much enthusiasm, but it is gaining adherents in several quarters. According to Joel Schatz of Oregon's energy planning office, Odum's work leads the way toward effective government planning in this age of economic uncertainty. "The more successful the United States is in maintaining or increasing its total energy consumption," he says, "under conditions of

To the credit of live tree posts

Present-day ecologists are by no means the first to see the value—the dollar value—in employing natural systems to do work for Man. Discussing the introduction of wire for fencing into the United States, Eric Sloane, in his book *Reverence for Wood*, mentions an address that was read before the Philadelphia Agricultural Society on January 2, 1816.

"The 1816 account spoke of 'living trees connected with rails of wire,' and true to the early American philosophy of looking far ahead, it compared the cost of wire fencing with wood fencing over a period of fifty years. It came to the conclusion that there was a cash saving of $1,329 per hundred acres enclosed. The plan, however, was indeed unique for it enabled the fence to *earn money!* Why plant dead posts in the ground and wait for them to rot? Why not plant live trees instead and let them bear fruit and nuts and firewood which would then give profit to the farmer? Using a hundred acres as an example, the Society suggested the following plan of live tree posts and showed what they might earn a farmer within fifty years (allowing no harvest for the first ten years of growth):

244 apple trees producing $1 per year		$	244
30 cherry trees " 50¢ per year			15
20 pear trees " 50¢ per year			10
10 plum trees "			3
10 shellbark trees "			10
50 chestnut trees "			12
5 butternut trees "			20
5 English walnuts "			5
20 walnut trees "			5
250 buttonwood trees (24 cords firewood taken from tops)			72
		$	396

multiplied by 40 years' harvests	$15,840
deduct the cost of wire rails	1,751
to the credit of live tree posts and wire fence in 50 years	$14,089"

declining net energy, the more rapidly inflation, un-employment and general economic instability will in-crease." Many people currently consider this disrup-tion only an economic crisis, says Schatz, rather than what he believes it really is: a symptom of a continu-ing and deepening energy crisis.

There are signs that the net energy approach is be-ing taken seriously even by the architects of Project Independence. Eric Zausner of the Federal Energy Administration says that net energy is a "useful con-cept" which is under investigation. "Net energy flows," he adds, "have practical implications in the new and exotic fuels, such as oil shale. With coal, there is no issue, since there is a net output of energy. But some of the new processes, such as shale oil processing in situ, net energy flow is a very important consideration in whether we should do it or not."

Congressman George Brown jr, a physicist from Southern California and one of a bare handful of scientifically trained members of Congress, goes much further. He believes that the new Office of Technology Assessment in the Congress should undertake a broad energy analysis, encompassing the net energy approach, of the widespread implications of the administration's plans for Project Independence. "We must start with the assumption that the energy available to do work is declining. This one assumption, which is firmly based on the laws of physics, will revolutionize economic policy once its truth becomes known. . . . The implica-tions of the limits to growth of our economic systems are just beginning to be understood," says Congress-man Brown, pointing out that the net energy ap-proach indicates the inevitability of a national shift of emphasis toward a steady-state economy. "While this view is not yet widely held in Congress, the ranks of advocates are growing."

Since the Industrial Revolution, the Western world has been engaged in a great enterprise—the building of a highly complicated technological civilization. The Western "growth" economy (which today also charac-terizes Japan) has been made possible by seemingly endless supplies of inexpensive energy. One implica-tion of the net energy approach is that a vigorous and wide-reaching conservation program may be the only palliative for inflation.

Another implication is that the days of high growth may be over sooner than most observers have previ-ously thought. For it is increasingly apparent that today's energy crisis is pushing us toward a "steady-state" economy: No one yet knows what such an econ-omy will look like or what social changes will result. But it would seem to be about time to start thinking seriously about it.

The time may come when it simply isn't worth all the energy costs to do the work our society demands.

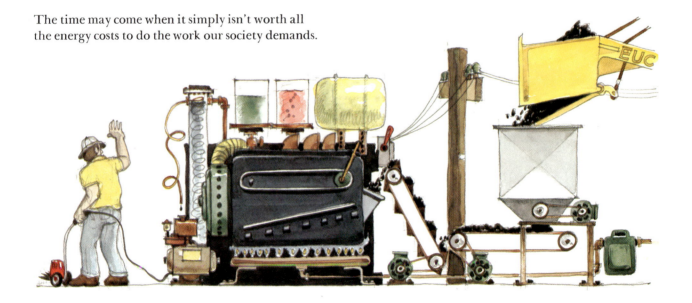

By Sam Love

An idea in need of rethinking: the flush toilet

Our present system is a major contributor to environmental decay and a waste of resources, but new ideas are proliferating

The Reverend Henry Moule's hellfire and brimstone sermons failed to make much of a mark on history, but his tinkering will never be forgotten in the annals of human sanitation. His most successful invention was the earth closet. Constructed by him in 1860, it consisted of nothing more than a wooden seat over a bucket and a hopper filled with dry earth, charcoal or ashes. The user simply pulled a handle to release a layer of earth from the hopper into the bucket. The container could be emptied at intervals.

Mr. Moule's original earth closet is a rather austere piece of household furniture, but later innovators loaded it with accessories. For example, a device could be added that released the earth each time a user rose from the seat. But the automatic earth release met with some opposition: "In sick rooms," according to one account, "this method of distribution of earth may be found objectionable, as more or less vibration follows the rising, and this is apt to disturb the nerves of a patient."

While sanitary historians may recognize Henry Moule's contribution, he is no longer a household word. Certainly he is not as well known as Thomas Crapper, the father of the flush toilet. In fact, while folk history is good to him, I am convinced he is a myth created by British author Wallace Reyburn, who wrote an amusing biography of him in 1969 entitled *Flushed with Pride*. Although the book and the history seem to be a complete figment of the author's imagination, many libraries, including the Library of

Makers used to decorate chamber pots with images of archenemies. In this case, target is Napoleon.

Congress, file their bibliographical cards for the book as if it were a serious historical treatise on the origin of the water closet.

Who actually invented the water closet is a mystery; its origins go far back in history. One of the earliest indoor bathrooms has been found by archaeologists on Crete. According to the bathroom history *Clean and Decent* by Lawrence Wright, the great palace of King Minos at Knossos included a water-supply system of terra-cotta pipes that some have judged superior to modern parallel pipes. One of the Knossos latrines appears to have sported a wooden seat and may have worked much like a modern flush toilet. Cities in the Indus Valley between 2500 and 1500 B.C. also had indoor bathrooms flushed with water. The waste was carried to street drains via brick-lined pits similar to modern septic tanks. Except for the briefly used water closet of Elizabethan times, such engineering did not appear in England until the middle of the 18th century.

Generally, the 18th and 19th centuries in Europe were dominated by the pan closet or the jerry pot. By 1800 many were elaborate, even to the extent of placing portraits of archenemies (Napoleon was a big hit in England) in the target area. After use, the pots were either emptied or concealed in commodes.

At first the contents of the urban jerry pots were collected by nearby farmers who were delighted to get nitrogen-rich organic fertilizer. But as London and other cities grew, the journey became uneconomical

A coordinator of Earth Day in 1970 and formerly the editor of Environmental Action *and a book* Earth Tool Kit, *Sam Love is an environmental consultant.*

Illustrations by John Huehnergarth

139

Future archaeologists might well misinterpret today's plumbing as a centralized food-distribution system.

and the waste was generally dumped in larger communal cesspits or in the nearest river. Today's modern sanitary system, with its maze of underground pipes, pumps and treatment techniques, is a direct descendant of the communal and private cesspits and open sewers which emptied into rivers. For centuries, water as a waste-removal vehicle functioned adequately from the urban resident's standpoint. Ecologically, the price may have been high, but urban users found it convenient because it allowed them to simply flush wastes and forget them. Only those people living downstream might be forced to question the wisdom of such a system.

Now, though, as cities grow larger and rivers become more saturated, increasing numbers of people are finding themselves living downstream. In area after area, urban growth is creating major water problems which are becoming front-page news stories. For example, Virginia's Fairfax County, a suburb of Washington, has been forced to declare a moratorium throughout most of the county on residential and commercial sewer applications.

A major villain in each case is the flush toilet. Of all home water users, the flush toilet is the biggest single consumer: The average North American family annually uses 35,200 gallons for toilet flushing.

In addition to water costs, the economic costs of the flush toilet and centralized waste treatment are rising. Currently, the investment in the utilities infrastructure in Western countries is around $500-$600 per person. This contrasts sharply with a country such as Tanzania, which in 1969 could spend only $8 per urban inhabitant. Thus, because of costs, the "modern" sanitary system, which Westerners now take for granted, is out of reach to most of the world's population. Reportedly, 70 percent of the human race does not even have piped water. The World Health Orga-

nization estimated in 1972 that only 8 percent of urban families in developing countries of Asia and Africa had access to a sanitary sewage system.

Moreover, energy costs of large centralized sewage-treatment systems are staggering. While the professional literature is slim in this area, one estimate is that, at full capacity, a 309 million-gallons-a-day waste-treatment system, such as that being built now for the Washington, D.C., area, will consume as much as 900,000 kilowatt hours of electricity, 500 tons of chemicals and 45,000 gallons of fuel oil daily. Some environmental groups, however, consider this estimate to be a low one and point out that, in any case, burning the sewage to produce 400 dry tons of sludge each day will create a major air pollution problem. Thus, even if the water required for the flush-toilet system were available in abundance, the growing scarcity of the other resources that support such a system is beginning to impose limits.

Already the flush-toilet, central waste-treatment system is in trouble. One response from toilet manufacturers was to begin marketing a "water-saver closet," which uses one-third less water than many older models now in use. Although major manufacturers have had water savers available for several years, an industry source says that these toilets account for no more than five percent of those installed today. He attributes the lack of sales to public apathy concerning

One new toilet design, which freezes wastes for later removal, had disadvantages to be worked out.

water problems and the slightly higher price of the water savers.

Even with water savers, however, many of the flush toilet's basic problems still exist, so some people in the field are actively pushing alternative methods of human waste disposal both on a public and a private level. Dr. John R. Sheaffer, a resource manager with the Chicago firm of Bauer, Sheaffer and Lear, contends that one possibility is simply to use the nutrient-rich sewage, after deodorizing and disinfecting it, to irrigate agricultural lands and let the water filter through the soil and into an "under drainage" system where purity can be monitored. The soil naturally cleanses the liquid wastes, except during freezing winter months, when the sewage can be stored for spraying on fields later.

Dr. Sheaffer's system has been tried in communities and found to work successfully. Bakersfield, California, and Abilene, Texas, are among larger cities that rely on land treatment of sewage. These systems use far less energy and chemicals than the advanced waste-treatment system, which tries to restore the waste water to its original quality. Michigan's Muskegon County recently put into operation a large (28-million-gallons-a-day) system using Dr. Sheaffer's "living filter" principle.

Among its advantages is the fact that the land treatment system lets man work with nature, not against it.

But its critics are quick to point out that land treatment requires large areas of land, a commodity that is also in short supply around large metropolitan areas. There is also concern among health officials that such systems might not screen out potentially harmful viruses, bacteria and industrial chemicals. Dr. Sheaffer's answer is that the water in projects he has worked with has always met pure-water specifications. In addition, the drainage system prevents salt build-up and waterlogging of soil.

For all its promise in cities that already have the plumbing, access to agricultural land and abundant water, land-treatment schemes fall short of meeting criticism that challenges the centralized waste-treatment approach with all of its piping, rights-of-way, energy use, water waste and control regulations.

One critic of the centralized flush-it-and-pass-it-on system, Berkeley architect Sim Van der Ryn, has imagined how future archaeologists, sifting through the material remains of our present culture hundreds of years from now, will interpret the curiously shaped ceramic bowl in each house, hooked up through miles of pipe to a central factory of tanks, stirrers, cookers and ponds, emptying into a river, lake or ocean. According to Van der Ryn their report might read:

> By early in the twentieth century, urban earthlings had devised a highly ingenious food production system whereby algae were cultivated in large centralized farms and piped directly into a ceramic food receptacle in each home.

A search for alternatives

The difficult challenge is to find a workable alternative. In a publication entitled "Stop the Five Gallon Flush!" the Minimum Cost Housing Group at McGill University's School of Architecture in Montreal examined systems from around the world that are designed for home use, and catalogued 52 of them from 11 countries. In their evaluation, the group steered clear of thinking of the modern flush toilet as "advanced," compared to a technology such as the pit latrine. As the researchers point out, "under certain conditions the latter is ecologically sound, cheap and quite safe."

What they found is a tribute to human ingenuity. For example, you can purchase a toilet from a Norwegian company for about $400 which uses an attached freezer to solidify the wastes so that there is no smell and no bacterial action. The toilet does require electricity, but no water or chemicals. The wastes are stored in a biodegradable plastic bag which can later be composted. At first the toilet suffered from a slight technological problem: The refrigerated air not only froze the waste, but it also chilled the seat, in turn

Flush toilets: a passing idea

chilling consumer interest. Now, however, freeze toilets stream warm air from the refrigeration unit's compressor over the seat to keep it warm.

If the freeze toilet doesn't light consumer fires, there are a variety of toilets that go to the other extreme; they incinerate the wastes with natural gas and/or electric heat. A Swedish design, the Pactor 101, utilizes the versatility of plastic to collect waste in a tube which is sealed by heat after each use to form a link in a large plastic "sausage." The chain is then stored in a removable plastic bag until it is discarded, along with other nonbiodegradable industrial age byproducts, somewhere in the great "away."

The World Health Organization, with headquarters in Geneva, has another, more ecological, approach: It offers plans for constructing a small-scale plant that can recover methane gas from human and animal wastes. The gas can be used for cooking, heating or for power. Critical to the operation of such a unit is an abundance of manure so that animals, which produce larger quantities of manure than people, are essential to this approach. Horses and cows produce about 10 to 16 tons of waste per year, whereas humans add only 30 to 60 pounds per capita in the same time period. What humans lack in quantity, they make up in quality; our waste is rich in nitrogen and phosphorous, needed for biological digestion and methane production from materials such as cellulose, which have a high carbon content. The World Health Organization points out that a ton of manure can yield 65 to 90 cubic yards of gas per digestion cycle, depending upon the temperature. A cycle can be from 1 to 12 months. The initial costs of such systems are comparatively high, but operation and maintenance are insignificant.

For those without the necessary animals to support a methane toilet, the Swedes, who are undoubtedly

emerging as the leaders in the world's alternative-toilet development race, have come up with another design which uses virtually nothing as a transport medium, thus eliminating the problems created by moving wastes with large volumes of water. This toilet, manufactured by Sweden's Electrolux Company, utilizes a vacuum pipe to move wastes. Invented in the 1950s, it has been applied successfully in a number of different scales of operation, including railroad cars, a camp site with 83 toilets and a small community of 273 homes. The advantages of the system are that it requires only a small amount of water, less waste is created which has to be stored and removed, and smaller pipes can be used. Although cheaper to operate than a conventional system, its initial costs are high: A one-toilet installation costs about $1,200.

Other countries have also developed interesting designs which rely upon water, utilizing it much more efficiently. A Japanese model, made by Toto Ltd., takes the bold step of mating the standard washbasin with the standard toilet. The result is a freestanding unit which uses water from the sink, mounted on the top of the toilet tank, for flushing. The saving on water from this integration is around 25 percent. In addi-

A freestanding Japanese model saves water by mating a standard washbasin with a standard water closet.

tion, there are also savings in cost and space, since the two bathroom fixtures occupy the space normally required by one. The Minimum Cost Housing Group at McGill University has modified this design and cast it in sulfur concrete, an extremely cheap material, so that these toilets can be made for about $50. An English modification, marketed by Ideal-Standard Ltd. for less than $20 each, allows a person to selectively flush the toilet. The tank releases either one or two gallons depending upon the requirements. Uruguay has produced a flexible toilet tank which functions on the principle of the punching bag. It has virtually no moving parts and is activated when the user depresses a plastic cistern by hand so that water can flow into the downpipe. This gives the user control over the amount of water released.

Even these ingenious approaches to waste removal have their drawbacks, because they are either too expensive for much of the world's population, or use too much energy or water. But after a careful search for toilet alternatives, another approach to the waste problem is beginning to interest increasing numbers of people—composting.

The principle of using human waste or night soil as fertilizer has been known and utilized in some cultures for centuries, although it has been little used in the West. In the late 1930s Rikard Lindstrom, a Swedish art teacher, began experimenting with a toilet that would compost human waste for use on his garden. He was also motivated to work on the system out of concern for the sewage contamination of the Baltic bay near his home. The product of his work is the Clivus Multrum, a toilet which successfully composts wastes without water, electricity or chemicals. The name comes from *clivus,* which is Latin for "inclining," and *multrum,* which is Swedish for "composting room."

How the Clivus works

The device itself is a fiber glass container about nine feet long, three feet wide and five feet high. It contains three compartments, a top one for human waste, a middle one for vegetable scraps and other organic refuse, and a lower one which holds the finished compost. A vent pipe at the top of the composting chamber allows odors and gas to exhaust out the top of the house. The early Clivuses had to be installed in basements directly underneath the bathroom and garbage chutes, but a later model utilizes a screw transport to move wastes so that the toilets and composting chamber can be mounted at the same level. It also allows multiple toilets to be connected to the same Clivus. The Clivus is odorless, thanks to a unique design which utilizes the heat created by composting organic matter. The heated air in the chamber rises

What human waste lacks in quantity, compared to cows, it makes up in quality, being rich in nitrogen.

through the vent pipe, thereby creating a downdraft at the toilet stool and garbage chute. It is strong enough to pull the flame of a match downward when held over the toilet.

To get the composting process started, the bottom of the container must be lined with organic material such as peat, garden soil and grass clippings. After the initial loading the process continues indefinitely, producing several buckets of humus per year per person. The newly formed rich soil in the bottom chamber can be removed about once a year, after a startup period of about two years.

In Sweden and Norway more than a thousand Clivuses are in operation, and it has been given the blessings of the Swedish Ministry of Health. Some communities in Sweden even give Clivus owners a tax rebate because they reduce the cost of municipal services such as sewage and garbage collection. Extensive tests by Swedish health authorities have found that no harmful bacteria, viruses or parasites can withstand the year or so of heat and bacterial action produced by the composting process. Although tests indicate that the end product of the Clivus process is perfectly safe for garden use, *Organic Gardening and Farming* magazine recommends, as an extra safety precaution, that it not be used on edible root crops. It can be used on other plants.

The composting toilet is getting widespread use in Scandinavia, but only a few have been sold in the United States. A firm in Cambridge, Massachusetts, Clivus Multrum USA, Inc., has acquired a franchise for the system and is now producing them in a plant in Maine. Although costs are still high at about $1,500 per installation, this is expected to come down with mass production. Experiments are also under way to fabricate the toilet out of cheaper materials.

The state of Maine has recently rewritten its plumbing code to permit the installation of composting toilets. Some health authorities in other states are also allowing them to be installed experimentally.

Established and backed by Abby Rockefeller, the company she has created is staffed by people who promote the toilet with all the fervor that her ancestors used to sell Americans on Standard Oil. "I look at it this way," says Bob Pacheco, the installations director who, if possible, personally visits the site of each installation. "I don't like the idea of turning the oceans and rivers into open sewers. Every Clivus I install in a family dwelling could mean 40,000 gallons less sewage for Boston harbor or another body of water."

The Clivus can handle all human waste, including urine, plus table scraps and other organic material such as the contents of the vacuum cleaner bag, but it cannot handle too much water. As a result the "gray water" produced by washing dishes or hands must go into a conventional system. But Miss Rockefeller thinks she can solve that problem. Her next project is a greenhouse adjacent to her conventional frame house in Cambridge that will utilize waste water to grow plants. She has installed a Clivus in her house and reports no trouble after more than a year of operation. To get the composting process going, she dumped into her Clivus all the organic wastes from a neighborhood restaurant. She has also added earthworms and other creatures to see if they can tolerate the heat and speed of the decomposition process.

The initial costs may appear prohibitively expensive, yet it is already competitive in areas where steep sewer hookup fees are required for conventional toilets. As mass production and alternative materials bring the Clivus' price down, it will be even more attractive. In addition, a group that Sim Van der Ryn works with in California, the Farallones Institute, is experimenting with ways people may build their own composting toilet. Their initial model can be built for less than $100 out of concrete blocks.

Some may view the composting toilet as simply a throwback to the outhouses of the past and reject it, but that would be shortsighted. Its time appears near at hand, as "No swimming, fishing or boating" signs pop up with increasing frequency on the banks of our rivers. With no connections to external networks, no moving mechanical parts, and its useful by-product, the composting toilet is a beautifully simple piece of technology of which a society could be proud.

Many benefits would accrue if we used our heads instead of using our rivers as the great "away."

It's safe again for swimming, fishing or boating

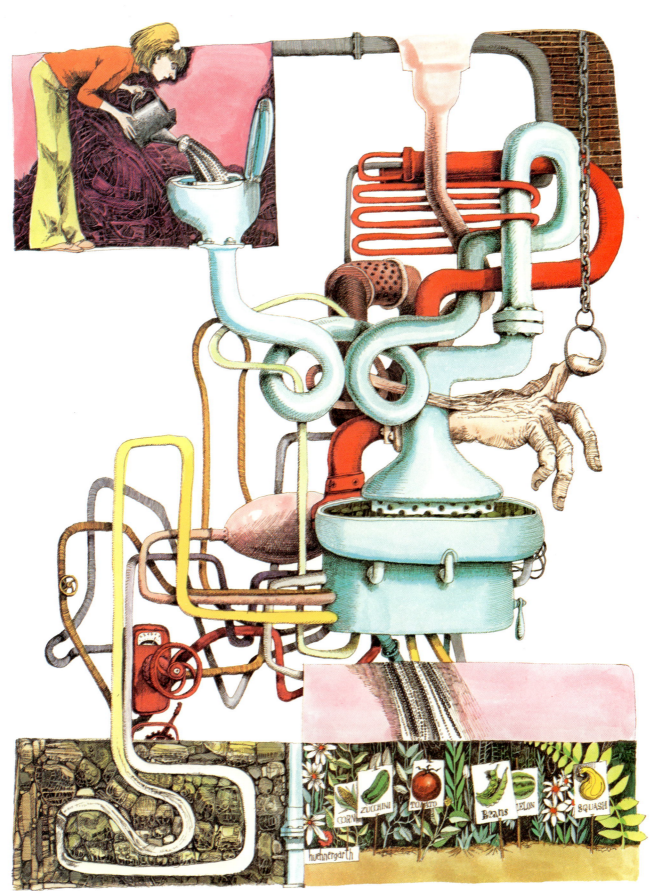

There are ways—some less complex than above—
to design toilets that serve more than one purpose.

Huge new radio telescope array extends Man's celestial vision

Still listening, the ranks of antennas point skyward after a night monitoring the hiss of quasars, the most powerful emitters of radio signals in the universe. Since neither cloud nor sunlight interferes with

By John Neary

Photographs by Shorty Wilcox

On a remote desert in New Mexico,
giant ears are listening to signals which may
some day tell how universe was created

the wavelengths that interest astronomers,
observations continue rain or shine, night or day.

Imagine you are Galileo Galilei, and as you assemble what is to be the very first celestial telescope in the history of the world, you savor the prospect of turning the world on its scientific ear. That is precisely how it feels to be one of the scores of men and women at work on the Very Large Array, the biggest, most powerful and most sensitive radio telescope in existence.

This Y-shaped configuration of 27 giant antennas is now taking shape on the vast Plains of San Augustin, 52 miles west of Socorro, New Mexico. Jack Lancaster, Dick Thompson, Barry Clark, Carl Bignell and Bob Hjellming—to name just a few of the people involved in this $78-million project of the National Radio Astronomy Observatory—are as full of pride and enthusiasm as it is possible to be and still maintain a professional cool. The reason: they are convinced that the VLA is going to do for radio astronomy what Galileo's telescope did for optical study of the heavens.

Just as Galileo's refractor gathered more light and magnified the viewing angle more than the best optical instrument then available—which, in the early 17th century, happened to be the human eye—the VLA likewise will be able, by virtue of its huge dimensions and its supersensitive electronics, to gather in more radio waves from outer space, and discriminate among them with greater precision, than any similar device.

Though radio astronomy is still less than 50 years old, its practitioners have already been able to detect objects and discern phenomena which had been unknown—even unimaginable—to their optical brethren. The richness of the data they have accumulated is surprising (see SMITHSONIAN, May 1978 and November 1970), considering the low power of the radio waves themselves. While some celestial bodies function as powerful transmitters, the radio waves they generate are diminished by distance. Indeed, the total energy of all the signals that have struck all the antennas of all

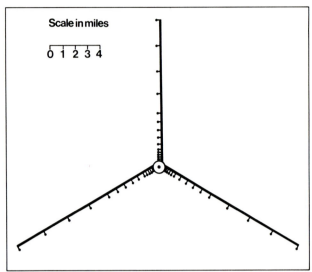

Two arms of VLA are 13 miles long; short arm, which points northward, is 11.8 miles long. Sensitivity and resolving power of the instrument when complete will permit observation of events near time of creation.

Bordered by massive peaks of Continental Divide, a group of antennas is readied for a look

the radio astronomers in the world since 1948, when the science really began to take off, is still equal to no more than the impact of a few snowflakes striking the Earth. Less poetically, what the antennas of radio astronomers pick up when aimed toward even the strongest radio source in space is about one-trillionth of a watt in signal strength, which is infinitesimal compared with even the weakest small-town or "ham" radio station.

Studying such evanescent phenomena may not be as difficult as counting the angels that can dance on the head of a pin, but it approximates the difficulty of, say, weighing them. The job obviously requires some extremely sophisticated and sensitive equipment. Thus it was that while scientists speculated about the existence of radio signals from space as long ago as 1890, when Edison made one of the first ventures to detect solar radio waves, it was not until 1932 that anyone actually found such signals.

The man who heard them—and indeed quite by accident—was Karl G. Jansky, a young Bell Telephone Laboratories engineer investigating the causes of interference in transoceanic radio-telephone communications. In addition to the static produced by such terrestrial sources as lightning flashes and the inner workings of the radio receivers themselves, Jansky kept picking up a persistent hissing. It varied in strength, depending on the time of day—and depending on where in the sky he aimed his antenna. Only after months of listening did Jansky realize that he must have tuned in on the world's oldest radio show: the

sibilant electronic utterance of the very heart of the Milky Way Galaxy.

Jansky did not know why the galaxy was making this racket, but we know now that every particle of matter in the universe radiates highly energetic electrons at radio frequencies. These emissions result from the inevitable spin-flips and collisions of the electrons composing the material in question—whether a jar of peanut butter or a collection of stars. The electron of a hydrogen atom, for example, spontaneously changes its orbital direction on the average of once every 11 million years. This reversal causes an energy loss, detectable on Earth—if the hydrogen exists in the form of a nebula in space—at the 21.3 centimeter wavelength. Such a reversal can be induced to occur more frequently, however, when one hydrogen atom bumps into another and *knocks* the electron into reverse—something a hydrogen atom can expect to experience once every 400 years.

Now it happens that space is almost entirely empty, but not quite. The air we breathe contains about 10-to-the-19th-power molecules in each cubic centimeter;

at a distant nebula. The full collection of dishes functions as single antenna 17 miles across.

Transporter shifts 213-ton dishes around like chessmen along some 38 miles of double-gauge tracks.

a cloud of hydrogen in space, on the other hand, contains only about 10 to 100 atoms—not molecules, but atoms—per cubic centimeter. However, space is enormous: a cloud of hydrogen can be ten light-years deep, meaning that each square-centimeter cross section would contain at least 10-to-the-20th-power atoms of hydrogen. Of them, some 10-to-the-10th-power atoms would undergo electron reversal at any given second. Taken altogether, the reversing electrons would produce a radio signal strong enough to be detected thousands of light-years away.

There are other kinds of electronic acrobatics going on in space that produce radio signals; the trick is to distinguish the signal, whatever its origin, from the noise the receiver itself makes. This the radio astronomer does by carefully matching his equipment's customary level of internal noise with the electronic blip he gets when he sweeps his antenna across the sky (or when the sky itself sweeps past a stationary antenna). The radio astronomer is not really listening to the sounds produced by his receiver; they are no more interesting than the hiss you pick up when you tune your stereo receiver to a spot between stations. Instead, he is interested in the power, frequency, wavelength, phase and polarization of the signals. Computers keep track of such data, as well as noting the time of day and where the radio telescope was aimed when it detected a given signal.

With a radio telescope of sufficient discrimination, the radio astronomer can then proceed to make maps of his sources, identifying them by signal strength or other characteristics.

Why radio telescopes? Because many of the things astronomers want to study in space simply cannot be examined optically. Dust and cosmic debris ofttimes restrict their vision in and around the spiral arms of our galaxy, and the nucleus is obscured by the blinding light of billions of stars. Radio waves at the longer wavelengths are not impeded by rain, snow, fog, sunlight or atmospheric turbulence. Then, too, some ob-

John Neary is a free-lance writer who now lives in Tesuque, New Mexico. His recent book, Whom the Gods Destroy, *is about madness.*

Standing inside the dish, deputy program manager Thompson and Vic Herrero, systems engineer, examine receiving apparatus. Here beams are focused, then amplified and transmitted to the computers.

When complete, 72 observing platforms will give astronomers a gourmet's choice of 351 combinations of dishes. Targets will vary widely in size, distance, composition and in signal frequency and wavelength.

jects, like "pulsating" collapsed stars (pulsars) and vast bodies of interstellar gas and organic molecules, radiate intensely only in the nonvisual parts of the spectrum. Radio telescopy will also have much to tell us about how quasars manage to generate their energy. These "quasi-stellar radio sources" produce enormous amounts of energy, as though all of the 250 billion stars in the Milky Way had been jammed into one fireball just a few light-years in diameter.

Despite all these advances, the limitations of radio telescopes have exasperated astronomers. Compared to the images obtainable from, say, the "Big Eye"— the 200-inch optical telescope on Mt. Palomar in California—the "pictures" from the best existing radio telescope look as if they were taken through the bottom of a pop bottle. As Thompson, VLA deputy program manager, says, "If you are using an optical telescope, the finest angular detail you can see is inversely proportional to the diameter of the mirror divided by the wavelength of light. The same thing is true of radio waves, which are several centimeters long—a hundred thousand times longer than waves of optical light. If you want comparable angular detail, you need a mirror a hundred thousand times wider than its optical counterpart. Physically, you couldn't construct a single telescope of such dimensions, but you can build a number of smaller ones and combine the signals."

This is precisely what the National Radio Astronomy Observatory, operated by the consortium of Associated Universities, Inc., for the National Science Foundation, is doing near Socorro. This broad, flat valley, once a Pleistocene lake bed, consists of at least half a million acres of ranch land, of which 3,500 acres

will be used by the VLA. The location was chosen for a number of reasons, but above all the high altitude, which offers minimal atmospheric interference and relative freedom from hurricanes or tornadoes; the southerly latitude, which provides increased sky coverage, particularly of the Milky Way's galactic center; and the remoteness from man-made radiation.

The VLA looks nothing like any popular notion of a telescope as you come upon it after driving through the Magdalena Mountains from town. In fact, an inquiry about the telescope itself is apt to draw a blank stare from the locals. But everybody seems to know about those big, gleaming white antennas—"You'll see 'em miles away!" Indeed you will, still diminutive on the horizon, like some Erector dream set made to order for a millionaire model buff. Then, as you draw nearer, the antennas loom larger on the sweep of the plains until they dwarf other structures—a cattle farmer's windmill and barn, and the VLA operations facilities.

The two-story control building, flanked by a cafeteria and a dormitory for visiting sky-gazers, is as no-nonsense inside as a police barracks. Already, although the VLA will not be finished until January 1981, the place is humming with scientists, engineers and technicians testing and calibrating their new baby.

One morning not very long ago, when the Magdalenas were shrouded in a mist of rain and fog, the VLA was busy scanning the surface of the sun. A 29-year-old array operator, Linda Sowinski, took us out to meet the newest of the huge antennas, Number 11, still undergoing an electronics shakedown. We wore hardhats, and climbing the 50 or 60 feet of open metal stairs to the "vertex room" was a somewhat dizzying experience. There was a pulsing sound in the vertex, the sound of the cryogenic pumps that keep a crucial portion of Number 11's electronics cooled to a frosty -427 degrees F. Alarm buttons were situated here and there around the structure—so that anyone on board when the big antenna begins to tip can let the operator know someone's there.

While the length of the radio waves studied means that individual dish-shaped "mirrors" do not have to be nearly so flawlessly smooth as an optical telescope's, the VLA has posed a substantial construction challenge. Two of its arms are 13 miles long; the third is 11.8 miles. The 213-ton aluminum ears—each 82 feet wide—must be movable and steerable, yet capable of performing in winds up to 40 mph and withstanding gusts of 125 mph at snow loads of 202 pounds per square yard. The Earth spins the installation in an arc beneath the heavens like a turntable, eventually moving the object of study beyond the field of view, but while it is in sight, refined electronic circuitry must keep the antennas locked on target and operating in unison. Some 85 percent of the celestial hemisphere, the sky over a given point on the Earth's surface, is accessible at any moment.

For a change of focus, the antennas (11 of the 27 are currently in operation, providing astronomers limited use of the facility) can be lifted from their pillars and moved by a 24-wheel, 60-ton transporter (p149) at up to five mph along a double pair of railroad tracks to any of 72 observing stations. At present, 55 of them are in place. There will be four basic configurations, approximately 13, 4, 1.2 and 0.37 miles long. Extended to its fullest, the array will see only the smallest objects and will be able to distinguish among components of radio sources no farther apart than 1/10 of a second of arc. When the antennas are clustered into their closest formation, the VLA will lose some of its resolving power—its capacity to separate one source of light

from another—but its sensitivity to continuous emissions of a given object will be greater.

Radio waves bounce off the concave surface of each antenna and strike a subreflector, which directs them to one of four sets of receivers, amplifiers and signal processors. Then they are picked up and transmitted to the central control building, where signals from all the antennas are combined and sent to the VLA's cerebral cortex, a battery of computers. The signals are carried not by ordinary electrical cable, but via waveguide; the waveguide is a buried copper-lined steel pipe 60 millimeters in diameter designed to handle 600,000 telephone calls at a time, and has the principal virtue of transmitting tremendous amounts of data without loss in signal strength. By matching up incoming data from pairs of antennas, 351 different pair-combinations can be set up.

"Billions of bits of information are coming in every hour," says the program director, Lancaster, and that is obviously beyond the capacity of any mortal arithmetician to manage. While an operator is in constant attendance, the job of running the VLA is given over to four minicomputer units which chat back and forth via teleprinter as they order the 'scopes around and sift through the masses of accumulated data. "Boss" oversees the two workhorses of the crew—"Cora," which collects the billions of signals, and "Corbin," which performs the staggering task of correlating it all—while "Monty," the fourth one, mon-

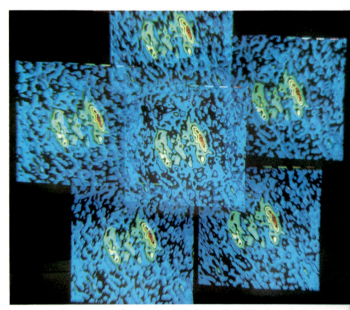

Computer data from VLA can be displayed visually in a variety of forms, such as the multiple-image map shown above. At right, programmer Jim Torson looks at high-resolution picture of distant sources.

itors all performances, including its own, instantaneously and with tireless vigilance.

The end product of all these labors is a curious mathematical map: a scroll of paper solidly covered with numbers, each representing the signal strength of an area just a few tenths of a second of arc in diameter. At the vast distances involved, this means the VLA is examining—in the case of the nearest spiral galaxy, the Andromeda Nebula—a location many hundreds of light-years wide, but still a pinpoint by astronomical standards. "We can make maps with four million numbers on them," says British-born astronomer Thompson. The computers will also conjure up a gaudy color video image of the radio source being studied, which the astronomers can then record with an instant camera for later reference. By virtue of the VLA's projected ability to detect the characteristic frequencies of key elements and molecules in space, the staff will eventually be able to map them as well.

The VLA is far more sensitive and easier to use than any other installation of its kind. It is instrumented so that an observer can switch among four different frequencies in about 60 seconds instead of having to make awkward, time-consuming changes in equipment. Early in December 1976, a month after formal program observations began, spectra from a celestial x-ray source were obtained in a few hours; heretofore, such observations might have taken months or years. Since there are always more astronomers with

critical projects in mind than there is observing time on existing instruments, such celerity is highly desirable and long overdue.

Indeed, few aspects of astronomy will be untouched by this splendid new instrument. Astronomers have been wondering for some time whether there is an active center in our galaxy which expels gas and produces a high flux of energy in various parts of the electromagnetic spectrum. The galactic nucleus lies in the direction of the constellation Sagittarius, and is invisible in ordinary light because thick clouds of interstellar dust get in the way. Radio waves, however, penetrate the dust easily. They reveal a radio source buried in the complex of clouds called Sagittarius A, and though that area does not appear as bright as the centers of other galaxies, it does still exhibit a rapid outflow of gaseous material. Thus it appears that the nucleus of the Milky Way Galaxy was once like the most active ones we see elsewhere.

The new facility has attracted many talented staff and visiting astronomers from all over the United States and the world. Scientist Bignell, a 34-year-old Canadian, moved himself and his family from the NRAO headquarters in Charlottesville, Virginia, to Socorro. To Bignell, the VLA "allows us to probe beyond our own Earth, to understand—in a very esoteric way— what's happening in the universe." Bignell and his colleagues are chasing some very big cosmological questions: How did the universe originate? What is its

structure? Is it positively or negatively curved? Will it collapse some day or go on expanding forever, or does it pulsate on a time scale of tens of billions of years? When these astronomers predict the VLA may see to the very limits of the universe, the mind does boggle a bit, because the notion seems to contradict the very meaning of the term universe. What lies beyond those limits? Is there anyone who understands these contradictions? "I don't know anybody who does, but there can only be one universe as far as we physically are concerned," Bignell replies. "There is no window to the other side."

The man in the street might well ask what this has to do with him. The answer is—maybe everything. Among various molecules found in interstellar gas clouds is some complex organic material, and astronomers hope that they will even find amino acids, the basic building blocks of life. Finding them would be of major philosophical as well as scientific importance because, according to theory, interstellar gas clouds now and then condense into stars and their associated planets. The Earth itself is supposed to have resulted from such a condensation and so may have been endowed at birth with the materials from which life evolved. The organic compounds in the nuclei of your cells and mine may have been made in interstellar space five billion years ago.

Then there are the mysterious quasars, some of which appear to be flying apart at speeds greater than light. Since physics is based on the postulate that nothing can go faster than light, the experts are scrambling for ways to explain these apparent hyperluminal velocities. Hjellming, an NRAO senior staff scientist who is with the VLA, says that if it could be established that "some things *do* move faster than the speed of light, there is possibly no more revolutionary finding we could come up with." Of course, he quickly

adds, the phenomenon may be nothing more than an optical illusion of sorts. Unaccountably, too, as we have seen, quasars radiate as much light and as many radio waves as entire galaxies. According to Hjellming, they would have to convert up to 20 to 25 percent of their mass into energy in order to produce the findings obtained by the VLA—yet the most efficient fusion process known would yield a mass conversion ratio of only 10 to 15 percent. Proof that quasars do immolate themselves in this way, and that the readings are not simply being misunderstood, would require profound modifications of physical law. The prospect doesn't bother him.

"Physics," says Hjellming, "has been thoroughly dull for the last 10, 15 years. We've proved quarks exist, and found a few more particles, and that's about all." The VLA, he believes, will agitate his profession considerably. "The astronomical laboratory is the best place to find things we don't expect. The reason I'm an astronomer is that the most interesting unsolved problems—pulsars, quasars, black holes, the geometry of space—lie in this natural realm and it's cheaper to examine them in this laboratory." Indeed, no physicist can produce comparable effects on Earth.

"But nature has no problem producing such things and on a galactic scale," Hjellming explains. "If we can find out how nature does it, it would be fantastic. When one is in one's cups, one says one is working on the energy problem."

Hjellming ruminated on yet more riddles the VLA might help astrophysicists to solve. Because quasars are so many billions of light-years away—and that means so many billions of years back in time—they could tell us a great deal about physical conditions at the birth of the universe. "To be able to see out as far as one can see anything! To turn the cosmological clock back!" He believes that if we can say anything about how quasars age, we can say what the universe was really like and how it evolved. "The ultimate would be to find some cut-off. No more stars, no galaxies, *nothing*. At that point, we would be studying objects closer to T-equals-zero than anything around."

T-equals-zero: the birth date of the universe, when all the stuff that would make up everything from the tiniest meson to Man himself was first created. "One has an urge to try to overthrow laws," he admits as he chalks complex diagrams on the blackboard of his Socorro study. "That's the reason we are in this business. We will find things going on that we never even guessed." In short, things beyond imagination.

Earth's rotation causes star streaks in this time exposure. Red lights alert low-flying aircraft.

By Dennis Farney

Ominous problem: what to do with radioactive waste

*More nuclear power plants mean more
of the most lethal and long-lasting of poisons,
and scientists disagree about their disposal*

They call it "the thousand-year problem."

It begins with a rusty-brown fluid that roils and churns inside its great underground tank, boiling in the heat from some inner fire. This dark liquid doesn't look especially sinister, but drop for drop it is one of the most hazardous, long-lived substances on Earth.

It is "high-level" radioactive waste, produced when the spent fuel of nuclear reactors is recycled. The fuel is dissolved in acid and the reusable uranium and plutonium are laboriously separated out. What remains in the end is a liquid so laden with radioactive substances that it will self-boil for years from the heat generated in decaying. Depending upon the tank design, the waste is either cooled artificially or simply allowed to boil (after much of the heat-producing strontium 90 and cesium 137 have first been removed for separate storage). At the Atomic Energy Commission's Hanford works in Washington, a million-gallon waste tank produced and stored under current procedures, would contain roughly 250 or more times the strontium 90 released by the Hiroshima bomb—and this after about 95 percent of the strontium had already been removed.

There are 65 million gallons of waste at Hanford, stored in about 150 underground tanks. Most tanks contain a good deal less than the above amount of strontium. There are some 22 million gallons elsewhere stored in giant underground tanks—most of it the byproduct of U.S. nuclear weapons-making over three decades. And, by the year 2000, the growing use of nuclear power for electricity is expected to generate the equivalent of 60 million gallons more. (There will be more signs like those above). This waste will be at least 10 to 30 times as radioactive as that at Hanford.

To contemplate this growing accumulation in terms of its outermost *potential* for harm—to man and to the intricate life chains of the Earth—is to conjure up problems so large as to be almost incomprehensible.

Consider:

• Many of the radioisotopes within the waste do decay in short order to relatively harmless levels. An example is zirconium 95, which has a half-life of only 65 days. This means that half of a given amount will decay within the first 65 days, half of the remaining half within the next 65 and so on.

But three are very long-lived. Strontium 90 and cesium 137 both have approximately 30-year half-lives; there is so much of them within the waste that they will have to be isolated from the environment for 600 to 1,000 years. A third substance, plutonium 239 (which escapes recycling in small quantities) has a fantastically long half-life of 24,000 years. It will have to be contained for at least 250,000 years.

• Each of these substances presents its own hazards, and some are less serious than others. Plutonium's radiation is weak, incapable of penetrating even a sheet or two of newspaper. But if you inhaled even one dust particle of plutonium you would be in grave danger of lung cancer. What plutonium dictates, then, is containment; it must simply be bottled up.

Cesium emits a type of radiation which can penetrate anything short of a thick shield of lead or con-

Mr. Farney has covered a wide range of environmental and political topics for the Wall Street Journal *and edits features in the paper's Washington office.*

156

crete. Cesium, however, is chemically similar to potassium, so that, if ingested, it will be excreted by the body within a few weeks.

Strontium also is responsible for a penetrating type of radiation. Like cesium, it gives off great amounts of heat as it slowly decays. In addition, it is chemically similar to calcium and, if ingested, lodges in bone cells to bombard surrounding tissue with radiation for years. It is this deadly combination that makes it the most hazardous of the three.

• The standard unit of measurement for quantities of radioactivity is the curie, and one way to express the pollution potential of a radioactive substance is in the amount of water required to dilute one curie to drinking water purity. The amount necessary for one curie of strontium 90: about ten billion gallons. By the year 2000, the generation of electric power in U.S. nuclear reactors will have accumulated ten billion curies of strontium 90. An AEC computer has calculated what it would take, theoretically, to dilute these ten billion curies to drinking water purity: roughly one-fortieth of all the water in all the oceans, rivers, lakes and streams on the face of the Earth.

A *potential* problem, however, can often loom all out of proportion to a *realistic* problem. Radioactive waste becomes a threat only if it escapes into the biosystem; with no other environmental hazard has there been such "determination to minimize [this] risk at almost any cost," says a National Academy of Sciences report. The waste becomes a threat of the gravest sort if some cataclysm catapults it into the upper atmosphere to rain down as global fallout. That kind of cataclysm is extremely unlikely and the AEC's ultimate goal is to transform its waste into non-liquid forms deposited in invulnerable locations.

Simplifying the AEC's task is the fact that the volume involved is relatively small. All the waste produced by all the domestic U.S. reactors for the rest of this century theoretically could be stored, after solidification, in a single warehouse 200 feet on a side and $12\frac{1}{2}$ feet high.

So much for the good news. The bad news is that the military waste, having been produced by less sophisticated chemical methods than the coming domestic waste will be, is more of a volume problem. And both the military waste and the domestic waste are going to require a "warehouse" that remains leakproof, tamperproof and foolproof for lengths of time that, in human terms, approach forever.

Whole empires have risen and fallen in a fraction of the time the strontium and cesium will have to remain sealed away. The entire recorded history of mankind is but a fraction of the 250,000-year storage time of plutonium. Neanderthal man appeared only about 75,000 years ago. The implications have reminded one thoughtful nuclear scientist of one of man's most gripping legends—Faust, who bargained his soul to the devil in exchange for power. The scientist wondered: Are short-lived man and the ephemeral institutions he creates equal to the demands of the fissioned atom?

"We nuclear people have made a Faustian bargain with society," wrote Alvin M. Weinberg, then director of the Oak Ridge National Laboratory, in *Science* in 1972. "On the one hand we offer—in the catalytic nuclear burner—an inexhaustible source of energy. . . . But the price we demand of society for this magical energy source is both a vigilance and a longevity of our social institutions that we are quite unaccustomed to. . . . Is mankind prepared to exert the eternal vigilance needed. . . ?"

Photographs by Fritz Goro   *Painting by Ron Miller*

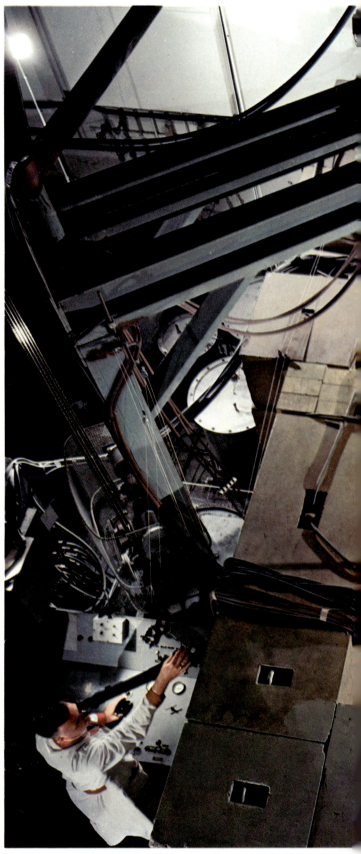

To Weinberg personally, the bargain seemed well worth making. Nevertheless, he argued that this decision is really "trans-scientific"—so fundamental, so bound up in questions of ethics and ultimate values that only society as a whole should make it.

Today, with an added incentive in the form of the energy shortage, this society and others are nearing definitive commitments to the Faustian bargain. In some ways this commitment has been preceded by the kind of national debate that Weinberg thought necessary. There has been a great deal of discussion of reactor safety; there has even been some debate over such relatively esoteric problems as that of "nuclear blackmail" by terrorists who might threaten society with stolen plutonium. But, curiously, there has been relatively little public debate about the long-run implications of nuclear waste. It remains the province of experts and their views are nowhere near unanimous.

To AEC Chairman Dixy Lee Ray, the waste is "the biggest non-problem we have"—one "readily solvable" through any of a number of techniques. This spring the AEC hopes to announce plans for a man-made facility which could accommodate all the commercial waste generated for the rest of the century. Meanwhile, it is investigating "ultimate" solutions that range from entombing the wastes deep within the earth to rocketing them into outer space.

To Hannes Alfven, Nobel Prize-winning physicist at the University of California, San Diego, "a very large production of nuclear energy necessarily means the mass production of radioactive poisons in quantities which are terrifying." Until a few years ago, Alfven endorsed nuclear fission as a solution to global energy needs; now, largely because of the waste problem, he argues for a moratorium on fission reactors. He explains that nuclear fission dictates safety requirements so stringent that "no acts of God can be permitted."

Scientist at left peers through fortresslike walls at glowing radioactive cores in a research reactor

at Brookhaven National Laboratory, where tests have been made to bake wastes into a ceramic form.

Somewhere in the middle is Ralph E. Lapp, of the original Manhattan Project and today an energy consultant to the nuclear industry. Waste disposal "is just not in the same class as some other problems," he says. "It's not as dynamic as the problems associated with reactor safety," and there remains adequate time to solve the problem. Still, "I worry about it."

What worries him is that more and more nations are producing more and more waste at an increasing rate. As late as 1970, nuclear reactors produced only one percent of U.S. electrical power. Today the figure is five percent; the AEC projection for 1980 is 20 percent and for the year 2000, 60 percent. Abroad, reactors will be operating in about 30 nations by 1976.

Logically, the growing accumulation of waste should be treated as a planetary problem by some international organization. But in the real world, practices considered questionable by some nations are being used routinely, or at least being considered for use, by others. The Soviet Union, for example, is reportedly considering injecting high-level wastes deep into a water-bearing sandstone formation. Japan is looking around for a small island or two to use for storage, although just about any Japanese island will be vulnerable to earthquakes, tidal waves and typhoons. The U.S. program is among the most scrupulous and most advanced in the world, yet even here waste disposal remains at a rather low priority.

Senator Frank Church of Idaho has calculated that in the AEC's first 25 years it spent billions to develop the production side of the nuclear industry, but a mere $50 million on the waste problem. In fiscal 1975, the agency plans to spend about $29.5 million for waste management—less than eight percent of the $385.5 million budgeted for civilian reactor research and development and less than the additional $52.9 million for reactor safety activities.

A case of human error

This country began generating waste in 1944, when reactors at Hanford secretly began making plutonium for the atomic bomb. Of those hectic days, Chairman Ray said, "It was believed that the best way to handle radioactive wastes would be, put them into a tank in the ground, the tank would gradually corrode, and the material would gradually leak into the soil, and the soil would be the burying place." As a result of that decision—and the fact that the practice of putting waste in tanks continued long after the original naïveté about the hazards of waste had faded—the AEC today is stuck with some 85 million gallons of military-related waste. Although it will remain hazardous for centuries, it is occupying tanks with useful lives of about 30 years.

Radioactive waste

In eerie cavern of a salt mine in Kansas, the Atomic Energy Commission experimented with natural

The oldest of those tanks are now wearing out—and leaking. To date the AEC has experienced 17 leaks at Hanford and six at Savannah River. The most serious occurred at Hanford last spring, when a leaking tank went undetected from approximately April 20 to June 8. About 115,000 gallons of high-level waste soaked into the ground. This included an estimated 14,000 curies of strontium 90 and 40,000 curies of cesium 137.

Of course, the leak of tank 106 T can be seen as an apparent demonstration of how the escape of a potentially grave amount of waste need not necessarily lead to grave consequences. So far as it can be determined, no waste came within 100 feet of the local aquifer.

Still, even Pollyanna herself would be hard-pressed to whip up enthusiasm for such accidents. Partly as a result of them, the AEC began about nine years ago to solidify its military waste within tanks, using a process that evaporates it down to an intensely radioactive "salt cake." By the time the AEC catches up to current production (in 1977 or so), it will have some 380,000 tons of radioactive salt on its hands, and no one is quite sure just what will be done with it. At the least it will be less vulnerable to accidents.

The AEC simply got behind on its military waste. It does not intend to make the same mistake with the commercial waste, now totaling a mere 600,000 gallons but beginning to accumulate. AEC regulations do require contractors to solidify the commercial waste soon after it emerges from the reprocessing plant. One process would convert it from an acid solution to a granular substance that looks like a washday detergent. Others also feasible would yield glass or a ceramiclike material. Within ten years after reprocessing, the contractor is to pack the solidified waste into metal canisters and transport them to the AEC inside enormous lead "casks" that contain their radiation. What the AEC will do with the canisters for the next 249,990

years is certainly a question that intrigues scientists.

Some have seriously proposed that society create a new kind of "priesthood" to watch over the waste, much as medieval monks watched over mankind's written history in the Dark Ages. Presumably, this priesthood would have to be supranational in character and somehow insulated from the rise and fall of nations through the centuries. Other scientists think the solution lies not so much in recruiting priests but in making a storage vault that not only endures for millennia but also remains so conspicuous that future generations will never lose track of it: something along the lines of the great pyramids.

The AEC's position is that neither a perpetual priesthood nor a moratorium is warranted. ". . . Some consider [the waste] the Achilles heel of nuclear energy," Commissioner William O. Doub has testified before Congress. ". . . However, a course of action is available to us which will provide safe storage . . . for an extended period . . . while still making it possible to develop truly permanent storage and to transfer the waste to it." This refers, of course, to the AEC plan to store solidified commercial waste in a highly retrievable form inside a sturdy man-made structure while the agency continues to investigate permanent solutions. This approach does buy time. Yet in a sense it also represents an embarrassing retreat from two "permanent" solutions the AEC had been advancing when the 1970s began.

Then the solution to at least part of the problem of its military waste seemed to be "Project Bedrock." The 20 million gallons or so of the waste at Savannah

rock-salt formation as final resting place for nuclear
waste, but unforeseen difficulties developed.

River would be pumped into a man-made cavern deep
below the site. If all went well, the concept might then
be applied to the Hanford waste as well.

But a problem developed before the idea had gone
much beyond the theoretical stage. The proposed
cavern would lie about 500 feet below the Tuscaloosa
aquifer, a great underground reservoir that supplies
fresh water to much of South Carolina and Georgia.
Could the AEC be absolutely certain the waste
wouldn't someday pollute the aquifer? After initially
defending the concept in the face of mounting alarm
and criticism, the AEC has now pigeonholed it, probably for good.

The seeming solution to the commercial waste appeared to lie in an abandoned salt mine a half-mile
outside the county seat town of Lyons, Kansas. There,
a thousand feet below, the AEC proposed, if tests
proved favorable, to bury all the commercial waste
produced for the rest of this century.

Scientific advisory committees had recommended
burial of solidified waste in bedded salt as the safest
current alternative. Bedded salt deposits are among
the most stable geologic structures known. Since salt
is highly soluble in water, the mere presence of it automatically denotes the absence of water—in the case of
the deposits under Lyons, for some 250 million years.
In addition, rock salt roughly equals concrete as a
radiation shield and is so plastic under heat and stress
that fissures from an earthquake would be self-healing.

Even so, political opposition began to build in Kansas. The AEC strongly defended its Lyons site, until a
disturbing discovery was made. Less than a half-mile

away from the agency's proposed repository was a still-
active salt mine where owners had previously experimented with a hydraulic fracturing mining technique.
In one such experiment, the operators had "lost"
175,000 gallons of water. No one could be sure just
where it had gone and thus no one could be absolutely
sure that this and other mining techniques hadn't
compromised the geological integrity of the AEC's
mine. After weighing these findings, the AEC pulled
out of Lyons.

Of the three types of man-made facility it is now
considering, the simplest would seal individual canisters of waste inside 35-ton steel casks and arrange the
casks on individual saddles on the surface of the
ground. The result would be an eerie tableau a little
reminiscent of the monoliths of Easter Island. Each
cask would heat up from the thermal energy generated by the decaying radioisotopes inside, but natural
convection would keep temperature within bounds.
Each cask probably would be surrounded by a concrete housing to improve radiological protection and
encourage air circulation.

The second concept would place the canisters inside
a kind of superwarehouse, again designed in such a
way that natural air currents would cool the casks.

The third approach would place the canisters in
basins of circulating water. The water would be
chilled and there would be backup cooling systems
available if this primary system failed. One disadvantage of this approach is that it would require more
extensive monitoring and mechanical maintenance.

As for permanent disposal solutions, an AEC contractor, Battelle Pacific Northwest Laboratories, has reported these preliminary evaluations:

Outer Space. Despite the obvious appeal of this idea, it seems likely to remain impractical for a good long while. For one thing it now costs about $1,000 to put a pound of payload in an Earth-escape trajectory. A single 1,000-megawatt reactor will produce something like 70 pounds of solidified waste a year and safety considerations would dictate another 700 pounds of shielding. Thus the total annual cost per reactor would be about $1.4 million.

There is also a question of safety. As the Battelle report puts it, "there seems to be a degree of uncertainty as to whether . . . a trajectory can be achieved with sufficient accuracy to insure that a capsule will not come back to earth in an unplanned manner."

Polar Disposal. There still remain great uninhabited land masses, like Greenland and Antarctica, of seemingly little economic significance. Why not haul the wastes there? If simply deposited on the surface of the ice they would melt their way down to bedrock within a few years—and there would be absolutely no need for a backup cooling system! But, Battelle argues, too little is known about such things as the movement of glaciers in these areas. Then, too, burial of wastes in Antarctica would require amending an international treaty that now bars the disposal of atomic wastes there.

Seabed Disposal. European nations already have deposited some relatively low-level wastes at sea. So did the United States in years past, although AEC policy now forbids this. It has been suggested that high-level waste might be deposited in underwater valleys, on deep abyssal plains or on the sea floor in areas where high sedimentation rates would soon bury them. But a seabed repository would be very difficult to monitor, and it would be so hard to guarantee that

something wouldn't go wrong that the idea seems likely to remain little more than a scientific curiosity.

Transmutation. The ancient alchemists who sought to change base metals into gold anticipated this concept. The modern idea is to bombard the wastes with neutrons inside a reactor and thus transmute them into shorter-lived or even harmless substances. "Transmutation may prove to be one of the best methods for treating long-lived radioactive wastes," Battelle reports. But the problem is that existing fission reactors don't do a very good job of altering cesium 137 or strontium 90. Fusion reactors (SMITHSONIAN, December 1972) do look promising, but it may be decades before they are operating.

Geologic Disposal. Despite the fiasco at Lyons, burial in bedded salt still looks promising. Although it is far from recommitting itself to this approach, the AEC is checking out virgin salt beds in Kansas and New Mexico. One variation on the geologic disposal theme would be to create a bedrock cavern—by mining, drilling or even exploding an underground nuclear device—and then introduce wastes that are so hot thermally that they would melt the surrounding rock and form a rock-waste matrix.

Conceivably, any of these concepts could prove out and thus rewrite the terms of mankind's Faustian bargain. Pessimists should recall that even the legend of Faust itself has been rewritten in a fundamental way.

In the 16th-century accounts Faust comes to horrible ends. In one version, the devil carries him off; in another, the Evil One wrings his neck. But the early 19th-century Faust of Goethe, the Faust we know today, ends much more happily. Through sheer wile, strength of character and the love of a beautiful maiden, Faust is able to enjoy the devil's power and yet escape his clutches. Social historians say that as Man's philosophic outlook gradually evolved, the legend evolved with it.

Optimists must ask: Cannot Man, through ingenuity and the help of technology, win his own bargain with the atom? Can he not enjoy its almost unlimited power and yet avoid its almost immortal pollution? It is a question all bound up with the needs of an energy-hungry planet and the silent presence of generations still centuries away from being born. And a question that, as yet, awaits a final answer.

Several proposed disposal schemes appear in the artist's composite: Huge concrete canisters lined with steel could become the nuclear age version of Easter Island monuments; deep ocean burial and deposition in polar ice caps have been suggested, along with idea of shooting wastes into space by means of a rocket.

People and History

In the honeymoon flush of getting *Smithsonian* under way, we staff members often came up with some splendid rationalizations for our choice of types of articles and of articles themselves. These criteria generally were rerationalized as we got into month-by-month production, for the realistic demands of meeting the schedule, of avoiding conflicts in subject matter and of attracting readers. The infant magazine was in no position to reject a sure-fire article in favor of a might-be article simply because the latter hewed to theoretical standards of "purity" worked out months before.

Still, the standard for history-people subjects is fun to review. We would be relevant, we vowed, back in those days of magazine gestation. History, just for history's sake, didn't belong here. History that added a new dimension of understanding with which to meet today's problems . . . now, *that* was what we were after. We would remind people that the world was troubled by pollutions of various kinds in the past, and seemed to cope with them somehow. Crime in the streets was rampant in Hogarth's England, yet British justice is an inspiration. Traffic made life unbearable in ancient Rome, yet it got straightened out one way or another. Political corruption plagued the United States in the late 19th century, yet reformers managed to appear in the nick of time and we survived. There is nothing really new—and we should gain hope with that.

The trouble with articles about straight history is that they often fail to tingle the toes with the excitement of discovery. And as we got into production a number of articles came our way which were not obviously relevant—but certainly aroused interest. Moreover, we tended to avoid saying No to a Smithsonian-based topic. And there were various anniversaries to which we felt we should give a nod. There was, in fact, the Bicentennial. Any Revolutionary War subject was assured of serious consideration.

So the magazine slipped into a more flexible, more tolerant, more comfortable editorial position. If we could react to a proffered article with interest and surprise—"Gee, I didn't know *that*!"—after all, *that* and revealing it was what the magazine and the Institution was about. It the subject was pre-photographic history and amusing, it might be illustrated with cartoons. If the articles were simply excellent, that was enough.

Here you have examples. Bronowski's Copernicus sprang from a Smithsonian lecture and was simply excellent. O'Donnell's Paul Revere was a refreshing Bicentennial piece, so it ran with Arnold Roth's hilarious cartoons. Wittenberg's article on Harlem photographer James Van DerZee caught little-known nuances of an under-reported facet of history. "Gee," we say as we read it, "I didn't know *that*!" The insight into child rearing in New Guinea is fascinating Smithsonian anthropology. And the late Al Capp's appreciation of the late Rube Goldberg began as a critique of a Smithsonian exhibit and turned into a wonderfully grouchy assessment of the modern world.

Where, then, is the relevance? As you read of the past and of the people of our Earth, you find all is richly relevant. They sharpen your concern over topics that deserve it. They stir your interest in the unfamiliar and your pleasure in new views of the familiar. They produce the delight and substantial satisfaction of discovery.

—Edwards Park
Board of Editors

A Star was born: *Smithsonian* staffer Meredith White rides the Smithsonian's original Star "safety" bicycle, an overnight success built in 1881 by millionaire manufacturer Hezekiah Smith. From "Hezekiah Smith, builder of a 'safety' bicycle" February 1972 pp. 70-74.

By J. Bronowski

The heavens were brought down to earth by Copernicus the humanist

Amid the bustling ferment of Renaissance thought, this modest, committed man brought a human perspective to astronomy

The facts of Copernicus' life may seem modest (SMITH-SONIAN, March 1973) and his character obscure to us. But we know that Copernicus the astronomer was also a humanist gentleman and I want first to transmit the broad and even romantic sense of humanism in that description. I want to begin with the tang and taste of the age, its almost physical sense of bursting from the monastery back to nature, which is so vivid in the Renaissance.

Movements that claim to go back to natural ways of thinking usually turn out to have a bias against science, and humanism was no exception. The father and fountainhead of the movement, Petrarch in the 14th century, had such an antipathy toward scientific techniques that he even disliked medical men. Nevertheless, one of Petrarch's good friends, Giovanni de' Dondi, was a doctor, and a fine mechanic into the bargain; he was nicknamed dell'Orologio because he spent 16 years, during a busy medical and university practice, in making a beautiful astronomical clock at Padua. The original clock is lost, but it has been possible from the drawings to make a copy which is now in the Smithsonian Institution in Washington (see page 168).

It is a mechanical model of Ptolemy's system, with seven faces on which the seven planets of antiquity (Mars, Jupiter, Saturn, the Moon, Mercury, Venus and the Sun) run on geared sets of wheels that trace out their epicycles. We do not know when the clock was lost; it may be that Leonardo da Vinci saw it, since there is a drawing of his that looks very like the mechanism designed to carry Venus.

I linger on de' Dondi's clock because I want to bring home the age's sense that the starry heavens are a work of art, and a divine inspiration for the poet and the scientist alike. Petrarch could not be expected to find that in the classical authors that he admired and re-introduced: They were Latin, and came from a culture that had little head or taste for science. But a hundred years later, the movement of humanism to the Greek classics recovered a culture with a different outlook, in which science in general and astronomy in particular had been highly regarded. Humanism in the 15th century was preoccupied with Greek as a language and with Greek ideas.

Copernicus was not at the hub of humanism in Krakow—an eastern frontier town at the edge of Europe, as we are still reminded by the trumpeter who blows the hours from the Cathedral tower to commemorate a Tartar raid. One of his objectives in going to Italy was certainly to learn Greek, and probably to learn Greek in a scientific context; it had just been introduced, for example, at the medical school in Padua. Indeed, it has been suggested, and supported by astronomical evidence, that Copernicus had already convinced himself that the earth moves around the sun, and that he went to Italy to learn Greek specifically to find sources in Greek thought—in Aristarchus of Samos, for example, and in Pythagoras.

At this point it is right to ask: But was not Greek

The late Jacob Bronowski, distinguished mathematician/biologist, was the creator and host for the internationally acclaimed BBC television series, "The Ascent of Man." This article is based on a lecture given April 24, 1973, at the Smithsonian.

A radiant, stylized portrait of the astronomer is the motif for a Polish poster, one of many on display in that country (see pages 48-49) as it celebrates Copernicus' 500th anniversary.

science known in Europe before the Renaissance, before Petrarch even? Surely Ptolemy was known, surely Euclid and Galen were known. And surely already by 1270 Thomas Aquinas had turned Aristotle into a household oracle and a Christian.

Indeed, that is so; the books of these men were read and revered in Europe, having been translated first into Arabic and thence into Latin during the Moorish occupation of Spain. But that roundabout and narrow channel had produced a tradition dominated by one Greek thinker, Aristotle, in all fields of science. A central thrust in humanism is the revolt against Aristotle, and this is true whether we interpret humanism broadly as I am doing, as a thirst for the whole wealth of knowledge, or strictly as an academic program of reform in education. For example, when the founder of the new alchemy, Paracelsus, showed his contempt for medical dogmatism by publicly burning a standard textbook in Basel in 1527, he chose the *Canon of Medicine* by Avicenna, an Arab follower of Aristotle.

Since what we would call the scientific establishment based itself on Aristotle, the up-and-coming young men avid for new ideas naturally turned to Plato. The masterly translation of Plato was begun by Marsilio Ficino in the 1460s and finally published in 1484; he had trained himself for it on the instructions of Cosimo de' Medici, who had made Florence a home for Platonists. These events had two effects on the development of science and its conjunction with humanism—one direct and one indirect.

The direct effect was to make science more mathematical, since Plato was much concerned with geometrical notions. Aristotle's insight had been into differences of quality; he was a naturalist by temperament, a lover of taxonomic systems, and that was the mood of science and medicine before 1500. In contrast, Platonism brought in a more quantitive manner, in which general principles were expected to satisfy specific tests, so that the detail of nature became significant for scientists as well as artists.

The new temper is evident in the work of Leonardo da Vinci, who wanted his drawings of a machine or a flower not only to look right but to work right. Aristotle has no sense of mathematics as a dynamic description; for example, he thinks of an eclipse of the moon as an inherent property of the moon, not as an effect of its motion. The idea that the world is in movement that can be pictured mathematically had to come from the Platonists. Later, when Galileo in

The faces of Giovanni de' Dondi's 14th-century clock traced the epicycles of Ptolemy's seven planets.
This replica stands in the Smithsonian Institution.

his *Dialogue on the Great World Systems* explained the Copernican system, he repeatedly stressed his debt to Plato.

The indirect effect of the Florentine school of Platonism is more subtle and harder to trace, though I think it no less important. There is an underlying sense of mystery in Plato, and even in the Greek fascination with mathematical relations. It was therefore foreseeable that the new Platonism in Florence and elsewhere leaned to mysticism and in time became obsessed by it. When Cosimo de' Medici's buyers came back to Florence from Macedonia with a manuscript of the fabled Hermetic texts, which were supposed to be pre-Christian prophecies by an Egyptian magus called Hermes Trismegistos, he had Ficino put Plato aside and translate them first. Their influence was immense, for they gave to nature a numinous quality, a sacred but vibrant life, which fitted the breathless adventure of the Renaissance. They are quoted in this sense by Copernicus in a well-known passage in *De revolutionibus orbium coelestium*:

> In the center of all rests the Sun. For who would place this lamp of a very beautiful temple in another or better place than this, wherefrom it can illuminate everything at the same time? As a matter of fact, not unhappily do some call it lantern; others, the mind, and still others, the pilot of the world. Trismegistus calls it a visible God.

However, we must not let this single passage lure us to believe that Copernicus drew much on the Hermetic texts or on Ficino's own rapturous essays on the sun; he did not. But there is no doubt that the appeal of Copernicus' system was heightened by an enthusiasm for the astrological power of the sun that came from the Hermetic texts. The fact is that until 1600 humanists knew Ficino better than Copernicus, and were quick to recognize his touch. For instance, when Giordano Bruno lectured on Copernicus in Oxford in 1583, his hearers ignored the science but were sharp to spot the quotations from Ficino.

Mysticism and science

The mystical fantasies in neo-Platonism seem to us now merely superstitious, and to obscure the science as they did for Bruno's audience at Oxford. But this is too simple a view. The neo-Platonists were fascinated by the relations between nature and Man, and they were too sophisticated to think that they could be controlled by the primitive and beastly magic that was current in the Middle Ages. They looked for more subtle influences in nature, such as the influence of the planets; and since those could not be browbeaten or

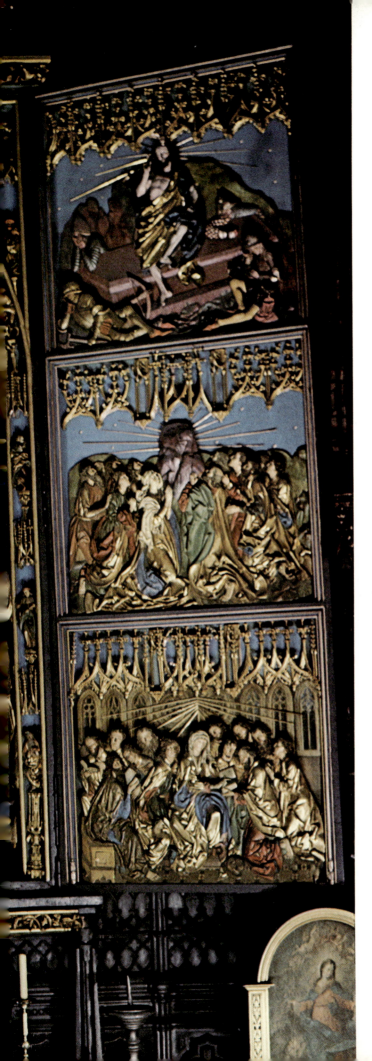

controlled by Man, they wanted to understand nature so that they might fit their actions to the propitious moments that she presented.

In this way, they moved away from the medieval concept of black or Satanic magic, which seeks to force nature out of her course, to a new concept of white or natural magic which is content to exploit her laws by understanding them. I believe that this change in the means by which the mind hopes to master nature was an important influence of humanism on science which took place in Copernicus' lifetime.

Humanism in any sense is by origin an academic movement, because the sources at which it seeks its new knowledge are classical texts. But it would be unrealistic to ignore the strength that it drew from its popular appeal. Erasmus and Martin Luther were contemporaries of Copernicus, and showed before he published his book that the attack on authority needs a public that has the means to judge for itself—needs the printed book above all. Petrarch in the 14th century could find a poetic following in manuscript, but the sweep of humanism a hundred years later needed the backing of print; for lack of that, Leonardo da Vinci was forgotten much as William Blake was later. A list of the books printed in 1543, the same year as Copernicus' *De revolutionibus*, is fascinating: It includes the anatomical drawings of Andreas Vesalius, the first Latin translation of the mathematical works of Archimedes, and the attack on Aristotle's logic by Petrus Ramus which did so much to change methods of reasoning and of education.

A new picture of the world was forming in the public mind—a new geography that made Ptolemy old-fashioned, and a new cosmology that made him seem literal, formalist and unimaginative. What spread the new picture through Europe as if it had wings was the printed word; for example, Galileo's *Dialogue* in 1632 was sold out before the Inquisition had time to seize the copies.

But there was also a popular element in the formation and the nature of Copernicus' picture which has been neglected and which I want to stress. Consider what Martin Luther said about it before the book ever got into print. Here, he said in his *Table Talk*, is a "new astronomer who wants to prove that the Earth goes round, and not the heavens, the Sun and the Moon; just as if someone sitting in a moving wagon or

Copernicus knew the huge wooden triptych in Krakow's St. Mary's Church, carved by a German, Veit Stoss. It is a spectacular example of the new perspective of space in religious art, a style later banned when the Church grew alarmed over secularization.

The Krakow triptych comes alive in the detailed portraits of everyday citizens that were carved on the reverse side of the outer panels. This realism, the desire to capture a particular moment

ship were to suppose that he was at rest, and that the Earth and the trees were moving past him."

Luther was an earthy man, by no means an intellectual, and his earthy comparison was also made by others. Yet think how surprising it is in an age when the laws of motion were unknown, and dynamics was not understood. The principle that the motions Luther describes are equivalent is usually called Galilean relativity; Luther is speaking 25 years before Galileo was born. How had it come about that Copernicus could place his mind's eye at the sun and see the earth from it, and that much less mathematical minds could grasp what he was doing and see it as he did?

The question seems far-fetched today, because we have lived with perspective drawing for 500 years, and therefore find it easy to shift our viewpoint in imagination. But that was not so when Copernicus grew up. Perspective was a new art then that had been cultivated by the *Perspectivi* in Italy early in the century. Albrecht Dürer, who was a contemporary of Copernicus, had to travel to Italy to learn "the secret art of perspective." Copernicus himself was fortunate in seeing perspective at first hand as a popular art in the huge carved and colored wooden triptych in St. Mary's Church in Krakow which Veit Stoss finished about 1489 (see pages 170 - 171).

Such simple and almost primitive church pictures had changed the perception of space in the 15th century. Before that, sacred pictures were flat and static because they represented a god's eye view. Perspective is a different conception, mobile and human, a moment in time that the artist has caught with a glance from where his eye happens to stand. This sense of the temporal and human pervades the picture: In the Krakow triptych it comes alive in the portraits of city worthies, the everyday people who stand around the holy figures. After the coming of Luther, the Church of Rome grew alarmed at this secularization of the heavens and at the Council of Trent expressly forbade it in sacred paintings. It is an element in Copernicus' view of nature, for although he is usually accused of removing Man from the center of the universe, in fact he moved him into the heavens. His system abolished the distinction between the terrestial sphere and the crystal spheres beyond the moon, and made the heavens earthy.

The humanism that I have traced in Copernicus' outlook was a broad and, at the last, even a popular mode of thought. There was also, however, a narrower and specific form of humanism directed to a reform of the curriculum. In this sense, humanism was pursued in the particular study of grammar, rhetoric, poetry, history and normal philosophy. In time it mounted a formidable attack on the syllogistic logic of Aristotle. But it failed to find an alternative in science to Aristotle's mode of reasoning from the general to the particular until it inspired Francis Bacon.

Nevertheless, academic humanism established results in one of its disciplines which had a far-reaching effect on science and on society together. It came in the most unlikely way from the study of Latin and Greek, which stimulated in literary scholars a feeling for exactness as passionate as that which the new-found mathematics stimulated in scientists. As a result, they learned to analyze old texts precisely enough to date them. Their discovery that this could be done, and how to do it, has a right to be ranked as a scientific discipline, a kind of literary archaeology. And like the

in time, in contrast to the traditionally flat, static, sacred art, secularized the heavens and indirectly paved the way for the new perspectives of science in the Renaissance.

more usual archaeology, it uncovered fakes: For example, it enabled Isaac Casaubon in 1614 to prove that the Hermetic texts had been forged in Christian times.

But a far more upsetting discovery had been made before that in the 15th century. It was made by the pioneer of the method, Lorenzo Valla, an early humanist who scandalized his contemporaries by his epicurean and irreverent ways. In 1439 he electrified the Christian world by proving that a number of revered church documents had been forged, probably in Rome in the eighth century. The most important of them was the Donation of Constantine, by which that emperor, who died in the year 337, was supposed to have granted the Popes temporal dominion in and beyond Rome. We have perhaps grown cynical now about the shuffling of treaties, and do not expect states to be scrupulous in their quest for power. But in 1439 it was catastrophic to learn that the spiritual head of the Church was sustained by fabricated documents.

The moment was a watershed for intellectual leadership in Europe, because it identified scholarship with exact truth. That had not been the character of academic disputation in the established tradition of scholasticism, nor was it prominent in the Aristotelian way of doing science. Of course, Aristotelian and Thomist science offered explanations for natural phenomena, but these explanations were not expected to have the precision of detail and sharpness of fit that Valla's literary archaeology had shown to be possible and definitive. It was not self-evident and not a foregone conclusion that the lesson would be picked up by scientists, and singled out so that it became a crucial part of their method.

There is a case for saying this was the most profound influence of humanistic scholarship on science.

The preoccupation with the exact detail of truth created a different ethic for science: In the long run, it shifted the pursuit of science from results to methods, and the personality of the scientist from a finder to a seeker—characteristically, we now call his work *research*. In this way science becomes an activity which demands for its collective success that all those who practice it share and adhere to certain values. As a particular case, the critical need for the detail of truth has forced the scientific community to insist that ends must not govern means: There are no supreme ends— only decent and honest, namely truthful, means.

Had the Church drawn the same lesson from the scandal of the Donation of Constantine, there might have been no reason for it to part company from science. Instead, Valla was long persecuted, and 150 years later Cardinal Bellarmine still castigated him as *praecursor Lutheri*, a man who opened the way for Luther. By then the Copernican world system had been made a religious issue; Bellarmine had a finger in the trial of Bruno and in the first proceedings against Galileo, and science in Italy was doomed.

Copernicus was a silent man, but a committed one. He believed that his world system was true, and no ground of expediency persuaded him to say less. More is at stake here than belief in any one truth: Copernicus' attitude implies that truth exists in nature absolutely, and cannot be established or overturned by any authority other than the study of nature herself. In this simple and rational faith, Copernicus was a humanist pioneer who created his science from a base of philosophy as Isaac Newton did in a later age, and Albert Einstein in ours.

'On the eighteenth of April, in Seventy-five...'
Longfellow didn't know the half of it

'Hardly a man is now alive/ Who remembers ...' the name of Paul Revere's horse, for one thing, or the true facts of his midnight ride

Revere, "with muffled oar," was rowed to Charlestown, but signal lanterns were hung *before* he left Boston.

There was Traveller and Man o' War and also Paul Revere's horse, but it's doubtful that Paul Revere himself knew the nag's name. He was in a hurry when he borrowed the horse on the night of April 18, 1775, for his famous midnight ride which warned the patriot Minute Men that the British were marching on Lexington and Concord. Twenty years after his historic gallop through the Massachusetts countryside, Revere could only recall that he rode "a very good horse."

In 1860, Henry Wadsworth Longfellow penned his beloved poem, *Paul Revere's Ride,* and described "a steed flying fearless and fleet," but neglected to mention its name. The poet used Revere's own account of the ride as a reference, and if Revere didn't know his horse's name, how could Longfellow know it?

Longfellow might have decided to allow the steed to remain anonymous, because in that poem he had already used and abused his poetic license until it was in danger of being revoked. Longfellow was a fine poet but a poor historian, and because of him generations of Americans have swallowed a conglomeration of falsities about the ride.

For example, the poet convinced most people that Revere, "impatient to mount and ride," waited in Charlestown for a lantern signal from the Old North Church in Boston which would indicate that the British were on their way. The truth is that Revere was still in Boston when the signal was flashed. He had requested a friend to hang the lanterns for the benefit of patriots over in Charlestown. Then, "with muffled oar," Revere was "silently rowed to the Charlestown shore" by two other friends.

When he got there, Revere learned that the Charlestown men apparently were confused by the "one, if by land, and two, if by sea" signal and had not departed for Lexington. He immediately located a horse and rode away. It should be noted that the lantern

By Richard W. O'Donnell
Drawings by Arnold Roth

signal was wrong anyway. General Joseph Warren, the patriot leader who sent Revere to Lexington, assumed that the redcoats were going to start toward Lexington by way of the Charles River. So the "two if by sea" signal was given. But the British rowed only a short distance, then made the rest of the trip on foot.

Longfellow's poem claims that Paul Revere shouted his "cry of alarm to every Middlesex village and farm." Revere himself may have deceived Longfellow on this point, for in his account he wrote that after leaving Medford (known as Mistick in those days) he "alarmed almost every house" on the way to Lexington. Among other things, Paul was a part-time poet, so it is possible that he used some of that poetic license himself.

Revere did not shout "The British are coming!" But don't blame Longfellow for this, for he never used the line in his poem. Paul did announce that "the Regulars are coming out" when he arrived in Lexington. The British Regulars, about 700 strong, had indeed come out on Boston Common before crossing the Charles and assembling in East Cambridge for their march to destroy ammunition stores. Their patrols were out that night and Paul, perforce, should have proceeded quietly.

The route he took was not the same one that the troops followed. They marched directly over a main road. Hence there was little reason for Revere to alarm the citizens along most of his route, because the British weren't coming their way at all.

Revere had made an earlier, less publicized gallop over practically the same route on Easter Sunday, April 16. In Lexington, he had informed the Minute Men of British plans to raid Concord. The three-day alert made it possible for a large share of the ammuni-

The author lives in Derry, New Hampshire, when he's not in Boston, writing articles for the Globe.

"The fate of a nation was riding that night," but the "fearless and fleet" steed went unnamed.

If Revere had raced about shouting his head off, he
would have been nabbed before he got to Lexington.

Paul never "came to the bridge in Concord town." He was seized by the British—and spilled everything.

tion to be moved to Groton, a few miles away, along with a cannon that the British especially wanted.

Why, then, did Revere need to make a second ride to Lexington? Primarily, to warn two revolutionaries, Samuel Adams and John Hancock, to leave town. Had they stayed, they would have been arrested. Revere arrived at the Hancock-Clark house where the two were holed up, gave his message and sat down to a midnight snack. Then William Dawes, the ancestor of Coolidge's Vice President, Charles G. Dawes, showed up. He had made a similar ride from Boston—but almost four miles longer—and people have wondered why he has never received equal billing with Revere.

Dawes was slow. He left Boston two hours before Revere departed Charlestown and arrived in Lexington 15 minutes after him. True, Dawes was delayed by British patrols, but then, so was Revere.

After Dawes joined Revere at the Hancock-Clark house, Adams and Hancock decided that the two men should ride on to Concord with word of the British march. They set off on the Concord road and were joined by Dr. Samuel Prescott. And people complain that *he* never gets the credit he deserves for that night.

The truth is, Prescott doesn't deserve the same fame as Revere—or Dawes, for that matter. He only galloped into the act by accident. He was returning from a visit with his girl friend—"a Miss Mulliken"—in Lexington, caught up with Revere and Dawes, and asked if he could ride along. A lot of people were visiting girl friends that April night. Hancock had been sitting up with "the beautiful Dorothy Quincy" when Revere arrived, and, in fact, they were having a lovers' spat while history was erupting all around them. They kissed and made up that night, although later Dorothy maintained that "At that time I should have been very glad to have got rid of him."

When Dawes and Prescott detoured briefly from the Concord road to alert the Minute Men of Lincoln, the only patriot they found awake was one Nathaniel Baker. He was holding hands with a fair maid—and her name was Elizabeth Taylor.

Back on the Concord road, the three riders were approached by a patrol of six British officers. Dawes turned quickly, dashed back to Lexington and there reined in so abruptly that he tumbled off his horse. Prescott jumped a fence and got away to Concord to

The truth about Paul Revere

deliver the message. Revere was captured. A pistol was placed against his head, and he was ordered to talk. With deep regret it must be revealed that the great patriot spilled everything. He gave such a detailed account of his glorious gallop that if Longfellow had only been there to take notes he might have written a more accurate poem.

At about 3 A.M., the British officers heard the sound of shooting and released Revere and four other men they had picked up, so they wouldn't be handicapped by prisoners in the event of a battle. Revere headed back to Lexington where he helped Hancock and Adams get away. The battle there did indeed break out, but not for several hours.

The exact route of Paul Revere's ride can never be duplicated again. At its very start, in City Square, Charlestown, a "Do Not Enter" sign blocks the entrance to Main Street, which Revere traveled. Subway stations, rotaries and all sorts of new twists and turns

have completely altered the route and, at the end of his ride, Revere might have trouble finding the Hancock-Clark house, since it has been moved.

Revere was paid four or five shillings for his ride, having been hired by Boston patriots to do the job. He couldn't return to Boston for a year after that April night and lived in Charlestown until the British left the city in 1776.

As for that horse, it seems that Revere got it from Deacon John Larkin of Charlestown, who, in turn, borrowed it from his father, Samuel. It was a little brown mare, and it was never returned to its owner; after Revere's arrest, he was ordered to turn it over to a British officer whose mount was worn out. That was the last ever seen of the illustrious animal.

In 1925 a direct descendant of Paul Revere apparently made a donation to a Charlestown historical group to pay for the horse. But what was the animal's name? Some historians insist on Scheherazade, others on Dobbin. A distinguished historian suggested the horse be called Sparky because Longfellow referred to "the spark struck out by that steed in his flight."

Forget all these unworthy names. The official genealogy of the Larkin family includes the following: "Larkin, Samuel, born Oct. 22, 1701; died Oct. 8, 1784, aged 83; he was a chairmaker, then a fisherman, and had horses and stable. He was the owner of 'Brown Beauty,' the mare of Paul Revere's ride, made famous by Longfellow's poem. The mare was loaned at the request of Samuel's son, Deacon John Larkin, and never returned to her owner."

If you happen to be near the route traveled by Paul Revere some April 18th, or even think you are, listen closely to the spring winds in the trees. Forget the clamor of jets overhead, the cars going by. If you're alert, you'll hear Brown Beauty gallop by you in the midnight darkness.

"So through the night rode Paul Revere;
And so through the night went his cry of alarm . . .

. . . to every Middlesex village and farm—"
but what about the horse that made it all possible?

'Absolutely, Dr. Franklin?'

Two knowledgeable ghosts case modern America with incredulity and some feeling of regret

Because it was the evening of July 2, precisely 200 years after the act of "Independency" had been introduced to Congress in Philadelphia; and because I had been working with blinding intensity to finish my article, *Sociopolitical Repercussions of 1776*, for an erudite biweekly, I was hardly surprised to see the two figures. I had approached my dark red Volkswagen in the university parking lot, and there they sat, in the back seat, as though they owned the car. I could make out, in silhouette, the long hair and strange spectacles of Dr. Franklin and the strong profile of Mr. Jefferson. Unbelievable, shocking, disorienting—but really not surprising in this especial case.

"Gentlemen," I said, "I am honored." I bowed and inserted myself behind the wheel. "You are comfortable?" I asked.

"Comfortable and highly curious," said Jefferson. His manner was far younger than Franklin's and contained a hint of shyness. "What is this vehicle, Professor? Some sort of sedan chair?"

"It is an automobile, sir," I said. "As the word suggests, it moves by itself, thanks to an engine that runs on the explosion of gases."

"'Auto-mobile,' eh? Yes, yes. Splendid! Can you make it go?"

I turned the key and shifted into low. The car had barely moved when Jefferson positively shouted from the back seat: "Stop! Stop! This is too marvelous to pass without having a dash at it! I must try it, sir! And our United States manufacture this?" he mused.

"The United States manufacture a great many automobiles, sir," I said, falling into the old plural usage of the nation's name, "but as it happens, this one was made in—ah—part of the German states."

"Good God! What Hessian princeling could prove so intelligent as to produce this machine?"

"They have changed, sir," I said.

Under my direction, Jefferson drove confidently out of the university grounds and toward the Thruway. Franklin, alone and slightly white-knuckled in the back seat, peered from his windows with growing excitement. "The lights, sir!" he exclaimed. "The colors and words of light. What wizardry is this?"

"Electricity, Dr. Franklin," I answered. "It has been put to use since you brought it from the lightning."

"Ah, I had a feeling. How wondrous it looks! But I cannot well read these messages. What do these words *mean*? There: 'Chick-n-Eat' and in the distance, 'Drive-in-Movie.' Do we speak our old language still?"

"Barely," I admitted, translating as best I could. Both forefathers seemed amused by the coinages, but rather bewildered by elisions and abbreviations. My explanation of "Motel" was greeted with cheers from these amazingly uninhibited guests. But "Bar-B-Q" baffled them. I pointed out that brevity in signs was essential in the world of 1976. "You will see why soon."

For by then Thomas Jefferson was nearing the Thruway and with some help mastered the approach. But at the first sight of thousands of cars hurtling past, he came to a shaky stop.

"I never imagined such speed," Jefferson said. "Professor, you shall drive us now." And so, on the 20-minute journey toward my suburb, the two figures were free to stare and to ask questions.

"I understand that the speed of your life requires you to read gibberish," Franklin said. "But why read at all? Why not invent some device that will bring voices to you with messages of importance?"

Of course I switched on the car radio. A voice proclaiming the best used car deal in town filled the sedan. Franklin and Jefferson were again delighted—but concerned with the fatuousness of what was being said.

"It *must* be said," I told them, "to pay for using the

'Positively,
Mr. Jefferson!'

By Edwards Park

device. Otherwise it would be too expensive." I went on to describe television ("What a sensible word," Franklin put in, "and what a shame to call it 'TV' ").

"There are no rules of—of *deportment* in television?" Jefferson asked.

"We cannot have that sort of control and still maintain our concept of democracy," I said.

"And what is your concept?" asked Franklin.

I thought quickly, feeling the same pressure as a freshman in an oral exam. "Broad freedoms of choice, opportunity and enterprise. We feel we should start from an equal base."

Franklin nodded toward Jefferson. "You see, Tom? For all your doubts, you've had history on your side."

"But who rules, sir? Who rules?" asked Jefferson.

"The people rule through their representatives—at least, that's the idea."

"We know the *idea*, sir. What of the *reality*?"

Soon I was deep in a discussion of lobbyists, pressure groups; of logrolling, vote-swapping, petty graft; of primaries, conventions and smoke-filled rooms.

"Complexity upon complexity," murmured Franklin, his age plainly showing in his voice. "I have a certain appreciation for the—ahem—necessary deviousness of politics, and so has my young friend. But the convolutions that our government now sees fit to go through to obtain relatively simple results would astonish Machiavelli. You have complicated much that should have been simple. . . ."

". . . And simplified—by retaining—much that has always been too complex," added Jefferson. "The Constitution, for example. Have you rewritten it?"

"No, sir!" I cried. "Amended, but not rewritten."

"But why in the world *not*?" demanded Franklin. "This is hardly the same world."

"It is a sacred document, Dr. Franklin. It is enshrined in our hearts."

"God's wit! What secrets does it tell you? How far does it propel you toward . . . toward whatever you are seeking? What *are* you seeking, fellow American?"

I thought frantically, then was inspired: "Life, liberty and the pursuit of happiness!" In the rearview mirror I saw Jefferson nudge Franklin.

There was silence in the car as the traffic flashed by. I found my exit and swung off the Thruway, heading toward our four-bedroom split-level.

"No sunset," murmured Jefferson. "This accursed haze blocks it and stings my eyes. No birds, either."

"No trees for them," Franklin replied. Both were talking more to each other than to me. They stared at the houses. "All alike," said Jefferson.

"Funny smell to them," said Franklin.

"Hamburgers," I said, then quickly described them: "sort of a 'Bar-B-Q.' "

"This is life, liberty and the pursuit of happiness?" Franklin asked a little testily. He put the question to Jefferson, so I gratefully remained silent. But then, around the corner came my younger son, Ned, pedaling his new ten-speed bike. Before I could stop them, the two forefathers leapt out and ran toward the boy.

I saw an exchange of coin, then the two were off, Jefferson pedaling, Franklin astride the bar, the bike weaving erratically down the residential street.

"What a couple of kooks," Ned said as I came up. "They told me this was the ultimate vehicle in efficiency and simplicity. 'Just what we have striven for,' one said to the other. And they've given me about $500 worth of antique gold for it. Far out!"

In the distance, the two figures wove through the thickening mists of twilight, and I faintly heard a voice—Franklin's: ". . . Pursuit of happiness sir! Pursuit of happi. . . ." They were gone.

"Yes, son," I said. "Far out!"

In *The Artist in His Museum*, Peale displays Long Room of his museum, world's first with the avowed purpose of education. Peale started the painting, son Titian finished it.

By Lillian B. Miller

The Peale family: a lively mixture of art and science

A record of the artist and his many gifted children is recorded on microfiche by the Smithsonian's National Portrait Gallery

His children, like the institutions he founded, were "tender young plants," and Charles Willson Peale, artist, museum keeper and patriarch, nurtured them all so that they would grow in a proper—that is, natural—direction. As a result, the Peale family has become one of America's most famous clans, as interesting in their achievements as the Adamses or Jameses were in theirs. The publication in microfiche of the Peale Family Papers this spring by the Smithsonian's National Portrait Gallery throws new light on this extraordinary dynasty.

Charles Willson Peale's life bridged two centuries, but 18th-century ideals and practices influenced it greatly. Born in 1741 in Queen Anne's County in the royal colony of Maryland, he died in Philadelphia in 1827—just before his hero Andrew Jackson took over the Presidency and gave his name to a new democratic age. During his long life, Peale painted more than a thousand portraits and miniatures of men and women of the Revolutionary generation. He also delivered numerous lectures and published treatises on natural history, health and domestic happiness, helped to found institutions for the encouragement of the arts, created in Philadelphia the first scientifically organized museum to be open to the American public on a regular basis (opposite), and educated his numerous progeny in such a way that most of them continued his interests in art, science and museology.

Thrice widowed (he was courting a prospective fourth wife when he died at 86), Peale sired 17 children, 11 of whom survived to adulthood. The first four, all of whom died in infancy, were given unexceptionable Anglo-Saxon names. With the fifth he began naming them after famous artists and scientists: Raphaelle, Angelica Kauffmann (an 18th-century Swiss-born painter), Rembrandt, Titian Ramsay I (he died at 18), Rubens, Sophonisba Angusciola, Rosalba Carriera and Vandyke (both of whom died before the age of two), Charles Linnaeus, Benjamin Franklin, Sybilla Miriam, Titian Ramsay II and Elizabeth DePeyster (with the last his second wife, Betsy DePeyster, finally revolted and said, in effect, no more outlandish names).

It is not strange to include a family among Peale's many achievements. In Colonial America, learning took place within the context of a total household environment. The home was the source of attitudes, values, manners and vocations passed from one generation to another. As an 18th-century father, Peale was as concerned for his children's education as he was for the shape of his museum or the quality of a portrait—perhaps more so. Educated in the writings of French and English Enlightenment philosophers and scientists, he shared Rousseau's conviction that children should be led "to the paths of Virtue with a Chain of Flowers," that education provided the answer to most of society's ills. Just as he planned his museum so that its organization as well as its exhibits would instruct the public in nature's order and harmony, so he created a family structure that would allow his children to develop freely within a discipline imposed by an understanding of nature's laws. Typically, Peale presented his third wife (p. 185), early in their marriage, with two books to prepare her for the role of stepmother. One was a collection of devotional meditations relating the wonders of nature to the wisdom and power of God. The other was a volume of Robert Donovan's *Natural History of British Insects* which he chose, perhaps, to demonstrate the fineness of natural design—to show how even the smallest creatures are beautiful in structure and function.

Peale was convinced that individuals could use their reason to understand what was good and to act accordingly. In his autobiography, compiled a year before his death, he wrote: "Shame if properly seasoned is a greater scourge than the birch." Parents, he felt, should teach by example, sharing their children's interests while involving them in family activities. Just as nature presented models of social organization and cooperation among animal and plant life, so parents, by behavior and attitudes, presented models that any child with "reasoning faculties" could follow.

Historian of American Culture at the Smithsonian's National Portrait Gallery, the author is editor of the microfiche edition of the Peale Family Papers.

Charles Willson Peale and family

Peale's sense of familial responsibility began before he reached his tenth birthday. His father, a country schoolteacher in exile from England for embezzling post office funds, died and left the family almost penniless. As the oldest child, Charles was required to help his mother, who became a seamstress. At 13 he was apprenticed to a saddlemaker, and at 20 he opened his own shop, married and took on as helper his younger brother James. Later, when he turned to portraiture, he taught James the art of painting in miniature, believing that anyone could learn to paint if he or she understood the rules. In his domestic portrait, *The Peale Family Group* (c. 1772), we see him teaching another brother, St. George, how to draw (opposite).

Peale's enterprises frequently turned into games. When he decided to learn French in 1774, he had his family and students join him in his studies around the candles during the winter evenings. Fines were paid by those who made the mistake of speaking English. "An accident, or a joke," he later reported, "produced many fines, and the amount went to furnish cakes for the company. Time passed pleasantly on . . . as is always the case with those who have much to do."

Another game helped to move Peale's exhibits from his painting gallery to the Hall of the American Philosophical Society, the site of his new museum. Aware that all boys love a parade, he enlisted the neighborhood youngsters into a "cavalcade." Each was entrusted with a specimen appropriate to his size. Only a "young alligator" was lost and one glass broken, and the parade provided effective publicity for the museum, soon to be one of the most influential of its time.

Peale's children enjoyed the same combination of fun and work in their home. In their father's painting room they were given a rigorous course in drawing; in his carpentry shop the boys learned how to handle tools and work in wood. As they grew older, Peale's seven sons worked in the museum, helping with the machinery, gathering specimens and taking care of their preservation.

When the family later moved their living quarters to Philosophical Hall, the children received a social experience. Mechanics such as Isaiah Lukens and Burgess Allison came to show off their inventions; Alexander Wilson participated in their pursuit of natural history and shared their musical and literary interests (as well as their enthusiasm for the revolutionary Tom Paine); visiting French scientists loftily discussed nature's wonders and the benefits of free thought.

One of the most exciting events for the Peale family was a farmer's discovery of mastodon bones in Ulster County, New York, in 1801. Peale hurried to the site and bought the bones and the right to dig for more. Returning with equipment and accompanied by Rembrandt, his second-oldest son, he exhumed the heavy bones of the mammoth creatures—a scene later recorded in his painting, *Exhuming the Mastodon* (detail, p. 191). One of the reconstructed skeletons brought crowds of curious visitors to the museum; the other gave Rembrandt and his younger brother Rubens an opportunity to travel in Europe exhibiting it.

Alert to any opportunity to bring his children forward, Peale in 1795 took advantage of his warm friendship with President Washington to arrange a sitting for 17-year-old Rembrandt, who had just been commissioned to paint the great man's portrait. Then he decided to join Rembrandt in the painting room and, while painting what would be his seventh portrait of Washington, also engaged him in conversation to ease his shy son's embarrassment. At the second sitting, Peale's brother James and eldest son Raphaelle joined the group, thus giving rise to Gilbert Stuart's famous pun that Washington was "in danger of being *Pealed* all around."

Father and son see Washington differently

The sittings resulted in two interesting portraits (p. 189). Intent upon producing a good likeness, Rembrandt painted a direct and vivid—almost brutal—portrait of an aging subject as seen through young eyes. The elder Peale, filled with sentiment for an old friend and a sense of Washington's meaning for the nation, softened and idealized his subject, presenting him as the embodiment of republican virtue: dignified, assured, benevolent.

Pressures within the crowded Peale household must have created problems for some of the youngsters. Those who temperamentally resembled their father probably felt little tension. Rembrandt (1778-1860) was fascinated by his father's activities in the painting room, carpentry shop and museum. Together father

Charles Willson Peale painted *The Peale Family Group* c. 1772 and put himself in it, bending over brother St. George (left), who is sketching their mother (far right). Brother James smiles; above him stands sister Margaret Jane. Charles' first wife, Rachel, is in center with baby girl. Sister Elizabeth Digby sits next to mother. Peggy Durgan, nurse to five Peale children, stands.

INA Corporation Museum

Museum of Fine Arts, Boston

Betsy DePeyster was C.W.P.'s plump, willful second wife. This 1795 miniature is by brother James.

Hannah Moore, a gentle Quaker, was Peale's third wife. He painted this portrait in 1816.

Charles Willson Peale and family

The Detroit Institute of Arts,
Dexter M. Ferry jr. Fund

Second son Rembrandt, to
Peale the most talented, did
this self-portrait in 1828.

Private collection—Kennedy Galleries, Inc.

Peale painted Angelica Kauffmann Robinson,
eldest of four daughters, and husband Alexander. She
was named after famous 18th-century Swiss artist.

In Peale's famed trompe l'oeil *The Staircase
Group,* oldest son Raphaelle climbs while
Titian I, who died at 18, peeks. Painting was
set in museum doorway with a real wooden step
projecting beneath it. George Washington,
passing it, is said to have nodded to the boys.

The Philadelphia Museum of Art, George W. Elkins Collection

Collection of Mrs. Norman B. Woolworth

Rembrandt painted his younger brother Rubens, with America's "first" geranium (1801) as a tribute to Rubens' deep interest in botany.

Dietrich Collection, Philadelphia

Charles Linnaeus Peale, C.W.P.'s wayward son, chose soldier-adventurer's life.

The Pennsylvania Academy of the Fine Arts

Benjamin Franklin Peale, next-to-youngest son, was a mechanical engineer.

The American Museum of Natural History

Titian Ramsay Peale II, youngest son, became a naturalist-illustrator.

and son read Matthew Pilkington's *Gentleman's and Connoisseur's Dictionary of Painters* (1770), so vital a volume in the Peale household that important family dates were recorded on its flyleaves. Captivated by the romance of the artists' lives, Rembrandt (opposite, top left) thought of himself as participating in a great Renaissance tradition. Perhaps one of his greatest disappointments would later be the fact that the American public did not look upon artists with the same awe.

Rembrandt took advantage of every opportunity to study art. At eight he began to draw; by 13 he had painted a self-portrait. He became a student at classes organized by his father and other Philadelphia artists and also studied the chemistry of pigments at the University of Pennsylvania's new medical school.

Before leaving for Europe with Rubens to exhibit the second mastodon skeleton, Rembrandt painted the charming picture of his younger brother holding a geranium plant (above). Later study in France and Italy contributed to his development of a romantic style that would be praised by French artists and presumably Napoleon himself. While abroad, he perfected a painting technique and palette that filled him with enthusiasm. "My tints," he wrote home in 1808, "surpass the finest complexions and equal what the imagination can conceive." The elder Peale agreed. When he returned to painting landscapes and portraits late in life, he adopted his son's innovations.

Rembrandt's driving ambition was to paint a perfect interpretation of Washington and he gave careful study to the extant portraits. Then, in a three-months'

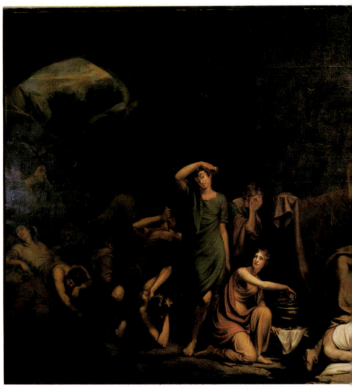

Rembrandt Peale's *The Court of Death* was hailed as a "Great Moral Painting" as it toured

frenzy of effort, he produced a composite portrait which he and many of his contemporaries believed truly represented the first President. Painted in 1823, it now hangs in the restored Old Senate Chamber of the U.S. Capitol Building. He made many replicas of this composite, encasing some of them in a painted stone surround, which earned them the name "Porthole" Washingtons.

Rembrandt's *Court of Death* (1820) received widespread acclaim. During its first 13-month tour of American cities, the canvas (above right) earned more than $9,000 in admission receipts and clergymen preached its moral message. But the Peales were never practical businessmen, and Rembrandt's life as founder and proprietor of the Baltimore Museum (now the Municipal, or Peale, Museum) and as portrait painter was marked by struggle.

In later years, Rembrandt published essays in the *Crayon,* one of America's first art journals, and presented illustrated lectures on Washington's portraits which brought him notice as one of the country's oldest living artists. But the full extent of his achievement cannot be measured until his work has been carefully catalogued and evaluated.

Rembrandt's older brother, Raphaelle (1774-1825) was the tragic figure in the household. Full of impish humor (p. 186) and artistic genius, he never was able to earn a living by his art. In the absence of commissions, he turned his imagination to helping his father in the invention of stoves, fireplace improvements and wooden bridges, and in the mounting of the larger animals in the museum. In 1803, John I. Hawkins, the English inventor, allowed Raphaelle to take his physionotrace—a profile-cutting machine—with him on an extended Southern trip. The device was a huge success and Raphaelle made a small fortune cutting thousands of profiles. But he spent it quickly, and for the

most part he, like other family members, faced constant financial crises.

As Raphaelle's hands became more arthritic (perhaps, he felt, from frequent immersion in the strong arsenic solutions needed to preserve his father's specimens) and, as a combination of alcoholism and gout made steady work impossible, he grew more dependent on his father. His major artistic expression became the still life, which he painted with such "exactness of finish" as to convince his father that if the young man could develop "confidence" and paint portraits, "no artist could be [his] superiour in that line." "They must feel happy," Peale wrote to his troubled son, "who communicate happiness to their near and dear connections, and thus draw on them the esteem and honor of a deserving public."

Raphaelle never became "celebrated by his pensil," but today his few portraits still extant and his exquisite still lifes are treasured.

Handicapped since childhood by poor eyesight, Rubens Peale (1784-1865) never learned to paint formally. Instead, he turned to botany, mineralogy and museum management. In 1810, when the elder Peale decided to retire to a farm in Germantown, he left the Philadelphia Museum in Rubens' hands, in return for a yearly allowance. Rubens continued the educational mis-

The Detroit Institute of Arts, gift of George H. Scripps

The New-York Historical Society

the country, illustrating the transience of life
and earning more than $9,000 for the artist.

Charles Willson Peale's last portrait of George
Washington idealized his old and intimate friend.

sion of the museum, but made some changes for the
sake of profit. Although he introduced theatrical entertainments, his experimental demonstrations with
gas, machinery and chemicals were thoroughly scientific. The art of museum keeping became synonymous
with the family name.

In 1822, Rubens took over the Baltimore Museum
from the less businesslike Rembrandt. Three years
later, he opened a museum in New York, which
spawned an offshoot in Utica. Enormously successful,
the museum succumbed to the economic crisis created
by the Panic of 1837. Rubens did not rail at fate; instead, he quietly retired to a Pennsylvania farm. Here
he spent the next three decades growing wheat, vegetables and fruit, carrying on experiments in mesmer-
ism and, at 80, he turned to the painting of still lifes.

Titian Ramsay I (1780-1798) was a genius in the
museum and a favorite companion of his father (p.
186). He wrote an unpublished manuscript on the art
of miniature painting and was at work on a manuscript on the insects of North America (p. 190) when
he died of yellow fever.

His namesake, Titian Ramsay II (1799-1885), painted meticulous watercolors of flora and fauna and
served as naturalist-artist on the Long Expedition of
1819-1820 and Wilkes Expedition of 1838-1842 (p. 190).

The Historical Society of Pennsylvania

Rembrandt painted Washington at the same time—
1795—and described him as looking "dismal."

National Agricultural Library, Historic and Rare Book Collection

Before dying of yellow fever, Titian I made this insect drawing, here published for first time.

Titian Ramsay II's *Lepidoptera* illustration is also reproduced below for the first time.

The American Museum of Natural History Library

In between, he ran the Philadelphia Museum in co-operation with his elder brother Franklin.

He too was a victim of circumstances when his report on *Mammalia and Ornithology* (of the Wilkes Expedition) was suppressed by Wilkes before it could be distributed and another study was substituted. Moving to Washington, D.C., to organize and arrange the expedition's collections, he was further disappointed when in 1846 he failed to receive appointment as curator of the newly established Smithsonian Institution. Two years later, he became an Assistant Examiner at the Patent Office, where he worked for a quarter-century, never rising much higher. A gifted photographer and artist, he wrote and illustrated a catalog of *Lepidoptera* of the New World (below left).

Cultural force amidst commerce

Benjamin Franklin (1795-1870) was the most mechanical and perhaps the most musical Peale (p. 187). Unlucky in a cotton-manufacturing enterprise, he co-managed the museum with Titian after their father's death. While Titian worked in the preserving room and attended to the scientific organization, Franklin specialized in mechanical exhibits. One was a large working model of a locomotive, another a huge magnet capable of lifting 300 pounds. He lectured at the Franklin Institute on new inventions and in 1833 joined the U.S. Mint, where he eventually became Chief Coiner. Here he developed many innovations.

Charles Linnaeus (1794-1832), named for the great Swedish naturalist, was the family rebel and scorned a museum career (p. 187). Apprenticed to a printer, he ran away to sea and a life of adventure in the War of 1812 and South American revolutions. His father, a pacifist despite (or perhaps because of) his own experience in the Revolution, was outraged at his son's adoption of the "murderous, miserable" life of a soldier, "whether by land or sea." He would have preferred Lin an "honest man conducting a small manufactory than . . . *the greatest general in the United States.*"

None of Peale's sons achieved great financial success; with the exception of the unmanageable Lin, they did achieve artistic and scientific renown. After the War of 1812, the country was caught up in a rapidly expanding economy. Land, industry, commercial growth captured the American imagination. But art and science were as important for the young Republic as commerce and politics. What the Peales represented in the midst of enormous materialistic concentration was a continuation of the concern for culture which the Enlightenment had fostered.

As Peale put it to Jefferson, his lifelong friend, "the attainment of Happiness, Individual as well as Public, depends on the cultivation of the human mind."

Charles Willson Peale's *Exhuming the Mastodon* (detail).

A great painter, a royal naturalist on wild Missouri

Plains Indian life, customs and combat
as recorded in the 19th century by
Prince Maximilian and Karl Bodmer

Among the trappers, boatmen and frontiersmen boarding the steamship *Yellowstone* in St. Louis on April 10, 1833, none stood out so exotically as a middle-aged minor German prince and his companions, a young Swiss artist and a family retainer who acted as general factotum. The ship belonged to John Jacob Astor's American Fur Company and it was to visit the company's posts along the reaches of the wild and sometimes wide Missouri, carrying provisions and a year's supply of trade goods for bartering with Indians.

The aristocrat, Alexander Philip Maximilian, 50, Prince of Wied-Neuwied, was traveling with Karl Bodmer, 24, an artist of outstanding vitality and talent, and David Dreidoppel, his man of all work, a real-life, earlier version of Jules Verne's Passepartout. They were to be gone for more than a year.

Maximilian, scientist as well as nobleman, a naturalist, ethnologist and explorer who had established his reputation with the publication of a book on his Brazilian expedition of 1815-17, was setting forth on part of the trail pioneered by Lewis and Clark a quarter of a century earlier, to study the Plains Indians of the American West.

His book on his American experience, published in 1843, was to become a standard reference work for scholars, an important and unusually readable contribution to aboriginal science. Bodmer's extraordinary paintings appeared in the book's various editions as copperplate engravings, hand-tinted in special editions. Together, the text and engravings constitute a record of early trans-Mississippi exploration that is

At Fort Clark, Maximilian and Bodmer (right) are welcomed by Mandans and Minnetarees.

generally considered to be second in importance only to the journals of Lewis and Clark. The Bodmer watercolors themselves, hidden away on the Wied estate in Germany, dropped out of sight until they were brought to the United States in 1953 for a traveling exhibition under the auspices of the Smithsonian.

Adapted from *People of the First Man*, © by Davis Thomas and Karin Ronnefeldt, editors. Watercolors © by the Northern Natural Gas Company of Omaha

Now, Davis Thomas and Karin Ronnefeldt have taken sections of Maximilian's book, added extensively to them from his unpublished handwritten field journal of 500,000 words, and had made new reproductions from Bodmer's original watercolors, together presented in a sumptuous volume, *People of the First Man: Life Among the Plains Indians in Their Final Days of Glory*, to be published this month by E.P. Dutton & Co. Following are excerpts and illustrations from the book.

By Alexander Philip Maximilian, Prince of Wied-Neuwied

St. Louis to Fort Union
April 24, 1833

We saw the chain of the Blacksnake Hills, but we met with so many obstacles in the river that we did not reach them till towards the evening. Near to the steep bank a trading house had been built, which was occupied by a man named Roubedoux, an agent of the Fur

Company. [Joseph Robidoux's post is now the site of the city of St. Joseph.] When the steam-boat lay to, between 500 or 600 paces from the trading house, some of the *engagés* [virtually indentured employees] of the company came on board, and reported that the Iowa Indians, whose village was about five or six miles distant, had made an incursion into the neighbouring territory of the Omahas, and killed six of these Indians, and brought in a woman and child as prisoners, whom they offered for sale. Major Dougherty, to whose agency the Iowas belong, landed to rescue the prisoners, but they returned at eleven o'clock at night, without having accomplished their object, because the Iowas, fearing his reproaches, had completely intoxicated both themselves and their prisoners.

May 25, 1833

On a point of land, at the left hand, round which the Missouri turns to the west, we saw the buildings of Sioux Agency; the *Yellowstone* saluted the post with several guns, and was welcomed to the fort by the hoisting of a flag, while the whole population, about fifty in number, chiefly consisting of Sioux Indians, were assembled on the beach.

The Dakotas, as they call themselves, or the Sioux of the French, are still one of the most numerous Indian tribes in North America. They are divided into branches which speak the same language, with some deviations. Three principal branches live on the Missouri, *viz.*, the Yankton, the Tetons, and the Yanktonans.

The Yanktons live in Sioux Agency, or the furthest down the Missouri, among which tribe we now were. All these Dakotas of the Missouri, as well as most of those of the Mississippi, are only hunters, and, in their excursions, always live in portable leather tents. All these Indians have great numbers of horses and dogs, the latter of which often serve them as food. The Dakotas on the Missouri were formerly dangerous

Mato-Topé (the four bears), second chief and a hero of the Mandan nation, he provided Bodmer with a noble subject and Maximilian with tales and details.

enemies to the Whites, whereas now, with the exception of the Yanktonans, they bear a very good character, and constantly keep peace with the Whites. Such of these Indians as reside near the Whites, are frequently connected with them by marriages, and depend on them for support. They then become negligent hunters, indolent, and, consequently, poor.

May 30, 1833

Before six, in the evening, we reached the mouth of the Teton River which the Sioux call the Bad River. The steamer had proceeded a little further, when we came in sight of [Fort Pierre], to the great joy of all.

The Sioux, who live on Teton River, near Fort

Fort Clark from the east bank of the Missouri. The
Indians used the iced river as a thoroughfare to
reach firewood groves and winter village downstream.

Pierre, are mostly of the branch of the Tetons; though
there are some Yanktons here. Like all the North
American Indians, they highly prize personal bravery,
and, therefore, constantly wear the marks of distinction which they have received for their exploits;
among these are, especially, tufts of human hair attached to their arms and legs, and feathers on their
heads. He who, in the sight of the adversaries, touches
a slain or a living enemy, places a feather horizontally
in his hair for this exploit. They look upon this as a
very distinguished act, for many are often killed in the
attempt, before the object is attained. He who kills an
enemy by a blow with his fist, sticks a feather upright
in his hair. If the enemy is killed with a musket, a
small piece of wood is put in the hair, which is intended to represent a ramrod.

June 18, 1833

At half-past seven we passed a roundish island covered
with willows, and reached then the wood on the western bank, in which the winter dwellings of part of the
Mandan Indians are situated.

Above 600 Indians were waiting for us. Close to the

beach, the chiefs and most distinguished warriors of
the Mandan nation stood in front of the assembly
of red men, among whom the most eminent were
Charata-Numakschi (the wolf chief), Mato-Topé (the
four bears), Dipauch (the broken arm), Berock-Itainu
(the ox neck), Pehriska-Ruhpa (the two ravens), and
some others.

The view of the prairie around Fort Clark was at
this time highly interesting. A great number of the
horses were grazing all around; Indians of both sexes
and all ages were in motion; we were, every moment,
stopped by them, obliged to shake hands, and let them
examine us on all sides.

June 24, 1833

Following the numerous windings of the Missouri,
from one chain of hills to another, we reached, at seven
o'clock in the evening, the mouth of the Yellowstone,
a fine river, hardly inferior in breadth to the Missouri
at this part. A little further on lay Fort Union, on a
verdant plain, with the handsome American flag,
gilded by the last rays of evening, while a herd of horses
grazing animated the peaceful scene.

The Company maintains a number of agents at these different stations; during their stay they marry Indian women, but leave them, without scruple, when they are removed to another station, or are recalled to the United States. The lower class of these agents, who are called *engagés* or *voyageurs*, have to act as steersmen, rowers, hunters, traders, &c., according to their several capabilities. They are often sent great distances, employed in perilous undertakings among the Indians, and are obliged to fight against the enemy, and many of them are killed every year by the arms with which the Whites themselves have furnished the Indians. Some of the agents of the fur company winter every year in the Rocky Mountains.

Wild beasts and other animals, whose skins are valuable in the fur trade, have already diminished greatly in number along this river, and it is said that, in another ten years, the fur trade will be very inconsiderable. As the supplies along the banks of the Missouri decreased, the Company gradually extended the circle of their trading posts, as well as enterprises, and thus increased their income. Above 500 of their agents are in the forts of the Upper Missouri, and at their various trading posts; and, besides these individuals, who receive considerable salaries (for it is said that the Company yearly expend 150,000 dollars in salaries), there are in these prairies, and the forests of the Rocky Mountain, beaver and fur trappers, who live at their own cost; but whose present wants, such as horses, guns, powder, ball, woollen clothes, articles of clothing, tobacco, &c. &c. are supplied by the Company, and the scores settled, after the hunting season is over, by the furs which they deliver at the different trading posts. Many of these, when not employed in hunting, live at the Company's forts. They are, for the most part, enterprising, robust men, capital riflemen, and are able to endure the greatest hardships.

Daybreak at Fort McKenzie, August 28, 1833, brought with it a war party of some 600 Assiniboins and

Fort Union to Fort McKenzie
July 6—August 9, 1833

[Although in years to come steamboats would eventually venture farther upstream on the Missouri, in 1833 Fort Union was the head of steamboat navigation on the river. Cargoes destined for posts farther west had to be transported either overland by pack train or upriver by keelboat.

The keelboat Flora that carried Maximilian and his party upstream measured sixty feet overall and had a beam of sixteen feet.]

Crees who attacked an encampment of Blackfeet just outside the Fort. Bodmer's dramatic re-creation of the battle captures the chaos, fury and savagery described in Maximilian's dramatic description.

Fort McKenzie
August 15, 1833

Our residence was besieged all day long by Indians who were attracted by our drawing and writing. They said about Mr. Bodmer, after he had executed a portrait, that he could "write" well.

In the evening, we went to the tents of the Indians, where we saw at least six women whose noses had been cut off. This is the way in which the Piegans and other Blackfeet nations punish the infidelity of their women, a hideous disfigurement.

August 28, 1833

At break of day, we were awakened by musket-shot, and Doucette entered our room, crying, "Levez-vous, il faut nous battre," on which we rose in haste, dressed ourselves, and loaded our fowling-pieces with ball. When we entered the court-yard of the fort, all our people were in motion, and some were firing from the roofs. On ascending it, we saw the whole prairie covered with Indians on foot and on horseback, who were firing at the fort; and on the hills were several detached bodies. About eighteen or twenty Blackfoot tents, pitched near the fort, the inmates of which had been singing and drinking the whole night, and fallen into a deep sleep towards morning, had been surprised by 600 Assiniboins and Crees. When the first information of the vicinity of the enemies was received from a Blackfoot, who had escaped, the *engagés* immediately repaired to their posts on the roofs of the buildings, and the fort was seen to be surrounded on every side by the enemy, who had approached very near. They had cut up the tents of the Blackfeet with knives, discharged their guns and arrows at them, and killed or wounded many of the inmates, roused from their sleep by this unexpected attack. Four women and several children lay dead near the fort, and many others were wounded. The men, about thirty in number, had partly fired their guns at the enemy, and then fled to the gates of the fort, where they were admitted. They immediately hastened to the roofs, and began a well-supported fire on the Assiniboins.

In the fort itself all was confusion. If the men had been mustered and inspected, it would have been found that the *engagés* had sold their ammunition to the Indians; they were, therefore, quite unprepared to defend themselves, and it was necessary, during the combat, to distribute powder as well among the Whites as the Indians.

Assiniboins and Crees vs. Blackfeet

Mr. Mitchell and Berger, the interpreter, were employed in admitting the Blackfeet women and children, who were assembled at the door of the fort, when a hostile Indian, with his bow bent, appeared before the gate, and exclaimed, "White man, make room, I will shoot those enemies!" This exclamation showed that the attack was not directed against the Whites, but only against the Blackfeet. Mr. Mitchell immediately gave orders to his people to cease firing; notwithstanding this, single shots continued to be fired, and our Blackfeet were not to be restrained, nay, ten or twelve of our people, among whom were Doucette and Loretto, went into the prairie, and fired in the ranks of the Blackfeet, who were assembling, and every moment increasing in numbers. Loretto had shot, at the distance of eighty-six paces from the pickets, the nephew of the Assiniboin chief, Minohanne (the left-handed), and this was the only one of the killed whom the enemy were unable to carry away, for we saw them lay many others on their horses, and take them off. In the fort itself only one man was wounded, having had his foot pierced by an arrow, and likewise a horse. . . .

When the Assiniboins saw that their fire was returned, they retreated about 300 paces, and an irregular firing continued, during which several people from the neighbourhood joined the ranks of the Blackfeet.

A Mandan warrior spends days and nights in ritualistic obeisance before deities symbolized by effigies.

Although tepees were used on hunting trips, Mandans and Minnetarees, sedentary tribes, enjoyed better permanent homes than other Plains tribes. Lodges were built of heavy timber, wickerwork and sod.

While all this was passing, the court-yard of the fort exhibited very singular scenes. A number of wounded men, women, and children, were laid or placed against the walls, others, in their deplorable condition, were pulled about by their relations, amid tears and lamentations. The White Buffalo, whom I have often mentioned, and who had received a wound at the back of his head, was carried about, in this manner, amid singing, howling, and crying; they rattled the schischikué in his ears, that the evil spirit might not overcome him, and gave him brandy to drink. He himself, though stupefied and intoxicated, sung without intermission, and would not give himself up to the evil spirit.

Otsequa-Stomik, an old man of our acquaintance, was wounded in the knee by a ball, which a woman cut out with a penknife, during which operation he did not betray the least symptom of pain. Natah-Otann, a handsome young man, with whom we had become acquainted, was suffering dreadfully from severe wounds. Several Indians, especially young women, were likewise wounded. We endeavoured to assist the wounded, and Mr. Mitchell distributed balsam, and linen for bandages, but very little could be done; for, instead of suffering the wounded, who were exhausted

by the loss of blood, to take some rest, their relations continually pulled them about, sounded bells, rattled their medicine or amulets, among which were the bears' paws, which White Buffalo wore on his breast.

A spectator alone of this extraordinary scene can form any idea of the confusion and the noise, which was increased by the loud report of the musketry, the moving backwards and forwards of the people carrying powder and ball, and the tumult occasioned by above twenty horses shut up in the fort. The enemy gradually retreated, and concentrated themselves in several detachments on the brow of the hill, and this gave us an opportunity to open the gate, with due precaution, and view the destroyed tents and the bodies of the slain. The Indian who was killed near the fort especially interested me, because I wished to obtain his skull. The scalp had already been taken off, and several Blackfeet were engaged in venting their rage on the dead body. The men fired their guns at it; the women and children beat it with clubs, and pelted it with stones; the fury of the latter was particularly directed against the privy parts. Before I could obtain my wish, not a trace of the head was to be seen.

At the very beginning of the engagement, the Black-

On the wild Missouri

feet had dispatched messengers on horseback to the great camp of their nation, which was eight or ten miles off, to summon their warriors to their aid, and their arrival was expected every moment.

From the place where the range of hills turns to the Missouri, more and more Blackfeet continued to arrive. They came galloping in groups, from three to twenty together, their horses covered with foam, and they themselves in their finest apparel, with all kinds of ornaments and arms, bows and quivers on their backs, guns in their hands, furnished with their medicines, with feathers on their heads; some had splendid crowns of black and white eagles' feathers, and a large hood of feathers hanging down behind, sitting on fine panther skins lined with red; the upper part of their bodies partly naked, with a long strip of wolf's skin thrown across the shoulder, and carrying shields adorned with feathers and pieces of coloured cloth. A truly original sight! Many immediately galloped over the hill, whipped their tired horses, in order to take part in the engagement, shouting, singing, and uttering their war-whoop; but a great part of them stopped at the fort, received powder and balls, and, with their guns and bows, shot at the disfigured remains of the Assiniboin who was slain, and which were now so pierced and burnt as scarcely to retain any semblance of the human form. As the Indians near the fort believed themselves to be now quite safe, they carried the wounded into the leather tents, which were injured and pierced through and through by the enemy's balls, round which many dead horses and dogs were lying, and the crying and lamenting were incessant.

Fort McKenzie to Fort Clark
September 14—November 8, 1833
[Maximilian turned his face downstream. His new plan was to ship down the Missouri past Fort Union to Fort Clark and there emulate Lewis and Clark

by spending the winter living with the Indians.

All told, Maximilian and his two companions were to spend nearly five-and-a-half months at Fort Clark, living through an unusually brutal winter under primitive conditions. Over the months the white population fluctuated at about a dozen, sometimes less, which was just as well since the fort was frequently on starvation rations, and, as a result, Maximilian contracted scurvy. Despite the bitter cold, food shortages and his illness, however, the prince worked away through the winter with his usual diligence. All winter long a procession of Indians trooped through the Europeans' drafty quarters and posed for hours on end as the artist worked on their portraits.]

April 14, 1834
A main point now was my recovery, which was singularly rapid. At the beginning of April I was still in a hopeless condition, and so very ill, that the people who visited me did not think my life would be prolonged beyond three or, at the most, four days. The cook of the fort, a Negro from St. Louis, one day expressed his opinion that my illness must be the scurvy, for he had once witnessed the great mortality among the garrison of the fort at Council Bluffs, when several hundred soldiers were carried off in a short time. He said that the symptoms were in both cases nearly similar; that, on that occasion, at the beginning of spring, they had gathered the green herbs in the prairie, especially the small white flowering *Allium reticulatum*, with which they had soon cured the sick. I was advised to make trial of this recipe, and the Indian children accordingly furnished me with an abundance of this plant and its bulbs: these were cut up small, like spinage, and I ate a quantity of them. On the fourth day the swelling of my leg had considerably subsided, and I gained strength daily. [Maximilian departed from Fort Clark three days later.]

April 18, 1834
The weather was favourable, though there was a strong wind from the southwest. Some cannon-shot were fired by the fort as a farewell salute, and we glided rapidly down the beautiful stream of the Missouri.

[Maximilian's voyage down the Missouri to St. Louis was accomplished in the company of Bodmer, Dreidoppel, a crew of four Company *engagés*, the two caged bears, and occasional river passengers. After an absence of 13 months the party arrived in St. Louis on May 27, 1834. The great adventure was over.]

Bodmer's paintings were not only ethnographically accurate, they were also pure, decorative works of art, as in portrait of the Mandan, Flying Eagle.

By Tom Crouch

December: diamond anniversary of Man's propulsion skyward

The sage of the Smithsonian did not get off the ground, and the press hooted. Then, quietly, two 'nobodies' began to fly

Dr. Crouch is associate curator of astronautics at Smithsonian's National Air and Space Museum. Robert Osborn was the subject—and artist—for an article on airplanes in December 1976. His wartime cartoons helped teach safety to U.S. Navy pilots.

Shortly after 2:30 on the afternoon of December 8, 1903, the steam tugs *Bartholdi* and *Joe Blackburn* pulled away from a wharf at the foot of Eighth Street in southwest Washington with a large, flat-bottom houseboat in tow. The two vessels moved downstream through blocks of floating ice to an anchorage off Arsenal Point, near the confluence of the Potomac and Anacostia rivers. A midday calm had given way to winds gusting up to 20 miles an hour—hardly ideal conditions for workmen struggling to bolt a cruciform tail and four large wings to a steel-tube fuselage mounted on a catapult on the roof of the houseboat.

Langley's houseboat is towed down the Potomac while workers assemble Great Aerodrome on catapult.

Charles Matthew Manly was obviously in charge of the operation. For the past five years Manly had served as chief aeronautical assistant at the Smithsonian Institution. He took particular care with these final preparations, for he was about to trust his life to the ungainly machine resting on the launcher. If the events of the next few hours unfolded as planned, Charles Manly would become a very famous man indeed—the pilot of the world's first successful powered, heavier-than-air flying machine.

The director of the project, Samuel Pierpont Langley, watched the activity from the houseboat's deck. Secretary of the Smithsonian Institution since 1887, Langley was widely recognized as the nation's unofficial chief scientist. He had thrown over an embryonic career in architecture to pursue his first love, astronomy, after the Civil War and had become interested in flight in 1886, when he attended a lecture on aeronautics. He was inspired to undertake a lengthy series of experiments, and their results convinced him that human beings could fly.

When Langley's data and conclusions were published in 1891, some colleagues questioned the care with which he had conducted the experiments. The Secretary came to believe that redeeming his reputation required a practical demonstration of the validity of his conclusions. Between 1887 and 1891 he had constructed more than 100 rubber-band-powered flying models sporting various wing, tail and propeller combinations. None met his expectations.

Langley then turned to larger models, with wingspans of up to 14 feet. These could be propelled by light yet powerful steam engines. With Smithsonian funds he mounted a five-year effort that culminated in successful flights of two unmanned models—resembling giant dragonflies—for distances of up to 4,200 feet in May and November 1896. These flights silenced those skeptics who had questioned the quality of Langley's experimental data. Moreover, newspapers and popular magazines reported the flights and turned the Secretary into a celebrity. Thousands felt that the age of flight was close at hand and that Langley would inaugurate it.

Immediately after those 1896 flights of his models, the Secretary announced that he had decided to halt aeronautical experiments. In reality, he had begun a serious search for funding. By 1898, with the assistance of his friend Charles Doolittle Walcott of the U.S. Geological Survey, Langley obtained $50,000 through the War Department's Board of Ordnance and Fortification, the agency charged with the development of new weapons.

Langley aimed at enlarging the size of his successful models roughly four times with as few changes as possible. The unmanned craft had been inherently stable, a requirement for all free-flying model aircraft. Langley, who feared that a pilot would be unable to cope

Charles Manly, pilot, and Dr. Samuel P. Langley.

Illustrations by Robert Osborn

Manly, stripped to union suit, enters cockpit . . .

. . . flips into the Potomac after being launched . . .

with rapid shifts in the winds aloft, planned to retain this stability in the Great Aerodrome. The craft would include a movable tail to control altitude, and a rudder, but it would normally fly straight and level. Once the machine had provided the minimum demonstration, Langley planned to devise a suitable control system for it.

In one area, Langley's engineers broke new ground. The steam power plants that had propelled the small craft would be replaced by an internal combustion engine. A one-quarter-scale model was built to test the use of this power. For the Great Aerodrome, Stephen M. Balzer, a New York machinist and instrument maker, developed a five-cylinder rotary engine that operated intermittently, generating only four hp. Manly took delivery of the power plant and transformed it into a water-cooled radial, producing an impressive 52 hp.

By the fall of 1903 the old models had been successfully reflown, and the new one-quarter scale machine had made a brief flight. On October 7, the crew was ready for a manned launch. After a preliminary engine run-up, the Great Aerodrome shot down the rail—and fell into the water "like a handful of mortar," in the words of one Washington reporter. Manly and Langley laid the blame on the catapult mechanism. They repaired the aircraft and modified the launcher for another attempt.

Final preparations for the second test flight on December 8 must have been particularly tense for Langley who, at the age of 69, stood at the pinnacle of his career, and who had chosen to expend 50,000 of the taxpayers' dollars and an additional $20,000 in Smithsonian private funds on a project that many felt was doomed. A small group of invited witnesses joined Langley on board the houseboat. Dr. F. S. Nash, an

Army contract surgeon, was present in case an emergency should arise.

By 4:30 the winter sky was darkening rapidly, and shifting gusts made it impossible to keep the boat heading into the wind. In a hurried conference, Langley and Manly agreed that the test could not be postponed. It might be weeks before the weather improved, and funds were not available to allow for such a delay.

Manly quickly stripped off his outer clothes. He would make the flight dressed in a union suit, stockings, light shoes and a cork-lined jacket. Whether he succeeded or failed, he faced the prospect of a landing in the frigid Potomac and he had no intention of being weighed down by heavy garments.

The young engineer stepped through the tangle of brace wires and struts into the small fabric-sided cockpit. He seated himself on a board facing the right side of the machine, his hands resting on two small wheels mounted on the right wall of the cockpit. These controlled the up-and-down motion of the tail and operated the rudder on the underside of the fuselage. Before Manly ran up the engine, the invited guests joined members of the Washington press corps in a number of small boats. These provided a good view and put them in position to offer assistance should rescue attempts be required.

... and, warmed by drink, produces well-chosen words.

Satisfied with the sound of the engine and the operation of the controls, Manly gave the signal for release at 4:45. He sped down the 60-foot track, felt a sharp jerk and immediately found himself staring straight up at the sky as his aerial steed flipped on its back and dropped into the water.

Manly hung from the cockpit sides with his hands and entered the water feet first. In spite of his precautions, he found himself trapped beneath the surface with the cork-lined jacket caught on a metal fitting. Ripping the garment off, he struggled through the maze of broken wood and wire only to reach the surface beneath an ice block. He dived down, finally emerging in free water some distance from the floating wreckage, just in time to see a workman plunge under the remains of the machine in a rescue attempt. Both men were quickly fished out of the water and carried to safety aboard the houseboat. Manly was uninjured but so frigid that Dr. Nash was forced to cut the clothing from his body.

Moments later, wrapped in warm blankets and fortified with whiskey, this genteel son of a university president startled the group by delivering a "most voluble series of blasphemies." Samuel Pierpont Langley's 20-year drive to develop a flying machine was halted.

The reaction to the disaster of December 8 was as immediate and harsh as Langley had feared it might be. Newspapermen, bitter over the Secretary's policy of secrecy, were little disposed to show mercy. A dramatic photograph showing the shattered aircraft falling toward the water appeared in the Washington *Evening Star*. Once considered the best hope for achieving flight, the machine was now dubbed "Buzzard" and "Mud Duck." Congressmen, ridiculing the expenditure of government funds on flying-machine projects, argued that a regiment of Langley machines "would not conquer the Fiji Islands, except, perhaps, by scaring their people to death."

On December 9, the morning after the Langley catastrophe, one of the men who would prove Langley's critics wrong boarded a train in Dayton, Ohio. Orville Wright faced a two-day journey to Kitty Hawk, a small fishing village and life-saving station on the Outer Banks of North Carolina. He carried with him new propeller shafts that would be fitted to another flying machine that had been conceived and constructed far from the glare of publicity that then surrounded Langley.

During the trip from Dayton, Orville had read the news stories of Langley's disaster. These accounts came as no surprise to him, for he and his older brother Wilbur had long believed that there was little hope for success with the Langley machine.

Still, both brothers must have felt a great deal of

sympathy for the older man. As Wilbur Wright recalled three years later, "The knowledge that the head of the most prominent scientific institution of America believed in the possibility of human flight was one of the influences that led us to undertake the preliminary investigation that preceded our active work. He recommended to us the books which enabled us to form sane ideas at the outset. It was a helping hand at a critical time and we shall always be grateful."

Sons of a United Brethren minister, the Wright brothers were members of an extremely close Midwestern family, and were far removed from the urbanity of Dr. Langley. Aged 29 and 25 in 1896, they were still family-bound. For several years of his young manhood, Wilbur, the elder, remained unemployed, a semi-invalid because of an ice-hockey accident. Orville, who left high school before graduation, had tried his hand at a variety of tasks, but had achieved little financial success.

Their second joint venture (the first was printing), the Wright Cycle Company, provided a reasonable income and an outlet for their mechanical interests, but left the brothers with a great deal of free time, particularly during the winter.

The year 1896 was a crucial one for the brothers. Magazines and newspapers had been carrying reports of men taking to the skies. In Germany, Otto Lilienthal was concluding his sixth successful season of trials with a series of manned hang gliders. By the time of his death in a glider accident in August of that year, he had convinced most obstinate doubters that human beings could fly on wings of their own construction.

Octave Chanute, a world-famous civil engineer, was

emulating Lilienthal that summer at an aerial-experiment station on the Lake Michigan sand dunes near Miller, Indiana.

Their interest whetted by published reports, the Wrights spent the next three years slowly absorbing the flying-machine and bird-flight literature available at home and in the local library. A letter to the Smithsonian Institution produced suggestions for further reading. Correspondence with Chanute cemented a friendship with this man who was to become their chief confidant.

Though the aeronautical literature of the period was a confusing mix of speculation and theory, one of the early marks of the Wright genius was their ability to winnow a few useful ideas from this contradictory morass. It was clear to them, for example, that the flight tests of manned gliders, as advocated by Lilienthal, offered a more rational path to success with a powered machine than did the use of scale models. Moreover, they believed that the practical success of Lilienthal guaranteed the accuracy of the air-pressure tables that he had developed for use in planning the wing-surface area of a flying machine. Chanute had suggested the most efficient aircraft structure in his classic biplane glider of 1896.

More important than these bits of information, however, was the fact that their review of previous work in aeronautics enabled the Wrights to identify the most troublesome problem that had blocked the route to success for others—control.

The Wrights recognized the almost universal search for a system of automatic stability as a blind alley that had led and was leading virtually all other aeronauti-

Back in Dayton, the Wrights seemed to mark time.

Brothers made crucial discoveries

cal experimenters, including Langley, astray. The brothers were resolved that their pilot would be in absolute command of the motion and attitude of his machine at all times.

It had long been recognized that the presence of a horizontal elevator would enable an aircraft to climb or dive, while a vertical rudder could be used to keep the nose of the craft pointed in the desired direction. The longitudinal, or roll, axis was another matter, however. Most of the inventors who had tackled the problems of flight prior to the Wrights saw such control as necessary only to correct for the rise or fall of wing tips struck by gusts. They assumed that the aircraft could be turned to the right or left by the action of the rudder alone.

As experienced bicycle riders, the Wrights realized that bicycles and airplanes are not naturally stable platforms. Rather, the operator must maintain equilibrium or he will fall. Such a craft cannot negotiate a sharp turn simply by angling a front wheel or a rudder. In order to maintain balance, it is necessary to lean into the turn. In the case of the airplane this requires a dip of the wing tip in the direction of the turn. Thus the Wrights sought a method of dipping or raising either wing at will, whereas other experimenters searched for a device to counter such an action. This realization of the necessity for active longitudinal control set the two Daytonians apart from other flying-machine innovators.

Wing warping was the Wrights' answer. If a helical twist could be imparted to the wings, the shift in pressure would force one wing tip down and the other up. They first applied the technique in a small kite built during the summer of 1899, then planned the construction of a man-carrying device embodying the same principle.

As they prepared to enter the active phase of their work, the Wrights were only four years from ultimate success. Lilienthal, Langley, Chanute and others had struggled unsuccessfully for decades to develop a powered flying machine. The Wrights would accomplish the task in seven years, only four of which were devoted to active trials.

The wing-warping system allowed the Wrights to operate gliders with much larger wingspans than those of other designers. The performance of these craft astounded Chanute and everyone else who visited the camp near Kitty Hawk. Yet the Wrights were so dissatisfied at the close of the 1901 season that they seriously considered abandoning aviation. They had failed to achieve the results predicted by their calculations. Ultimately unwilling to walk away from the puzzle, they undertook a series of wind-tunnel tests in order to check the validity of the Lilienthal air-pressure tables on which they had based their preliminary performance computations.

This episode is the clearest example of the intuitive engineering genius that the Wrights brought to bear on the problems of flight. While the renowned Langley clung to cut-and-try empiricism, the self-educated Wrights broke entirely new ground with their homemade wind tunnel. Their 1902 glider, which embodied the corrected wind-tunnel data, performed spectacularly and enabled the Wrights to modify their control system. They realized that they stood very close to final success and turned their attention to the propul-

with their novel wind tunnel.

Wrights controlled tilt of wings by warping them.

sion system. Unable to locate a suitable lightweight engine at a reasonable price, they designed a four-cylinder power plant. Constructed by Charles Taylor, a mechanic in the bike shop, the engine was in many respects quite primitive, producing roughly 16 hp when first started, but dropping to about 12 hp after a minute or so of operation.

In the matter of propellers, the Daytonians were far in advance of their fellows. The brothers were the first to understand that an aircraft propeller is not an "air screw" in a literal sense. Rather, it is a rotary wing, the lift of which draws the airplane forward.

With their new engine and propellers on hand, and work on the structure of the large aircraft nearing completion, the Wrights began planning for their fourth season at Kitty Hawk. This year, 1903, they would expand their camp with the addition of a new shed to supplement the original building constructed in 1901. For the first time, they would be flying two machines, the 1902 glider having been refurbished for practice flying while the powered machine was being put together.

The brothers arrived at their Kitty Hawk camp at 1 P.M. on September 25, 1903. They had originally chosen this site after correspondence with Chanute, U.S. Weather Bureau officials and local residents. Attracted by reports of steady winds to keep their gliders aloft, hills from which to launch them and isolation that would permit them privacy, the brothers were to develop an affection for the self-reliant "Kitty Hawkers" (as they called them).

The Wright camp was situated just north of the Kill Devil Hills, a range of sand hummocks that derived its name, according to one account, "because sailors say it is enough to kill the devil to navigate this part of the [Albermarle] sound." The Wrights' only immediate neighbors were the crew of the Kill Devil Hill Life Saving Station, located roughly a mile from their camp. The closest population center, the small village of Kitty Hawk, lay some four miles to the north. Kitty Hawk boasted its own life saving station, a U.S. weather bureau, a post office serviced by a small mail boat from Manteo, and scattered houses.

But living conditions on the Outer Banks shocked the brothers. Sand sifted through the smallest cracks. Mosquitoes, as Orville reported in 1901, "chewed us clear through our underwear and socks. Lumps began swelling up all over my body. . . . Misery! Misery!"

On arrival in 1903, the brothers discovered that a storm had lifted their original hangar from its foundations. Having just repaired it and completed a second shed, they were promptly assaulted by a ferocious gale. By November, cold weather had set in. In a letter to his father and sister, Wilbur commented that "In addition to . . . 1, 2, 3 and 4 blanket nights, we now have 5 blanket nights, & 5 blankets & 2 quilts. Next come 5 blankets, 2 quilts & fire; then 5, 2, fire & hot water jug. . . . Next comes the addition of sleeping without undressing, then shoes & hats, and finally overcoats."

A makeshift stove constructed from a carbide can provided heat, but filled the building with smoke so thick that when the brothers sat down to eat, the soot on the ceiling began dropping onto their plates. They added legs, chimney and dampers to the stove, which eased the situation.

In spite of the difficulties, the Wrights forged ahead with trials of the 1902 glider and worked to complete the powered machine. By early November, as Manly and Langley were waiting for a break in the weather over the Potomac, the brothers were encountering problems with a rough-running power plant and damaged tubular propeller shafts that eventually forced Orville's quick return to Dayton to supervise work on a new set of solid spring-steel shafts.

Finally, on December 14, preparations seemed complete. The toss of a coin determined that Wilbur

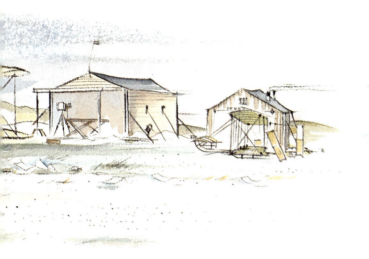

Orville, rushing new shaft to Kill Devil (at far left, Osborn gets literal) Hills, had read of Langley failure.

would have the honor of the first full trial of the powered machine. The craft lifted off on this occasion, but nosed up too sharply and fell to earth, causing slight damage. Three days later, with repairs complete, they were ready for a second trial.

The morning of December 17 dawned cold. The puddles of standing water had frozen overnight, and a 27-mile-an-hour wind was blowing from the north. Hoping that the wind might abate, the brothers enjoyed a leisurely breakfast and remained indoors until 10 A.M., when they decided to make the trial.

They hung out a signal to summon the volunteer ground crew from the Kill Devil Station. The Wrights then maneuvered four 15-foot sections of two-by-four, the tops of which had been sheathed in metal, to a level area some 80 feet west of their buildings. The aircraft, which would ride along this takeoff rail on a truck constructed of two modified bicycle hubs, was then taken out of the hangar and prepared for flight.

Work in the biting cold was difficult, requiring frequent retreats to the comfort of the carbide-can stove, but by the time John Daniels, W. S. Dough and A. D. Etheridge arrived from the Kill Devil Station, preparations were nearing completion. Two visitors, W. C. Brinkley from Manteo and young Johnny Moore from Nags Head, accompanied the lifesavers. Robert Wescott, who had remained on duty at Kill Devil, watched the proceedings through a spyglass, while four miles away Captain S. J. Payne, chief of the Kitty Hawk Station, was also training his telescope on the men clustered around the plane.

At about 10:30 A.M., a few drops of gasoline were pumped into each cylinder. The coil box for starting was attached. The engine was allowed to run for several minutes while Wilbur and Orville discussed the situation. One of the witnesses years later recalled that "we couldn't help notice how they held on to each other's hand, sort o'like they hated to let go; like two

folks parting who weren't sure they'd ever see each other again."

Finally, the two shook hands and Orville climbed into place beside the engine, prone on the lower wing with his feet braced against a board tacked to the trailing edge. His hips lay in a cradle free to move from side to side. To bank to the right, or to raise the left wing tip, he would shift the cradle to the right. This action would impart the correct warp to the wings and turn the rudder to the proper angle. With his left hand Orville grasped the elevator level that would, he hoped, control the rise or fall of his machine.

His right hand operated a second lever that had only three positions. In the "off" position, it was pointed slightly to the right over the leading edge. When pushed straight forward, it opened the cock connecting the half-gallon gasoline tank to the engine and permitted starting. When Orville was prepared to begin the flight he would pull the lever to the left, slipping a line that bound the aircraft and the truck to the rail and permitting them to move forward. At the same time, a stopwatch, the anemometer that served as an airspeed indicator, and the engine-revolution counter were set in motion. The lever was not a throttle, for the engine had only two speeds, on and off. Upon landing, however, the pilot would shove the control to the right to shut off the gas and kill the engine.

With Orville in place, Wilbur walked to the cluster of witnesses. Daniels was dispatched to man the camera pointed at the end of the rail. The elder brother now suggested that the men "not look too sad, but . . . laugh and holler and clap . . . hands and try to cheer Orville up when he started." Wilbur then took up a position by the right wing tip, replacing a low wooden bench that had supported the wing up to this point.

At 10:35 Orville moved his right hand toward his left and the craft began to move slowly into the 27-mile-an-hour wind. Wilbur had little trouble keeping up with the slow forward speed of the machine. As it rose into the air after a 40-foot run, Daniels clicked the shutter just as everyone broke into cheers on cue.

The airplane rose and fell erratically as it sailed forward. After 12 seconds of flight it struck the sand at a point about 120 feet from where it had left the rail. It hadn't taken very long and the machine hadn't traveled very far, but it had undeniably risen from the ground and flown forward under its own power, landing at a point as high as that from which it had taken off. On this isolated North Carolina beach, a man had flown.

The small crew carried the aircraft back to the rail for a second trial, then retired to the shed for a bit of warmth. At 11:20 the group emerged from the building and Wilbur took his place on the machine for a flight 75 feet longer than the first. Twenty minutes later Orville made his second trial, which lasted 15 seconds and covered a little more than 200 feet. At about noon Wilbur tried again, turning in the best performance yet, a spectacular 852 feet in 59 seconds.

The men carried the airplane back to camp. As they clustered around it, a gust of wind caught the machine and sent it tumbling. Daniels went head over heels through the wood and wires, suffering severe bruises. When the airplane came to rest it was extensively damaged. Once the witnesses had helped drag the wreckage into the hangar, they returned to the station. One of them then raced down the beach toward Kitty Hawk. When he encountered Captain William Tate, in whose home the Wrights had lived during their first experiments, he was yelling excitedly, "They have done it! They have done it! Damned if they ain't flew!"

The Wrights ate an unhurried lunch, then strolled up to Kitty Hawk themselves, calling on old friends in the village to confirm the reports of their success, but not before sending a telegram to their father. The message, slightly garbled, was received in Dayton at 5:25 that evening:

Success four flights thursday morning all against twenty one mile wind started from Level with engine power alone average speed through air thirty one miles longest 57 seconds inform Press home Christmas.

Orevelle Wright

The two aircraft of December 1903 were to remain inextricably linked for almost 50 years. Following its final crash on December 8, efforts were made to pull the Langley Aerodrome from the Potomac mud. In so doing, the machine was completely smashed, only the engine remaining undamaged. With the funds left in the Aerodrome account, Manly ordered at least the fuselage refurbished. All parts were placed in storage in the hope that someday trials could be resumed. Following Langley's death in 1906, his old friend and successor, Charles Walcott, revived the dream of flying the Great Aerodrome.

In 1913 Walcott established the Langley Aerodynamical Laboratory at the Smithsonian. The new organization was designed to spearhead American theoretical flight research. Dr. Albert F. Zahm, a onetime friend of the Wrights who had become one of their bitterest enemies, was placed in charge of the new organization. Zahm inherited the Aerodrome and

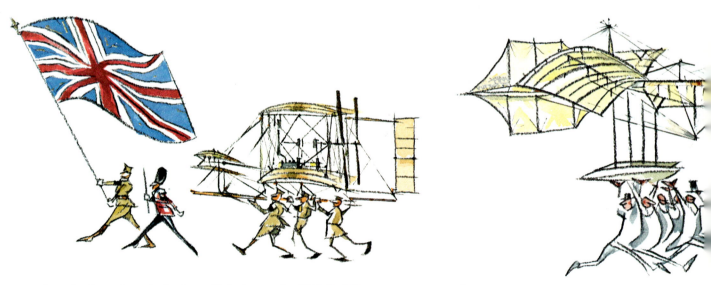

America kept Langley's plane; Britain got the Wrights', but not permanently.

determined that the time had come to prove that the craft could have flown. Glenn Curtiss, who was at the time being sued by the Wrights for having infringed their basic aeronautical patents, was chosen to rebuild and test the Great Aerodrome.

Orville Wright can hardly be blamed for interpreting the Smithsonian's actions as a breach of ethics. Should the Aerodrome fly, Curtiss would be able to claim that the Wright machine had not been the first capable of flight with a man, thus winning an enormous advantage in court.

Curtiss did rebuild the airplane, incorporating a great many major and significant alterations reflecting the advance of aeronautics since 1903. The rebuilt and much altered Aerodrome did, in fact, make a number of short hops. It was later returned to the Smithsonian, where it was restored to the 1903 configuration and placed on exhibit. Smithsonian publications began to describe the Aerodrome as "the first aeroplane in . . . history . . . capable of flying with a pilot and several hundred pounds of useful load."

Wilbur Wright had died of typhoid in 1912, leaving Orville to fight the patent suits and defend their priority as the first to fly. Orville was naturally incensed by the Smithsonian's refusal to accept their valid claims to the invention of the airplane. As early as 1910, Walcott had made it apparent that the Institution had little interest in exhibiting the Wright 1903 machine. This rebuff, complicated by Walcott's later sponsorship of the Langley Aerodrome and the favoritism shown toward a business and legal opponent of the Wrights, guaranteed that the 1903 airplane would

not find a home in the National Museum until amends had been made.

The original Wright Flyer was first rebuilt for exhibition at the dedication of new buildings at the Massachusetts Institute of Technology in 1916. It was exhibited periodically at aeronautical events until 1928, when Orville, convinced that the Smithsonian would not change its position on the priority of the Langley over the Wright machine as the first aircraft capable of flight, ordered the 1903 Flyer sent to England where it was exhibited for more than a decade in London's Science Museum, before being moved into underground storage for safety during World War II.

In 1942 Charles Abbot, Walcott's successor, was finally able to satisfy Orville as to the Institution's change of heart. Six years later the priceless 1903 Flyer was returned to the United States and given a place of honor in the Smithsonian Arts and Industries Building with a formal presentation on December 17, 1948 —11 months after Orville's death.

Visitors now enter the National Air and Space Museum through a gallery entitled "Milestones of Flight." The 1903 Wright Flyer, the world's first airplane, holds the central position, hanging suspended in the center of the area, surrounded by other air and space vehicles that have carried mankind on a journey begun at Kill Devil Hills. Nestled in an upper corner of the gallery, above the Flyer, is the fifth of Langley's steam-powered flying models. Both aircraft serve as reminders of the tragedy and triumph experienced by the first generation that took to the skies on fragile wings fashioned by the human mind and hand.

By Clarissa K. Wittenberg

An intimate record of how it was in yesterday's Harlem

Starting out at 14, in 1900, James Van DerZee painstakingly constructed a gallery of middle-class blacks who made their own society

For almost three-quarters of a century—he is now 89—James Van DerZee has with rare artistry compiled a sweeping photographic survey of a way of life among black people of Eastern America, and particularly Harlem, that is unique and irreplaceable. It is both a historical record of archival value and an achievement of disciplined and feeling art. Van DerZee is only now beginning to be recognized as one of the notable photographers of middle-class people of the country.

Regenia A. Perry, Associate Professor of African and Afro-American Art at Virginia Commonwealth University in Richmond, in the introduction to a portfolio of Van DerZee's photographs (published by Graphics International Ltd., Washington, D.C.) from which this article is largely illustrated, says:

"The message of Van DerZee's photography is a universal one. To the black viewer he provides revealing glimpses of the people and activities in America's most unique black community, which are bound to instill an element of pride and self-respect. To the nonblack viewer Van DerZee's photographs represent Afro-Americans from a dignified, graceful, and impressive point of view which should dispel existing misconceptions. Above all, Van DerZee is a photographer of people and his works are both raceless and timeless." Says Dr. Perry, "Van DerZee's photographs are labors of love both for the profession and for his people."

Clarissa K. Wittenberg is a free-lance writer and an editor of the new Washington Review of the Arts.

The Van DerZee men, Lenox, Massachusetts, 1908, a time when there were few black families in the town. Proud father John is flanked by James, on his far right, and by two younger sons, Walter and Charles.

Although he photographed the people of rural Virginia around the turn of the century, and of Lenox, Massachusetts, where he was born, his photographs of Harlem—an unparalleled historical and social record —draw the most attention. Harlem is unique. To describe it as a section of Manhattan about five miles square in size, with almost a half-million black residents, is to miss its essence. Harlem is the most significant black community in the United States. It is a cultural capital. There is a myth of Harlem that is greater than Harlem itself.

Van DerZee has been uncommonly able to capture both the people who helped to shape the myth and the ordinary citizens who made up the underlying community. His photographs are unusual, but in many cases his subjects were not. All across the country, wherever black families live, subjects such as his may be found in family scrapbooks. Tuskegee Institute year-

Wedding day, Harlem, 1926. The superimposed image of the little girl in the foreground is an example of Van DerZee's interest in technique and experiments in multiple-image photography.

books show many women as lovely as his, many young men as dignified and proud. His work, however, has the considerable added dimension of his creative ability and his high standards. Van DerZee's professional attitude, his careful preservation of his work, the dating and signing of each glass plate and negative, have contributed to the development of a valuable historic record of the heart of a society within a society.

Van DerZee was born in 1886 in Lenox, Massachusetts. His father had become the sexton of the wealthy Trinity Church and his parents had moved there from New York where they had served as butler and maid to General Ulysses S. Grant.

James was 14 when he saw an advertisement that would change his life. A camera was offered as a premium to anyone who could sell 20 packets of perfume. His mother and his aunts bought the sachets and he waited expectantly for the camera. Finally several packages arrived containing a camera, glass plates, clearing solution and developer. Two cardboard **boxes** covered with wax were to serve as trays. Van DerZee learned the directions by heart, but was never able to obtain a picture. Later he bought a better camera and his career began.

In 1906 he moved to New York and soon noted that

In 1925, Van DerZee brought his equipment out and combined in this panorama two of

During a family visit to Lenox, in 1909, Van DerZee composed this portrait of his wife and child.

An affluent side of the Harlem of 1938 is shown in this study of an elaborately furnished apartment.

his major interests, his love of children and of community life in the special place called Harlem.

One view of the black experience

unless the newspaper said "elevator work," "porter" or "waiter," men of his color would not be hired. He played piano and violin with Fletcher Henderson's band. The income was unreliable and he found a job at $5 a week as an assistant in a department store photographic concession. He left in 1916 to open his own studio on 135th Street in Harlem.

Although he took pictures for hack licenses, school graduations, weddings, funerals, lodges and clubs, he gave each commission serious attention. He spent hours on many sittings and his pictures of groups and individuals reflect this care. Everyone came to him, scholars who needed portraits for their books, entertainers, politicians and sports figures. The churches of Harlem were valuable customers. He was often

Van DerZee was a familiar figure in the busy streets of Harlem, lugging his cumbersome equipment on assignment or in search of outstanding subjects. Here, he caught classic expression of the Jazz Age.

Daddy Grace, one of Harlem's charismatic religious leaders, posed frequently for the Van DerZee lens.

In Harlem, in 1915, Van DerZee made this portrait of his cousin, Suzie Porter, dressed for the opera.

Lenox, Massachusetts, 1905—a quiet town in a gentle time; a lady sits for a matriarchal portrait.

A Garveyite family, Harlem, 1924. Marcus **Garvey** led a movement calling for return of blacks to Africa.

"Harlem Renaissance" of Twenties and Thirties was mainly literary, but it was also a time for vibrant theater, musicals, nightclubs, as exemplified by this lovely dancer, on left, and the actor, above.

called to take pictures of their mortgage burnings, their dedications and their ministers, charismatic figures such as Daddy Grace and Father Divine.

Van DerZee took his camera and his plates out into the streets and shot pictures of children at play, of boys racing for a water wagon on a searing hot day. He went to barber shops and ladies' hair salons at teatime.

Van DerZee's portraits of women are particularly beautiful. "Women . . . women . . . what can I say . . . a lot of beauty." They posed in their best dresses (often straight from Paris), their hair arranged, their eyes glowing. One beauty came before a costume party gowned entirely in crepe paper. Although some were posed in the studio, many were photographed in their own homes, giving us an unusual glimpse of their lives.

Fame came late to Van DerZee and he accepts it with some amazement and good grace. He never made much money, he took too many pictures for the joy of it, gave too many away. He was working almost in isolation, doing mail-order restoration of old photographs, when Reginald McGhee, then doing research for *Harlem on My Mind*, an exhibit at New York's Metropolitan Museum of Art in 1969, walked down Lenox Avenue and saw his window filled with old photographs.

Soon afterward, McGhee and Charles Inniss obtained a grant from the New York State Council on the Arts and founded the James Van DerZee Institute Inc. to promote Van DerZee's work, as well as that of other black photographers.

Van DerZee has lived his life with the people whom he photographed, grieved over their funerals, and celebrated their weddings. His record of Harlem is extraordinary, all of his work important in documenting a vital part of America's history.

"It's a hard job," he says philosophically, "to get the camera to see it like you see it. Sometimes you have it just the way you want it, and then you look in the camera and you don't have the balance. The main thing is to get the camera to see it the way you see it."

Although he made "calendar" pictures to order, this 1923 study was an exercise in pure composition.

By Al Capp

I remember Rube, the Chaplin of the funny pages

A tribute to the one and only Goldberg, he of the many inventions, by his cantankerous colleague from Dogpatch

In the early '30s Rube Goldberg was to the young comic artist what Chaplin was to the young comic then and earlier; he was the Master, at the peak of his powers. But to newspaper publishers Goldberg had become a problem. The problem wasn't that he didn't continue to be funny. He was funnier than ever. It was that publishers were no longer sure that readers wanted fun on the funny pages. As we entered the '30s a new element had entered the funnies: misery. And it was going well.

A stunted and sanctimonious little orphan named Annie, a mirthless accident-prone detective named Dick and a Cro-Magnon named Joe whose daily adventures didn't end as Goldberg's did, in creating hilarity, but in creating anxiety, were worrying millions of newspaper readers into rushing out, day after day, to buy the papers that carried them. And a hell of a lot of good that did them. The next day matters of course would get worse, and the next day, and the next, but readers never learned. Every poll and survey proved that misery sold more papers than merriment, and publishers began asking themselves if Rube Goldberg's cartoons were worth the space they occupied and the money they cost, merely to make people feel fine, when it was clearly better business to make them feel frustrated and frenzied.

This new element on the funny page was called "suspense." I was in my early 20s then, working for one of the new "suspense" strippers as an assistant. I wrote, drew and hand-delivered the strip for $22.50 a week while he blew thousands a week trying with no success to make an impression on a new movie·cutie pie, Marlene Dietrich. I still think of him. He is dead now. I never thought of him then as a comic artist, nor do I remember him as one now so much as a salesman of cheap thrills and maudlin sentimentality.

Back then, though, they were household words. Back then, remember, the comic strip was the TV soap-opera series of its time. Comic strips were as inevitable and as necessary in the lives of most Americans as "Laugh In" and "Bonanza" are today, and their creators were as celebrated and beloved as their stars. None however was as celebrated and beloved as Rube Goldberg. He was not only our greatest cartoonist, he was our greatest after-dinner speaker (and he still is); he was big, handsome, radiant and rich, he exuded good-nature, good humor and goodwill and so the man I worked for—"Mr. Cheap and Maudlin"—hated his guts.

This was why: Rube and my boss were under contract to the same syndicate (an agency that sold and

distributed newspaper features to newspapers for a percentage of the take, over and above the basic guarantee). The syndicate's guarantee to Goldberg was opulent, one of the highest in the field, and it had been in effect for many years with one or two to go. Yet, practically, it amounted to little more than a gentlemanly understanding. Goldberg's cartoons over the years had earned comfortable sums over and above the guarantee shared by the syndicate and Goldberg.

But the new "suspense" strips were already cutting into Goldberg's list of newspapers, and there was no telling how far the trend would go. At the time I'm writing of, it was generally known that the syndicate was making every effort to persuade my boss to renew his contract, and he was demanding an even more opulent guarantee than Goldberg's, for a longer time, a guarantee of more sales effort on his cartoons.

It was an illuminating time for me. Raw and undernourished though I was, I was importantly involved in as dramatic a transition period in my profession as the shift from silents to talkies was in films. My heart

Rube Goldberg demonstrates his own invention—a life-sized portrait-maker—as part of a comprehensive display of his work at the Smithsonian's Museum of History and Technology, starting November 24. He sits on a pneumatic cushion (A), forcing air through a tube (B) which moves forward an ice boat (C) armed with a lighted cigar (D). This bursts a balloon (E), convincing a jittery dictator (F) that he's been shot. He falls backward on a bulb (G) which snaps the picture.
The resulting portrait appears on page 224.

Assured a full measure of fame for his own cartoon creation, hard-muscled, soft-headed Li'l Abner, Al Capp deplored the sad turn in comics from fun to maudlin misery and suspense.

221

Rube Goldberg's world

Although I was on the winning side, I hated to see Goldberg's side lose. The side of laughter and irony and wit. It seemed to me that he could survive and prosper again, if he would combine comedy with the new element of suspense, if he'd change from pure comedy to comic melodrama.

Then one day I saw by the papers that Goldberg had changed. But alas, beyond recognition. Suddenly, in the last year of his contract, in what was clearly a last, frantic effort, "Mike and Ike," "Boob McNutt," "Life's Little Jokes" and the stunningly sensible "Inventions" vanished and "Doc Wright" appeared. The Doc was a Lincolnesque character—selfless, heroic, kindly, philosophical; in short, an asphyxiating bore. He reeked with the sanctimoniousness Goldberg had always ridiculed.

Goldberg trying to become a mirthless maudlin "suspense" cartoonist was as hopeless as Bernard Shaw trying to become Lawrence Welk. He didn't have the talentlessness for it. I was convinced that "Doc Wright" (and Rube Goldberg) would indeed vanish if I didn't save them. This was comparable to the Republic of Chad being convinced that Red China would be vanquished unless it saved her.

He agreed to see me because he remembered me as the Kid he'd met at my boss' studio, whose job was cleaning up the strips. When company came, my boss'

was with the comedy of Rube Goldberg, yet for that $22.50 a week I was devoting my gifts to the sort of "suspense" strip that was inexorably ousting him from paper after paper. If I describe my gifts at the time as considerable I'm not being immodest. I'm giving the Kid I was then his due. A year later I was doing "Li'l Abner." It was considered, from the beginning, as seductive a "suspense" strip as there was and funny enough to be referred to in *Time* as in the "tradition of such great masters as Rube Goldberg."

Rube's alarm clock, a model displayed at the Smithsonian, is activated by a 6 a.m. garbage man. He lifts an ash can, causing mule to kick statue of Indian warrior, whose arrow punctures an ice bucket. Ice cubes fall on false teeth, making them chatter and nip elephant's tail. He raises his trunk in pain, pressing lever that starts toy maestro leading quartet in a sad song. Sentimental girl's tears water flowers which grow and tickle man's feet. His laughter triggers gong and slides the sleeper into slippers on wheels—and thus into a cold shower. Four more Goldberg cartoons appear opposite.

AT 6:30 WEIGHT (A) AUTOMATICALLY DROPS ON HEAD OF DWARF (B), CAUSING HIM TO YELL AND DROP CIGAR (C), WHICH SETS FIRE TO PAPER (D) - HEAT FROM FIRE ANGERS DWARF'S WIFE (E) - SHE SHARPEN'S POTATO KNIFE (F) ON GRINDSTONE (G) WHICH TURNS WHEEL (H) CAUSING OLIVE SPOON (I) TO DIP REPEATEDLY INTO OLIVES - IF SPOON DOES NOT LIFT AN OLIVE IN 15 MINUTES, CLOCK (J) AUTOMATICALLY PUSHES GLASS-CUTTER (K) AGAINST BOTTLE AND TAKES OUT CHUNK OF GLASS BIG ENOUGH FOR YOU TO STICK YOUR FINGER IN AND PULL OUT AN OLIVE.

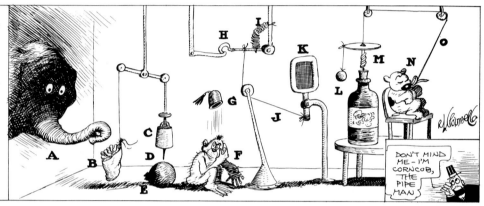

ELEPHANT (A) EATS PEANUTS (B) - AS BAG GETS LIGHTER WEIGHT (C) DROPS AND SPIKE (D) PUNCTURES BALLOON (E) - EXPLOSION SCARES MONKEY (F) - HIS HAT (G) FLIES OFF AND RELEASES HOOK (H), CAUSING SPRING (I) TO PULL STRING (J), WHICH TILTS TENNIS RACKET (K) - RACKET HITS BALL (L), MAKING IT SPIN AROUND ON ATTACHED STRING, THEREBY SCREWING CORKSCREW INTO CORK (M) - BALL HITS SLEEPING DOG (N) WHO JUMPS AND PULLS CORK OUT OF BOTTLE WITH STRING (O) - MY, HOW SIMPLE!

DON'T MIND ME - I'M CORNCOB, THE PIPE MAN

PROFESSOR BUTTS FALLS ON HIS HEAD AND DOPES OUT A SIMPLIFIED CAN-OPENER WHILE HE IS STILL GROGGY. GO OUTSIDE AND CALL UP YOUR HOME. WHEN PHONE BELL RINGS, MAID (A) MISTAKES IT FOR AN ALARM CLOCK - SHE AWAKENS AND STRETCHES, PULLING CORD (B) WHICH RAISES END OF LADLE (C). BALL (D) DROPS INTO NET (E) CAUSING GOLF CLUB (F) TO SWING AGAINST BALL (G), MAKING A CLEAN DRIVE AND UPSETTING MILK CAN (H). MILK SPILLS INTO GLASS (I) AND THE WEIGHT PULLS SWITCH ON RADIO (J). WALTZING MICE (K) HEARING MUSIC AND PROCEED TO DANCE, CAUSING REVOLVING APPARATUS (L) TO SPIN AND TURN. SPIKES (M) SCRATCH TAIL OF PET DRAGON (N) WHO IN ANGER EMITS FIRE IGNITING ACETYLENE TORCH (O) AND BURNING OFF TOP OF TOMATO CAN (P) AS IT ROTATES. WHEN NOT OPENING CANS, THE DRAGON CAN ALWAYS BE KEPT BUSY CHASING AWAY INCOME TAX INVESTIGATORS AND PROHIBITION OFFICERS.

RING! DING! A-LING!

WHEN YOU FIND YOU'VE LOST YOUR COLLAR BUTTON AGAIN, YOU WAVE ARMS IN ANGER-FIST (A) PRESSES BULB (B) AND SQUIRTS WATER (C) INTO EYE OF YIFFIK BIRD (D) - BIRD IS TEMPORARILY BLINDED & WALKS OFF PERCH (E), FALLING INTO CAR (F) OF SCENIC RAILWAY (G) - CAR DESCENDS, CAUSING CORD (H) TO TILT BAR (I) - WOODEN FINGER (J) PRESSES REFEREE DOLL (K) MAKING IT SAY "PLAY BALL" - PITCHER (L) OF MIDGET GIANTS GRABS BALL (M) WHICH IS ATTACHED TO HANDLE OF PHONOGRAPH (N) AND WINDS UP - PHONOGRAPH RECORD ASKS; "WHERE IS AT?" - PHILOSOPHER FATHER (O) OF PITCHER, WHO IS EVEN SMALLER THAN HIS SON, IS PUZZLED OVER QUESTION AND WALKS AROUND TRYING TO FIGURE IT OUT - HE IS SO ABSORBED IN PROBLEM, HE WALKS UNDER BUREAU (P) AND BUMPS INTO COLLAR BUTTON (Q), YELLING "OUCH" AND SHOWING YOU WHERE COLLAR BUTTON IS.

PLAY BALL

WHERE IS AT?

BENNY SENT ME

Rube Goldberg's world

orders were for me to stop writing or drawing, pick up an eraser, rub, and not do anything else, until they left. The '30s were a time when it was thought to be as suicidal for a cartoonist to admit that he had an assistant as for a movie idol to admit that he had a wife.

Rube's studio was elegant, orderly and decorated with pictures by other great men and pictures of Rube with other great men. I remember that when I was shown in, he was on the phone, talking to his syndicate about a request from some city in the Midwest, a two-day journey by train, for a personal appearance on some important public occasion. He grunted and asked if it would help Doc Wright with the local paper. The answer must have been that nothing would help Doc Wright because Rube grunted again and said something like to hell with it.

I began by saying that I thought he was the funniest cartoonist in the world and that the world still wanted fun and that, although it *was* true that "suspense" suddenly sold more papers than fun, I was convinced that the public still wanted to laugh and that if he *combined* his comedy with the new "suspense," "Doc Wright" could sell more papers than anything.

Rube said he'd think it over and to call him back in a few days. I did. He said he thought he'd better work it out himself. I was left with a theory.

And so, instead of working it out with Rube Goldberg in "Doc Wright" in my spare time, I worked it out alone. I combined the fun I'd learned to love in Goldberg's cartoons, with "suspense," and that combination of farce and melodrama made "Li'l Abner."

Is this, then, a story that ends by proving the Kid was right, and the Master was wrong? No. That isn't the end of the story. It's a long story—it goes on from the '30s to the '70s, and it ends by proving that the best the Kid could do was adjust to a temporary (40-year) situation, but that the Master had been right from the beginning, and that his only mistake was deigning to adjust to a passing (40-year) fad that deserved only his contempt.

"Doc Wright" vanished from the comic page, and Rube switched to the editorial page. In 1948, he won the Pulitzer Prize. In 1964, he left the editorial page and switched to sculpture (opposite page). If there was a Hogarth prize for sculpture, he'd win it today, at 87.

His greatest victory, however, is over all the suspense cartoonists, the pollsters, the publishers who claimed that Goldberg's day—the day of pure fun—was over. The tormented orphan, with her Afro hairstyle and her Orval Faubus life-style survives. The dauntless Dick and the uneducable hillbilly, too. But the others are all pure Goldberg: "Beetle Bailey" although he is a WASP; "B.C." is pure Goldberg, although a bit less lusty; "Peanuts" is pure Goldberg, although a bit diluted; Feiffer's cartoons are "Life's Little Jokes" all over again, although they pretend not to be by use of bits of New Left slogans and jargon popular in Brooklyn Heights psychiatric circles; "Pogo" now is pure Goldberg, the only one that is frequently every bit as good.

The grandsons of "Boob McNutt" have overcome.

Self-portrait of the artist at his present age, 87, was snapped by his invention (pages 220 & 221). Author of many books, Rube recently gained new prestige as a sculptor. Opposite: a bust of himself.

Text and photographs by E. Richard Sorenson

Growing up as a Fore is to be 'in touch' and free

Film studies of a hunting-gardening culture in Papua New Guinea disclose remarkable child-rearing practices

Untouched by the outside world, they had lived for thousands of years in isolated mountains and valleys deep in the interior of Papua New Guinea. They had no cloth, no metal, no money, no idea that their homeland was an island—or that what surrounded it was salt water. Yet the Fore (*for'ay*) people had developed remarkable and sophisticated approaches to human relations, and their child-rearing practices gave their young unusual freedom to explore. Successful as hunter-gatherers and as subsistence gardeners, they also had great adaptability, which brought rapid accommodation with the outside world after their lands were opened up.

It was alone that I first visited the Fore in 1963—a day's walk from a recently built airstrip. I stayed six months. Perplexed and fascinated, I returned six times in the next ten years, eventually spending a year and a half living with them in their hamlets.

Theirs was a way of life different from anything I had seen or heard about before. There were no chiefs, patriarchs, priests, medicine men or the like. A striking personal freedom was enjoyed even by the very young, who could move about at will and be where or with whom they liked. Infants rarely cried, and they played confidently with knives, axes and fire. Conflict

between old and young did not arise; there was no "generation gap."

Older children enjoyed deferring to the interests and desires of the younger, and sibling rivalry was virtually undetectable. A responsive sixth sense seemed to attune the Fore hamlet mates to each other's interests and needs. They did not have to directly ask, inveigle, bargain or speak out for what they needed or wanted. Subtle, even fleeting expressions of interest, desire and discomfort were quickly read and helpfully acted on by one's associates. This spontaneous urge to share food, affection, work, trust, tools and pleasure was the social cement that held the Fore hamlets together. It was a pleasant way of life, for one could always be with those with whom one got along well.

Ranging and planting, sharing and living, the Fore diverged and expanded through high virgin lands in a pioneer region. They hunted out their gardens, tilled them while they lasted, then hunted again. Moving ever away from lands peopled and used, they had a self-contained life with its own special ways.

The underlying ecological conditions were like those that must have encompassed the world before agriculture set its imprint so broadly. Abutting the Fore was virtually unlimited virgin land, and they had food plants they could introduce into it. Like hunter-gatherers they sought their sources of sustenance first in one locale and then another, across an extended range, following opportunities provided by a providential nature. But like agriculturalists they concentrated their effort and attention more narrowly on selected sites of production, on their gardens. They were both seekers and producers. A pioneer people in a pioneer land, they ranged freely into a vast territory, but they planted to live.

Exploring, two youngsters walk confidently past men's house in hamlet. Smaller women's house is at right.

Close, constant body contact, as between this baby and older girl, creates security in Fore children.

Cooperative groups formed hamlets and gardened together. When the fertility of a garden declined, they abandoned it. Grass sprang up to cover these abandoned sites of earlier cultivation, and, as the Fore moved on to other parts of the forest, they left uninhabited grasslands to mark their passage.

The traditional hamlets were small, with a rather fluid system of social relations. A single large men's house provided shelter for 10 to 20 men and boys and their visiting friends. The several smaller women's houses each normally sheltered two married women, their unmarried daughters and their sons up to about six years of age. Formal kinship bonds were less important than friendship was. Fraternal "gangs" of youths formed the hamlets; their "clubhouses" were the men's houses.

During the day the gardens became the center of life. Hamlets were virtually deserted as friends, relatives and children went to one or more garden plots to mingle their social, economic and erotic pursuits in a pleasant and emotionally filled Gestalt of garden life. The boys and unmarried youths preferred to explore and hunt in the outlying lands, but they also passed through and tarried in the gardens.

Daily activities were not scheduled. No one made demands, and the land was bountiful. Not surprisingly the line between work and play was never clear.

The transmission of the Fore behavioral patterns to the young began in early infancy during a period of unceasing human physical contact. The effect of being constantly "in touch" with hamlet mates and their daily life seemed to start a process which proceeded by degrees: close rapport, involvement in regular activity, ability to handle seemingly dangerous implements safely, and responsible freedom to pursue individual interests at will without danger.

While very young, infants remained in almost continuous bodily contact with their mother, her house mates or her gardening associates. At first, mothers' laps were the center of activity, and infants occupied themselves there by nursing, sleeping and playing with their own bodies or those of their caretakers. They were not put aside for the sake of other activities, as when food was being prepared or heavy loads were being carried. Remaining in close, uninterrupted physical contact with those around them, their basic needs such as rest, nourishment, stimulation and security were continuously satisfied without obstacle.

By being physically in touch from their earliest days, Fore youngsters learned to communicate needs,

Dr. Sorenson, director of the Smithsonian's National Anthropological Film Center, wrote The Edge of the Forest *on his Fore studies.*

desires and feelings through a body language of touch and response that developed before speech. This opened the door to a much closer rapport with those around them than otherwise would have been possible, and led ultimately to the Fore brand of social cement and the sixth sense that bound groups together through spontaneous, responsive sharing.

As the infant's awareness increased, his interests broadened to the things his mother and other caretakers did and to the objects and materials they used. Then these youngsters began crawling out to explore things that attracted their attention. By the time they were toddling, their interests continually took them on short sorties to nearby objects and persons. As soon as they could walk well, the excursions extended to the entire hamlet and its gardens, and then beyond with other children. Developing without interference or supervision, this personal exploratory learning quest freely touched on whatever was around, even axes, knives, machetes, fire, and the like. When I first went to the Fore, I was aghast.

Eventually I discovered that this capability emerged naturally from the Fore infant-handling practices in their milieu of close human physical proximity and tactile interaction. Because touch and bodily contact lend themselves naturally to satisfying the basic needs of young children, an early kind of communicative experience fostered cooperative interaction between infants and their caretakers, also kinesthetic contact with the activities at hand. This made it easy for them

Learning to be a toddler, a Fore baby takes its first experimental steps. No one urges him on.

to learn the appropriate handling of the tools of life.

The early pattern of exploratory activity included frequent return to one of the "mothers." Serving as home base, the bastion of security, a woman might occasionally give the youngster a nod of encouragement, if he glanced in her direction with uncertainty. Yet rarely did the women attempt to control or direct, nor did they participate in the child's quests or jaunts.

As a result Fore children did not have to adjust to rule and schedule in order to find their place in life. They could pursue their interests and whims wherever they might lead and still be part of a richly responsive world of human touch which constantly provided sustenance, comfort, diversion and security.

Learning proceeded during the course of pursuing interests and exploring. Constantly "in touch" with people who were busy with daily activities, the Fore young quickly learned the skills of life from example. Muscle tone, movement and mood were components of this learning process; formal lessons and commands were not. Kinesthetic skills developed so quickly that infants were able to casually handle knives and similar objects before they could walk.

Even after several visits I continued to be surprised that the unsupervised Fore toddlers did not recklessly thrust themselves into unappreciated dangers, the way our own children tend to do. But then, why should they? From their earliest days, they enjoyed a benevolent sanctuary from which the world could be confidently viewed, tested and appreciated. This sanctuary remained ever available, but did not demand, restrain or impose. One could go and come at will.

In close harmony with their source of life, the Fore young were able confidently, not furtively, to extend their inquiry. They could widen their understanding as they chose. There was no need to play tricks or deceive in order to pursue life.

Emerging from this early childhood was a freely ranging young child rather in tune with his older and younger hamlet mates, disinclined to act out impulsively, and with a capable appreciation of the properties of potentially dangerous objects. Such children could be permitted to move out on their own, unsupervised and unrestricted. They were safe.

Such a pattern could persist indefinitely, re-creating itself in each new generation. However, hidden within the receptive character it produced was an Achilles heel: it also permitted adoption of new practices, including child-handling practices, which did *not* act to

In infancy, Fore children begin experimental play with knives and other lethal objects. Sorenson never saw a child warned away or injured by them.

perpetuate the pattern. In only one generation after Western contact, the cycle of Fore life was broken.

Attuned as they were to individual pursuit of economic and social good, it did not take the Fore long to recognize the value of the new materials, practices and ideas that began to flow in. Indeed, change began almost immediately with efforts to obtain steel axes, salt, medicine and cloth. The Fore were quick to shed indigenous practices in favor of the Western example. They rapidly altered their ways to adapt to Western law, government, religion, materials and trade.

Sometimes change was so rapid that many people seemed to be afflicted by a kind of cultural shock. An anomie, even cultural amnesia, seemed to pervade some hamlets for a time. There were individuals who

Babies have free access to the breast and later, like this toddler being helped to kernels of corn by an older girl, can help themselves to whatever food is around—indulged by children and grown-ups.

On the way to hunt birds, cuscus (a marsupial) or rats, Fore boys stride through a sweet-potato garden.

A girl goes over a garden stile. Gardens are fenced to keep pigs out of the hamlet's plantings.

appeared temporarily to have lost memory of recent past events. Some Fore even forgot what type and style of traditional garments they had worn only a few years earlier, or that they had used stone axes and had eaten their dead close relatives.

Remarkably open-minded, the Fore so readily accepted reformulation of identity and practice that suggestion or example by the new government officers, missionaries and scientists could alter tribal affiliation, place names, conduct and hamlet style. When the first Australian patrol officer began to map the region in 1957, an error in communication led him to refer to these people as the "Fore." Actually they had had no name for themselves and the word, Fore, was their name for a quite different group, the Awa, who spoke another language and lived in another valley. They did not correct the patrol officer but adopted his usage. They all now refer to themselves as the Fore. Regional and even personal names changed just as readily.

More than anything else, it was the completion of a steep, rough, always muddy Jeep road into the Fore lands that undermined the traditional life. Almost overnight their isolated region was opened. Hamlets began to move down from their ridgetop sites in order to be nearer the road, consolidating with others.

The power of the road is hard to overestimate. It was a great artery where only restricted capillaries had existed before. And down this artery came a flood of new goods, new ideas and new people. This new road, often impassable even with four-wheel-drive vehicles, was perhaps the single most dramatic stroke wrought by the government. It was to the Fore an opening to a new world. As they began to use the road, they started to shed traditions evolved in the protective insularity of their mountain fastness, to adopt in their stead an emerging market culture.

The coming of the coffee economy

"Walkabout," nonexistent as an institution before contact, quickly became an accepted way of life. Fore boys began to roam hundreds of miles from their homeland in the quest for new experience, trade goods, jobs and money. Like the classic practice of the Australian aborigine, this "walkabout" took one away from his home for periods of varying length. But unlike the Australian practice, it usually took the boys to jobs and schools rather than to a solitary life in traditional lands. Obviously it sprang from the earlier pattern of individual freedom to pursue personal interests and opportunity wherever it might lead. It was a new expression of the old Fore exploratory pattern.

Some boys did not roam far, whereas others found ways to go to distant cities. The roaming boys often sought places where they might be welcomed as visitors, workers or students for a while. Mission stations and schools, plantation work camps, and the servants' quarters of the European population became way-stations in the lives of the modernizing Fore boys.

Some took jobs on coffee plantations. Impressed by the care and attention lavished on coffee by European planters and by the money they saw paid to coffee growers, these young Fore workers returned home with coffee beans to plant.

Coffee grew well on the Fore hillsides, and in the mid-1960s, when the first sizable crop matured, Fore who previously had felt lucky to earn a few dollars found themselves able to earn a few hundred dollars. A rush to coffee ensued, and when the new gardens became productive a few years later, the Fore income from coffee jumped to a quarter of a million dollars a year. The coffee revolution was established.

At first the coffee was carried on the backs of its growers (sometimes for several days) over steep, rough mountain trails to a place where it could be sold to a buyer with a Jeep. However, as more and more coffee was produced, the villagers began to turn their efforts to planning and constructing roads in association with neighboring villages. The newly built roads, in turn, stimulated further economic development and the opening of new trade stores throughout the region.

Following European example, the segregated collective men's and women's houses were abandoned. Family houses were adopted. This changed the social and territorial arena for all the young children, who hitherto had been accustomed to living equally with many members of their hamlet. It gave them a narrower place to belong, and it made them more distinctly someone's children. Uncomfortable in the family houses, boys who had grown up in a freer territory began to gather in "boys' houses," away from the adult men who were now beginning to live in family houses with their wives. Mothers began to wear blouses, altering the early freer access to the breast. Episodes of infant and child frustration, not seen in traditional Fore hamlets, began to take place along with repeated incidents of anger, withdrawal, aggressiveness and stinginess.

So Western technology worked its magic on the Fore, its powerful materials and practices quickly shattering their isolated autonomy and life-style. It took only a few years from the time Western intruders built their first grass-thatched patrol station before the Fore way of life they found was gone.

Fortunately, enough of the Fore traditional ways were systematically documented on film to reveal how unique a flower of human creation they were. Like nothing else, film made it possible to see the behavioral patterns of this way of life. The visual record, once made, captured data which was unnoticed and unanticipated at the time of filming and which was simply impossible to study without such records. Difficult-to-spot subtle patterns and fleeting nuances of manner, mood and human relations emerged by use of repeated reexamination of related incidents, sometimes by slow motion and stopped frame. Eventually the characteristic behavioral patterns of Fore life became clear, and an important aspect of human adaptive creation was revealed.

The Fore way of life was only one of the many natural experiments in living that have come into being through thousands of years of independent development in the world. The Fore way is now gone; those which remain are threatened. Under the impact of modern technology and commerce, the entire world is now rapidly becoming one system. By the year 2000 all the independent natural experiments that have come into being during the world's history will be merging into a single world system.

One of the great tragedies of our modern time may be that most of these independent experiments in living are disappearing before we can discover the implications of their special expressions of human possibility. Ironically, the same technology responsible for the worldwide cultural convergence has also provided the means by which we may capture detailed visual records of the yet remaining independent cultures. The question is whether we will be able to seize this never-to-be repeated opportunity. Soon it will be too late. Yet, obviously, increasing our understanding of the behavioral repertoire of humankind would strengthen our ability to improve life in the world.

Any child and any adult, related or not, may get along in a Fore hamlet. The secret: interaction—and trust.

The Arts

Smithsonian's coverage of the arts—fine, decorative, performing and architectural—is both eclectic and topical, which is to say there are no limitations.

The editorial insistence is to identify and explain, in clear, uncluttered language, those exhibitions, performances, and artists—of outstanding cultural importance or, perhaps, of more ephemeral interest—having to do with popular culture as it is perceived at the moment.

Some such moments have a way of persisting through history and so become part of the lasting record of world culture. One can hardly assume, for example, that a nomadic steppes tribesman living 700 years before Christ had it in mind to create a high work of art when he designed a metal bit for a horse. And yet, as exemplified by our story on Scythian gold, such metalwork is today prized for the dazzling beauty of its design and must be accorded the same kind of admiration as, say, a stone carving on the face of a Gothic cathedral or an apple as painted by Cezanne.

To keep in touch with the best of what is going on— often a controversial decision—*Smithsonian* maintains a close watch on schedules of forthcoming exhibitions at American and foreign museums. So, foreign as well as domestic periodicals and announcements are regularly reviewed. In this way many outstanding exhibitions mounted in foreign countries and scheduled to appear later in the United States have been covered in Europe and have therefore been ready for release in conjunction with the American opening. *Smithsonian* makes it a point to list the itinerary for traveling exhibits so that readers may be aware of a show in their vicinity or one that will be coming there. Stories must be planned long in advance, the writer commissioned, the photographer selected.

The range of arts stories is wide and catholic, ranging from the masters of past time to living artists, from community activities involving the arts, to cultural institutions, to music, the theater, the arts of crafts to the craft of art. When an artist is of interest equal to the work itself, we are able to present an article such as Tom Prideaux's on the actress Ellen Terry. John Russell's exposition of the later works of Henri Matisse, a summation of the illuminating grace of a world master, is notable for its quiet knowledge, comprehension and clarity. The article by Jean Stratton on the drama of the deaf explicates a new form of theater art. The fanciful world of the Lalannes, as portrayed by Robert Wernick, deals with art that is meant simply to amuse, by no means a minor form of creativity in the world's history. With Benjamin Forgey's essay on the genius of Isamu Noguchi we are in touch with efforts of one of the world's most creative sensibilities. Russell Lynes's article on New York's World Trade Center considers not only the substance of this massive addition to the city, but also its effect on the occupants and the city itself. And, in Dora Jane Hamblin's presentation of Venice and its troubles we are face to face with a work of art that is an entire city and what can happen to it through the depredations of both man and nature.

In its selection of arts articles *Smithsonian* strives to achieve, and it is not an easy goal to reach, the kind of quality Samuel Johnson spoke of when he said that what one looks for is ". . . that comprehension and expanse of thought which at once fills the whole mind, and of which the first effect is of sudden astonishment, and the second rational admiration."

—Bennett Schiff
Board of Editors

Detail of *May Sartoris* illustrates the dramatic style of 19th-century British painter Sir Frederic Leighton, one of four artists featured in an exhibit entitled "Victorian High Renaissance." From "Re-creation of Olympus on high, heroic days of Victoria's reign" December 1978 pp. 48-57.

By Tom Prideaux

Ellen Terry wowed the New World onstage–and off

A queen of the theater, golden-haired and gifted, a luminary of the English stage, came trembling to America—and triumphed

When Ellen Terry, making her first voyage to America, arrived in New York harbor at dawn on October 21, 1883, it seemed to the swarm of welcoming reporters that the ruling queen of the English stage half expected to be shot at sunrise. She was edgy and scared.

Before the S.S. *Britannic* docked, Ellen and her great partner, Henry Irving, were transferred to a private yacht where the interviews were to be held. It was a gala event, for Irving was bringing from London his celebrated Lyceum Theater company for its first U.S. tour. Many of the reporters expected to be high-hatted by the glamorous acting team. But Irving charmed them at once with his modesty and excellent cigars, not to mention the cold chicken, champagne and band provided by his American manager.

While the band played "Rule, Britannia," Ellen made her official entrance, a tall, golden-haired creature of 36, wrapped in tawny scarves and sashes, and looking, according to one reporter, like "a pre-Raphaelite saint." She had been warned that American reporters were devils, given to asking horrid questions, or disguising themselves as bellboys or waiters in order to spy on visitors. When they asked Ellen about the first role she was scheduled to play—Queen Henrietta in *Charles the First*—she grumbled that she disliked the part and couldn't imagine why she was playing it. When another reporter asked if he could send her friends back home a message, her blue eyes filled with tears, and she sobbed, "Tell them I never loved 'em so much as now."

After the interview Ellen and Irving took separate carriages, he to the Brevoort House on Fifth Avenue and she to the Hotel Dam (named after its owner) near Union Square. On the way Ellen's mood was not improved by noting "the muddy sidewalks and the cavernous holes in the cobble-paved streets," and, once inside her suite, she fell on the bed and wailed for two hours. Ellen had been stricken by acute homesickness; she had left a daughter and son, aged 13 and 11, in England, and now she felt bleakly isolated. Only when her maid, trying to cheer her, began to play "Annie Laurie" on the parlor piano—and play it abominably —did Ellen begin to laugh.

At that point, having exorcised her blues, Ellen commenced her long romance with America. All told, she was to spend some five years in the country, including seven tours with Irving and, in 1915, a final "reading" tour by herself.

America met Ellen at the peak of her career. Offspring of a Scotch-Irish theatrical family, she had made her stage debut at the age of nine, playing Shakespeare before Queen Victoria in London, and by 16 she had acted 50 different parts. She skipped school altogether, but from infancy she was soaked in Shakespeare. Her father taught her all the female roles, and she spoke them as naturally as she breathed. By the time she joined Irving, she was already an extremely popular actress. Bernard Shaw was to write ". . . every famous man of the last quarter of the nineteenth century—provided he were a playgoer—had been in love with Ellen Terry," and many of them, he added, "found in her friendship the utmost consolation one can hope for from a wise, witty and beautiful woman."

The reckless democrat

Ellen's style of acting was peculiarly suited to Americans. Its very simplicity reassured them that she was not putting on fancy airs or acting over their heads. Her lack of affectation, in fact, moved some critics to accuse her of not acting at all. They did her an injustice. For she was a deft technician who calculated every syllable, every pause and gesture, to give an illusion of spontaneity; she was a *trompe l'oeil* performer who made artifice seem real. Most important, her deep, slightly husky voice was an instrument for blessedly clear diction, which projected not only words but meanings. By making Americans really enjoy and understand Shakespeare, she banished their fears of being uncultured hicks.

Temperamentally, too, she was in tune with America. Optimistic, industrious and recklessly democratic, Ellen once said, "I have always thought it hard to find my inferiors," not meaning to abase herself but simply recognizing the innate worth of almost every individ-

Kerrison Preston, Esq.

Ellen's delicacy and tawny beauty were caught
in this portrait by her husband, G. F. Watts.

Ellen Terry in America: a romance

ual. Shaw had in mind her all-embracing cordiality when he wrote to her, "I am convinced that with you a human relationship is love or nothing."

Ellen's views of America were often patchy, seen from trains, or while rushing from stations to hotels to stage doors. But on longer stopovers she devoured the sights and made friends. No sight pleased her more than the new Brooklyn Bridge, especially when it glistened with ice and snow, "a gigantic trellis of dazzling white. . . ." Her memories of Brooklyn were enhanced by the famous pastor, Henry Ward Beecher, who, at 70, had never been to a theater until, with his wife, he saw Ellen and Irving in a play. "It burst upon my ripe old age," he wrote Irving, "as June would upon a Greenlander." He then invited the couple to a Sunday service in his Plymouth Church, followed by lunch in the Beechers' Brooklyn house.

Beecher, with his proud head and flowing locks, looked distinctly actorish—like Irving. But in spirit he was closer to Ellen. At heart a rule-breaker, he liked to romp with children at Sunday school picnics, and was as casual in his dress as he was cordial to everybody he met. Accused of seducing a friend's wife, he was finally cleared after lengthy litigation, but a cloud of scandal still hung over him, which threatened the spectacle of his sanctity but not his popularity. His wife, who bore him ten children, was steadfastly loyal, and held hands with him, Ellen noticed, at the luncheon table.

At first, Eunice Beecher was polite but aloof, probably in the belief that all actresses were sinful. It was also likely that she knew of Ellen's two children born out of wedlock (there had been obstacles that kept Ellen from marrying their father, with whom she lived in retirement for five years before they separated), all of which might make the pastor's wife uneasy with her theatrical guest. Yet before the visit ended, Eunice was reminiscing freely about her own strict girlhood, when

An entrancing subject for artists, Ellen was portrayed as Lady Macbeth by John Singer Sargent.

For years a senior writer for Life *and the author of books on art and the theater, Tom Prideaux's* Love or Nothing: The Life and Times of Ellen Terry, *is to be published this month by Scribner's.*

As Ellen was the Queen of the Western stage,
Sir Henry Irving was recognized to be the King.

her father once threw scalding soup at her neck because she was wearing a new blue silk dress with a modestly open collar. As the two women said good-bye, they both honored the occasion by crying.

From New York, Irving's show train took off for Philadelphia, the first lap on the tour, hauling nearly a hundred performers and technicians, tons of scenery and costumes for eight plays, including gas tanks for special lighting effects, and a thousand new wigs.

One of Ellen's favorite stops was Boston. Over the years she played there so many times that her memories were not always in chronological order, but she vividly recalled the witty, exuberant Mrs. Jack Gardner whose art treasures were housed, as they still are, in her incredible palazzo with its lofty courtyard, some of it transported stone by stone from Venice. Ellen gave special eye to John Singer Sargent's portrait of her hostess, gowned in tight-fitting black with no ornament except a rope of pearls around her wasp waist. A year after Sargent did Mrs. Jack, he painted Ellen as Lady Macbeth in her famous costume adorned with real beetle wings. A Boston oasis for Ellen was Oliver Wendell Holmes' house on Beacon Street. "Oh, the visits I inflicted on him," Ellen recalled. Since her visits were usually in winter, they moved their chairs close to

the fireplace and, as Ellen said, "At once it was four feet on a fender." Ellen could contribute to the literary chatter, for in London she mingled with Tennyson, Browning, Dante Gabriel Rossetti, Lewis Carroll, Wilde and Whistler.

In Chicago, which she had heard was barbaric, the audience greeted *Hamlet* ecstatically, and Ellen felt that her Ophelia had never been better.

After two days in Detroit, the company took a day off to sight-see near Buffalo, and Ellen began her long love-hate relationship with Niagara Falls. ". . . it became dreadful . . . I was *frightened* at it . . . wanted to follow the great flow of it." At another time she was overcome by its beauty, "with pits of color in its waters, no one color definite. All was wonderment, allurement, fascination." At her final visit it was "wonderful but not beautiful any more . . . the merely marvelous has always repelled me."

Moving to Toronto, Ellen indulged her enthusiasm for snow, and went tobogganing, accompanied by some young sportsmen. "I should say it was like flying! The start! Amazing! 'Farewell to this world,' I thought as I felt my breath go. . . . I rolled right out of the toboggan when we stopped. . . . Henry Irving would not come, much to my disappointment. He said that quick motion through the air always gave him the ear-ache."

After a week in Washington, where Ellen and Irving dined at the White House with President Chester A. Arthur, the company made a hit-and-run tour of five New England cities, while Ellen, needing a rest, stayed an extra week in the Capital.

Her first American tour, which wound up back in New York, ended in a flurry of farewell toasts and poems, and the beautiful news that the tour had grossed nearly a half-million dollars. To be sure, Ellen and Irving would return—again and again.

During the Lyceum company's second tour in 1884, Ellen wired the children's guardian to send one of them over to America. By not specifying which one, she wisely avoided any hint of favoritism. The guardian brought over Teddy, who arrived in time for Christmas dinner in Pittsburgh, and joined the company as a minor juvenile actor in Chicago.

Almost half American

In January 1888, while they were in New York, Irving and Ellen were dining at the Hoffman House, a Broadway hotel, and not rushing their meal because a terrific snowstorm had hit the city, and they assumed that their performance of *Faust* would be canceled. The wind reached 84 miles an hour. Electric light poles were blown down. Frost had cut off gas supplies. But, close to curtain time, a messenger ran into the

Onstage, the team of Terry and Irving. Was there an offstage romance? No one could ever say.

dining room, announcing that their audience had started to assemble. Hearing the news, a dozen male diners formed a rescue squad and took turns carrying Miss Terry on their shoulders for 12 blocks, or what might have been across the snow fields of Alaska, to the Star Theater. Ellen played to a very small audience, which included New York's Mayor and his daughter, but the show was a roaring success, and for once, in contrast to that epic blizzard of '88, the hellfires of *Faust* looked comfortably warm and cozy.

In the summer of 1893, the Lyceum stars, after a train ride across Canada, opened in San Francisco. No matter how often Ellen visited America, she reacted strongly to what she saw, for or against, or both. In California, she wrote, "For spite of fruits and flowers, the marvelous bay and the Golden Gate, there is printed on the face of the people, 'This-is-America-the-home-of-the-money-getter-Mammon-is-our-God,' and it spoils their faces and voices, although I *must* admit I don't think it spoils their hearts, for they are kindly to excess." In Mammon's hotbed she noted with approval that while in London the largest Lyceum receipts for a single night were £430, in San Francisco they exceeded £1,000 ($5,000).

Next on the route were one- or two-night stands in Portland, Seattle and Tacoma: "... Sleeping two nights in the Cars—(Oh, I don't like that.) I shall be glad to get to Chicago." She arrived there, via Minnesota, at the time of the nation's first great world's fair.

One of the reporters, who interviewed her on the train, wrote, "She persists in talking about her son, who has been very naughty and married a very beautiful and adorable girl." Then the reporter succumbed to Ellen herself, who was 46, extolling her "vast vintage of youth which mellows, not fades; she exults in her years, not shrinks at their approach." He noted further that she was "supple as a tiger," and her eyes

were "turquoise stars," and marveled that the "breezy creature sitting on the dusty floor of the car . . . could have a marriageable family. In proof, she called a dark-eyed girl from the compartment and introduced her as 'my daughter.' "

In Chicago Ellen received the news from her son that his new wife was pregnant. "Darling Boy," she wrote back, "I've just got your letter and May's postscript . . . I'm wishing nothing but that I were home—but that cannot be. Thank God, you are not both *here*, streaming about this unquiet galloping country. One wants extraordinary physical order to cope with America."

As for the world's fair, Ellen was too excited about being a grandmother to pay it much attention. She merely wrote, "This Chicago has gone mad over itself and its Fair—and certainly it has reason to be proud." She made no mention that she herself, in Sargent's portrait of her as Lady Macbeth, was hung at the fair. In fact, the big art exhibit might have seemed like old home week to Ellen, including as it did a dozen paintings by her London friends: Sir Lawrence Alma-

At height of American visit she displayed
chiseled beauty sparked by blue eyes, a face
that might have launched a thousand
ships on the oceans of applause it created.

Tadema, Ford Madox Brown, John Millais and her ex-husband, George Frederick Watts, at the time one of England's most successful painters, whom she married when he was 46. (She was 16; they separated within a year.)

On the next tour she and Irving played Washington again and dined at the White House, this time with Grover Cleveland, and then headed farther south. From New Orleans she wrote to her son, who had adopted the name Gordon Craig, "The *Sunny* South, indeed? They should call it the dusty South, I think. We have had a most uncomfortable but interesting week traveling in the Southern States. Poor places! Defeated (as *places*), all gone to bits and dust. No money to mend, to tinker, to repair, and keep in order stately homes and beautiful gardens. The people are very nice, but their houses are naught. In the North the houses are nice and (*some* of) the people are naught. . . . This hotel we are staying in has huge rooms, and I feel as if I were staying in modern Venice one moment, and then I'm reminded of Old Paris, again the dusty rooms and streets suggest Bloomsbury . . ." (a London enclave for intellectuals).

At this time, Ellen befriended two young actors in the company, Mr. and Mrs. Ben Webster III. Ben came from an old theatrical clan and his wife was to become the stage and screen star, Dame May Whitty. May was not always happy on her first American trip. She griped about the muddy, smelly streets, about a rat that crouched on the edge of her bathtub, and about Ellen Terry's little sideline project. At odd hours, Ellen was directing a one-act play about a medieval leper colony, written by Irving's son, Laurence, and performed eventually at a special matinee in Chicago. "We're rehearsing that filthy leper play," May wrote from New Orleans to a friend; it "takes up all our time, it's such a muddle owing to the erratic Nell's

stage management." May liked to tease Ellen and poke fun at her, but she admired her extravagantly. Thanks to May, we see how Ellen met a disaster that almost ended the leper play, and her career, altogether.

After leaving New Orleans for Memphis, the show train ran into a heavy storm, with floods and washouts along the line. The train had to crawl on a wooden trestle over a marshy area, where the rising waters began to cover the tracks. In one car Ellen and Irving gazed out at a parade of floating wreckage: fence posts, chicken coops, pots and pans, and, here and there, on a stray plank, coiled snakes.

The passengers knew that at any moment the wooden trestle might buckle, and the engine explode and sink with a sizzle, dragging all the cars to oblivion. According to May Webster's report, Edy rushed in from another car to comfort her mother, only to find her with her gloves neatly buttoned and tying on her veil. With perfect calmness, Ellen addressed her daughter: "Edy, darling! Hurry and dress yourself, we shall

Bernard Shaw wrote the play for her. Ellen promoted Carew to a starring role, and married him.

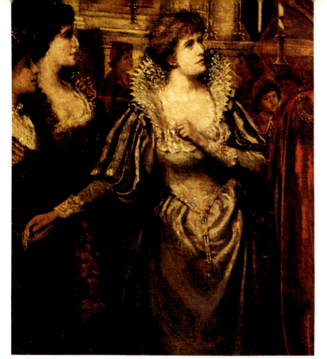

If walls could speak, this one surely would. Ellen, in full regalia, as painted by noted tragedian J. Forbes-Robertson, in Shakespearean scene, which today adorns a wall of The Players in New York.

probably have to swim." The company finally reached Memphis, late, hungry, but dry.

By now Ellen was saying, "I often feel that I am half American." In her mind, her tours were associated not only with her stage career, but with her family problems and emotional crises, many of which were played out against an American panorama. In Memphis she received a letter from her son, Teddy, hinting that he and his wife were about to separate, a prospect that dismayed Ellen because her own marriages had been so unsuccessful. A few weeks later she was further shocked by discovering that Edy, who seemed an aloof and starchy young lady, had fallen painfully in love with a married actor in the troupe. In Chicago, the "filthy leper play" came off far better than anyone expected. But two days later she learned that her beloved younger sister, "Floss," had died in childbirth in London. In Philadelphia an increasing chill in her long and loving relationship with Irving—though nobody knew how physically "loving" it had been—moved her to write her son, "I scarcely see much of Henry except in the confounded theater." And from Pittsburgh she wrote him, "I am as blue as indigo."

But on her next American tour in October 1899, her outlook changed. "New York is more marvelous than ever," she wrote to Teddy from the Plaza Hotel at Central Park and Fifth Avenue. (On this same site the present Plaza Hotel was built in 1910.) "We were knee deep in flowers, letters, gifts of all sorts before we had been here six hours."

Since Teddy had suddenly begun to show his striking talent in the visual arts, Ellen appointed herself his sales agent and took samples of his bookplates and illustrations to Scribner's, Harper's and other American publishers, and urged such stores as Brentano's and Wanamaker's to carry them. Temporarily, at least, Ellen and Irving felt closer to each other again, for America was their joint territory, crowded with memories. From Toledo, Ohio, Ellen wrote to George Bernard Shaw about the new play he had written for her, *Captain Brassbound's Conversion*. Ellen had been having reservations about its merits (she was right). A year later, she took her seventh and last U.S. tour with Irving, and felt the old thrill: ". . . lovely day . . . New York wondrously improved. . . ."

A blend of circumstances ended the partnership of Ellen and Irving. They parted amicably, she found work with other managements, and Irving, after several battles with illness, died in 1905. Ellen began to think more kindly of Shaw's play, and agreed to act in it. In the cast was a stalwart young man named James Carew, newly arrived in London, who played a secondary role of a naval officer. Ellen found him immensely attractive, and he was dazzled by her charm and eminence. In 1907 they took *Captain Brassbound's Conversion* on an American tour, with Jim Carew promoted to the title role. They were secretly married in Pittsburgh. Since Ellen was in her late 50s and he in his 30s, it was, perhaps, a foolish business. Yet they enjoyed two years or so of happiness, and remained good friends after they separated. Carew can rightly be called part of her American experience. He was born in Indiana.

Ellen ended her career as she started it: barnstorming—over land and sea—from the Palace Pier Theater at Brighton to Australia. Revisiting America, she trouped her one-woman Shakespeare show from New York to Seattle, where she had acted with Irving—only this time she ventured still farther to Vancouver, where her reputation for informality had obviously preceded her. "Ellen Terry is not coming to Vancouver to act," boasted a local paper, "she is coming to talk, chat, gossip (thank heaven not to 'lecture')."

Ellen died in 1928 in her ancient thatched cottage in Kent. Her memory was failing, but fragments of America turned up in her mind like colors in a kaleidoscope: the red brick sidewalks of Philadelphia and, as she once put it, "the low houses with their white marble cuffs and collars;" Chicago, when it was "snowing madly . . . marvelous;" West Point, where she and Irving performed *The Merchant of Venice* in a lecture hall and all the cheering cadets tossed their caps in the air; and New York, arriving there in a blue and gold October, and writing home to Teddy, "They are the wonderfullest people—the Americans."

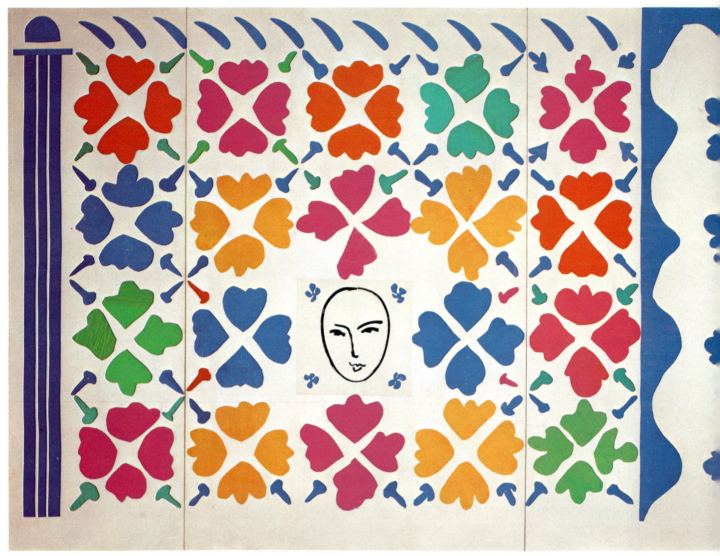

By John Russell

This inspired, efflorescent work, in which a
lively spontaneity exists alongside order, was

Final flowering
of Henri Matisse,
invincible artist

*In his last years, infirm but undaunted,
a grand master of the modern era
made great art with paper and scissors*

No one who was around at the time will ever forget
the impact of Matisse's cut-paper works of art when
they were first shown in Paris in 1949. It was as if
painting itself had been reborn. Matisse in arith-
metical terms was an old man—his 80th birthday fell
on December 31, 1949—but the cut-papers came
across with an effect of youth and exhilaration which
was all the more welcome at a time when there was
very little else in Paris to rejoice at.

For Paris in 1949 was an exhausted and a divided
city. Though virtually undamaged in World War II,
it was in physical terms a glum and shabby place in
which almost everything was in short supply. Five
years of German occupation had left a legacy of hatred
and recrimination, one which sundered Frenchman
from Frenchman.

Henri Matisse was as exempt from political feeling
as a man can be, and he certainly did not intend his
cut-paper compositions as an alternative to the dis-

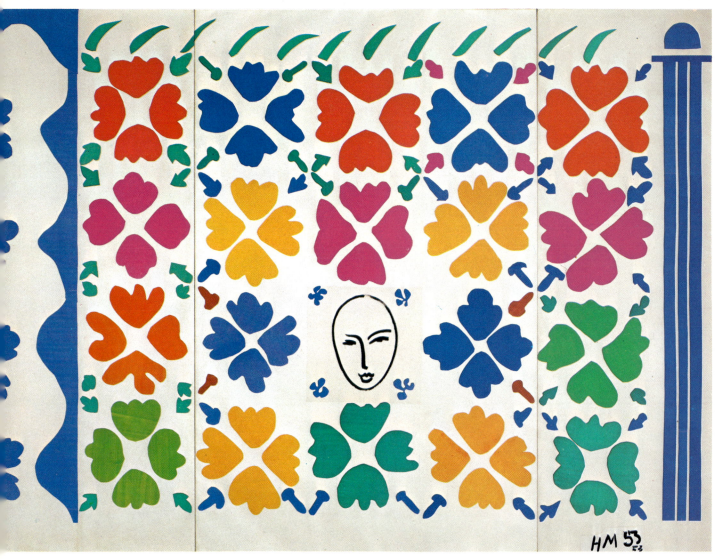

created by Matisse in 1953, when he was
84. He called it *Large Decoration with Masks*.

tresses of the day. But that is how they struck us, nonetheless. What they had to offer was in the highest sense a moral lesson. We felt about them as the German poet Rainer Maria Rilke had felt about a certain sculpture just 50 years earlier. "After this," he wrote, "we must live differently."

Matisse had done the right thing at the right time. He contributed to the convalescence of Europe in ways which can still be descried in the comprehensive exhibition of his cut-paper paintings which has been organized by Jack Cowart of the St. Louis Art Museum with assistance from John Hallmark Neff of the Detroit Institute of Arts. It will be seen initially at the National Gallery of Art in Washington from September 10 to October 23, 1977, and later in Detroit (November 23, 1977, to January 8, 1978) and St. Louis (January 29 to March 12, 1978).

Matisse had always intended his paintings to make people feel better. As early as 1908 he said that he

dreamed of an art which "could be for every mental worker, for the businessman as well as for the man of letters, for example, a soothing, calming influence on the mind, something like a good armchair which provides relaxation from physical fatigue." And the cut-papers can beyond a doubt be enjoyed in that way: more so, indeed, than most of Matisse's oils. Our cares vanish at once in the presence of those bright incorporeal scraps of paper, whereas when Matisse puts brush to canvass a sympathetic witness will sense the magnitude of the task which he has set himself. In the oils, the whole of art history is on his back; but what we see in the cut-papers is the art that conceals art.

But if the cut-paper compositions contributed to the convalescence of Europe, it is primarily because

New York Times art critic John Russell last wrote about Vollard in the July issue of SMITHSONIAN.

It can be relished just for color and shape,
but it's *Swimmer in the Pool.*

convalescence is what they are about. Matisse made them, that is to say, at a time when he had come back from the very edge of the grave and was in no state to make paintings in any other way. In 1941, when he was 71 years old, Matisse underwent a drastic and extensive internal operation. When it was over, and he was seen to be getting better, his nurses called him "the man who came back from the dead"; but for the rest of his life he was too weak to stand for long at a time and his powers of endurance in general were greatly diminished. Most men of his age and position would have settled for an honorable if precarious retirement. There was no reason, after all, for him to go on working. He had proved himself over and over again to be one of the great artists of all time—as an easel painter, as a muralist, as a sculptor, as a printmaker and, yet again, as a master of the illustrated book.

But he was hardly clear of the surgeon's knife

A daring summation in oil, the master's towering
Large Interior in Red, his farewell to easel painting.

Musée National d'Art Moderne, Centre Georges Pompidou, Paris

when he wrote to a friend that he had derived great moral benefit from the operation. "I see clearly, now," he said. "I have my whole career in focus, and its continuity, also." "Continuity" is the key word in that remarkable sentence. Matisse had always had a genius for continuity; or, to put it another way, continuity had always been fundamental to his genius. He knew when to concentrate on easel painting, and when to give it a rest. He knew when his ideas could best be put into sculpture, and he also knew when he was ready for a large-scale decorative scheme like the one for the Barnes Foundation in Merion, Pennsylvania. He was never idle, but what is more to the point in this context is that he seems never to have gone off on the wrong track. Continuity was fundamental to everything that he did; and continuity was nothing more than an instinct—infallible —for what he needed to be doing at any given time.

Even so, it was rash for him to speak of continuity in the spring of 1941. He had read in a medical textbook that even if he got through his operation he was unlikely to live more than another year or so.

Initially it meant a refusal to give in to nature. In this, he had Auguste Renoir in mind. Matisse had

Henri Matisse's final flowering

known Renoir towards the end of World War I, when Matisse was first living in Nice and Renoir was at Cagnes, a few miles away. "During those last years of his life," Matisse said later, "Renoir was just a bundle of pain. He had to be carried about in a chair. He fell into it like a dead man. His hands were bandaged, his fingers were twisted like the roots of a tree, he could no longer hold a brush. They used to have to push the brush through the bandages so that he could somehow get a hold on it. The first movement was so painful that he winced. But after half an hour, when he got going, he rose from the dead. I have never seen a happier man. And I swore that when the time came I, too, would have the courage to go on."

Continuity to Matisse meant carrying on with ideas that had haunted him all his life, but also finding a completely new way of expressing them.

Matisse got back to his home above the city of Nice just as soon as he could. Though he was without any kind of conventional religious belief, he did undeniably feel in his last years that fate was taking a hand in his affairs. By June 1941 he was painting and drawing again; and before long he was also at work on illustrated books (one of them already planned before 1941, the others new projects). Matisse never took a commission lightly; and the illustrations for the poems of Ronsard, in particular, occupied him on and off from 1941 to 1948. What had been intended as a book with 30 lithographed illustrations turned out to be a book with 126 of them, for Matisse even in old age was a prodigious worker. He went on doubling the stakes until in 1948 he painted one of the largest and most audacious of all his easel pictures: the *Large Interior in Red*.

This *Large Interior* can be construed as a majestic farewell to painting as Matisse had been practicing it since he was first given a box of colors in 1890.

Except that it includes no human figure, it is made up of just about everything that Matisse most liked to paint: an interior saturated with a single color, two strong tables with curvilinear legs, a tall thin Dutch chair to add a vertical emphasis, as many bouquets of flowers as the tables can carry, and two animal-skin rugs. The flatness of those skins has a vital part to play in the argument of the picture. Our instinct is to fill them out, as we fill out the idea of a tiger or a leopard if someone speaks of them in life. But their unwonted flatness makes us look more closely at all the other objects which are portrayed in the painting, and not least at the two pictures which hang on the wall. Matisse always enjoyed painting a picture-within-the-picture, and in this final summation of his endeavors as a painter he put in two of them side by side: a big painting of a pineapple on a chair and a no less imposing drawing in black and white. What Matisse went after in this big drawing was an alternative interior: one which would hold its own against the brilliant color of the rest of the painting and yet stick rigorously to black and white. Just how he achieved it is a miracle of midcentury painting.

There was no question, therefore, of any falling-off in Matisse's capacities. But there was a falling-off in his physical strength, and after the *Large Interior in Red* there was one of those natural pauses which had occurred after every great climax in his career. Nothing more could be done in that particular line. The practicalities of the Vence chapel—that sublime little building, a conjoined triumph of art, architecture and spirit, that Matisse engendered in the south of France—filled much of his time for the next three years. But there was a sense in which destiny had still some choosing to do on his behalf, and it was this choosing that led to the creation of the cut-papers.

Drawing on the idea bank

Three things were in question. One was the ambition for which he found words in 1943. "Everything seems to indicate," he said to the poet Louis Aragon, "that before long I shall start work on some large-scale compositions, as if I had my whole life before me, or the whole of another life." The second motor element in the cut-paper works was the idea bank which Matisse had been building up for years. They were ideas which didn't suit for easel painting, didn't suit for sculpture, and didn't suit for drawing in pencil or ink. And then there was a third factor: the grim one. Matisse just wasn't well enough, and would never again be well enough, to make major art in any of the ways that he had made it before. Only two possibilities were open to him: retirement or a new start. He chose the new start, and the cut-

248

Done in 1949, *The Dancer* evokes the essential ideas of freedom of motion and form which go with the title, but there is, also, the superb abstract design so typical of Matisse's late decorative paperworks.

paper "paintings" came as the result of that choice.

The technique in itself was not new to him. Already in 1933, when he was working on his mural for the Barnes Foundation, he realized that it would take forever to paint a full-size draft for every possibility that occurred to him. Yet at the same time he needed to think as much in terms of scale as of design. If he cut his design out of large sheets of painted paper he could adjust and revise and recombine as often as he pleased and with a minimal loss of time. He did find, however, that the cut-paper medium had a life, and almost a will, of its own. It was not content to be just a superior subterfuge. It was a medium in its own right, and quite possibly a medium of unguessed potential.

So he turned it over in his mind. He used it for a magazine cover, and he tried it out as a basis for a still-life painting, and gradually it became clear to him that it could bear the weight of ideas for which the slower, heavier, more conventional modes of expression were merely so many forms of inhibition. Cut paper set him free; in the 1940s he gave it its first big chance in the book which he called *Jazz*.

Jazz was something quite new for Matisse. It was the first of his books which was entirely his own invention. No great writer stood behind it. The texts were by Matisse himself. The images were without precedent in his work. They were built up by the cut-paper process, and they drew upon experiences which he had stored up for many years. Even the title was significant: "jazz" 30 years ago had a jaunty, off-beat, transatlantic implication which was quite contrary to the rules of the School of Paris. *Jazz*, in a word, was no less than a declaration of independence and Matisse did not make the choice lightly.

Matisse himself summed up the source material of *Jazz*. "The images in these lively and violent prints," he wrote, "come from memories of the circus, popular stories, and travel." This one sentence tells us to what an extent the cut-paper medium liberated Matisse from the inhibitions imposed upon him by high art and the French tradition.

But *Jazz* was not composed according to the principles of high art. Matisse took sheets of colored paper and he cut into them with scissors. Preliminary drawing as such had no part in the operation. He felt as if he were cutting into pure color, the way a sculptor cuts into marble. The scruples and inhibitions of high art dropped away, and he dipped into his unconscious with an unprecedented freedom.

It was on quite a small scale, however, in physical terms. There was no question, in *Jazz*, of the large-

The subject of this lyric work entitled *Women and Monkeys*, created in 1952, is incidental

scale compositions of which he had spoken in 1943 (*Jazz* came out in 1947). He could work on it in bed; for anything larger, other methods would have to be found. Luckily, he had at his disposal that most disinterested of assistants, Madame Lydia Delectorskaya. With her assistance he was soon able to work with a big pair of shears on very much larger sheets of painted paper. These were then pinned up and eventually transferred onto canvas under his direction. Many of them were very large indeed: 12 feet by 25 feet was nothing unusual, and the National Gallery of Art's *Large Decoration with Masks* (pp. 244-245) measures 139 by 393 inches. But one and all of them have it in common that they look as if they had been wished out of the air, instantaneously and without human intervention. Nothing could be further from the truth, of course, but the effect is what Matisse would have wanted.

The subject matter of these later and larger cut-papers is not as unexpected as the subject matter of *Jazz*. He had made botanical drawings which foreshadowed the adaptations of nature in the cut-papers, just as he had made sculptures which foreshadowed the poses of the heavy-limbed girls who move in and out of these new and colossal spaces. But there were monkeys and acrobats, masks and elements of architecture which have no parallel elsewhere in his work. There were abbreviations of form which remind us of how his teacher Gustave Moreau once said to him, "Matisse, you were born to simplify painting"; and there were large compositions in which for the first time in his life he came near to a decorative abstraction. Matisse was at a stage at which he was free to do whatever he liked, and in the cut-papers he found the ideal medium in which to do it.

These great works were soon shown here and there, all over the world, as occasion offered. The most important ones ranged in date between 1950 and 1954, though numerous trial runs dated from much earlier and certain tapestry designs done in 1946 were made from cut-paper cartoons.

It should be one of the merits of the upcoming exhibition that it promises us for the first time a comprehensive and informed study of exactly how well these great works are standing the test of time as physical objects.

How well they will last as physical objects is a matter for the specialists, and we must hope that the specialists will come up with the right answer, just as Matisse came up with the right answer when nature said to him "It's time you stopped painting," and he told nature what to do with her advice.

to what is, in its essence, a celebration of the singing spirit of the indomitable artist in his old age.

Galerie Beyeler, Basel

In a sideshow sequence in *Parade*, hands form designs on the tattooed man: butterfly and fire adorn legs; pumping heart is below large open mouth. Hands of other actors depict phrase, "New Deaf Dominion."

By Jean Stratton

The 'eye-music' of deaf actors fills stage eloquently

In its newest production, Parade, *National Theatre of the Deaf combines sign language, mime and humor to create unique drama*

Tension filled the crowded auditorium. Houselights dimmed, voices were stilled, and the audience readied itself for what was to follow. It was one of those tantalizing moments that occur just before any live performance, whether it be musical comedy, drama, opera, dance, even the circus. But this audience was about to experience a new type of theater, a very special blend of words and movement unlike any other seen before. The National Theatre of the Deaf was about to present its new production, *Parade* (the subject of the photographs on these pages), and any skepticism in the audience regarding deaf actors would soon dissolve in enthusiasm for the entertainment's swirl of color and movement and its panache.

It is also one of the rare occasions when the subject matter of an NTD production deals with deafness itself. In *Parade*, a professor recalls his own graduation from a high school of deaf students and remembers a march to Washington in which he participated. He tells the audience of the hopes and expectations the marchers had for their "New Deaf Dominion," a place where they would be free from the condescension and "special" treatment to which the deaf are frequently subjected, a place where they could be individuals and live as they wished and develop their own ideas.

As the professor reminisces, time suddenly freezes and we see the parade itself unfold—a montage of marches, rallies, speeches, demonstrations, dances, all with accompanying banners and floats, colorful costumes, and punctuated with stinging commentary on

the state of the world, both hearing and deaf. It is a parade into the past, too, as farcical sketches range from the Old West to Columbus' discoveries (see cover) to Biblical episodes, viewed from the vantage point of the deaf. More recent times are represented by a variety of comic vignettes and events—a carnival of the deaf filled with weird and wonderful characters: "As the Hand Turns," a special deaf soap opera; "The Adventures of Mr. Silence," the deaf version of Superman; and "Cinderella and the Magic Glove," a slapstick rendition of the fairy tale.

Throughout, emphasis is on the importance of sight to the deaf—for example, their visual rather than verbal language. The "star" of many sketches is the hand.

Indeed, central to any NTD production is the use of sign-mime, a combination of sign language and mime which is really a theatrical extension of the manual language by which many deaf people communicate. However, the spoken word is another element of these productions. Usually, three or four hearing speakers or narrators are integrated totally into the action of the play and speak the lines at the same time they are signed by the other actors. This alliance of speech and sign gives the NTD a unique place in theater history. The words increase the understanding of the sign (85 percent of the audiences are hearing and therefore do not know sign language), while the sign enhances the meaning of the words.

Help from The Miracle Worker

Parade is the NTD's 19th major production. Established in 1967 under the auspices of the Eugene O'Neill Memorial Theater Center, the company of deaf actors, numbering anywhere from 11 to 16, has given more than 1,500 performances. It has had 18 tours across the United States (including two Broadway runs and missing only four states), eight tours of Europe, Asia and Australia, and also visits to Israel and Canada. Critical acclaim has been nearly unanimous. Audiences increase every year, and the NTD has grown into one of the most consistently busy acting companies in the United States. As David Hays, award-winning Broadway scenic designer and now managing director of the NTD, says, "When funds are being curtailed elsewhere due to the economy, we're increasing our bookings by ten percent each year."

This is a far cry from what existed just nine years ago. Although amateur deaf acting companies abounded, there was no professional company. In fact, the thought of one would have seemed strange to many people. With the advent of *The Miracle Worker* in 1958, the play dealing with the life and ultimately successful struggle of Helen Keller to overcome both blindness and deafness, the idea of deaf theater took

Photographs by Bill Ray

253

The universe . . .　　　　　　*of the deaf . . .*　　　　　　*wants [you] . . .*

In a speech by Linda Bove, one sees that sign language, like all others, depends on context and flow. At far left, sign for universe could also be upswing of sign for "name." Third from left, sign is actually for "wish."

firm hold. In 1964 the Eugene O'Neill Memorial Theater Center was established in Waterford, Connecticut, to promote live theater in various ways.

When David Hays helped establish the O'Neill Center in 1964, he proposed the idea of a national deaf theater and the Center agreed to act as a sponsor. The Rehabilitation Services Administration of the U.S. Department of Health, Education and Welfare awarded the NTD a $140,000 grant for training, rehearsal and preparation for tours. On tour the company had to earn its own way. Contributions have been received from foundations and private donors, and the government has continued to fund the theater, seeing it as a means of creating pride among the deaf and of correcting public misconceptions. David Hays confirms what the NTD's backers have hoped. He observes that it "is the most successful social theater in America. In our plays, the social aspect is built in. The constant exposure of NTD has led to a revolution in the deaf world —their increased pride, self-image, demands."

For even today, the deaf are sometimes regarded as rather strange. The Old Testament found it necessary to warn against mistreatment: "Thou shalt not curse the deaf." The terms deaf-mute and deaf-and-dumb lead some people to believe deafness always includes an inability to speak. One who cannot hear has difficulty speaking clearly because he cannot hear the sounds he is attempting to form, but there is nothing wrong with a deaf person's vocal cords.

In the 18th century, in an effort to bring religious education to young deaf people who had been denied any education at all, a French priest, the Abbé Charles Michel de l'Eppé, constructed and codified a sign language based on the signs and gestures by which his pupils communicated with one another. It has been described as "a visual equivalent of spoken language . . . a true language, independent of speech and hearing, dependent instead on the hand and eye." An expanded form of this hand language is used today in the United States by many deaf persons to communicate with each other, and in an extended form to suit the purposes of the theater.

Once the NTD got under way, its artistic and theatrical goals became paramount. The staff set about gathering the best deaf actors they could find, and one of the first recruited was Bernard Bragg, already a professional. After graduating in 1952 from Gallaudet College in Washington, D.C. (the only accredited liberal arts college for the deaf), Bragg studied mime with Marcel Marceau in Paris and later toured the United States, performing in colleges and nightclubs and appearing in a television series, *The Quiet Man*. Tall, agile and good-looking, Bragg (p. 257) has been called "the man with the golden voice in his hands."

His versatility is given a splendid showcase in *Parade*. Enacting the pivotal role of the professor, whose reminiscences of the parade he embarked upon

Formerly a reporter with Life *magazine, Jean Stratton is now a free-lance writer based in New York.*

 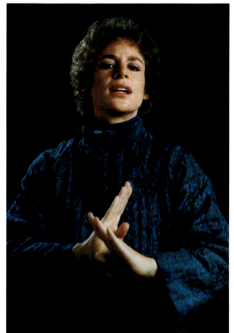 

At far right, she is finger-spelling and is seen between letters. A literal translation sounds awkward but, in colloquial English, she would be saying something like the sequence of words above these pictures.

as a young man form the basis of the play, Bragg also assumes other characterizations during the production. Moving easily from the role of an Indian in "How the West Was Won" to the husband of Madame Rose, the great deaf fortune-teller in "The Astounding Astonishing Carnival of the Deaf," he tops it off with a rousingly provocative "hand" striptease, concluding the routine with the removal of an imaginary glove. And what is undoubtedly one of the play's most affecting moments occurs when he sensitively describes his hopes and dreams for the "New Deaf Dominion, the city built by silent hands."

In 1967 the theater was ready for its first tour, its program a varied repertoire of poetry and short plays. Among them were adaptations of William Saroyan's *My Heart's in the Highlands* and Puccini's opera *Gianni Schicchi*; "Tyger! Tyger!" based on William Blake's *Songs of Experience*; and *The Tale of Kasane*, a Japanese Kabuki play. Audience reaction was almost completely favorable. Some playgoers confused the theater *of* the deaf with a theater *for* the deaf and were thus sometimes dragged to the theater, reluctantly but dutifully supporting what they thought to be a worthy cause. Occasionally, hints of condescension cropped up—the attitude of "Aren't they wonderful, in spite of their handicap!" But in most cases reaction was one of surprise and then delight with the NTD's innovative and vibrant performances.

Professional criticism, too, has been substantially approving, although on occasion the question is raised whether the sign becomes simply an illustration for the spoken word and unable to stand on its own merits. One critic referred to the social aspect of the NTD and wondered whether this became such an overriding issue that the performances would not measure up as valid theater. Such doubts, however, seem to have been answered by the increasing numbers of satisfied people who attend the performances.

Especially successful productions were adaptations of Sheridan's *The Critic*, Dylan Thomas' *Under Milk Wood*, and a striking performance of one of the oldest known literary works, *Gilgamesh*. Predating Homer by more than 1,000 years, it encompasses the life and struggles of the man-god Gilgamesh to achieve everlasting life. Directed by Larry Arrick (who also directed *Parade*), its bold imagery was suited to NTD's style. Director Arrick, who has been associated with the theater for nearly four years, describes the choice of *Gilgamesh* and the unique ability of the NTD in bringing this robust epic to life. "I was at the O'Neill with the National Theater Institute and suggested to David Hays a work of literature in which I was interested, *Gilgamesh*. It was a Sumerian composition, inscribed on clay tablets. It's mythic in nature, a series of poetic images. I was very excited by the possibilities of what could be done here. The company has extraordinary strength. They carve language in the air. Theatrically, their language is far more evocative than our speech is."

The NTD continued to "carve language in the air"

255

with television productions as well as stage works. Its interpretation of Dylan Thomas' *A Child's Christmas in Wales* with Michael Redgrave appeared as a CBS special. Prior to this, the company had also appeared in the NBC series, *Experiment in Television*. *Sesame Street,* the popular children's program, has also been a vehicle for deaf actors and actresses, and one, Linda Bove (pp. 254-255), has been a permanent resident of the "Street" for five years.

Petite, animated and dynamic, Linda is a vivid exponent of the NTD, an excellent example of the company's special aliveness. She wants to understand and to be understood and she expresses herself with constantly changing facial expression and body movement, as well as signing and speaking. On stage, moreover, she is exceedingly nimble, moving with a litheness and agility which is especially apparent in the gymnastics and tumbling in which nearly all of the members participate.

Nowhere is this more apparent than in her role in *Parade.* Portraying Billie Dove, the determined and persuasive leader of the deaf group, she must cover a wide range of mood and action. Called upon to dance, lead cheers and perform gymnastics, she invests all with a dashing exuberance. At the same time, during her efforts to encourage the group to achieve its goal and not lose hope, she brings insight and reflection to the more serious intent of the play.

In addition, the group has generated a spin-off from the main company—the Little Theatre of the Deaf, with two companies which visit schools, and perform in theaters and on *Sesame Street* each year.

And what of future direction for the NTD actors? In addition to the ensemble productions, there could be a place for these actors in other media also. Deaf characters frequently appear in various productions, and there seems no reason that these roles could not be undertaken by deaf actors. Such works as *Johnny Belinda* and *The Miracle Worker* are only two possibilities which come to mind. Some time ago, the television series *The Waltons* had a deaf character in its show. Television programming offers potential for deaf actors. In fact, there has already been a breakthrough. Linda Bove had a role in the popular daytime serial *Search for Tomorrow* for five months.

The former director of *Search for Tomorrow*, Bruce Minnix, believes strongly in the use of deaf actors in deaf roles. Describing the added realism they bring, he says, "Having a deaf actress play the role added reality to the production and to the other actors' roles."

Using a deaf actress presented a fascinating problem for the director. "For example," says Minnix, "Linda watches a hearing person very closely. Listening is the key. She could not be in a position where she couldn't see the other person's face. We had to make sure she was positioned so that she could always see the other people. And we widened shots to include her hands."

NTD director Larry Arrick also emphasizes the need for concentration and the propensity NTD actors have for it. "They must perceive, they must always be watching. This is an enormous demand. Exhausting."

Rehearsals last from 9 A.M. to 6 P.M., although the actors warm up with calisthenics at 7:30 so their day is even longer. Director and actors communicate primarily through an NTD interpreter, Nikki Kilpatrick. One of the hardest workers, she must be on call at all rehearsals to help with the director's changes and the actors' responses. Born to deaf parents, she learned to sign before she could speak, so that sign is quite literally her first language.

Translating a script into sign

Rehearsals can be frustrating. Words are not always readily translated into sign, and the NTD tries to avoid finger spelling since it is rarely effective dramatically. At times Bernard Bragg, who is sign master, is called upon to invent new signs. Playwright Jeff Wanshel, who helped create *Parade*, recalls just such a situation: "I can come up with a word or phrase—for example, the 'New Deaf Dominion'—and then find that no sign exists for it. Bernard Bragg may come up with one, but sometimes I have to change the word."

Developing and constructing an original production like *Parade* offers its own problems. The members of the company were heavily involved in the structuring of the play, contributing ideas and suggestions, objecting to and discarding others. "One of the problems with this particular original play," says Larry Arrick, "is that the subject is something I can only understand, not experience. It is a condition. I could stop up my ears with cotton, but it would not be the

Highlighting problem for deaf people in world of
sound is how to dance without music. In foreground

Bernard Bragg (on podium) directs while Julianna
Field and other cast members impersonate street traffic.

A Deaf Dominion would have its own soap operas.
In "As the Hand Turns," a nurse played by Julianna

Field and a doctor played by Joe Castronovo discuss
a crucial procedure through their surgical masks.

Deafness: "Suppose it is a calm day, absolutely still, not a twig or leaf stirring. To me it will seem quiet as a tomb though hedgerows are full of noisy but invisible birds. Then comes a breath of air, enough to unsettle a leaf; I will see and hear that movement like an exclamation. The illusory soundlessness has been interrupted. I see, as if I heard, a visionary noise of wind in a disturbance of foliage. Wordsworth in a late poem exactly caught the phenomenon in a remarkable line: 'A soft eye-music of slow-waving boughs. . . .' "

There is "eye-music" in all National Theatre of the Deaf performances—a ballet of darting fingers and a symphony of fluid motion. The theater is meant to be entertainment, but it is also communication, and true communication is more than just the transmittal of information from one person to another. To be truly effective it must connect and reach out, establish contact. The lines from Paul Simon's song first admonish, then implore:

People talking without speaking,
People hearing without listening . . .
Hear my words that I might teach you,
Take my arms that I might reach you.

Audiences seeing *Parade* or lucky enough to attend other National Theatre of the Deaf performances will know that they have been reached.

same experience. So I must try to impose a notion from my point of view on the piece. That, after all, is the point of the whole play. But the process takes a longer time, much longer, since the actors are involved so directly in the actual structure of the play. It can be tedious and time-consuming. Also it can be misleading. These actors are all graduates of college, so their experiences are not likely to be the same as those of all deaf people."

Arrick does not believe, as do some, that deaf actors are more expressive than others in face and body; they are, instead, different in their ways and means of expression. "It is essential for anyone working with them to acknowledge these differences and make them virtues." To do otherwise could border on condescension. Bruce Minnix noted the risk of this also. "We had to take care that we did not condescend and treat Linda as a child when we tried to catch her attention. Then, on the other hand, we could run the risk of ignoring it too much. The problem exists. We could be in danger of being too glib."

Group members are actors first, however. Arrick says: "Ego is an important element in an actor. Of course they're professionals and accept decisions for the good of the show. These actors have the same feelings any actor has, and they can be upset if their scene is cut, and resist. They are a company, however, in the real sense of the word. Part of the ego thing is 'I want to look good so I can get another job,' but these actors are assured of employment."

Inescapably, one is struck by the quietness of a rehearsal when the actors are signing and the director and the others listening and watching. Watching is vital for these actors—as it is for any deaf person. British author David Wright, who became deaf as the result of an illness at the age of seven, described the reliance on visual evidence by the deaf in his book

In *Parade*, Ed Waterstreet plays the role of Mr. Silence, the Deaf Dominion's equivalent of Superman.

Linda Bove, as chief proponent of Deaf Dominion, exults as *Parade's* final parade nears the White House.

By Benjamin Forgey

Isamu Noguchi's elegant world of space and function

Five-city tour will show work of a protean master of three-dimensional form who shapes both inner and outer environments

Model for playground and (below) its 1976 realization, Piedmont Park, Atlanta. "I like to think," Noguchi

A lot of things are coming together this spring for Isamu Noguchi. First, there will be the large exhibition of his sculptures and other projects that will go on a yearlong, five-city tour of the United States, beginning at the Walker Art Center in Minneapolis on April 23. Next month the artist will be in upstate New York to direct things as a group of huge gray blocks of Japanese granite, carved and treated in the singular Noguchi style, are hauled and hoisted into position atop a grassy hill at the Storm King Art Center (SMITH-SONIAN, March 1977). In June, one of Noguchi's magnificent stone monoliths will be among the major artworks to confront visitors as they walk for the first time into the new East Building of the National Gallery of Art in Washington. The crowning touch, though, is the 13-acre Civic Center Plaza in downtown Detroit (cover), even now nearing completion, which Noguchi designed almost in its entirety.

It is, in a sense, about time for all of this to happen. Noguchi is 73. He has been working as an artist, draftsman, potter, sculptor, furniture- and theater-designer, lantern-maker, landscape architect, form-giver and all-around space-shaper for more than half a century. Throughout much of this period his importance as an artist—not to speak of his greatness—has been only grudgingly acknowledged. It is as if there are too many Noguchis to hold in the mind. "With Noguchi," says Martin Friedman, director of the Walker Art Center, "you get the feeling of being in many places at once."

says, "of playgrounds as primers of shape and function; simple, mysterious, and evocative: thus educational."

Noguchi has been, and still is, one of the more enigmatic luminaries in the annals of art. His personality and its logical extension in the material world—his art itself—are each as incredibly durable as the stones he loves and searches for the world over. But the man and his art are also difficult and secretive, almost impossible to classify or to pin down. They project opposing qualities: solitude and charm, order and explosiveness, harmony and dissonance, affirmation and despair.

It is Friedman's contention (and certainly Noguchi's, too) that there is a profound intellectual and stylistic consistency in the work, an overriding sensibility that unites the apparently disparate parts. Thus the forthcoming exhibition, entitled "Noguchi: Imaginary Landscapes," will focus as much upon Noguchi's environmental projects, realized and unrealized, and his stage sets and playgrounds, as upon individual works of sculpture. The aim: to make clear their crossbreeding.

This view of the wholeness of Noguchi's varied and far-flung enterprise has the feel of a fundamental truth. Perhaps it is only now that we can begin to perceive this truth, because the dizzy swirl of art fashions has largely been stilled and the cannonades of avant-garde ideologies have largely lost their zip. Also, Noguchi has been strong enough to weather a long, stormy life. By design or by luck, he has lived to become an old master of modernism.

Noguchi was born in Los Angeles in 1904. His father was Yone Noguchi, a widely known Japanese poet. His mother was Leonie Gilmour, an American writer and translator whose father had fled from Northern Ireland and whose mother was part American Indian. Noguchi's parents met in New York, in 1903. Their short, unhappy union had far-reaching consequences for their son, contributing especially to the fierce sense of isolation he has carried with him through the restless peregrinations of his life.

Thomas B. Hess, writing an early appreciation of Noguchi as a modern artist in 1946, observed how Noguchi "has carried his exile inside him like his skeleton . . . and has fused in his art the East and the West as they were fused in his body." More recently, in the Walker exhibition catalog, Friedman writes that Noguchi "operates in a curious limbo, culturally and artistically. In America he is regarded as a Japanese sculptor, and in Japan he is perceived as American."

Noguchi himself, relaxing after lunch in his Long Island City studio one chilly day last January, stated tartly, with no prodding, "I am not a Japanese artist. I am an American." And yet, only a decade ago, in the opening paragraph of his autobiography, *A Sculptor's*

Benjamin Forgey, art and architecture critic for the Washington Star, *wrote about the art of Michael Singer in January* SMITHSONIAN.

The Illusion of the Fifth Stone, 1967-68, was done in Japan, to which sculptor returns annually.

Noguchi's own garden, across from his studio, with works executed

Noguchi: "The essence of sculpture is for me perception of space, the continuum of existence."

World, he had written: "With my double nationality and double upbringing, where was my home? Where my affections? Where my identity? Japan or America, either, both—or the world?"

Yone Noguchi returned to Japan the year Isamu was born. The mother followed in 1906, but the couple soon separated. Isamu grew up with his mother in Chigasaki, a village near the sea, seldom seeing his father. His education was irregular; he attended the local grammar school, and then commuted to a French Jesuit elementary school in Yokohama.

One year, when he was about ten, he was kept out of school and semiapprenticed to a cabinetmaker in Chigasaki. He "instilled in me a great feeling for materials and the use of tools," Noguchi was to tell art critic Katharine Kuh nearly 50 years later.

When Noguchi was 13 it was decided that he should continue his education in the United States, and his mother sent him alone to Indiana to attend an experimental school she had read about in a magazine, one that stressed farming, carpentry and other practical skills. Noguchi arrived there in 1918 in time for summer camp, but he soon found himself literally alone: the school had been taken over by the U.S. Army.

After a wild year of independence, during which he camped out with two custodians in one of the school's

from 1956 to present. Foreground:
Unmei, or—in Japanese—"Fate."

The base of a Noguchi sculpture is an integral part
of its conception, as in this untitled piece, 1968.

deserted faculty buildings, Noguchi was unofficially adopted by Dr. Edward A. Rumely, founder of the forsaken school, who became, in Hess' interpretation, the "first of a series of substitute 'fathers' for the homeless, very lonely, exiled child. . . . By now the irony of exile at home is established."

Noguchi's talent having already manifested itself, Dr. Rumely, against his better judgment, acceded to the young student's desire to become an artist. He got in touch with his friend Gutzon Borglum (the Mount Rushmore sculptor) and arranged to have Noguchi employed as an apprentice in his Connecticut studio. The experience did not work out—Borglum told Noguchi he would never be a sculptor—so Noguchi followed Rumely's advice and in 1923 began premedical studies.

Noguchi was also working in a restaurant at night. Even so, he enrolled as a part-time scholarship student in an East Village settlement school—the Leonardo da Vinci Art School—run by Onorio Ruotolo, who, convinced that he had a burgeoning genius on his hands, gave Noguchi a one-man show after only three months in the school. Needless to say, premed studies soon were dropped.

This experience did not work out, either. Noguchi recalls that by age 21 he had run the academic gamut and was "disillusioned." By that time he had begun to

look around Manhattan and had located those few places hospitable to the new modern art. The crucial eye-opener was the one-man exhibit at the Brummer Gallery in 1926 of work by Constantin Brancusi, the great Romanian sculptor. Noguchi had no doubts: "I was transfixed by his vision."

The crucial door-opener was Harry F. Guggenheim, who had seen a piece by Noguchi and suggested indirectly that he apply for a then-new Guggenheim fellowship for study abroad. Alfred Stieglitz wrote a recommendation for him, and he got the fellowship.

The day after he arrived in Paris in April 1927, Noguchi was seated at the Café Flore where, providentially, he met an acquaintance of Brancusi's. The day after that he visited the studio. Brancusi, then 51 and at the height of his powers (and his celebrity), told Noguchi that he did not accept students. Noguchi then asked if he needed a stonecutter. The great man agreed.

"Certainly I was no help to him whatsoever in the beginning," Noguchi later wrote, "and results could have been obtained without being so particular; but, no, it had to be done just his way no matter how long it took me to master it. The large saws he used must not be forced but gently cut of their own weight. The wide blade of the axe leaves its mark and that is how it should be left—the direct contact of man and matter."

In 1961 Noguchi bought a small factory building in Long Island City, since augmented by a second,

In just this spirit are Noguchi's great stone monuments made today. Unquestionably, Brancusi exerted a lasting influence upon Noguchi, who was deeply receptive to the older artist's philosophy regarding materials and their treatment in the hands of an artist, and who shared Brancusi's profoundly respectful attitudes toward ancient, archaic sculpture and artifacts.

It is a debt Noguchi repeatedly acknowledges, and yet it has perhaps been made too much of, for the differences are great. Brancusi himself had predicted one difference when he told Noguchi "how lucky were the young people of the new generation such as myself, who could look forward to uninhibited and true abstractions, not like himself who always started out from some recognizable image in nature."

Not only are Noguchi's anthropomorphic and morphological forms more elusive than they are allusive—in short, more abstract—but Noguchi's work has absorbed and transformed other lessons of the century. Probably the most important of these is his expanded conception of space, which he got indirectly from the Constructivists and directly from his old friend Buckminster Fuller, and his belief in the mythical, symbolical potential of forms, which he shares with dancer and choreographer Martha Graham.

But all of this was less than clear back in 1929, when Noguchi returned to New York. For the next 15 years his career would follow the peculiar pattern of advance into the world and retreat from it that started when he left Ruotolo's studio.

In New York the penniless virtuoso began to have a big success as a maker of portrait sculptures. Then, having put together enough money, he gave himself a grant to take a trip to the Orient. He made brush drawings in Peking under the informal tutelage of a Chinese master, Ch'i Pai-shih. In Japan Noguchi sought out a master potter, Uno Jimmatsu, and made terra-

cottas influenced by the ancient *haniwa* tomb figures.

Back in New York in 1932, he would have his first really important exhibition in 1934, a show teeming with ideas that was spitefully dismissed by major critics. Noguchi then went to Mexico, where he made an impressive 63-foot-long cement mural which, reflecting his personal bitterness and the mood of the Thirties, protested social injustice.

After Pearl Harbor, Noguchi was rudely awakened again to the split in his social identity and his very persona. He spent a painful sojourn as a voluntary internee at a camp for Nisei in the Arizona desert, building parks and playgrounds and participating in what

Noguchi's regard for and mastery of stone is evident in interlocking granite parts of *This Place*, 1968.

Cubic Pyramid, of highly polished granite, was done in 1969. Surface reflects light from studio windows.

Sky Mirror, 1967, is of basalt, its gleaming slanted top plateau contrasted with rough columnar surface.

which contains working space, an office, a kitchen and living quarters. This is part of the second one .

he, along with a few idealists in the bureaucracy, thought could be a valuable, if enforced, communal experiment. It was a prison camp. Even though he was a volunteer, it took him seven months to get out.

In any event, it was during the war, following his release from the internment camp, that Noguchi began to produce his first really major body of work, building upon his experiments of the early Thirties. In the following decade Noguchi began to create a world of somber, multivalent sculptures that would firmly establish the lineaments of his style and emotional range. He began to receive some serious attention. The Museum of Modern Art in New York included one of his

Three works in marble displaying
Noguchi's meticulous orchestration
of materials: above, *The Bow*,

of black petit granite and yellow
marble, 1969; *Spirit's Flight*,
1970, serpentine and carrara marble;

and *She* (small version), 1971,
black Austrian porticoi and
Portuguese rose aurora marble

bronzes, *Gregory* (opposite), in a 1946 exhibition called
"Fourteen Americans." He also resumed with great
intensity his involvement with Martha Graham, for
whom he has designed perhaps 20 highly effective sets,
and the world of modern dance.

In this sudden, powerful bursting out during the
1940s, Noguchi was not unlike other significant American artists of his generation such as the sculptor
David Smith or the painters Jackson Pollock, Willem
de Kooning, Mark Rothko and Barnett Newman. But
Noguchi did it with his own special inflection, as always, and he never got the critical attention or acclaim
that was accorded in time to these artists and those who
followed during the 1950s and 1960s.

One of the things held against Noguchi, although
not always verbalized, was that so much of his sculpture was made of stone when other modern sculptors
worked with steel and other, newer materials. Noguchi,
for his part, even today remains ambivalent about
using other materials, although he has placed large
steel sculptures in prominent locations in several of
our major cities.

Usually, when he does these larger things, the material is a question of scale, flexibility, structural necessity, efficiency and economics, all important parts of

Noguchi's approach to art. But stone and wood remain
somehow responsive to his vision in a way that most
other materials do not. In part, this has to do with
Noguchi's approach to nature: stone is closer to the
ancients, he feels, and stone is earth.

In our conversation last winter, he remarked that he
felt it had been an esthetic mistake to have had several
of his standing, totemic wooden pieces cast in bronze,
that it took something essential away from them. "It
was a tremendous advantage financially to do so, so I
succumbed," he said impassively. "But I like doing
things myself. I like the control. When something is
made directly, what it is, is. There's no camouflage."

We were sitting at a circular table in a kitchen nook
attached to the studio-offices he keeps in an industrial
sector of Long Island City, close by the East River. Not
far from Manhattan, but a world apart, dreary on the
outside, inside a Noguchi miracle—spacious, spare
rooms perfectly dotted with his sculptures, each as
good as the last. At our table, Noguchi raised his hands
quickly toward the enormous globular lamp, made of
an off-white, translucent Japanese paper stretched over
bamboo struts, that hovered above our heads—one of
his *akari* (Japanese for light) lanterns, which he has
been making since the early 1950s (p. 268).

sculpted in Italy in 1971 and measuring 46″ x 13″ x 22″. At right is an earlier and much-

noted work, *Gregory*, of bronze, in eight interlocking elements, 63″ x 16″ x 12″.

Wooden beam pierces *Stone of Spiritual Understanding,* created from aluminum and bronze, 1962.

Akari is a word that Noguchi says he "purloined." Its ideograph combines that of the sun and the moon. The lanterns that he has made under this insignia are indeed a fragile though not unimportant microcosm of the vast world of art that Noguchi has fashioned. They clearly relate to the interest in illumination that informs some of his best works dating back to the 1930s. Made to be carefully copied for sale at low prices, they demonstrate in a small way the same urge that the public playgrounds, plazas and gardens do in a big way.

Noguchi's sense of scale and space is perhaps unexcelled by any modern artist. Start with an *akari* lantern, about four feet high, in the curious, affecting shape of a square column twisted ever so slightly on a clear axis, bottom to top; jump to a gleaming stainless-steel pylon rising 120 feet in the air: the same form! The pylon, a marvel of engineering, a focal point of Noguchi's Civic Center Plaza in Detroit, fits its surroundings of sky and skyscrapers just as the lamp fits into a domestic interior.

The Detroit plaza, with its pylon, its graceful terracing down to the river, its sensitively chosen textures, its pyramid that doubles as a seating platform and its fountain, is but the more recent and more spectacular of Noguchi's public spaces. The stainless-steel struc-

ture, officially the Horace E. Dodge and Son Memorial Fountain (cover), is a genuine technological and financial amazement, containing 35 different light-and-water configurations and costing nearly $3 million.

Noguchi actually began working on these spaces back in the 1930s, long before he was able to connect with the means to put his ideas into practice. By now, however, he has sufficiently demonstrated his remarkable ability to modulate large spaces with the fidelity, control and sure intuition with which he invariably handles stone.

Perhaps now, with this spring into the public sun, Noguchi will begin to get credit for being the great artist and key national resource that he is. Obviously, he's slipped and stumbled along the way, as is human. But his art has the force of tremendous energy and range and courage. His space consciousness from the 1930s onward has anticipated enormous changes in art. His public projects—studies in ambition, creativity and, often, frustration—opened the terrain for the terrific amount of activity going on in this country today.

Ironically, the playgrounds, in many ways the most straightforward of Noguchi's imaginings, are an almost separate story of frustration: he has built but two —one in Atlanta (p. 260) and one in Japan—al-

In the studio, a lampland of standing and hanging lights, called *akari*, Japanese for illumination.

though he started dreaming of them and mapping them out nearly 45 years ago.

What the Walker Art Center is trying to stimulate with its show in Minneapolis is the process of seeing Noguchi whole (after the show closes there on June 18, it will travel to the Denver Art Museum, October 22-December 3; and then, in 1979, to the Cleveland Museum of Art, January 7-February 18; the Detroit Institute of Arts, April 10-June 10; and the San Francisco Museum of Modern Art, July 22-September 2). In the fall, a big book on Noguchi by Princeton art historian Sam Hunter should also contribute to this process—the first major work since Noguchi's own.

Noguchi at 73 still plays out the restless, driven, peripatetic pattern that has been his particular birthright. His studio in Long Island City, in addition to being the world's supreme Noguchi museum, is an office for planning, for "business," he says exhaustedly. "My solace has always been sculpture," he wrote ten years ago. It still is. He makes yearly trips to work near quarries in Italy and two or three trips a year to the island of Shikoku in Japan, where he lives and works with the master stonecutters.

Granite sculptures, tallest 16 feet, at Connecticut General Life Insurance Company, Bloomfield.

In front of Marine Midland Building, in heart of New York's downtown financial district, is *Red Cube*.

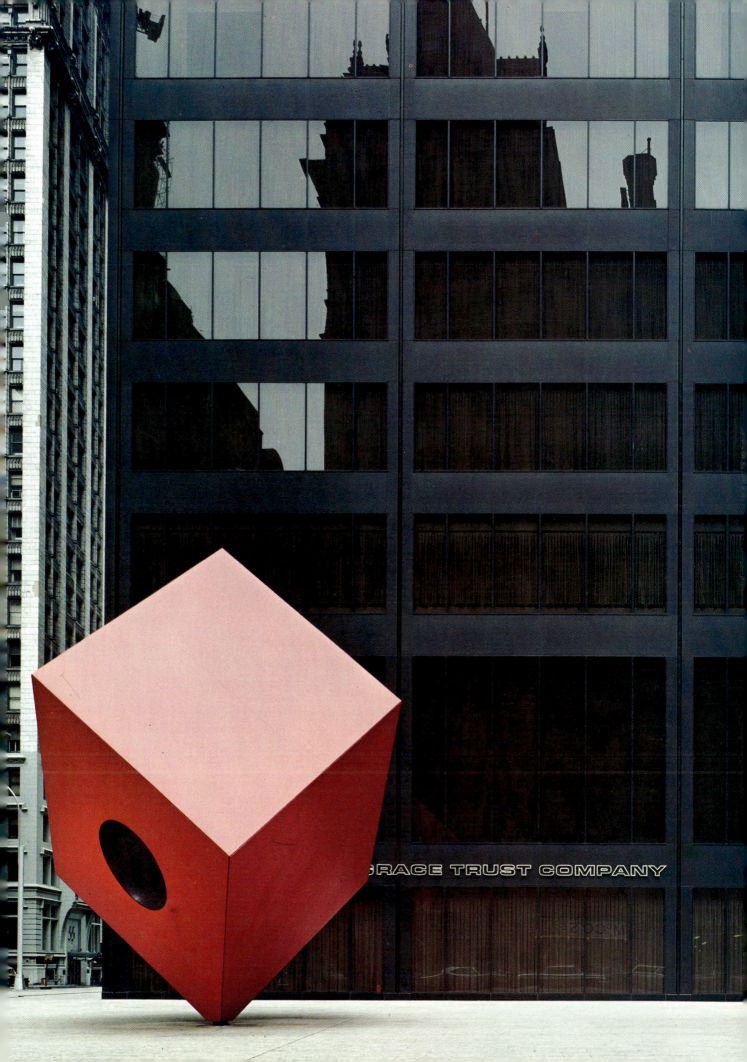

By Robert Wernick

Risible, visible— who cares as long as it's fun

Heads which are houses, fly-winged toilets, donkey-backed desks, ostrich bars and landscaped women are work of les Lalanne

The puckish humor and unbridled inventiveness of the French artists François-Xavier and Claude Lalanne have charted a unique area on the fringes of the art world.

"Art world" is not a phrase that means much to these polymorphous creators. François and Claude produce objects, known collectively as *les Lalanne*. They are generally objects that can be used, and they are also decorative and eye-catching. To the question, "But is it art?" they shrug their shoulders. Their work is shown in fashionable galleries and in museums. The first museum show in this country was at the Art Institute of Chicago in 1967; a forthcoming exhibit is slated for this Spring at the Art Museum of South Texas in Corpus Christi. Their art is meant to render service, give pleasure. The Lalannes see themselves in the tradition of the medieval craftsmen-painters who spent most of their time on workaday commissions like designing gigantic meat pies for official banquets. In that painstaking tradition, every Lalanne is well-made; the parts fit precisely. The Lalanne bathtub, to take one example, will not leak. And, being a Lalanne, it is unsurprisingly in the shape of a hippopotamus.

People love to bathe in the hippo. Marcel Duchamp's widow, a neighbor of the Lalannes, owns one, and she finds her water bills going sky high, because houseguests like John Cage, the composer, spend all day splashing around in it.

It is the mad logic of dreams turned meticulously into solid metal. Sometimes it is a simple pun, as

This is, well, a hippo. It is also a bathtub. And a washstand. It is to laugh. It pleases you,

when François got to brooding on the fact that 18th-century cabinetmakers used to make a type of desk called, because of its high steep form, a *dos d'âne* or donkey back. So he made a desk which not only had a donkey back, but a donkey head, legs, tail.

Or a natural form may suggest some human attribute, or vice versa. If you want a safe to store your valuables, you want an object suggesting massive strength. What could be better for the purpose than the Lalanne one—a barrel-chested gorilla?

since it keeps you in the swim. This one is
the bedroom of Marcel Duchamp's widow.

As in dreams, the Lalannes take an ordinary idea or image, play with it, rearrange it, transform it.

The Lalannes have been working together since the day in 1952 when they met at the opening of what was to be François' last exhibition of paintings. He had been struggling as a painter for several years, but to keep going he had had to take a variety of odd jobs. He had been a cowboy rounding up wild horses in the Camargue (the Rhone delta), a rug salesman, a guard at the Louvre.

Claude was a former art student who had worked for architects and sculptors but for years had led the conventional life of a housewife, raising three daughters.

Once together, they found they had a common taste and a common talent for putting odd things together in new and unusual patterns. They hired a studio and set up as decorators. They would take on any job, they said, that was too difficult for anyone else. No matter if they didn't know the necessary processes, they could learn as they went along. When they got

Photographs by Pierre Boulat

A plaster model of projected Lalanne head-houses designed for seaside resorts. The dining room is in the mouth; spiral stairways climb spinal cords; chimney in nasal passage, music room back of ear.

a commission for a glass background for gems in a jeweler's window, they had to run out and learn how to blow glass. They soon attained the required skills. Over the years they have acquired an immense technical expertise in handling all sorts of materials.

In a few years they were fashionable themselves. They did windows for Christian Dior. They made stage props for television and for the Opéra and the Comédie-Française.

There is a family resemblance to all Lalannes, but François and Claude each have a personal style and distinct method of working.

Claude works in apparently helter-skelter fashion. Her studio, she says proudly, is a mess. It is one immense clutter of leaves, flowers, vegetables, stuffed animals and bric-a-brac of all kinds, which she keeps around till she finds ways of combining them in strange and unexpected ways.

Claude works with metals. Her basic technique is the old one of electroplating, which was popular with both decorators and printers in the last century. It is a comparatively simple process. She takes a natural object like a leaf, sprays it with silver salts, then dips it in a bath of sulfuric acid and copper sulphate. At each end of the bath is a copper anode. She shoots an electric current through the bath, and a layer of copper forms all over the surface of the leaf. She later burns away the vegetable matter, bronzes the copper surface, and there she has a bronze leaf, ready to be soldered to other objects.

François' approach to his work is much more orderly, neat and intellectual. When he gets an idea, he jots down a quick sketch, which is eventually transformed into a precisely scaled drawing. Then he builds his armature of steel wire and cuts out pieces of paper which are placed over the armature where the metal surface is to be. He traces the paper shapes on copper or steel or what not, cuts them out, hammers and beats and burns them into shape, finally puts them all together, solders them, *et voilà*: a rhinoceros, or a centaur, or whatever form fancy has taken.

All of these fancies germinate and take shape in the Lalanne household, a splendid old stone farmhouse in Ury, at the edge of the Forest of Fontainebleau

Robert Wernick, who lives in Paris, wrote about Diego Giacometti in SMITHSONIAN, *June 1975.*

about 50 miles from Paris. Not all of them have yet gone out into the world; some exist only at the stage of sketches or plaster models. No golf course yet has had the vision or the cash to order the Feminine Landscape which François blocked out in 1974. This would be an artificial hill of gravel, covered with turf, anywhere from 60 to 600 meters long, in the shape of a reclining naked woman, with clumps of trees and bushes to represent the hair of her head and groin. It would put any male golfer on his mettle to hit a spoon shot straight and true between her billowing breasts. But the pleasure which has been denied to the golfers may be offered to automobile drivers, for François hopes to find a way to construct a Feminine Landscape alongside a new superhighway in the east of France to break the monotony which causes so many complaints from users of these roads.

Nor has there been an offer yet to put up a cluster of Lalanne head-houses, looking out to sea at some summer resort (p. 272). In these houses, the dining room is located, logically enough, in the mouth, the nasal passages provide a chimney flue, a spiral stair-

Claude's daughter Caroline is sculpted pregnant and with a cabbage for a head. The parent's concept.

But of course, a toilet, a fly-winged toilet of solid brass and cobwebby wings of Plexiglas.

Here is Caroline's real head, which is to say, in copper, made from wax-molded life mask.

273

Ministry of Health, Paris, ordered this bird, rejected it because some might take seed in bill for the Pill.

case winds around the spinal cord, a music room nestles just behind the left ear.

These are exceptions. Most Lalannes get snapped up almost as soon as they are dreamed up. They appeal to all sorts of people. They are fun to have around. Modernists and traditionalists can accept them with the same fond smile.

Georges Pompidou, the late president of France, put a Lalanne in the dining room of the Elysée Palace, the presidential residence in Paris. It consists of two porcelain ostriches looking at each other over their shoulders. Between their beaks is a metal tray on which glasses can be placed, as well as a large egg for ice or nuts; their bodies can be opened to be used as champagne coolers. When the more austere Giscard d'Estaing became president, he swept out most of Pompidou's far-out art. But he was amused by the ostriches: he has kept them on in one of the palace drawing rooms.

This general popularity is easy to explain. The Lalannes' combination of verbo-visual fireworks with meticulous craftsmanship is obviously influenced by the surrealists, but they wear their surrealism with a difference. The Lalannes don't go in for nightmares; they appear to have sweet dreams, though some of Claude's creations, like the pregnant woman whose head is a cabbage, have their inelegant sides as well. François' burly lumbering birds and beasts have a familiar barnyard air to begin with; they certainly don't mean us any harm. They have just enough of the bizarre to pique interest, stimulate a smile or a guffaw and perhaps a whole new association of ideas. They appeal to something childlike that lurks in all of us, a delight in the incongruous, a hankering for a world without the restrictive barriers of reason. No wonder virtually everyone likes them. No wonder Mrs. Duchamp's guests won't get out of that hippo.

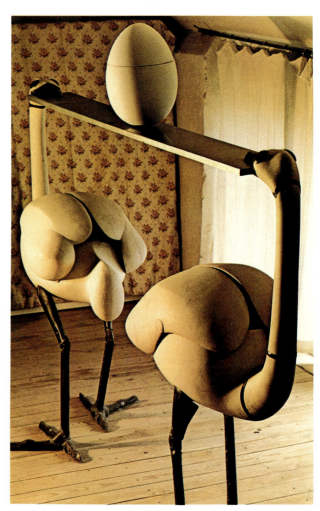

Ostriches of Sèvres porcelain form a fanciful bar. One example, is part of Presidential Palace furnishings.

This is a centaur, *évidemment, à la* Lalanne. Claude sits on it. François rests. They are happy, *non?*

Like a pair of giant exclamation points, the quarter-mile-high towers of the World Trade Center punctuate Lower Manhattan's evening skyline for commuters on the Staten Island Ferry.

By Russell Lynes

The architect was told '*world* trade' so he planned big

Eight hundred international organizations now occupy the controversial Center's 16 acres; here, a cultural observer casts a favorable vote

It is seven years now since the first tenants moved into New York's soaring, two-towered World Trade Center (WTC), time enough, so to speak, to get an idea of how it has settled in. There has been, of course, controversy from the day the project was first announced until right now (although, it must be said, on a decreasing scale). Among its critics were those who condemned the gargantuan structures for their dehumanizing effect on the area. Now, in answer at least to this point of objection, there is a new plaza—five acres of open space, at its heart a commanding fountain, a wide circle of polished dark brown granite. The tremendous ball of bronze (cover), a hazel iris at the fountain's center, is set to make one full turn an hour.

The function of the plaza, according to WTC chief architect Minoru Yamasaki, is a humane one, and it exists to afford respite for the urban spirit from the torments of hurry and crowding, a place of relaxation and casualness, a refuge. "Lower Manhattan is a tangle of narrow streets," he said as we looked west from the plaza on a windy March morning. "People can't help but jostle other people. They push each other off the sidewalks into the streets. What I wanted to do was to give them a paved garden, like San Marco, where they can spend a little time away from traffic, a place totally for pedestrians. Some of them have to get away from the tensions of their jobs, some from the monotony."

The analogy with Venice's Piazza San Marco is far-fetched physically and spiritually but not in intent. If San Marco is, as Napoleon called it, "the grandest

Photographs by Marvin E. Newman

Flags, uniforms, a brass band and a dwarfed crowd
marked dedication ceremony for plaza section.

Revolving doors spin shoppers, workers
into lobby of North Tower building

drawing room in Europe," the plaza at the World Trade Center may be the most awesome conversation pit anywhere. It is not quite as enclosed as it will eventually be when an 800-room hotel unfortunately will cut across the space between the towers, blocking the view of the harbor, but it has the sense of being what it is for the sake of people, not esthetics—the interplay of the personal and the monumental.

"The genius of the plan," an architect said to me, "is that Yamasaki decided on two tall and slender towers and not on one massive one, so that there is airiness rather than brutality about the open space."

The structure of the towers, each rising 1,350 feet, is unlike that of most skyscrapers. The exterior walls are not "curtains" hung on a steel cage. They are the supports that hold the buildings up and make them rigid. The steel columns, sheathed in aluminum and looking like silver ribbons that flow upward from the pointed arches at the base of the towers, are in fact cantilevered up from the foundations. They form a

truss which braces the buildings against strong winds on high. Together with the spandrels they constitute a sort of rectangular tube to which the open floors of the structure are attached. Unlike the cage construction with its structural interruptions of interior spaces, Yamasaki's supporting walls allow for far greater flexibility in how the interiors can be arranged and the whims of tenants met.

When Yamasaki, a native of Seattle whose offices are in suburban Detroit and whose elegant pavilions of commerce, transportation and learning are spread across the world (his biggest job at the moment is an airport for Saudi Arabia), received a letter from the Port Authority of New York and New Jersey in 1962, he thought there had been a mistake. It asked if he would be interested in developing a scheme for a projected World Trade Center and mentioned that what

Mr. Lynes, a cultural commentator, explored
the Cooper-Hewitt in Smithsonian, *November 1977.*

from fringes of the huge concourse that sprawls beneath the Center.

Feasting at Windows on the World restaurant is for the eyes as well as the taste buds—on a clear day.

they had in mind would be about a $280 million undertaking for construction alone. "My first reaction," he says, "was that an extra zero had been added. My colleagues didn't believe it either, so I called Richard Sullivan who signed the letter and asked him if it meant what it said. He said it did." Fifteen years later the cost had risen to over $900 million, including relocation, demolition and site preparation. There are now roughly 35,000 persons employed in the complex, which is five buildings in all—the two towers, the U.S. Customhouse and two additional nine-story business structures that wall off the plaza. It is estimated that 80,000 visitors come each day on business to see people who work at the Center. In addition to these are the sightseers who come to gape up at and down from the towers, still others who come to the restaurants and cafeterias and those who sit by the fountain in the plaza and eat out of paper bags. Some come to shop in the vast concourse beneath the plaza for flowers or books, groceries or clothes or anything else one expects to find in a sophisticated shopping mall. Others in the late afternoon come to the jazz and marching band concerts and other entertainments in the plaza, or pause there on their way home from work via the WTC rapid transit connections. These visitors add at least several thousand a day.

To talk with anyone who works for, not just at, the World Trade Center is to be showered with statistics. Depending on your temperament, it's either "Gee whiz!" or "God help us!"—disbelief or dismay. One is not likely to be indifferent, not, in any case, in the long shadows of the edifice itself. To wit: every night 600 women with dusters and sweepers move in to clean up the day's mess, and they are complemented by 400 men for the heavy work. A police force of 38 uniformed men keep their eyes and ears open 24 hours a day every day. These are in addition to at least 200 private security guards. The restaurants, about a dozen of them, serve 20,000 meals a day. There are 102 automatic elevators per tower. It takes 58 seconds in the

279

express elevator to get to the observation deck at the top of the South Tower or the Windows on the World restaurant at the top of the North Tower. It makes your ears pop. It is comparable to Rockefeller Center, for it is not just a piece of architecture, it is, like it or not, a place.

Beatrice Lillie is said to have asked when she boarded the RMS *Queen Elizabeth* some years ago, "When does this place get to England?" The analogy of the World Trade Center with a vast ship tied to the land seems to me more accurate than its comparison with a small city. It is self-contained; it has no sprawl, at least not yet. Curiously, no one in this place which is dedicated to maritime concerns, surrounded by the waters of the harbor and suckled by freighters, mentioned its likeness to a great ship. Its first-class tenants occupy its uppermost floors and eat in its loftiest restaurants. Its crew is "below" in its engine rooms (its refrigerator plant must be the largest in the world). Its crow's nest is the observation deck on the top of the South Tower; its promenade is the plaza. If it should float down the harbor and out to sea, some of its critics would be pleased, but its friends would understand.

It is what its name says it is, a center for world trade. A glance at its tenants' directory confirms this: import-export firms, shipping companies, freight forwarders, customhouse brokers, cargo inspectors, marine insurance brokers, international bankers, steamship agents. There are offices promoting the ports of Seattle, Boston, Baton Rouge and others. There is a World Trade Institute that "offers courses, meetings and seminars on all aspects of international trade for all levels of management."

The tenants have different reasons for how far up in the twin Towers of Babel with their "confusion of tongues" they want their offices. An official at the World Trade Department of the Port Authority said:

Bright-coated floor brokers (shirt-sleeves are taboo) huddle at trading ring to buy, sell with "open outcry" everything from butter to zinc on world's largest trading floor in Commodities Exchange Center.

Miró tapestry brings brilliance and a Spanish accent; windows have been criticized as too delicate.

Concourse is a boulevard linking WTC buildings, the shopping mall and rapid transit systems.

Guiding Red by Helen Frankenthaler blends with sun patterns for cathedral mood in the South Tower.

"One Japanese company hired a soothsayer to throw dice to determine what floor they should have their offices on. They wound up in the nineties." There is more cachet to higher than lower and somewhat less convenience. Getting from building to building and access to the shopping and eating concourse is quicker from the lower floors. To get to the upper offices one changes from an express to a local elevator at one of the "skylobbies" (one on the 44th and one on the 78th floor) where there are restaurants, beauty parlors, a smoke shop and banks. The views of the harbor and its surroundings, which include a good deal of New Jersey as well as New York's five boroughs, are of course best seen aloft, from where the Statue of Liberty looks the size of a desk ornament. The top offices are not infrequently above the clouds, like an airplane that got stuck, and there is no telling short of a phone call or a wet visitor if it is raining below.

The critical reception of the World Trade Center has been by no means all enthusiastic. It has drawn a hail of arrows, some of them with flattering bouquets attached to their shafts. It has been called "kitsch" architecture by a critic who praises the Chrysler Building, perhaps unmindful that the generation of critics before his thought *it* unspeakably vulgar. It has been scored by pundits who say that the skyscraper is doomed, the very same critics who deplore the death of the center of cities because of sprawl and no open space for human dalliance. There are critics who deplore what they call the "daintiness" of Yamasaki's arches and the delicate quality of his detailing, to which Yamasaki replies by quoting Emerson: "The line of beauty is the result of perfect economy." To be sure, the arch has an almost timeless respectability both for its structural economy and as a line of beauty. The Bauhaus and its "functionalists" gave it a bad name for 30 or so years, but in the last few, less didactic decades the arch has been reemerging.

A building that everyone likes does not exist unless it has been standing for a very long while and has become part of everyone's visual vocabulary. A landmark building is architecture encased in time and sentiment and, with luck, style. A contemporary building that the public likes and the critics do not has at least an equal chance of survival with one the critics and dilettantes like and the public does not—I'd say a better chance. If that is so, I'll place my chips on the World Trade Center.

As someone said to me, "We know that the WTC is there for sure because somebody had to climb it!"

An escalator carries Jersey-bound commuters and their newspapers to tube beneath the Hudson

By Dora Jane Hamblin

Maladies of Venice: decay, delay and that old sinking feeling

The city is not necessarily doomed, but those who seek to save her will have to do better than in the past. It may happen

Reports of her death have been exaggerated, but there is no doubt that regal Venice, the dowager empress of the Adriatic, is desperately ill.

Her lovers, and the merely curious, call upon her assiduously: five million or so a year. They admire the Titians and Tintorettos, misquote Shakespeare at the Rialto Bridge, feed the messy pigeons in front of that ultimate Byzantine monument, St. Mark's Basilica. Most go home happy, all unaware that Venice still has no viable sewer system, that almost 58 percent of the dwellings have no central heat, that more than one-third of the population has fled across the famous lagoon in less than 25 years to the relative comfort of dry apartments on the mainland.

Yet even the most art-drenched tourist must see the deterioration. Blocks of weathered Istrian stone slip periodically from their moorings beside the stations of the *vaporetti,* or water buses, and subside into the canals. Church facades crack down the middle. Eroded marble reliefs lack noses and fingers, and pigeons nest quietly behind the ears of sculptured saints. Plaster falls from exterior walls of once-glorious palaces on the Grand Canal, exposing the damp brick beneath. First floors, too wet for habitation, are closed off and their windows boarded up.

Winter's cold and damp settle on Grand Canal, veiling church of Santa Maria della Salute in fog.

All this despite the fact that, for more than a decade, millions of dollars have been borrowed, begged, donated or appropriated to save the city. The big trouble is that the dowager's doctors have been paralyzed by the complexity of the illness. A strangling bureaucracy at all levels (the national government, the regional government, the city administration), convoluted politics and stridently competing aims and claims have induced Italian administrators to behave like lifeguards arguing over who should throw out the cork ring—and who will have to pay for it if it doesn't work. Meanwhile, would-be rescuers from UNESCO, the United States, half of Europe, even Japan, Iran and Brazil, not to mention thousands of concerned Italian citizens, are constrained to dance around the perimeter alternately urging haste and crying "shame" at too-hastily conceived cures.

The shocking state of Venice might have remained only a local sorrow had it not been for the big flood of 1966. Eleven years ago this month, heavy storms spread havoc across much of northern Italy, drove the Arno River out of its banks to devastate Florence, and sent more than six feet of high water rampaging through the homes, shops and piazzas of Venice.

At first, both Italian and world attention focused on Florence, but within weeks a cry for aid came from the lagoon city. Led by UNESCO, dozens of private organizations rushed to help: from the United States the Committee to Rescue Italian Art (CRIA) and Colonel James A. Gray's International Fund for Monuments (IFM); Great Britain's Venice in Peril Fund and Italian Art and Archives Rescue Unit; hastily formed committees in West Germany, France, Yugoslavia, Australia and other countries; plus a host of Italian public and private institutions. In the years since the flood, this cadre of international volunteers has done wonders and spent from 3.5 to 4 million dol-

Color photographs by Dmitri Kessel

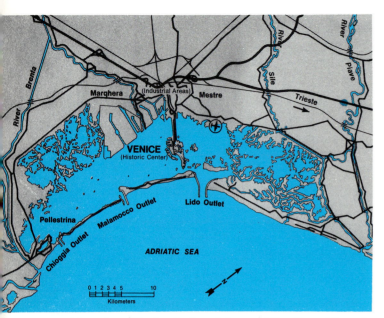

Map shows Venice, industrial areas (Marghera, Mestre) and three channels linking lagoon with Adriatic.

lars in the process. This year, 33 groups from 13 nations are funneling funds and experts into the rescue. The Italian financial contribution (from ten distinct groups) ranks second only to that of the United States.

Thousands of square yards of frescoes and paintings have been restored. Churches have been renovated and structurally repaired, palaces put in order, bridges and facades cleaned. All this is wonderful, but it is in a sense only cosmetic. What good to save the treasures, if the whole city is doomed to wash away or perish in its own pollution, erosion and neglect?

The basic cure for Venice is a job only Italians can do, and it has become a classic case of the collision of warring interests: ecologists versus industrialists, city planners versus regional planners, developers versus preservationists. It is, to be fair, a staggering problem; "Everything that must be done in Venice must be done at the same time," complains the hard-working Communist assistant mayor, Gianni Pellicani.

Venice has been in peril, no doubt, since the first settlers sank wooden piles into the ooze of the lagoon in the fifth century A.D. and decided, against all odds, to build a city there. They had astonishing luck for centuries, grew rich and powerful, famous and decadent. Venice was the longest-lived republic the world had ever known, until it fell in 1797 to Napoleon, who then handed it over to Austria. In 1866 it was incor-

Dora Jane Hamblin, who lives in Italy and writes frequently for SMITHSONIAN, *is a former* Life *bureau chief and the author of* That Was the LIFE.

porated into the brand-new Italian unified state, and lurched uncertainly into the more complex perils of the 20th century.

In the middle of World War I the renowned Venetian Arsenal, which since the 12th century had mass-produced men-of-war and armaments, closed down and turned 8,000 men out of work. A group of local patriots, led by Count Giuseppe Volpi and including members of the Cini and Gaggia families, rushed to the rescue with a plan: Venice could once again become an important port, an industrial center, if it would build modern facilities. The men placed their dream on the mainland, on the other side of the causeway which Austria had built in 1846 to connect the island city for the first time with terra firma.

The new industrial zone, called Porto Marghera, was created by filling in about 500 hectares (1,235 acres) of mud flats. It thrived and attracted the beneficent attention of Mussolini. As Marghera grew, an adjoining tiny community called Mestre became its bedroom. By 1927 these satellite areas had grown important enough to be incorporated into "Greater Venice," which included the historic center and the islands of the lagoon.

Venice survived World War II relatively unscathed, though Marghera was bombed, and shortly after the war a second industrial zone grew up nearby. This one took another 500 hectares of what Venetians call the *barene*, or mud flats, and gobbled up twice that amount of adjacent farmland. Petrochemical, aluminum and other heavy industries, shipyards and oil refineries went up. The three ancient channels of Chioggia, Malamocco and Lido, which link the lagoon with the Adriatic Sea, were deepened to facilitate

The Piazzetta di San Marco was submerged by highest waters in recorded history: the floods of 1966.

access to the factory areas. Tourists suddenly were treated to the sight of 60,000-ton tankers cruising through the Giudecca Canal less than a hundred yards from the Doge's Palace.

For a while in the 1950s it seemed that happy days were here again. Employment on the mainland rose steadily; a third and even more gigantic industrial zone was projected. Yet in the rush of postwar building, some of it illegal and some just ineptly designed, the face of Venice began to change. The clashingly modern railway station in the center and a towering, ugly parking garage across from it were joined by several architecturally unsuitable hotels and innumerable "elevations," *i.e.*, extra floors perched atop older existing buildings. Rich foreigners rushed to acquire palaces or a piece of a palace, as did rich Italians for whom "a second home in Venice" seemed desirable.

There were a few danger signals. Some days the sun was obscured by pollutants either from within the city or from across the lagoon. Fish began to vanish from the canals. Pieces of stone—small, at first—began to fall from buildings. Most ominous of all was the increasing incidence of *acque alte*, or high waters. Venice has always been subject to exceptionally high tides, caused by meteorological events such as low-pressure systems or scirocco winds from the southeast which fill the Adriatic gulf to overflowing. These are dramatic but less dangerous in the long run than smaller, but more frequent, inundations. *Acque alte* are described specifically as tides of 1.1 meters, or about 43 inches higher than a so-called "normal" tide reference-level established in 1897. In the 20th century their occurrence increased, and waters of three and a half feet or higher have come with monotonous regu-

Ancient breakwater that protects Venice from sea has been neglected, was badly battered in 1966.

Experimental model of inflatable dam proposed by Pirelli/Furlanis to seal off channels in high tides.

A forlorn relic, this gondola was thrown up on the pavement by one of Venice's periodic storms.

287

Seen from Venice, the industrial zone of Marghera
darkens the evening sky with smoke and fumes.

Motorboats and steam launches congest the Grand
Canal, making waves that weaken foundations.

larity. Even more alarming was the increasing difference between high and low water. The highs were higher and the lows were lower.

Although not immediately apparent to tourists, these fluctuations create near-intolerable problems for Venetians. In high water the boats have trouble getting beneath small bridges, and in low water even emergency craft—fire and ambulance boats—cannot navigate the smaller canals. Furthermore, the exaggerated changes between high and low cause structural damage. Stone, wood, even brick, will survive for a long time if they are either totally wet or totally dry. But the alternation of wet-and-dry, dry-and-wet, sharply increases the disintegration of the basic fabric.

Complicating the phenomenon was the now-celebrated "subsidence" of the city. Greater Venice was plagued by the existence of about 20,000 deep artesian wells dug to suck up water for public use and for the needs of the increasingly greedy industries on the mainland. As this sustaining underground water table fell, so did the lagoon bed above it.

Oceanographers, marine biologists, even ordinary Venice-lovers with boats knew what was wrong: Man had tampered too long and too drastically with the delicate balance of the lagoon and its underpinnings. When the Venetian Republic was at its height, the

Its refineries and other industries provide jobs
for Venetians, but are a source of pollution.

most powerful citizen in it, after the Doge himself,
was the Superintendent of the Waters. His authority
was awesome: he could forbid fishermen to dam the
lagoon to make hatcheries; he could keep people
from building on or filling up the vast mud flats into
which the incoming tides rushed twice a day, and
from which they retreated, slowly, when high tide
was over; he oversaw the cleaning and dredging of
the 160-plus large and small canals of the city.

The happy Venetians of that era had no need for
man-made sewers because the unimpeded tides came
rushing, sucking, evacuating, twice a day. They tended their seawalls carefully, and were so jealous of
their limpid waters that they forbade housewives and
their slaveys even to beat rugs on balconies, for fear
dust would fall into the canals where gondolas plied.

Beginning in the 19th century, after the Austrian
occupation, it all changed. For whatever reason, Venice began neglecting its seawalls, left its small canals
undredged. Then the industrial zones filled in 2,500
acres of mud flats, the escape valve of other days, and
a projected third zone was planned to take away far
more. Other acres were filled in to let the town of
Mestre grow and to build the airport. By one expert
evaluation, an incredible one-fourth of the total area
of the lagoon has now been closed to the tides. At the

Artesian wells, which have lowered the water
table, will be replaced by aqueducts such as this.

Decaying housing, such as this in the Ghetto Nuovo (New Ghetto), is another severe problem

same time, all the channels have been deepened, and a new tanker canal dredged from the Porto di Mala-mocco to the industrial zone is 40 feet deep. Water rushing through such deep channels has an erosive effect on everything from seawalls to basements, and with the escape hatch of the *barene* so restricted, it has trouble getting out before the next high tide.

When the flood came in 1966, many conservationists and ecologists, both Italian and foreign, were secretly relieved. Now, they thought, at last Rome and the rest of the world would pay attention. The late René Maheu, director-general of UNESCO in Paris, instantly offered his own services, and the concern of the organization, to the stricken city. Within months that body had set up an office in Rome to coordinate international aid to both Florence and Venice. The mere existence of the office, plus some exuberant journalism, convinced most Italians and a great part of the Western world that UNESCO was at the ready with "an international loan" of millions, just as it rushed to the rescue of Egyptian treasures when the Aswan Dam was built.

UNESCO officials today deny that there ever was such a loan, or even the offer of one. The organization did help raise money to enable Venice's Super-intendent of Galleries and Monuments to catalog and restore the most gravely endangered major works of art. Money came to help set up a restoration laboratory in the monastery of San Gregorio, and to support an international advisory committee to direct the salvation work. Maheu devoted a great part of the last ten years of his life to lobbying and working for an effective campaign to save the city.

Five years after the flood, the Italian Senate finally passed a special statute to safeguard Venice. That was in December 1971, but the statute had not yet passed the lower house when the government fell and the

Venice law was lost among 3,773 others under consideration at the time. Not until April 1973, almost seven years after the flood, did a national law finally pass both houses. It was a painfully obvious compromise between the interests of industry and the preservation of the historic center. It postponed development of the "third zone," but it approved completion of the hotly opposed (by ecologists and hydrologists) deep tanker canal. It threw a bone to labor by guaranteeing that the 40,000 to 50,000 jobs in the Marghera-Mestre area would be maintained. It directed that sewers be built, polluters controlled, artesian wells capped and replaced by aqueducts, home heating switched from oil-based fuels to non-polluting methane gas or electricity.

The law was specific about expenditures. Half a billion dollars would be raised and divided roughly into thirds: one-third for the national government, to repair seawalls and bridges, to combat damage done by high water and to construct barriers in the channels as a defense against high tides; one-third to the regional government, charged with devising anti-pollution measures and building aqueducts and a

Thousands of workers have moved to better quarters on the mainland, commute back to jobs in Venice.

sewage-treatment system; one-third to the city of Venice for restoration of decayed housing, palaces, bridges and monuments in the historic center and on the islands of the lagoon.

The latter job turned out to be far more complex than it seemed because of the shift in population from "old Venice" to the mainland. In 1945 the historic center boasted 180,000 residents and the mainland 83,000. But today the balance has shifted, aided by the departure of well over 80,000 Venetians to the mainland, so that almost two out of three citizens of 'Greater Venice' live within the industrialized zones.

Six months after passage of the law, Italy issued a loan contract described as a "prefinancing loan . . . in connection with the preservation project of the city of Venice." Banks all over the world rushed to take up the issue, at favorable terms to Italy, and very quickly one of the biggest loans ever arranged on the Eurodollar market was accomplished.

Then, to the consternation of many, the money didn't go to Venice. For one reason: no official governmental body, on any level, was ready with precise plans for how to spend it. No serious organization

Slums, not palaces, are reflected in the refuse-filled waters of a canal well away from the tourist beat.

Moved inside for study, decapitated horse is one of four above portal of St. Mark's. Whether Greek or Roman, they were taken to Constantinople, later carried off to Venice at the end of Fourth Crusade.

Ghostly under plastic, angels from St. Mark's
facade have been relegated to roof for restoration.

will leave such sums lying about, so the Eurodollar
loan—it was generally suspected—was used to help
prop up the staggering *lira*.

At the risk of boring everybody, it must be explained that passage of a special law in Italy com-
mits the state, but also indicates primarily *intent*. To
implement the Special Law on Venice required sup-
plementary issuance of guidelines called *indirizzi*. A
government led by Mariano Rumor had some *indirizzi* ready in October 1974, but the government
fell four days before the crucial vote. Twenty-three
months had dragged by between passage of the Special Law and the final appearance of *indirizzi* in the
spring of 1975, endless months during which endless
committees had endless meetings.

After the *indirizzi* must come detailed plans and
projects for each particular segment of the total problem. And at every turn the warring elements, both
political and economic (leaving out for the moment
the artistic and historical), collide.

Item: Industrialists insist that Venice needs more
and more jobs on the mainland.

Supporters of the historic center counter that most
of the present industrial workers come from surrounding mainland areas rather than from Venice
itself, and statistics confirm their view: every day
about 24,000 residents of Mestre and its surroundings
commute back to the historic center to work, while
only 1,700 go the other way to mainland jobs.

Item: What to do about deteriorating housing in
the center, substandard conditions which forced Venetians to go to the mainland in the first place?

Everyone agrees that the commuting workers should
be brought home again and the exodus halted. But no
one agrees on how to do it.

The ruling Communist-Socialist city administration is determined to renovate housing for workers

Three horses of the Quadriga, as they are called,
are in place. Missing is one on opposite page.

Interior of the late Baroque church of San Stae,
on Grand Canal, is being restored with Swiss funds.

and prevent speculators from buying up and restoring property which then might become too expensive for the working class. To this end they have set up rigid rules which make it almost impossible for even an owner to fix up his own property. The result has been a private paralysis which compounds the official one, and an explosion of illegal alterations on the part of those rich or influential enough to risk a fine.

Item: Control of high water. In the wake of the flood, in 1969, the Italian government set up a laboratory with the high-flown title of Institute for the Study of the Dynamics of Large Masses. Its chief was a U.S.-trained oceanographer, Roberto Frassetto, who for six years labored mightily with the help of nearly 200 scientific and technical volunteers from all over the world, an IBM computer, and an offshore research platform from which they made field measurements of water levels, currents, waves and tides.

The Institute tested and evaluated a dozen systems for preventing *acque alte,* everything from placing maneuverable barriers in the Adriatic channels to actually raising the land mass. The latter involved a technique called mud jacking, in which a resilient substance is pumped deep into the subsoil to support and raise land levels and the buildings on their backs.

Much more public attention has been devoted to the series of proposals to close the three seaward channels in case of high tide by man-made barriers. One, developed by the Pirelli/Furlanis Consortium, would anchor giant hot-water-bottlelike structures to the bottom and inflate them when necessary (p. 287). Another would install pivotal metal discs which would be raised or lowered. An international tender was extended for proposals, and by the end of 1976 six firms had submitted plans which are currently under study.

Many oceanologists, hydrologists and Venetian citizens hope the decision will never be made. Further tampering with the natural passages, they argue, would only increase the erosive action of incoming tides; besides, it would impede the outrush of the tides, upset the flushing action and set up stagnation which would become a breeder of disease.

What should be done, ecologists say, is clear and simple: restore the old channels to their previously much shallower depths, abolish the tanker canal and serve the industries with overland oil pipelines, liberate the thousands of acres of *barene* now enclosed for fish hatcheries or the proposed development of the "third zone" (now temporarily halted), dredge the silt-and-garbage-filled secondary canals. Also, restrict the size, speed and traffic patterns of the public and private motorboats which churn through the main thoroughfares, throwing up lashings of waves and the pollution of their motors.

Item: Pollution of air and water. Conservationists blame the industrial zones, industrialists blame Venice itself. Some restorers agree with the industrialists. Even so august a witness as Sir Ashley Clarke, former British ambassador to Italy and now a vice chairman

The Arsenal, restored with Italian private funds, built the fleets with which Venice ruled the seas.

International Fund for Monuments has made possible restoration of the church of San Pietro di Castello.

of Britain's Venice in Peril Fund, holds that "Prevailing winds carry industrial pollution inland, not across the lagoon to the historic center."

Yet on any day when the wind blows from the wrong direction, or when there is no wind at all, towering columns of yellow and red and black effluent from the mainland are visible in the historic center, and spread over the city "like an airborne mattress," in the words of a stern *Italia Nostra* conservationist.

Air pollution levels, now measured and infrequently reported by city authorities, instead of by the ecologists who set up the system, seldom reach the danger point for long periods of time. But, say conservationists, if the official level (a very permissive .30 parts of sulfur dioxide for every million volumes of air) is exceeded for only one half hour every week, it attacks the stone, marble, brick and bronze of which Venice is made.

Lagoon Venetians have done their part. In response to provisions of the Special Law, they dutifully converted home heating from oil-based to methane fuels. They were supposed to get 40 percent of the cost back from the state, and about one-third of them have been reimbursed, but the other two-thirds are still waiting.

On the mainland, however, the local health officer in 1973 ordered workers in Porto Marghera to wear gas masks to protect them from clouds of nitrogen oxide, sulfur dioxide, phenols, cyanide, formaldehyde, ammonia, methacrylic acid, vitriol and phosgene—the latter a gas used to poison people on purpose during World War I. The workmen largely ignored the order ("gas masks are uncomfortable") and the state failed to enforce it. Even now, ominous little news items buried at the bottom of newspaper columns report that 10 or 15 or 20 workers were carted off to the hospital for treatment after they had inhaled too many fumes of one kind or another.

Throughout the dragging months and years, international crusaders and UNESCO have maintained a stiff upper lip, and in their annual reports have dwelt upon whatever accomplishments they could claim. They have been unfailingly polite to the Italian bureaucracy, although noting from year to year that "We regret this new delay," "What is needed is no possibility of further delay. . . ." and so on.

Sir Ashley Clarke and Venice in Peril Fund came to rescue of San Niccolò dei Mendicoli (background).

John McAndrew, head of Save Venice, Inc., near church (opposite page) which American group saved.

Their faith may be rewarded. Inner-city pollution has definitely been reduced by the switch to methane. Many artesian wells have been capped, and one new aqueduct has been completed to bring water from the Sile River to the gulping mainland factories (p. 45). A second aqueduct is on the drawing board, and four pilot sewage plants are in various stages of development. The first doesn't work very well, but maybe the builders will learn by doing.

Italian authorities claim proudly that almost one-third of the total allocation of money has been made (although one-third of that is being held in reserve to cover tenders for the ill-conceived effort to close the channels). Much of the money is being consumed in studies and drawing-board work.

But an international training course for the care and cure of ailing stone, organized and sponsored by UNESCO, is now being held annually in Venice. Then there is the new restoration laboratory in San Gregorio. Eventually the world's aspiring restorers may learn there how to save everything from canvas to marble to wood to glass.

And there has been no disastrous flood in more than a decade. The *acque alte* have receded in intensity if not in frequency, and new scientific measurements indicate that the subsidence of the city has stopped. It might even be rising almost imperceptibly, as underground waters begin to fill the gaps made earlier by the gulping artesian wells.

Finally, no mere foreigner should ever discount the Italians' genius for the last-minute save. If they didn't invent *The Perils of Pauline,* they should have: nobody else is so expert at cutting the bonds of the lady just before the train thunders through, or in leaping from the top of a burning building into a fortuitously passing hay wagon.

Sometimes the save is done thoughtfully instead of instinctively. An organization called the Friends of Museums and Monuments of Venice currently transports children from the industrial zone to the historic center to see the glories of St. Mark's, San Rocco, the Doge's Palace, the Rialto Bridge. The volunteers who run the tours report that 85 percent of these children, Venetians by definition and separated by only 15 minutes of public transport from the historic center, had never seen it before. If these children learn to love old Venice, and if politicians and technicians of all orders can solve one of the knottiest problems of the 20th century, then *La Serenissima* will, truly, rise again.

Glistening restoration of church of Santa Maria dei Gesuiti gives no hint of its once-parlous state. U.S. funds kept it from falling into canal.

USSR lends its dazzling Scythian gold for American exhibitions

By Rudolph Chelminski   *Photographs by Lee Boltin*

It will be seen at New York's Metropolitan Museum of Art, later in Los Angeles, revealing work of ancient steppe nomads

"The Royal Scythians," wrote Herodotus, "guard their sacred gold with most especial care, and year by year offer great sacrifices to its honor."

The father of history, as Cicero later called him, was correct. Toward the middle of the fifth century B.C. he had come to the Greek settlement of Olbia on the north shore of the Black Sea, one of the many commercial outposts thrown off from the motherland in those days. The purpose of his visit north, to the very edge of the civilized world, beyond which lay vast stretches of untracked land peopled by the most fantastic and frightening of barbarians—bald people! goat-hooved people! cannibals!—was to gather material for what was to become Book Four of his history of the Greek and Persian wars.

Of all the populations of the steppe above Olbia, the Scythians were by far the most important in Herodotus' time. For a few hundred years these fierce mounted nomads ruled the plain like invulnerable pirates, growing unconscionably rich from booty taken in battle, tribute exacted from more sedentary folk and trade with the Greek colonies. The Scythians had no towns, no temples, no large possessions: Everything they valued had to be small enough or mobile enough to accompany them in their seasonal wanderings. And what they treasured above everything was gold.

Scythian gold was not accumulated and secretly hoarded, but carried on one's person, grandly ornamental, a sign of importance and accomplishment. The Scythians wore gold combs in their hair, gold rings on their fingers, and gold in endless combination as necklaces, bracelets, earrings and headgear. Gold plaques were sewn to their finest clothing. Beautiful gold totem animals, fastened to the centers of their shields, protected them from danger.

The Scythian gold which remains today—only a tiny portion has survived the systematic looting of their tombs over the centuries—constitutes one of the principal national treasures of the Soviet Union. Many Americans have marveled at this trove on its home grounds in the USSR, but during the next few months a great many more will be able to see a portion of it in this country. On April 29 the Metropolitan Museum of Art in New York will open an exhibition called "From the Land of the Scythians," a comprehensive selection of ancient Scythian, Altaic, Urartian and Sarmatian artifacts sent here by the Soviet government under the current cultural exchange

Golden stag, 12½ inches long, was fastened to a shield; antlers are exaggerated to emphasize strength. Found in 1897, this is pure Scythian work of the late seventh or early sixth century B.C.

agreement. About half of the exhibition will consist of Scythian gold objects, including all of those shown in these pages, but there are also remarkable works in bronze, wood, felt, horn and iron. After the show closes in New York on June 29, it will go to the Los Angeles County Museum of Art. In exchange, the Metropolitan is sending 100 masterpieces of European and American painting from its own collections for exhibition at the Pushkin Museum in Moscow and the Hermitage in Leningrad.

What impressed Herodotus about the Scythians, and what made him decide to devote virtually all of Book Four to them, was that they had won a great military victory in favor of Greece.

What had happened was that the Scythians, against all expectations and precedent, ruined the huge offensive which Darius the Great of Persia began leading against them in 514 B.C. as part of his master plan for subduing Greece. The Scythians controlled the grain and livestock traffic from the rich steppe (today's Ukraine) which kept food-poor Greece alive. By clobbering these insolent horsemen—and who could resist an army 700,000 strong—he could starve Greece into submission. Darius and his host lumbered across the

Bosphorus, angled north across Thrace and present-day Bulgaria, crossed the Danube and invaded Scythian territory, spoiling for a fight. In what must have been history's first example of the now well proven Russian tactic of scorched earth, the Scythians gave Darius a bitter pretaste of Napoleonic and Hitlerian futility: They retreated, keeping one day ahead of the sluggish Persian machine, burning crops and plugging wells, then turning at odd moments to make vicious, slashing attacks against the aggressor's flanks. As week after week passed—Darius had confidently told his rearguard at the Danube crossing-point that he would be back within 60 days—the bloodied Persian frustration grew along with the soldiers' hunger and thirst. Finally, the nonplussed Darius resolved to send a messenger to Idanthyrsus, the Scythian king.

"Thou strange man," he protested, "why do you keep on flying before me, when there are two things you might do so easily? If you deem yourself able to resist my arms, cease your wanderings and come, let us engage in battle. Or, if you are conscious that my

Mr. Chelminski's most recent SMITHSONIAN *article was on Hitlerian art in the February issue.*

Mare with suckling foal, a cow and a calf (above) are among domestic scenes of inner ring of pectoral.

The outer ring has scenes of more violent activity: griffins attacking a horse (center), a panther

strength is greater than yours—even so you should cease to run away—you have but to bring your Lord [meaning himself] earth and water, and to come at once to a conference."

Idanthyrsus answered with another speech of his own, which ended with some succinct advice: "Go weep." Which, we may safely assume, was the nomadic equivalent of "Get lost." Puzzled and exhausted, Darius gallantly left his sick and wounded behind and scrambled for the Danube. With him he bore the Scythians' only tribute: a bird, a mouse, a frog and five arrows. "These men do indeed despise us utterly," he concluded.

If Herodotus felt gratitude to these cavaliers for having saved Greece, we of the 20th century may be thankful that they evidently believed in a form of life after death. The beyond, as the Scythians apparently conceived it, was quite like life on Earth, and to deal with it every man would need to carry with him everything he held to be most dear and most useful. As a result, all the Scythians—even the poor, sedentary ones who tilled the soil, but especially the warriors and their chiefs—had elaborate burials which mirrored their living environments. If Soviet archaeologists

Easily the most spectacular of recent finds (it was excavated in 1971), this 12-inch gold pectoral is of Greek workmanship, executed for the Scythians in the fourth century B.C. Details shown below.

and a lion attacking a boar (right). Separating the two openwork rings is a band of exquisitely worked

flowers and tendrils. The 48 figures were cast individually and soldered to the twisted gold frame.

301

with wooden lances atop their mounts and propped up in a circle around the grave—ghostly riders of a ghostly honor guard.

Who were the Scythians? Many theories have been offered over the years and some, at least, have now been eliminated. There is general agreement that they were of neither Asiatic nor Finno-Ugric stock, as had been occasionally presumed. All the signs now point to an Indo-European origin; more specifically, they were northern Iranian. The ancestors of the Scythian nation took to the immense sweep of the Eurasian plain, which stretches from the Danube all the way to the interior of China. Over the centuries this steppe has been like a gigantic vein flowing with different tribes and races, touching and mingling, bumping into

have discovered the skeletons of simple farmers with bronze and clay vessels placed next to them, they have also unearthed tombs of kings and princes which are nothing short of fabulous. The burial mounds were the Scythians' pyramids.

Their funeral customs as described by Herodotus were striking by any measure. The harsh conditions of nomadic life on the steppe seem to have created a most exacting loyalty to chieftain and king, one which demanded that many of his subjects join him in his grave. A Scythian of great importance was embalmed at his death (an herbal mixture of chopped cypress, frankincense, parsley seed and anise seed was stuffed in the abdominal cavity, after which the body was encased in wax) and taken around his territory for 40 days. The cart bearing his body was followed by ostentatiously grieving subjects, who engaged in all manner of self-mutilation and choruses of wailing, shouting and jingling bells. The burial chamber was dug deep below ground level, buttressed by wooden beams and topped off with an immense earthen mound. Inside the tomb the chieftain was dressed in his finest gold-sewn clothes, surrounded by his gold treasure and left with his weapons to defend it.

But he did not go to the afterlife alone. Far from it. It was common practice for the ruler's favorite concubine and closest servants to be sent with him, persuaded by the gentle art of strangulation and themselves adorned in their best gold. Accompanying them all on their voyage were his horses, put to ritual death—as many as 360 have been found in a single grave—and lain around them in procession, themselves bedecked in leather and gold and felt. One final practice completes the macabre picture: One year after a king's death, up to 50 of his young bodyguards would be volunteered for strangulation, along with a similar number of horses. They were then impaled

This gold comb, reflected in a mirror to show both sides, is from the fourth century B.C. The men wear Scythian costumes, but the Greek goldsmith who made it gave two of them Greek armor (opposite).

Siberian burial mounds of the Royal Scythians' distant relatives. The stars of the show, though, are unquestionably the fruit of the digs in the Black Sea area southeast of Kiev.

The Animal Style is exactly what its name implies: endless representations of deer and eagle and panther and lion and all the other creatures (sometimes imaginary, as griffins) which the Scythians would have encountered in their wanderings. Dr. Yaroslav Domansky, a member of the Hermitage's prehistoric culture department, suggests a twofold use for this bestiary: first, as a protective personal totem, such as a stag in the middle of a shield; and, second, as pure decoration, for which any kind of animal at all could serve to bedeck clothing, quiver or saddle. Being mounted nomads, the Scythians perforce had to limit themselves to relatively small objects, so nothing of their art is grandiose in size. As usually happens in illiterate cultures, the Scythians had an acute visual sense which enabled them to bring extraordinary excitement and grace to the animals they represented.

each other in periodic migrations, swirling apart and often gathering their forces to slaughter each other.

Contemporary Soviet scientists deliberately limit the term "Scythian" to the tribes which settled north of the Black Sea, as described by Herodotus. Other related tribes also roamed the steppe, and similar burial mounds exist by the thousands deep into Siberia and the region of the Altai mountains, near the present Sino-Soviet border. It was, in fact, from Siberia that the first inklings of a previously unknown ancient art began reaching the modern world: the Animal Style.

In 1715, Peter the Great and the Empress Catherine I received as a gift, on the birth of their first son, a large number of decorative gold ornaments, all of them covered with intricate designs of animal forms. Peter was so taken by these curiosities that he issued an order forbidding the common practice of grave-robbing and the melting down of the historical artifacts for common gold. In the years since, the objects found in tombs of the Black Sea Scythians and related tribes to the east have grown into the stunning collections now found in the Hermitage in Leningrad and the Lavra Museum in Kiev, the two principal sources for the show at the Metropolitan.

This is not the first time that the Soviets have parted with some of their Scythian treasures for the benefit of foreign viewers (there have been Scythian shows in France, Holland, Italy, Japan and elsewhere), but the Metropolitan's selection is by far the largest. It is also the first one ever to be lent to the United States.

"If you only knew how hard it was to give all of them up," said Dr. Boris Piotrovsky, director of the Hermitage. "I cried big tears."

To show the scope of the Animal Style discoveries in the Soviet Union, Piotrovsky has included both pre- and post-Scythian objects, as well as many from the

The enigmatic scenes on this vase have had many interpretations including the one in the text.

Scytho-Siberian plaque from Peter the Great's collection depicts combat between tiger and monster.

Panther shield totem is among strongest examples of Animal Style (early sixth century B.C.).

Head of Athena, inspired by statue in the Parthenon, adorns Greek-made pendant (fourth century B.C.).

Much of what is known about the way the Scythians looked and dressed has been learned from such

It may be presumed that the Animal Style originally began with bone and wood carvings, later replaced by gold, but except for the Altai burial mounds in Siberia, where perpetual freezing preserved much wood, felt, leather and other organic matter, none has survived. The famous recumbent stag shield centerpiece (pp. 298-299), though undoubtedly a casting by the "lost wax" technique, bears strong resemblance to the inclined planes of a wood carving. The stag's beautiful and quite realistic rendering is set off by the surprisingly fanciful continuation of the antlers all the way down the back, an exaggeration by which the artist underlined the essence of the animal's strength.

The same reinforcement of a totem's magic protection is seen in the panther shield centerpiece (p.305); in most ways it resembles a normally fierce, fang-baring panther, but its significance is restated in the tiny panthers twisted head-to-tail at the beast's feet and along its tail.

The greatest period of purely Scythian artistic creation seems to have been the sixth century B.C., after their defeat of the Cimmerians and before their own

finds as this marvelously detailed gold and silver
cup, executed by Greeks in fourth century B.C.

downfall at the hands of their tough eastern cousins,
the Sarmatians. Both the panther and the stag are of
this period. By the fifth century B.C., though, Greek influences began to appear in the gold art, and they only
grew stronger with the passing of time. Wealthy Scythians, obviously charmed by the high level of craftsmanship and sophistication of the Greek artisans in
towns like Herodotus' Olbia, began ordering from
them, as well as from their native artists.

A good example of a Scythian "mail order" from
Greek craftsmen is the astonishing comb (pp. 302-303).
Discovered in the Solokha barrow near the Dnieper
River some 180 miles south of Kiev, it depicts violence,
a recurrent and important theme in Scythian art.

The violence on the comb is purely human: Three
Scythians, one mounted, have at each other, above a
small frieze of recumbent lions. Both the horseman
and the warrior on the right, whose mount has been
slain (note the blood flowing from his neck wound),
wear Greek helmets and are protected by armor; the
foot soldier on the left rushing to help his mounted
chief wears the simple Scythian caftan and is helmet-

The fourth-century B.C. grave of a young Scythian
woman is reconstructed as it was found in 1971.

less. The scene shows, as Dr. Domansky points out, that by then it had become common for certain Scyths to buy Greek armor, as well as Greek art.

The famous cup from the Kul Oba dig (p. 304), made of electrum (a natural gold-silver alloy), is adorned with a marvelously realistic relief showing scenes which until recently had been described as mere stray vignettes of Scythian life: two men conversing, one apparently probing for the other's aching tooth, one dressing another's wounded leg and the last stringing a bow by bending it under his leg. But one final element had been missing until now: a more accurate interpretation of the four vignettes. Dr. Piotrovsky today believes that the riddle has been puzzled out by Dmitri Rayevsky, his colleague in the Moscow Institute of Ethnography. Far from being random scenes of life on the steppe, Dr. Piotrovsky says, the vignettes represent a Greco-Scythian legend of the founding of the Royal tribe, a variant which has the Scythians descending from Hercules. Having fathered three male children by a strange half-woman, half-serpent goddess, Hercules directed that she give them each a chance to string his bow when they grew to manhood. He who succeeded would be worthy to lead the tribe. Suddenly the vignettes offer an easy meaning. The two big brothers have a try at the bow, but one—ouch—gets it in the mouth when he can't hold the tension any longer, and the second received his punishment in the leg. Little brother squats resolutely on the ground and manages to string the bow. In the last scene he is seen as the new king, being invested by a priest.

The brilliant pectoral (pp. 300-301), the supreme example of Greek workmanship in service to the Scyths, was found only in 1971 in the great Bliznitsa dig just south of the Sea of Azov. Each part was cast separately and then carefully soldered into place. The three rows each depict a different aspect of the Scy-

thians' experience: man and animal, floral and vegetable nature, and, finally, the recurrent theme of violence. In the peaceful first row, two Scythians work together on a sheepskin shirt, while two others milk ewes and horses, goats, cattle and ducks gambol. Bits of the original enamel still remain on the floral arrangement of the second row. In the third, griffins, lions and panthers attack luckless horses and a wild boar, while dogs chase rabbits.

By 300 B.C. the declining Scythians had suffered the fate of their victims the Cimmerians. They were pushed from the steppe by the even more warlike Sarmatians, who had impressed Herodotus by the fighting quality of their women—descended, he said, from the legendary Amazons and able to hold their own with the best of male soldiers. The Scythians' last refuge was in the confines of the Crimean peninsula, but by 106 B.C. the last of them disappeared, swept clean from the slate of history. The cruel logic of the steppe eventually held good for their conquerors, the Sarmatians, too: the Huns, the most terrible and powerful of all the mounted tribes, destroyed them in turn.

As the years pass, the continuous Soviet digs into the still untouched Scythian burial mounds will doubtless help to define the exact limits of their territory, the dates of their ascendency and decline, and the correlations between the many tribes of the Eurasian plain. Perhaps a few more masterpieces like the pectoral or the panther shield totem will be unearthed. In contrast to the outright plundering of the time of Peter the Great, Soviet archaeologists now approach each new dig with a traditionally painstaking scientific precision which often, happily, can be helped along with such modern conveniences as tractors and bulldozers to do the brute work of sweeping away the huge dirt caps from the tombs. And modern science has still further shortcuts up its sleeve: According to Mrs. Oksana Ganina, director of the Lavra Museum in Kiev—the principal beneficiary of recent Royal Scythian discoveries—the Kiev Cybernetics Institute is working on a metal-detecting sounding device to help archaeologists put priorities on the approach to specific burial mounds.

"That will help, of course," she says with something very close to resignation, "but there are thousands and thousands of unopened barrows, not only here, but in Siberia as well. All of them will probably be investigated some day. But not, I am afraid, in our lifetime."

In this enlarged detail from a fourth-century B.C. gold clothing ornament, found in the Crimea in 1830, two Scythians share the same drinking horn exactly as in a ritual described by Herodotus.

Smithsonian highlights 1970-1980

In the September 1976 issue, the recently re-opened Arts and Industries Building evokes the spirit of the 1876 Philadelphia Centennial.

April 1970	First issue of *Smithsonian* magazine
October 1970	Woodrow Wilson International Center for Scholars welcomes first fellows
January 1972	The Renwick Gallery opens
April 1972	Pandas Hsing-Hsing and Ling-Ling arrive at the National Zoo; August 1975 Zoo opens Conservation and Research Center in Front Royal, Virginia; July 1976 the William M. Mann Lion/Tiger Exhibit; May 1979 Beaver Valley
July 1972	Chesapeake Bay Center for Environmental Studies becomes separate Smithsonian bureau
July 1972	The National Portrait Gallery opens "If Elected. . . . Unsuccessful Candidates for the Presidency;" July 1973 "The Black Presence in the Era of the American Revolution;" September 1978 "Facing the Light: Historical American Portrait Daguerreotypes"
April 1973	National Museum of History and Technology (now National Museum of American History) presents the Hall of News Reporting; June 1976 "Nation of Nations;" December 1977 "Atom Smashers"
May 1973	The Freer Gallery of Art celebrates its 50th anniversary
July 1973	Smithsonian Astrophysical Observatory joins with Harvard College Observatory to form the Center for Astrophysics
October 1974	Hirshhorn Museum and Sculpture Garden opens
October 1974	National Museum of Natural History opens "Ice Age Mammals and the Emergence of Man;" August 1976 "Insect Zoo;" October 1977 "Splendors of Nature"
April 1976	National Collection of Fine Arts (now National Museum of Ameri-

September 1976 issue also pictures visitors in the newly opened Air and Space Museum's Rocketry and Space Flight Gallery.

Visitors arrive at twilight for their first glimpse of the rich collection of modern art at the Hirshhorn Museum and Sculpture Garden (cover, December 1974).

can Art) presents "America as Art;" October 1976 "Robert Rauschenberg;" October 1978 "Perceptions and Evocations: The Art of Elihu Vedder"

May 1976	"1876" opens in Arts and Industries Building
July 1976	National Air and Space Museum opens
October 1976	Cooper-Hewitt Museum of Design and Decorative Arts opens in New York City
November 1976	The National Gallery of Art presents "Treasures of Tutankhamun;" June 1978 East Building opens
May 1979	Center for Astrophysics installs Multiple Mirror Telescope on Mt. Hopkins, Arizona
August 1979	Museum of African Art joins Smithsonian

Miró tapestry on wall, Noguchi sculpture at left in East Building court, June 1978.

Knife-edged angles define the National Gallery of Art's East Building, June 1978.

In the December 1978 issue, Smithsonian Secretary S. Dillon Ripley introduces nine then-directors of museums, with examples from the collections. From left: Mr. Ripley, Marvin Sadik, Mel Zisfein, Al Lerner (in front) and Tom Lawton, Theodore Reed, Porter Kier, Otto Mayr, John Kinard and Lisa Taylor.

The Institution's Magazine

Smithsonian magazine's curiosity is perhaps matched only by that of its parent Institution. In fact, it has been said that the magazine's coverage includes "anything that the Institution is interested in, might be interested in, or ought to be interested in."

And the Institution is interested in nearly everything. For instance, it preserves some 78 million specimens in more than a dozen major museums and collections. More than just a delight to visitors, these collections are the foundation for the Institution's vast array of scientific research programs and cultural and historical studies.

In such photographs as these, *Smithsonian* reflects the scientific, historical, and artistic interests and concerns of the Smithsonian.

The figurehead and pegbox of a 1717 *viola de gamba*, opposite, from "Restoring to antique instruments their looks—and voices," August 1970. Over, gleaming steam engine harks back to the 1876 Philadelphia Exposition, from "1876, its artifacts and attitudes, returns to life at the Smithsonian," May 1976. The crested hoatzin, page 317, is one of the more striking species of birds to be found in the Amazon basin biosphere, from "A timely reprieve or a death sentence for the Amazon," October 1977. Pages 318-319, the January 1977 issue's "Supreme Court of the United States: the staff that keeps it operating" describes what goes on behind the scenes at the summit of judicial power in the United States.

Picture Credits

Front Matter
p. 2-3 Peter Jackson; 8-9 Kjell B. Sandved; 12 *The Races of Europe,* Carleton Stevens Coon, 1939, page 24, fig. 1, Neanderthal Man in Modern Dress; 13 Susanne Page; 14 Robert P. Sharp; 15 (top) Sigrid James; (bottom) © 1978 Jill Krementz; 16 U.S. Navy Photo; 17 (left) Smithsonian Institution; (top & bottom) Kenneth M. Towe; 18-19 Val E. Lewton; 20 Smithsonian Institution; 21 Margaret Brown; 22 Yoichi R. Okamota; 23 National Zoo, photo by Ilene Berg.

Wildlife and Environment
p. 24 © Dan Guravich; 26-35 Robert Osborn; 36 P. W. Grace/Photo Researchers; 38-39 Tony Florio/Photo Researchers; 39 Anthony Merciaca/Photo Researchers; 40 (left) Thomas W. Martin/Photo Researchers; (center) Townsend P. Dickinson/Photo Researchers; (right) Leonard Lee Rue, III/Bruce Coleman, Inc.; 41 (left) Delbert Rust/Photo Researchers; (center) S. J. Kraseman/Photo Researchers; (right) Phil A. Dotson/Photo Researchers; 42-43 George Laycock/Photo Researchers; 44-45 Daniel Owen Stolpe; 52-59 Fred Gwynne; 60 Frank White; 61-63 Edward S. Ayensu; 64 (left) Edward S. Ayensu; (right) William S. Justice, M.D.; 65 (left) Kjell B. Sandved; (right) Edward S. Ayensu; 66-67 Kjell B. Sandved; 68-77 Farrell Grehan; 78-82 Russ Kinne/Photo Researchers; 83 Norman Myers/Bruce Coleman, Inc.; 84 Animals Animals/Stouffer Enterprises; 88-57 Russ Kinne/Photo Researchers; 88-89 Yoichi R. Okamoto; 90-91 © 1979 Durward L. Allen; 92 NASA; 93-99 © 1979 Durward L. Allen; 100-105 Brenda Losey-Tilley.

Energy and Technology
p. 106 John Huehnergarth; 108 Smithsonian Institution; 109-115 Robert Osborn; 116-118 Chuck O'Rear; 119 USDA, photo by Howard Heggestad; 120-121 Emery Industries, Inc.; 122 *Nature Science Annual*/1976 Edition, photograph by Ken Kay, © 1975 Time, Inc., Time-Life Books, publisher; 123 Ross Chapple; 124 Captain Per E. Meidel, courtesy Gotaas-Larsen, Inc.; 124-125 Pierre Mion; 126 UPI; 126-127 Pierre Mion; 127-130 Pierre Mion; 130-131 Wide World Photos; 132-138 Jan Adkins; 139-145 John Huehnergarth; 146-147 © 1978 Shorty Wilcox; 148 (left) Beveridge & Associates; 148-155 © 1978 Shorty Wilcox; 156-161 Fritz Goro; 163 Ron Miller.

People and History
p. 164 Charles H. Phillips; 167 Copernicus Society of America; 168 Smithsonian Institution, photo by Edwin A. Battison; 170-171 CAF Press-Photo Agency; 172-173 From *Wit Stwosz* © 1964 Oficyna Wydawnicza, Auriga, Wydawnictwa Artystyczne i Filmowe, Warszawa; 174-179 Arnold Roth; 180-181 © Peter Angelo Simon; 182 Courtesy of the Pennsylvania Academy of the Fine Arts; 185 (top) courtesy of The New York Historical Society; (left) INA Corporation Museum; (right) Courtesy, Museum of Fine Arts, Boston; 186 (top left) Courtesy of the Detroit Institute of Arts; (bottom left) Private collection, courtesy of Kennedy Galleries, Inc., New York; (right) Philadelphia Museum of Art, The George W. Elkins Collection; 187 (left) Collection of Mrs. Norman B. Woolworth, courtesy of Coe-Kerr Gallery; (top right) The Dietrich Brothers Americana Corporation; (center right) Courtesy of the Pennsylvania Academy of the Fine Arts; (bottom right) Courtesy of The American Museum of Natural History; 188-189 Courtesy of the Detroit Institute of Arts; 189 (top) Courtesy of The New York Historical Society; (bottom) The Historical Society of Pennsylvania; 190 (top) National Agricultural Library, Historic and Rare Book Collection; (bottom) Courtesy of The American Museum of Natural History; 191 The Peale Museum, Baltimore; 192-201 The InterNorth Art Foundation; 202-211 Robert Osborn; 212-219 James Van DerZee; 220-222 Lee Boltin; 223-224 © Rube Goldberg, permission granted by King Features Syndicate, Inc.; 226-233- E. Richard Sorenson.

The Arts
p. 234 Kimbell Art Museum, Fort Worth, Texas; 237 John Donat; 238 The Tate Gallery, London; 239 The Bettmann Archive; 240 The Raymond Mander and Joe Mitchenson Theatre Collection; 241 The Meserve Collection; 242 Derek Bayes; 243 Copied by Henry Groskinsky; 244-245 National Gallery of Art; 246 Musée National d'Art Moderne, Centre Georges Pompidou, Paris; 247 Steven Sloman; 249 Collection of Robert Motherwell; 250-251 Ludwig Collection; 252-259 Bill Ray; 260-261 (top) Lee Boltin; (bottom) Isamu Noguchi; 262 (bottom) © 1978 Andrew Popper; 262-267 Lee Boltin; 268 (top) Lee Boltin; (bottom) Ezra Stoller © ESTO; 269 Ezra Stoller © ESTO; 270-275 Pierre Boulat; 276-283 Marvin E. Newman; 284 Dmitri Kessel; 286 (top) Beveridge & Associates; 286-297 Dmitri Kessel; 298-309 Lee Boltin; 310-312 Robert C. Lautman; 313 (top) Yale Joel; (bottom) Robert C. Lautman; 314 Lee Boltin; 315 Charles H. Phillips; 316 Robert C. Lautman; 317 Loren McIntyre; 318-319 Yoichi R. Okamoto.

Gatefold
1970 Dr. John F. Eisenberg; Terence Spencer; Lee Boltin; Crawford H. Greenewalt; Lee Boltin; Eliot Elisofon; Lee Boltin; Federal Water Quality Administration/EPA; Lee Battaglia.
1971 Bjorn Reese; Gjon Mili; Judson E. Vandevere; Fritz Goro; Frank Greenwell; Archives of American Art, photograph by Charles H. Phillips; Kjell B. Sandved; Yoichi R. Okamoto; Lee Boltin; Robert Osborn; Loomis Dean; William K. Sacco.
1972 Dmitri Kessel; Charles H. Phillips; Farrell Grehan; Loomis Dean; National Museum of American Art, Smithsonian Institution; Don Carl Steffen; Barbara Fahs Charles; Lee Balterman; Terence Spencer; Dmitri Kessel; Robert C. Lautman; René-Jacques, Paris.
1973 Photograph by Eliot Elisofon, Museum of African Art, Eliot Elisofon Archives; Arthur Sirdofsky; Richard Bell and Jeremy Grimsdell; "Horse Attacked by Jaguar" (detail) by Henri Rousseau, Pushkin Museum, Moscow; Carl Mydans; © 1973 John Reader; Terence Spencer; Paul D. Harwood; Dmitri Kessel; Basil Williams; Carl Mydans; Photograph by Nina Leen.
1974 Howard Sochurek; David Lees; Takeyoshi Tanuma; Pierre Boulat; John Blaustein; A. Y. Owen; Terence Spencer; © Dan Guravich; Alfred Eisenstaedt; Don Carl Steffen; Lee Boltin; Yale Joel.
1975 Bill Ray; George Silk; Art by Max Ernst, photograph by Vincent Miragelia; Lee Boltin; George Silk; Tom Nebbia/D.P.I.; Thomas J. Watson, Jr.; © Charles E. Rotkin, PFI; A. Y. Owen; Carl Mydans; W. B. Park; Kjell B. Sandved.
1976 Henry Groskinsky; Dmitri Kessel; Bill Ray; Henry Groskinsky; Robert C. Lautman; A. Y. Owen; John Huehnergarth; © 1976 Stephen Green-Armytage; George Silk; Yoichi R. Okamoto; Yee Boltin; Robert Osborn.
1977 Yoichi R. Okamoto; Miami Seaquarium, photograph by Bill Hunter; Pierre Boulat; James R. Buckler; © 1977 Christopher Springmann; Lee Boltin; The Meserve Collection; Dmitri Kessel; George Silk; Loren McIntyre; Dr. Sung-Yang Lee; Telegraph Sunday Magazine.
1978 Marvin E. Newman; © Dan Guravich; Marvin E. Newman; © 1978 Andrew Popper; Robert C. Lautman; Dmitri Kessel; © 1978 Shorty Wilcox; Peter Jackson; Thomas D. Mangelsen; Lee Boltin; Dmitri Kessel; Kimbell Art Museum, Fort Worth, Texas.
1979 © John Reader; Keystone-Mast Collection, California Museum of Photography, University of California, Riverside; T. S. Satyan/Black Star; Farrell Grehan; Gary Ladd; © 1979 John Reader; Christopher Casler/Camera 5; Ralph Crane; China Pictorial; National Museum of American Art, Smithsonian Institution; Seth Joel; Marvin E. Newman.
1980 NASA; The Metropolitan Museum of Art, Anonymous Gift, 1964.

Jacket
Lee Boltin; James R. Buckler; China Pictorial; Ralph Crane; Crawford H. Greenewalt; Farrell Grehan; Peter Jackson; Dmitri Kessel; Gary Ladd; Nina Leen; David Lees; Loren McIntyre; The Meserve Collection; National Museum of American Art; Marvin E. Newman; Bill Ray; John Reader; Kyell B. Sandved; George Silk; Terence Spencer; Christopher Springmann.

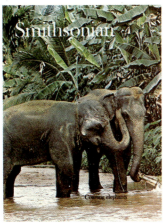

April 1970

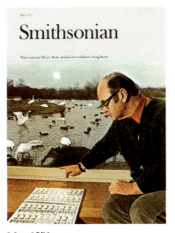

May 1970

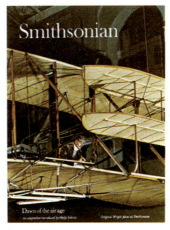

June 1970

July 1970

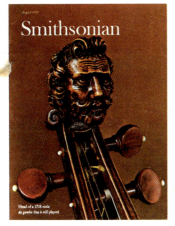

August 1970

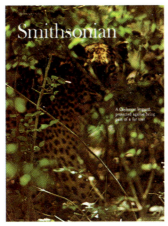

September 1970

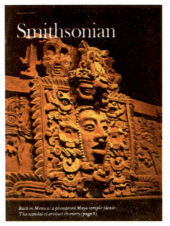

October 1970

November 1970

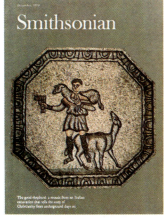

December 1970

January 1971

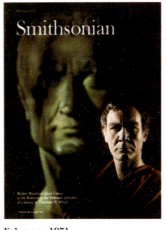

February 1971

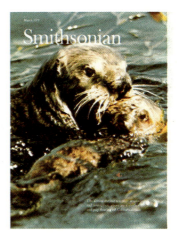

March 1971

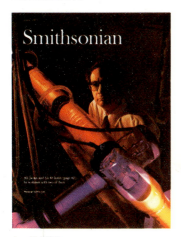

April 1971

May 1971

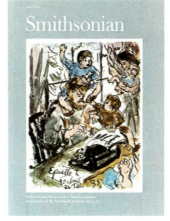

June 1971

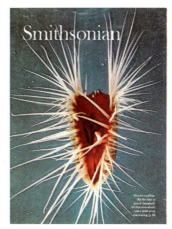

July 1971

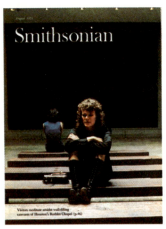

August 1971

September 1971

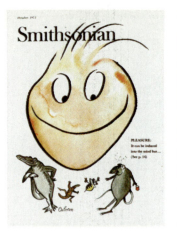

October 1971

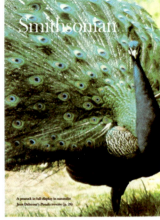

November 1971

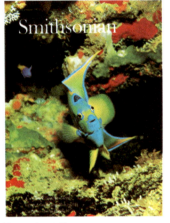

December 1971

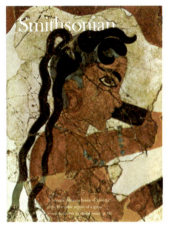

January 1972

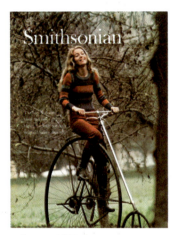

February 1972

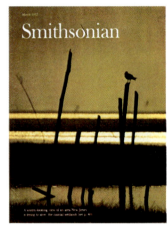

March 1972

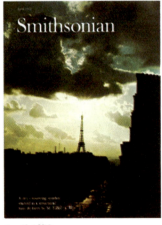

April 1972

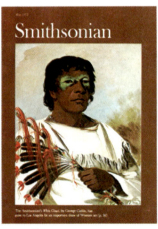

May 1972

June 1972

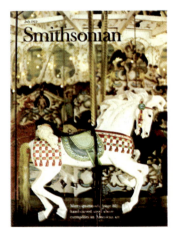

July 1972

August 1972

September 1972

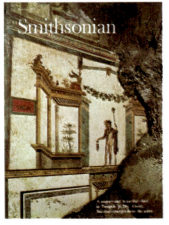

October 1972

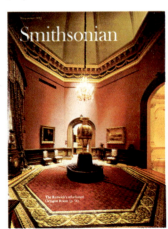

November 1972

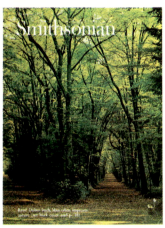

December 1972

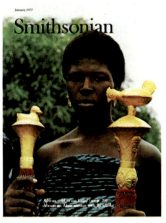

January 1973

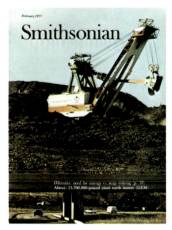

February 1973

March 1973

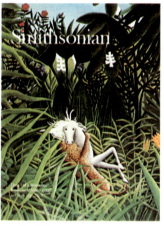

April 1973

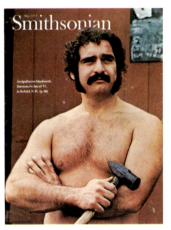

May 1973

June 1973

July 1973

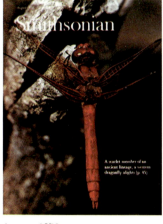

August 1973

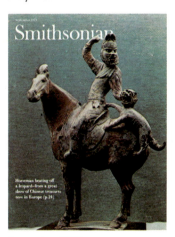

September 1973

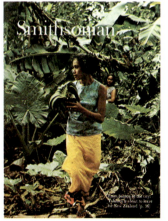

October 1973

November 1973

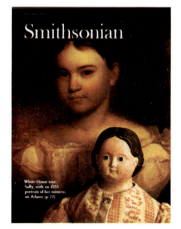

December 1973

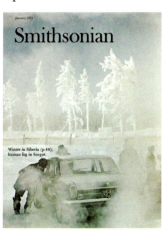

January 1974

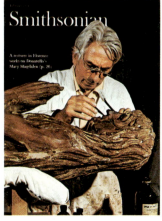

February 1974

March 1974

April 1974

May 1974

June 1974

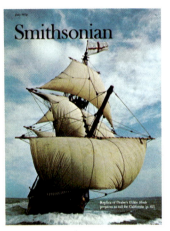

July 1974

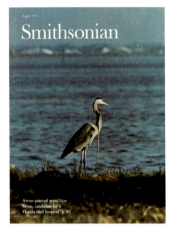

August 1974

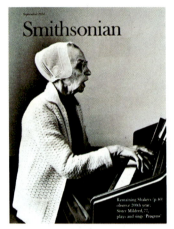

September 1974

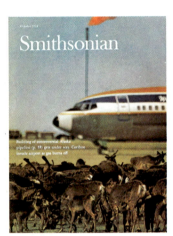

October 1974

November 1974

December 1974

January 1975

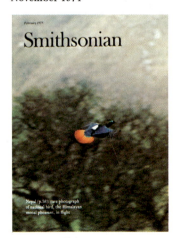

February 1975

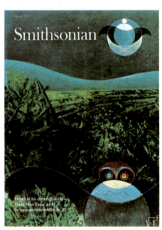

March 1975

April 1975

July 1977

August 1977

September 1977

October 1977

November 1977

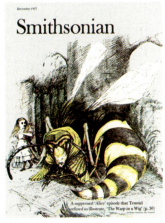

December 1977

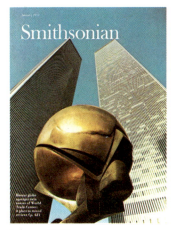

January 1978

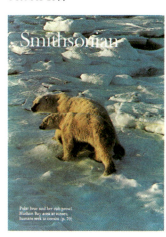

February 1978

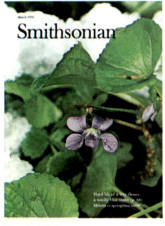

March 1978

April 1978

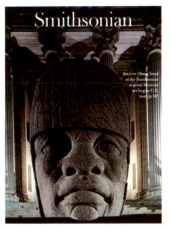

May 1978

June 1978

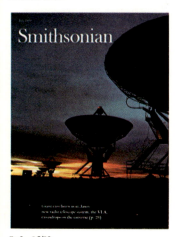

July 1978

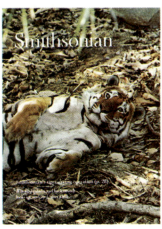

August 1978

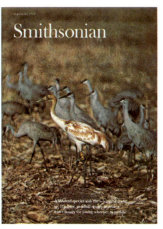

September 1978

October 1978

November 1978

December 1978

January 1979

February 1979

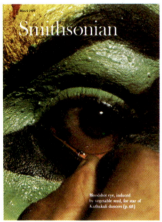

March 1979

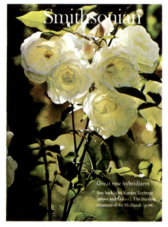

April 1979

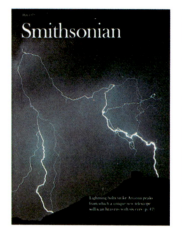

May 1979

June 1979

July 1979

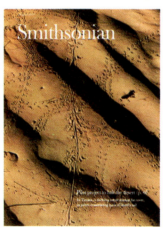

August 1979

September 1979

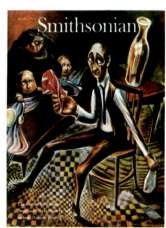

October 1979

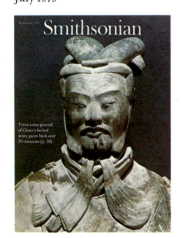

November 1979

December 1979

January 1980

February 1980

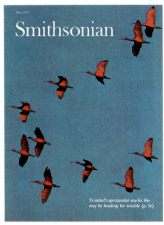

May 1975

June 1975

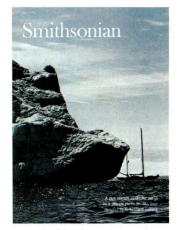

July 1975

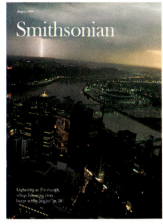

August 1975

September 1975

October 1975

November 1975

December 1975

January 1976

February 1976

March 1976

April 1976

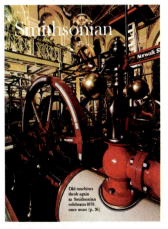

May 1976

June 1976

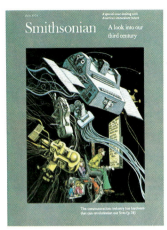

July 1976

August 1976

September 1976

October 1976

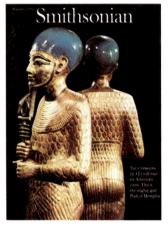

November 1976

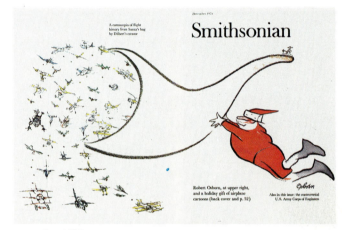

December 1976

January 1977

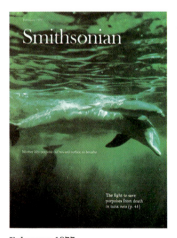

February 1977

March 1977

April 1977

May 1977

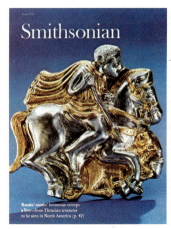

June 1977